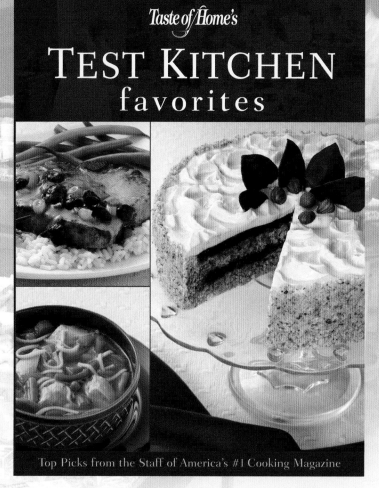

Taste of Home's
TEST KITCHEN
favorites

Top Picks from the Staff of America's #1 Cooking Magazine

Pictured on the Cover: Cranberry Pork Chops (p. 103), Classic Chicken Noodle Soup (p. 73) and Hazelnut Mocha Torte (p. 258).

Test Kitchen Staff Shares Their All-Time Favorites!

OUR TEST KITCHEN STAFF goes to great lengths to make sure the recipes that appear in *Taste of Home* magazine and its "sister" publications are guaranteed to be great.

With more than 20,000 recipes published in our magazines and books each year, it's no wonder these talented food folks are constantly asked by curious friends, family and co-workers to divulge what dishes they make in their own homes.

After years of informal recipe swaps, we compiled 498 of our staff's most tried-and-true dishes in this special collection—*Test Kitchen Favorites*!

You'll not only find previously published reader recipes that our Test Kitchen staff relies on most but also dishes from their personal recipe boxes at home. They've enjoyed making, eating and sharing these treasured dishes with family and friends for years ...and now you can, too!

Editor: Jean Steiner
Art Director: Lori Arndt
Cookbook Project and Recipe Editor: Janet Briggs
Executive Editor/Books: Heidi Reuter Lloyd
Senior Editor: Julie Schnittka
Proofreader: Julie Blume
Editorial Assistant: Barb Czysz
Graphic Art Associates: Ellen Lloyd, Catherine Fletcher

Food Editor: Janaan Cunningham
Associate Food Editors: Coleen Martin, Diane Werner
Assistant Food Editor: Karen Scales
Senior Recipe Editor: Sue A. Jurack
Test Kitchen Director: Mark Morgan
Senior Home Economists: Peggy Fleming, Pat Schmeling,
Amy Welk-Thieding
Test Kitchen Home Economists: Sue Draheim, Tamra Duncan,
Erin Frakes, Nancy Fridirici, Karen Johnson, Wendy Stenman
Test Kitchen Assistants: Anita Bukowski, Suzanne Kern, Rita Krajcir,
Kris Lehman, Sue Megonigle, Betty Reuter, Megan Taylor

Food Photographers: Rob Hagen, Dan Roberts, Jim Wieland,
Grace Sheldon
Food Stylists: Kristin Arnett, Sarah Thompson, Joylyn Trickel
Set Stylists: Jennifer Bradley Vent, Julie Ferron, Stephanie Marchese,
Sue Myers
Photographers Assistant: Lori Foy

Chairman and Founder: Roy Reiman
President: Barbara Newton
Senior Vice President, Editor in Chief: Catherine Cassidy

Taste of Home Books
© 2005 Reiman Media Group, Inc.
5400 S. 60th St., Greendale WI 53129
International Standard Book Number: 0-89821-455-6
Library of Congress Control Number: 2005929210
All rights reserved. Printed in U.S.A.

To order additional copies of this book,
write *Taste of Home* Books, P.O. Box 908, Greendale WI 53129.
To order with a credit card, call toll-free 1-800/344-2560
or visit our Web site at www.reimanpub.com.

Taste of Home's
TEST KITCHEN
favorites

Table of Contents

Behind the Scenes of Our Test Kitchen

How It All Began

Our Test Kitchen had humble beginnings with a staff of just one, our first food editor, Annette Gohlke. She tested the recipes in her home kitchen and drove the finished dishes 30 miles to the office, where a taste panel evaluated them. For contests, the panel took a field trip to Annette's kitchen. The best recipes were then published in the food section of *Farm Wife News* magazine, now called *Country Woman*.

That first magazine has since been joined by four food publications—*Taste of Home* (the No. 1 cooking magazine in the country), *Quick Cooking*, *Light & Tasty* and *Cooking for 2*. We also feature reader recipes in seven more of our magazines and in our cookbooks.

We built our first Test Kitchen in 1981 and added our fourth kitchen in 2004. Three of those kitchens are in the company's main office and one is inside the Reiman Publications Visitor Center in downtown Greendale. Our staff of 25 now includes food editors, home economists, recipe editors, food stylists and editorial assistants!

So how does a recipe get published in one of our many publications? It all begins with the recipes our talented readers submit for magazine contests and other special features. Turn the page to tag along on a photo journey as one reader's recipe travels from submission to publication.

Our first food editor, Annette Gohlke, tested recipes at home from 1972 until 1981.

After driving 30 miles to the office, Annette presented the recipes she prepared to a taste panel.

At the start of the day, our newest and largest test kitchen is in perfect order. It has four commercial refrigerators, nine ovens with three warming drawers, six sinks and dishwashers, and three microwaves.

Over 130,000 visitors a year watch home economists at work in our Reiman Publications Visitor Center Test Kitchen. A large overhead mirror provides spectators with a clear view.

With Annette's urging, our first Test Kitchen was built in 1981 and recently updated. Its wallpaper and fruit decor inspired its nickname, the "apple" kitchen.

The First Cut

For our 28 contests a year, recipes are sorted into categories before they are reviewed by the home economists. As you can see in the photo below, our call for recipes elicits many responses. In fact, our most popular contest—the "Cookie of All Cookies" contest—had over 34,000 recipe submissions!

Let's say our reader's recipe stands out from the other contest submissions. First, it needs to be checked against all of the previously published recipes in our database—30,000 recipes and growing! Once it's made that cut, a test sheet is created and groceries are ordered so our recipe can be tested.

Speaking of groceries, the four Test Kitchens go through about 356 dozen eggs a year, almost 200 pounds of chicken breasts, about 250 pounds of ground beef, 260 bags of chocolate chips and over 225 pints of heavy whipping cream! We usually order groceries twice a week.

Readers love our recipe contests, as you can see by the piles of submissions Wendy Stenman is wading through.

About **34,000** recipes poured in for the cookie contest, overwhelming Coleen Martin and the rest of our staff.

Food staff members Diane Werner, Peggy Fleming and Janaan Cunningham review recipes to narrow down the selection.

Using published recipes as a comparison, Wendy Stenman and Sue Jurack check the accuracy of a submitted recipe's cooking method.

Sorting boxes of reader recipes into food categories (salads, main dishes, desserts, etc.) sure keeps Kris Lehman and Suzanne Kern busy!

At the Visitor Center, Sue Megonigle mixes up a batch of *MMM*minnesota Munchers, the grand-prize winner of the cookie contest, for eager visitors to sample.

The Testing Process

A home economist will prepare our recipe, which is evaluated by a taste panel. Generally, there are about 45 recipes tested per contest. Each recipe tester prepares more than 900 recipes a year. Between tests and retests, our staff prepares between 6,000 and 8,000 recipes yearly.

Before testing, a home economist will review our recipe for sound cooking techniques and, if necessary, research the recipe and cooking method. Then she writes up the recipe on a test sheet, which she'll refer to when cooking in the kitchen.

The test sheet contains information about who submitted the recipe, ingredients and cooking directions. The tester will note food brands on the test sheet, cooking times and temperatures, pan sizes, volume of the recipe, and the size and color of the finished food. She also attaches a digital photo of the final food and any additional comments.

In the end, the test sheet is a complete record of how our recipe was tested and how it performed in the kitchen.

The Test Kitchen staff spends a busy day testing the narrowed-down recipe entries in a strawberry contest.

Taking a minute to share a chuckle, our food staff knows that all work and no play...would make for a very long day!

Prepping the food our home economists will use for testing is part of Anita Bukowski's responsibility.

A taste panel, made up of home economists, magazine editors and recipe editors, evaluates the prepared food. Each taster takes only a few bites of each dish and writes down his or her comments.

Making the Grade

A home economist presents the food to the panel, which evaluates our recipe based on taste, appearance, mass appeal and preparation. We generally have taste testing in the morning and afternoon. In a single day, we may evaluate recipes for five different publications.

For each contest, eight to 12 recipes are selected as winners and runner-ups. When we are sampling all of those recipes, we are actually only tasting a very small portion—about two to three bites.

But those 6,000 to 8,000 recipes a year create quite the stack of dirty dishes. We use over 8,000 dish towels and 425 rolls of paper towels in a year, along with 50 bottles of dishwashing liquid and 125 containers of dishwasher detergent!

Sue Draheim, Tamra Duncan and Karen Johnson evaluate the food before presenting it to a taste panel.

After tasting, the food is laid out for one final evaluation by the food staff.

At the end of the day, the Test Kitchen is anything but in perfect order. Look at those dirty dishes!

Picture-Perfect

Whew, our recipe has made it through the testing procedure and is now ready for recipe editing. This is where ingredients are double checked for accuracy and the method is finalized into the Reiman recipe style. More than 3,000 recipes are edited in a year.

After recipe editing, our recipe is sent to the photo studio for a little pampering and its "glamour shot."

The food stylist, set stylists and photographers will present our recipe in its best possible light. Over 2,700 recipes a year pose for the cameras.

Our recipe and its photo makes another stop at editing for one last review before going to the editorial department to prepare it for its magazine or book debut.

Out of the thousands of dishes we keep on hand, Janet Briggs, Janaan Cunningham and Sue Myers select those to best complement a particular food.

Stephanie Marchese creates an eye-pleasing setting for the selected dishes, including picking tablecloths, silverware and props.

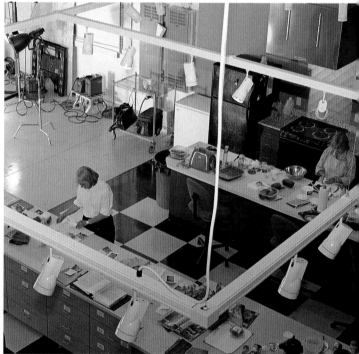

Three Sets and a food preparation area make up our recently remodeled photo studio, where all of our food photos (including those for this book) are taken.

Putting the finishing touches on the food, Kristin Arnett and Sarah Thompson make sure it's picture-perfect.

The Final Leg

The editors work with the art directors on layouts and design. In addition to generating articles and other information for magazines and books, the editors read each recipe for clarity and accuracy.

Our recipe is now ready to move on in the form of a laser. (A laser is the paper print of a magazine spread that has been laid out with all type and photos in their appropriate positions.) The Test Kitchen and Editorial staffs read over 1,700 laser pages a year for accuracy and clarity. Once the laser has been stamped final, our recipe is ready to be published and sent to our magazine subscribers.

As you can see, our recipe has a long way to travel before being printed in one of our Reiman publications. But this gives our readers piece of mind because they know it will turn out perfectly every time they make it themselves at home. It's guaranteed good!

APPETIZERS
and BEVERAGES

Vegetable Appetizer Pizza

This appetizer pizza always turns out colorful and flavorful. I've found that it's a company favorite. —*Betty Reuter*

    3 tubes (8 ounces *each*) refrigerated crescent rolls
    2 packages (8 ounces *each*) cream cheese, softened
  2/3 cup mayonnaise
    1 tablespoon dill weed
    4 medium fresh tomatoes, seeded and chopped
    2 cups chopped fresh broccoli
    3 green onions, thinly sliced
    2 cups sliced fresh mushrooms
  1/2 medium green pepper, chopped
  1/2 medium sweet red pepper, chopped
    1 can (2-1/4 ounces) sliced ripe olives, drained
    2 cups (8 ounces) shredded cheddar cheese

1 Unroll crescent roll dough and place on two greased 15-in. x 10-in. x 1-in. baking pans. Flatten dough, sealing seams and perforations. Bake at 400° for 10 minutes or until light golden brown. Cool.

2 In a small bowl, blend cream cheese, mayonnaise and dill. Spread over crusts. Top with vegetables, olives and cheese. Cut into bite-size squares. Refrigerate until serving. **Yield:** about 96 appetizer servings.

Crunchy Snack Mix

Sweet and crunchy, this snack mix is great for a party or to enjoy while watching TV. Brimming bowls are always emptied in no time. —*Janet Briggs*

    1 cup packed brown sugar
  1/2 cup butter
  1/2 cup light corn syrup

    1 package (12 ounces) Crispix cereal
  1-1/2 cups coarsely chopped walnuts

1 In a saucepan, bring the brown sugar, butter and corn syrup to a boil over medium heat, stirring occasionally. Spread cereal in a large roasting pan. Pour syrup mixture over cereal and stir until well coated. Sprinkle with nuts and stir.

2 Bake at 250° for 1 hour, stirring every 15 minutes. Spread on waxed paper to cool. Break apart and store in airtight containers. **Yield:** 15 cups.

TEST KITCHEN TIP
Janet likes to vary the nuts is this mix. Almonds go very well, and sometimes she uses a 10-ounce can of mixed nuts.

Elegant Cheese Torte

(Pictured on page 15)

This is a Christmas lifesaver! The cheese torte is very elegant-looking, plus it serves a crowd. I make it every year for the holidays.
—Coleen Martin

4 packages (8 ounces *each*) cream cheese, softened
1 cup butter, softened
2 teaspoons coarsely ground pepper
1 jar (5-3/4 ounces) stuffed olives, drained and chopped
8 cups (32 ounces) shredded sharp cheddar cheese
3/4 cup apple cider
2-1/4 teaspoons paprika
1 cup chopped pecans, toasted
Additional stuffed olives *or* grapes, optional
Assorted crackers

1 In a large mixing bowl, beat the cream cheese and butter until smooth. Remove 3-1/2 cups to a small bowl; stir in pepper and set aside. Fold olives into remaining cream cheese mixture. Spread evenly over the bottom of a 9-in. springform pan; set aside.

2 In another large mixing bowl, beat cheddar cheese, cider and paprika on low speed for 1 minute. Beat on high until almost smooth.

Spread half over olive layer. Top with peppered cheese mixture. Top with remaining cheddar mixture. Cover with plastic wrap; refrigerate for 6 hours or until firm.

3 Place on serving plate and remove sides of pan. Press pecans into top; garnish with additional olives or grapes if desired. Serve with crackers. **Yield:** 24-30 servings.

TEST KITCHEN TIP
Coleen often cuts this appetizer into smaller wedges to give as hostess gifts or bring to smaller parties.

Sausage Wonton Stars

I like to make a batch of these cheesy pork-filled cups for guests and family. If I don't need the whole batch, I'll freeze the extra and just reheat them as a special treat for my husband and me.
—Anita Bukowski

1 package (12 ounces) wonton wrappers
1 pound bulk pork sausage
2 cups (8 ounces) shredded Colby cheese
1/2 medium green pepper, chopped
1/2 medium sweet red pepper, chopped
2 bunches green onions, sliced
1/2 cup ranch salad dressing

1 Lightly press wonton wrappers onto the bottom and up the sides of greased miniature muffin cups. Bake at 350° for 5 minutes or until edges are browned.

2 In a large skillet, cook sausage over medium heat until no longer pink; drain. Stir in the cheese, peppers, onions and salad dressing. Spoon a rounded tablespoonful into each wonton cup. Bake at 350° for 6-7 minutes or until heated through. **Yield:** about 4 dozen.

Pear Pistachio Pita

This recipe makes a fun and deliciously different appetizer or snack! Pears and pistachio nuts are a surprising and satisfying combination.
—Stephanie Marchese

2 tablespoons olive oil
2 teaspoons crushed garlic
4 whole pita breads (6 inches *each*)

1 cup (4 ounces) crumbled blue cheese
2 medium pears, peeled and sliced
1/2 cup chopped pistachios

1 In a bowl, combine the oil and garlic; brush on top of each pita. Arrange oil side up on an un-greased baking sheet. Sprinkle with cheese, pears and pistachios.

2 Bake at 375° for 8-10 minutes or until pears are tender. Cut into wedges. **Yield:** 24 appetizers.

STEPHANIE MARCHESE

Being Italian herself, it's no surprise that Stephanie mainly prepares Italian dishes for her family. Favorites of her husband, two children and two stepdaughters include pasta with homemade "sugo" (sauce) and all different kinds of lasagna. It wasn't until she joined our Test Kitchen staff more than 14 years ago that she really became interested in cooking. She also enjoys gardening, photography and spending time outdoors when the weather is nice.

Garden Salsa

Garden-fresh tomatoes and subtle seasonings make this salsa a real summer treat. I enjoy it so much, though, that I frequently whip it up year-round.
—Rita Krajcir

6 medium tomatoes, finely chopped
3/4 cup finely chopped green pepper
1/2 cup finely chopped onion
1/2 cup thinly sliced green onions
6 garlic cloves, minced
2 teaspoons cider vinegar
2 teaspoons lemon juice
2 teaspoons olive oil
1 to 2 teaspoons minced jalapeno pepper
1 to 2 teaspoons ground cumin
1/2 teaspoon salt
1/4 to 1/2 teaspoon cayenne pepper
Tortilla chips

In a large bowl, combine the first 12 ingredients. Cover and refrigerate until serving. Serve with chips. **Yield:** 5 cups.

EDITOR'S NOTE: When cutting or seeding hot peppers, use rubber or plastic gloves to protect your hands. Avoid touching your face.

Pepper Poppers

These creamy and zippy stuffed jalapenos will kick-start any party! I always am sure to make plenty, because they go fast.
—*Diane Werner*

- 1 package (8 ounces) cream cheese, softened
- 1 cup (4 ounces) shredded sharp cheddar cheese
- 1 cup (4 ounces) shredded Monterey Jack cheese
- 6 bacon strips, cooked and crumbled
- 1/4 teaspoon salt
- 1/4 teaspoon chili powder
- 1/4 teaspoon garlic powder
- 1 pound fresh jalapenos, halved lengthwise and seeded
- 1/2 cup dry bread crumbs

Sour cream, onion dip *or* ranch salad dressing

1 In a large mixing bowl, combine the cheeses, bacon and seasonings. Spoon about 2 tablespoonfuls into each pepper half. Roll in bread crumbs.

2 Place in a greased 15-in. x 10-in. x 1-in. baking pan. Bake, uncovered, at 300° for 20 minutes for spicy flavor, 30 minutes for medium and 40 minutes for mild. Serve with sour cream, dip or dressing. **Yield:** about 2 dozen.

EDITOR'S NOTE: When cutting or seeding hot peppers, use rubber or plastic gloves to protect your hands. Avoid touching your face.

Antipasto Appetizer Salad

Serve this with a slotted spoon as an appetizer or over torn Romaine lettuce to enjoy as a salad. I like it with toasted baguette slices on the side.
—*Tamra Duncan*

- 1 jar (16 ounces) roasted sweet red pepper strips, drained
- 1/2 pound mozzarella cheese, cubed
- 1 cup grape tomatoes
- 1 jar (7-1/2 ounces) marinated artichoke hearts, undrained
- 1 jar (7 ounces) stuffed olives, drained
- 1 can (6 ounces) pitted ripe olives, drained
- 1 teaspoon dried basil
- 1 teaspoon dried parsley flakes

Pepper to taste
Toasted baguette slices *or* Romaine lettuce, torn

1 In a large bowl, combine the first nine ingredients; toss to coat. Cover and refrigerate for at least 4 hours before serving.

2 Serve with baguette slices or over lettuce. **Yield:** 6 cups.

Orange Fruit Dip

The fruit I serve with this wonderful dip varies depending on the season. Our favorite, though, continues to be Granny Smith apples. —*Joylyn Trickel*

        1 cup sugar
        2 tablespoons plus 1 teaspoon cornstarch
    1/4 teaspoon salt
        1 cup orange juice
    1/2 cup water
    1/4 cup lemon juice
    1/2 teaspoon grated orange peel
    1/2 teaspoon grated lemon peel
Assorted fresh fruit

1 In a small saucepan, combine the sugar, cornstarch and salt; stir in the orange juice, water, lemon juice, and orange and lemon peels until blended. Bring to a boil; cook and stir for 2 minutes or until thickened.

2 Cover and refrigerate until chilled. Serve with fruit. **Yield:** 2 cups.

TEST KITCHEN TIP

Cut a slice from both the lemon and orange used for the grated peel in the recipe, then slice the fruit for garnish.

Chai

Chai (rhymes with "pie") is the word for tea in some parts of the world...but in India, it's a spiced milk tea that's becoming more popular in North America. This recipe is just as tasty as any coffeehouse chai. —*Peggy Fleming*

        2 cups water
        2 individual tea bags
        1 cinnamon stick
        6 cardamom seeds, crushed
        1 whole clove
    1/4 teaspoon ground ginger

    2-1/2 cups milk
      1/3 cup sugar
    Sweetened whipped cream and additional cinnamon sticks, optional

1 In a small saucepan, combine the first six ingredients. Bring to a boil. Reduce heat; cover and simmer for 5 minutes.

2 Stir in milk. Return to a boil; boil for 1 minute, then strain. Stir in sugar until dissolved. Top with whipped cream and garnish with a cinnamon stick if desired. **Yield:** 4 servings.

White Bean Bruschetta

(Pictured on page 14)

This fabulous bruschetta has a Tuscan flavor. Quick and easy, I've made it many times to serve when entertaining guests.

—*Kristin Arnett*

 1 cup canned great northern beans, rinsed
   and drained
 3 plum tomatoes, seeded and chopped
 1/4 cup chopped pitted Greek olives
 6 tablespoons olive oil, *divided*
 1/4 cup fresh basil leaves, cut into strips
 1 tablespoon minced garlic
 Salt and pepper to taste
 1 French bread baguette, cut
   into 1/3-inch-thick slices
 1 package (5.3 ounces) goat cheese

1 In a medium bowl, combine the beans, tomatoes, olives, 4 tablespoons oil, basil, garlic, salt and pepper.

2 Place bread slices on an ungreased baking sheet. Brush with remaining oil. Broil 3-4 in. from the heat until golden, about 1 minute. Spread with cheese; top with bean mixture. Serve immediately. **Yield:** about 20 servings.

Avocado Salsa

We love to snack on this salsa whenever the "munchies" hit. It's great to make ahead and add the avocado just before serving.

—*Coleen Martin*

1-2/3 cups frozen corn, thawed
   1 can (2-1/4 ounces) sliced ripe olives, drained
 1/2 cup chopped sweet red pepper
   3 tablespoons chopped onion
   1 can (4 ounces) chopped green chilies
   2 garlic cloves, minced
   3 tablespoons olive oil
   2 tablespoons lemon juice
4-1/2 teaspoons white wine vinegar
 1/2 teaspoon dried oregano
 1/4 teaspoon salt
 1/4 teaspoon pepper
   2 medium ripe avocados
Tortilla chips

1 In a large bowl, combine the corn, olives, red pepper, onion and chilies. In a small bowl, combine the garlic, oil, lemon juice, vinegar, oregano, salt and pepper. Pour over corn mixture; toss to coat. Cover and refrigerate overnight.

2 Just before serving, chop avocados and stir into salsa. Serve with chips. **Yield:** about 3-1/2 cups.

Grilled Wing Zingers

My niece's husband loves to make these chicken wings, but we have to be careful because he's likely to add extra hot sauce!
—Karen Johnson

- 40 whole chicken wings (about 8 pounds)
- 2 cups packed brown sugar
- 2 cups hot sauce
- 1/2 cup butter, cubed
- 2 tablespoons cider vinegar
- 1/3 cup sugar
- 1/2 cup Italian seasoning
- 1/4 cup dried rosemary, crushed
- 1/4 cup paprika
- 1/4 cup chili powder
- 1/4 cup pepper
- 2 tablespoons cayenne pepper
- 1 cup blue cheese salad dressing
- 1/2 cup ranch salad dressing
- Celery sticks

1 Cut chicken wings into three sections; discard wing tip section. Set the wings aside. In a large saucepan, bring the brown sugar, hot sauce, butter and vinegar to a boil. Reduce heat; simmer, uncovered, for 6-8 minutes or until butter is melted and sauce is heated through. Cool.

2 In a gallon-size resealable plastic bag, combine sugar, seasonings and 1 cup sauce. Add chicken wings in batches. Seal bag; toss to coat.

3 Prepare grill for indirect medium heat. Grill wings, covered, over indirect medium heat for 35-45 minutes or until juices run clear, turning once and basting occasionally with remaining sauce.

4 In a small bowl, combine blue cheese and ranch salad dressings; serve with chicken wings and celery sticks. **Yield:** 25-30 servings.

EDITOR'S NOTE: 8 pounds of uncooked chicken wing sections (wingettes) may be substituted for the whole chicken wings.

White Chocolate Party Mix

The sweet and salty combination in this snack mix is awesome. I often send it to school in snack-size resealable plastic bags for a class treat or bake sale. When I take it to classroom functions, I eliminate the peanuts because of allergies.
—Coleen Martin

- 1 package (10 ounces) mini pretzels
- 5 cups Cherrios
- 5 cups corn Chex cereal
- 2 cups salted peanuts
- 1 pound chocolate M&M's
- 2 packages (10 to 12 ounces *each*) vanilla *or* white chips
- 3 tablespoons vegetable oil

1 In a large bowl, combine first five ingredients; set aside. In a microwave-safe bowl, heat chips and oil at 70% powder for 1-1/2 minutes, stirring once. Microwave on high for 5-10 seconds; stir until smooth. Pour over cereal mixture; mix well.

2 Spread onto three waxed paper-lined baking sheets to cool. Break apart and store in an airtight container. **Yield:** 5 quarts.

EDITOR'S NOTE: This recipe was tested in a 1,100-watt microwave.

Mocha Punch

This creamy drink is such a nice alternative to the typical fruit-based punch. I can't stop drinking it once I start!

—*Sue Draheim*

  1-1/2 quarts water
    1/2 cup instant chocolate drink mix
    1/2 cup sugar
    1/4 cup instant coffee granules
    1/2 gallon vanilla ice cream
    1/2 gallon chocolate ice cream
      1 cup heavy whipping cream, whipped
Chocolate curls, optional

1 In a large saucepan, bring water to a boil. Remove from the heat. Add the drink mix, sugar and coffee granules; stir until dissolved. Cover and refrigerate for 4 hours or overnight.

2 About 30 minutes before serving, pour into a punch bowl. Add ice cream by scoopfuls; stir until partially melted. Garnish with dollops of whipped cream and chocolate curls if desired. *Yield:* 20-25 servings (about 5 quarts).

Layered Oriental Dip

With tender chunks of chicken and oriental seasonings, this savory dip is simply yummy! It's a nice switch from taco dip and is always a hit at parties.

—*Wendy Stenman*

      1 cup chopped cooked chicken breast
    1/2 cup shredded carrot
    1/4 cup chopped unsalted peanuts
      3 tablespoons chopped green onions
      3 tablespoons reduced-sodium soy sauce, *divided*
      1 tablespoon minced fresh parsley
      1 garlic clove, minced
      1 teaspoon sesame seeds, toasted
      2 tablespoons packed brown sugar

  1-1/2 teaspoons cornstarch
    1/2 cup water
      2 tablespoons ketchup
  1-1/2 teaspoons Worcestershire sauce
    1/2 teaspoon cider vinegar
      2 drops hot pepper sauce
      1 package (8 ounces) reduced-fat cream cheese
Baked tortilla chips

1 In a large bowl, combine the chicken, carrot, peanuts, onions, 2 tablespoons soy sauce, parsley, garlic and sesame seeds. Cover and refrigerate for several hours.

2 In a saucepan, combine the brown sugar and cornstarch; stir in the water, ketchup, Worcestershire sauce, vinegar and hot pepper sauce until smooth. Bring to a boil; cook and stir for 1-2 minutes or until thickened. Cool for 5 minutes. Cover and refrigerate.

3 Just before serving, in a mixing bowl, beat cream cheese and remaining soy sauce until smooth. Spread evenly on a 12-in. serving dish. Cover with chicken mixture; drizzle with sauce. Serve with chips. *Yield:* 10 servings.

TEST KITCHEN TIP

If you are short on time, cook the chicken and make the sauce the night before you plan on serving this dip.

Crepes Florentine

Bring this spectacular appetizer to the table to cut into wedges, and you'll receive many compliments on the presentation! The rich Mornay-sauced spinach and creamy mushroom mixtures are beautifully layered between crepes.
—Sue A. Jurack

     2-1/2 cups milk
         4 eggs
       1/4 cup butter, melted
         2 cups all-purpose flour
       1/4 teaspoon salt
FILLING:
         8 tablespoons butter, *divided*
         5 tablespoons all-purpose flour
       1/4 teaspoon salt
       1/4 teaspoon pepper
Dash ground nutmeg
     2-1/4 cups milk
       1/3 cup heavy whipping cream
         1 cup (4 ounces) shredded Gruyere *or* Swiss cheese, *divided*
     1-1/2 cups finely chopped fresh mushrooms
         1 shallot, finely chopped
         1 package (8 ounces) cream cheese, softened
         1 egg
         2 packages (10 ounces *each*) frozen chopped spinach, thawed and squeezed dry
         2 tablespoons shredded Parmesan cheese

1 For crepes, in a large mixing bowl, combine the milk, eggs and butter. Combine flour and salt; add to milk mixture and mix well. Cover and refrigerate for 1 hour.

2 Heat a lightly greased 8-in. nonstick skillet; pour 2 tablespoons batter into the center of skillet. Lift and tilt pan to evenly coat bottom. Cook until top appears dry; turn and cook 15-20 seconds longer. Remove to a wire rack. Repeat with remaining batter, adding butter to skillet as needed. When cool, stack crepes with waxed paper or paper towels in between.

3 For filling, in a large saucepan, melt 5 tablespoons butter. Stir in the flour, salt, pepper and nutmeg until smooth; gradually add the milk. Bring to a boil; cook and stir for 2 minutes or until thickened. Reduce heat to low; stir in the cream and 3/4 cup Gruyere cheese. Cook and stir until cheese is melted. Remove from heat.

4 In a skillet, saute mushrooms and shallot in 2 tablespoons butter until tender. In a small mixing bowl, beat cream cheese and egg until smooth. Beat in mushroom mixture. Add enough cheese sauce to achieve a spreadable consistency. In a bowl, combine the spinach and 1/2 cup cheese sauce until blended. Add additional sauce if needed to achieve a spreadable consistency.

5 To assemble, on two greased 9-in. ovenproof pie or tart pans, layer a crepe, spinach mixture, another crepe, then mushroom mixture. Repeat five more times. Pour remaining sauce over the stacks. Sprinkle with remaining Gruyere and Parmesan cheeses. Dot with remaining butter. Cover and refrigerate for 1 hour.

6 Remove from refrigerator 15 minutes before baking. Bake at 350° for 55-60 minutes or until bubbly and golden and a thermometer reads 160°. Let stand for 5 minutes before cutting. Cut into wedges. **Yield:** 8-12 servings.

Tart 'n' Tangy Citrus Cooler

(Pictured on page 14)

This is a sweet and refreshing beverage that's perfect when cooling off in the shade. In summer, I make the sugar syrup in advance, so I can mix up a quick batch after we've been out in the sun. The syrup can keep for up to a week.

—Joylyn Trickel

6 cups water, *divided*
3 cups sugar
3 cups fresh lime juice *or* Key lime juice

3 cups orange juice
Crushed ice

1 In a large saucepan, bring 3 cups water and sugar to a boil; stir until sugar is dissolved. Cook and stir for 3 minutes. Remove from the heat; transfer to a bowl. Cover and refrigerate for at least 3 hours.

2 In a large pitcher, combine the sugar mixture, lime juice, orange juice and remaining water; stir well. Refrigerate until chilled. Serve over ice. **Yield:** 3-1/4 quarts.

Bread Bowl Fondue

This is a favorite appetizer that I often make for parties. The fondue can be made ahead and put in the bread just before baking.

—Karen Scales

1 round loaf (1 pound) unsliced bread
1/2 pound process cheese (Velveeta), cubed
2 cups (16 ounces) sour cream
1 package (8 ounces) cream cheese, softened
1 cup diced fully cooked ham
1/2 cup chopped green onions
1 can (4 ounces) chopped green chilies
1 teaspoon Worcestershire sauce
2 tablespoons vegetable oil
1 tablespoon butter, melted
Assorted fresh vegetables

1 Cut the top fourth off the loaf of bread; set top aside. Carefully hollow out bottom, leaving a 1/2-in. shell. Cube removed bread; set aside.

2 In a large bowl, combine the process cheese, sour cream and cream cheese. Stir in the ham, green onions, chilies and Worcestershire sauce. Spoon into bread shell; replace top. Wrap tightly in heavy-duty foil and place on a baking sheet. Bake at 350° for 60-70 minutes or until the filling is heated through.

3 Meanwhile, toss reserved bread cubes with oil and butter. Place in a 15-in. x 10-in. x 1-in. baking pan. Bake for 10-15 minutes or until golden brown, stirring occasionally. Unwrap loaf and remove bread top; stir filling. Serve with vegetables and toasted bread cubes. **Yield:** 5 cups.

Strawberry Lemonade Slush

This pretty slush was served at my baby shower. It's a perfect refresher for this type of event!
—*Sarah Thompson*

1 package (10 ounces) frozen sweetened
   sliced strawberries, thawed
3/4 cup pink lemonade concentrate
3/4 cup water
3/4 cup crushed ice
2 cups chilled club soda

1 In a blender or food processor, place the strawberries, concentrate, water and ice; cover and process until smooth. Pour into a 2-qt. freezer container. Cover and freeze for at least 12 hours or until icy.

2 Remove from freezer 1 hour before serving. Just before serving, transfer strawberry mixture to a large bowl; stir in soda. **Yield:** about 2 quarts.

Tomato-Onion Phyllo Pizza

With a delicate crust and lots of luscious tomatoes on top, this dish is a special one to serve to guests. Whenever I set it out at a party, it's one of the first platters to be emptied.
—*Janaan Cunningham*

5 tablespoons butter, melted
7 sheets phyllo dough (18-inch x 14-inch sheet size)
7 tablespoons grated Parmesan cheese, *divided*
1 cup (4 ounces) shredded mozzarella cheese
1 cup thinly sliced onion
7 to 9 plum tomatoes (about 1-1/4 pounds), sliced
1-1/2 teaspoons minced fresh oregano *or* 1/2 teaspoon dried oregano
1 teaspoon minced fresh thyme *or* 1/4 teaspoon dried thyme
Salt and pepper to taste

1 Brush a 15-in. x 10-in. x 1-in. baking pan with some of the melted butter. Lay a sheet of phyllo in pan, folding edges in to fit. (Keep remaining phyllo dough covered with plastic wrap to avoid drying out.) Brush dough with butter and sprinkle with 1 tablespoon Parmesan cheese.

2 Repeat layers five times, folding edges for each layer. Top with remaining dough, folding edges to fit pan; brush with remaining butter.

3 Sprinkle with mozzarella cheese; arrange onion and tomatoes over the cheese. Sprinkle with the oregano, thyme, salt, pepper and remaining Parmesan. Bake at 375° for 20-25 minutes or until edges are golden brown. **Yield:** 28 slices.

Marinated Mozzarella Cubes

I gave these as gifts one year for Christmas. The jar for my in-laws was gone before Christmas Day was over!
—*Suzanne Kern*

    1 pound mozzarella cheese, cut into 1-inch cubes
    1 jar (7 ounces) roasted red peppers, drained and cut into bite-size pieces
    6 fresh thyme sprigs
    2 garlic cloves, minced
1-1/4 cups olive oil
    2 tablespoons minced fresh rosemary
    2 teaspoons Italian seasoning
  1/4 teaspoon crushed red pepper flakes
Bread *or* crackers

1 In a quart jar with a tight-fitting lid, layer a third of the cheese, peppers, thyme and garlic. Repeat layers twice. In a small bowl, combine the oil, rosemary, Italian seasoning and pepper flakes.

2 Pour into jar; seal and turn upside down. Refrigerate overnight, turning several times. Serve with bread or crackers. **Yield:** 12-16 servings.

Coquilles St. Jacques ✓

I have served this first course at many winter dinner parties when fresh seafood is most plentiful. I serve the seafood mixture in natural scallop shells for a pretty presentation.   —*Sue A. Jurack*

1-1/2 pounds sea scallops, rinsed and patted dry
    3 shallots, finely chopped
    3 tablespoons butter
    2 cups dry white wine
  1/8 teaspoon salt
  1/8 teaspoon pepper

3/4 cup heavy whipping cream
  2 teaspoons cornstarch
  1 tablespoon water
  1 to 2 teaspoons lemon juice
  1 tablespoon minced fresh parsley

1 Cut scallops into three horizontal slices. In a large skillet, cook shallots in butter over low heat for 2-3 minutes or just until softened. Add the scallops, wine, salt and pepper. Bring just to a boil and poach for 1-2 minutes over low heat. Using a slotted spoon, remove scallops and drain on paper towels.

2 Boil poaching liquid, uncovered, over high heat for about 10-15 minutes or until reduced to 5-6 tablespoons. Add cream; return to a boil.

3 Combine cornstarch and water until smooth. Stir into sauce; cook and stir for 1-2 minutes or until slightly thickened. Reduce heat to low; adjust seasonings if desired. Return scallops to skillet and heat through. Add lemon juice and sprinkle with parsley. **Yield:** 6 servings.

TEST KITCHEN TIP
Once purchased, you can keep natural scallop shells year after year. After the dinner party, soak them, then use a soft brush to clean between the ridges and pop them into the dishwasher to clean them thoroughly.

Touch-of-Mint Iced Tea

This beverage is so refreshing on a hot summer day. It's a great way to use the mint that wants to take control of my garden.
—*Wendy Stenman*

6 cups boiling water
4 individual tea bags
1 cup packed fresh mint
3/4 cup frozen lemonade concentrate
Lemon slices and additional mint, optional

1 In a heatproof bowl or pitcher, pour boiling water over tea bags; cover and steep for 5 minutes. Remove tea bags. Cool for 15 minutes. Add mint; steep for 5 minutes. Strain.

2 Add lemonade concentrate; stir well. Cover and refrigerate. Serve over ice; garnish with lemon and mint if desired. **Yield:** 6 servings.

TEST KITCHEN TIP
Increase the number of tea bags for a stronger tea flavor.

Crab Triangles

I make these crisp seafood appetizers for many family gatherings. They can be made ahead and frozen, making them perfect for parties.
—*Patricia Schmeling*

1 package (16 ounces, 14-inch x 9-inch sheet size) frozen phyllo dough, thawed
1 package (8 ounces) cream cheese, softened
2 teaspoons milk
1/2 teaspoon prepared horseradish
1/4 teaspoon salt
1/4 teaspoon pepper

1 can (6 ounces) lump crabmeat, drained, flaked and cartilage removed
1 cup cooked small shrimp
2 green onions, finely chopped
1 tablespoon finely chopped almonds
1/2 cup butter, melted

1 Remove one wrapped phyllo roll from package and thaw according to package directions. Return remaining wrapped phyllo roll to freezer. Meanwhile, in a bowl, combine the cream cheese, milk, horseradish, salt and pepper. Add the crab, shrimp, onions and almonds; stir gently to coat.

2 Lightly brush one sheet of phyllo with butter. Layer with two more sheets of phyllo, brushing each sheet with butter. (Keep remaining phyllo dough covered with plastic wrap to avoid drying out.) Cut the layered sheets lengthwise into 2-in. strips. Cut each strip widthwise in half.

3 Place a heaping teaspoonful of filling in lower corner of each strip. Fold dough over filling, forming a triangle. Fold triangle up, then fold triangle over, forming another triangle. Continue folding, like a flag, until you come to the end of the strip. Brush end of dough with butter and press onto triangle to seal. Repeat with remaining ingredients.

4 Place triangles on ungreased baking sheets. Bake at 400° for 14-16 minutes or until golden brown. Cool on a wire rack. **Yield:** about 5 dozen.

Nutty Stuffed Mushrooms

Basil, Parmesan cheese and mushrooms blend together well, while buttery pecans give these delicious treats a surprising crunch.
—Julie Ferron

18 to 20 large fresh mushrooms
1 small onion, chopped
3 tablespoons butter
1/4 cup dry bread crumbs
1/4 cup finely chopped pecans

3 tablespoons grated Parmesan cheese
1/4 teaspoon salt
1/4 teaspoon dried basil
Dash cayenne pepper

1 Remove stems from mushrooms; set caps aside. Finely chop stems; place in a paper towel and squeeze to remove any liquid. In a skillet, saute chopped mushrooms and onion in butter for 5 minutes or until tender. Remove from the heat; set aside.

2 In a small bowl, combine the bread crumbs, pecans, Parmesan cheese, salt, basil and pepper; add mushroom mixture. Stuff firmly into mushroom caps.

3 Place in a greased 15-in. x 10-in. x 1-in. baking pan. Bake, uncovered, at 400° for 15-18 minutes or until tender. Serve hot. **Yield:** 18-20 servings.

Marinated Shrimp

My husband's cousin introduced us to this recipe. Every time I bring it to a party, everyone wants the recipe. It's so easy to prepare.
—Stephanie Marchese

1 pound cooked medium shrimp, peeled and deveined
1 small red onion, thinly sliced
2-1/2 teaspoons capers
1/3 cup canola oil
1/4 cup white wine vinegar
1/2 teaspoon salt
1/2 teaspoon celery seed

1 In a large bowl, combine the shrimp, onion and capers. In a jar with a tight-fitting lid, combine the oil, vinegar, salt and celery seed; shake well. Pour over shrimp mixture and toss to coat. Cover and refrigerate for 6 hours or overnight, stirring occasionally.

2 Using a slotted spoon, transfer shrimp mixture to a serving bowl. **Yield:** 8-10 servings.

EDITOR'S NOTE: Before using capers, turn them into a sieve and rinse with cool running water to remove excess salt or brine. Blot well with paper towels before using.

Cheese Ball Snack Mix

The chili powder and hot pepper sauce give some zip to this addictive snack mix. I eat it by the handfuls!
—*Sue Megonigle*

1-1/2 cups salted cashews
   1 cup crisp cheese ball snacks
   1 cup corn Chex cereal
   1 cup rice Chex cereal
   1 cup miniature pretzels
   1 cup chow mein noodles
1/2 cup butter, melted
   1 tablespoon soy sauce
   1 teaspoon Worcestershire sauce
1/2 teaspoon seasoned salt
1/4 teaspoon chili powder
1/4 teaspoon hot pepper sauce

1 In a large bowl, combine the cashews, cheese balls, cereal, pretzels and chow mein noodles. In another bowl, combine the remaining ingredients. Pour over cereal mixture and toss to coat.

2 Transfer to an ungreased 15-in. x 10-in. x 1-in. baking pan. Bake at 250° for 1 hour, stirring every 15 minutes. **Yield:** about 6 cups.

EDITOR'S NOTE: This recipe was tested with Planter's Cheeze Balls.

Onion Brie Appetizers

Puff pastry is filled with onions and Brie cheese for this recipe. These are wonderful appetizers that disappear fast! Caramelized onions add sweetness to these tasty bits.
—*Patricia Schmeling*

   2 medium onions, thinly sliced
   3 tablespoons butter
   2 tablespoons brown sugar
1/2 teaspoon white wine vinegar
   1 sheet frozen puff pastry, thawed
   4 ounces Brie *or* Camembert, rind removed, softened
   1 to 2 teaspoons caraway seeds
   1 egg
   2 teaspoons water

1 In a large skillet, cook the onions, butter, brown sugar and vinegar over medium-low heat until onions are golden brown, stirring frequently. Remove with a slotted spoon; cool to room temperature.

2 On a lightly floured surface, roll puff pastry into an 11-in. x 8-in. rectangle. Spread Brie over pastry. Cover with the onions; sprinkle with caraway seeds. Roll up one long side to the middle of the dough; roll up the other side so the two rolls meet in the center. Using a serrated knife, cut into 1/2-in. slices. Place on parchment paper-lined baking sheets; flatten to 1/4-in. thickness. Refrigerate for 15 minutes.

3 In a small bowl, beat egg and water; brush over slices. Bake at 375° for 12-14 minutes or until puffed and golden brown. Serve warm. **Yield:** 1-1/2 dozen.

Savory Party Bread

This easy but elegant-looking appetizer is so good warm when the cheese is nice and gooey. The sliced loaf fans out for a fun presentation. —Amy Welk-Thieding

　　1 round loaf (1 pound) unsliced sourdough bread
　　1 pound Monterey Jack cheese, sliced
　1/2 cup butter, melted
　1/2 cup chopped green onions
　　2 to 3 teaspoons poppy seeds

1 Cut the bread lengthwise and crosswise without cutting through the bottom crust. Insert cheese between cuts. Combine the butter, onions and poppy seeds; drizzle over the bread.

2 Wrap in foil; place on a baking sheet. Bake at 350° for 15 minutes. Uncover; bake 10 minutes longer or until the cheese is melted. **Yield:** 6-8 servings.

TEST KITCHEN TIP

The bread can be sliced and filled a day ahead. Right before company comes, melt the butter and add the green onions and poppy seeds.

SUE MEGONIGLE

Before coming to work at Reiman Publications 4 years ago, Sue worked in a daycare center, cooking for more than 100 hungry kids. She loved hearing the little ones frequently comment, "My mom can't cook like you!" This single mom, who is raising two teenage boys, especially likes baking up batches of homemade cookies. She also enjoys gardening and watching football.

Minty Orange Lemonade

I keep this refreshing beverage on hand in the refrigerator during the warm summer months. Friends and neighbors enjoy cool glassfuls when they stop by to visit. —Kristin Arnett

2-1/2 cups water
1-1/2 cups sugar
1-1/3 cups lemon juice
　3/4 cup mint leaves

2/3 cup orange juice
　4 teaspoons grated orange peel
　7 cups cold water
Orange slices and mint sprigs

1 In a large saucepan, combine water and sugar; bring to a boil. Reduce heat; cover and simmer for 5 minutes. Remove from the heat; add the lemon juice, mint, orange juice and peel. Let stand for 1 hour.

2 Strain and discard mint and peel. Add cold water; serve over ice. Garnish with mint and orange slices. **Yield:** 3 quarts.

BREADS

Raspberry Streusel Coffee Cake

Easter brunch would not be complete without this mouth-watering moist coffee cake. —*Patricia Schmeling*

3-1/2 cups unsweetened raspberries
1 cup water
2 tablespoons lemon juice
1-1/4 cups sugar
1/3 cup cornstarch
BATTER:
3 cups all-purpose flour
1 cup sugar
1 teaspoon baking powder
1 teaspoon baking soda
1 cup cold butter
2 eggs, lightly beaten
1 cup (8 ounces) sour cream
1 teaspoon vanilla extract
TOPPING:
1/2 cup all-purpose flour
1/2 cup sugar
1/4 cup butter, softened
1/2 cup chopped pecans
GLAZE:
1/2 cup confectioners' sugar
2 teaspoons milk
1/2 teaspoon vanilla extract

1 In a large saucepan, cook raspberries and water over medium heat for 5 minutes. Add lemon juice. Combine sugar and cornstarch; stir into fruit mixture. Bring to a boil; cook and stir for 2 minutes or until thickened. Cool.

2 In a bowl, combine the flour, sugar, baking powder and baking soda. Cut in butter until mixture resembles coarse crumbs. Stir in eggs, sour cream and vanilla (batter will be stiff).

3 Spread half into a greased 13-in. x 9-in. x 2-in. baking dish. Spread raspberry filling over batter; spoon remaining batter over filling. Combine topping ingredients; sprinkle over top.

4 Bake at 350° for 40-45 minutes or until golden brown. Cool on a wire rack. Combine the glaze ingredients; drizzle over warm cake. **Yield:** 12-16 servings.

Parmesan Herb Loaves

This is the perfect bread to make and let rise as I get other projects done or spend time with my family. It looks impressive and doesn't have a lot of ingredients. —*Amy Welk-Thieding*

2 loaves (1 pound *each*) frozen bread dough
1/2 cup shredded Parmesan cheese
1 tablespoon dried parsley flakes
1 tablespoon dried minced garlic
1/2 teaspoon dill weed
1/2 teaspoon salt
2 tablespoons butter, melted

1 Place dough in two greased 8-in. x 4-in. x 2-in. loaf pans. Thaw according to package directions. In a small bowl, combine Parmesan cheese, parsley, garlic, dill and salt. Brush dough with butter; sprinkle with cheese mixture. Cover and let rise in a warm place until nearly doubled, about 2-1/2 hours.

2 Bake at 350° for 20-25 minutes or until golden brown. Remove from pans to wire racks to cool. **Yield:** 2 loaves.

Triple-Berry Muffins

(Pictured on page 33)

I love all kinds of fresh berries, and this muffin recipe deliciously showcases them. Sometimes I substitute chopped blackberries for the blueberries.
—*Janaan Cunningham*

    3 cups all-purpose flour
1-1/2 cups sugar
4-1/2 teaspoons ground cinnamon
    3 teaspoons baking powder
  1/2 teaspoon salt
  1/2 teaspoon baking soda

    2 eggs
1-1/4 cups milk
    1 cup butter, melted
    1 cup fresh blueberries
  1/2 cup fresh raspberries
  1/2 cup chopped fresh strawberries

1 In a large bowl, combine the first six ingredients. In another bowl, beat the eggs, milk and butter; stir into dry ingredients just until moistened. Fold in berries.

2 Fill greased or paper-lined muffin cups three-fourths full. Bake at 375° for 18-20 minutes or until a toothpick comes out clean. Cool for 5 minutes before removing from pans to wire racks. **Yield:** about 1-1/2 dozen.

TEST KITCHEN TIP

Place the fresh strawberries in the freezer for about 15 minutes before you chop them. It makes them easier to chop.

Maple Oat Bread

The first time I made this old-fashioned oat bread, it was a hit with my family. It's been popular with them ever since.
—*Janet Briggs*

    1 cup old-fashioned oats
    1 cup boiling water
    1 package (1/4 ounce) active dry yeast
  1/3 cup warm water (110° to 115°)
  1/2 cup maple syrup
    2 teaspoons canola oil
1-1/2 teaspoons salt
3-1/2 to 4 cups all-purpose flour
TOPPING:
    1 egg white, lightly beaten
    2 tablespoons old-fashioned oats

1 Place oats in a blender or food processor; cover and process for 6-7 seconds or until coarsely chopped. Transfer to a small bowl; add boiling water. Let stand until mixture cools to 110°-115°. In a large mixing bowl, dissolve yeast in 1/3 cup warm water; add syrup, oil, salt, oat mixture and 2 cups flour. Beat until smooth. Stir in enough remaining flour to form a soft dough.

2 Turn onto a lightly floured surface; knead until smooth and elastic, about 6-8 minutes. Place in a greased bowl, turning once to grease top. Cover and let rise in a warm place until doubled, about 1 hour.

3 Punch dough down. Turn onto a lightly floured surface. Shape into a flattened 9-in. round loaf. Place in a greased 9-in. round baking dish. Cover and let rise until doubled, about 45 minutes. Brush with egg white; sprinkle with oats.

4 Bake at 350° for 30-40 minutes or until golden brown. Remove from pan to a wire rack to cool. **Yield:** 1 loaf (16 slices).

Olive and Tomato Bread

This savory bread has a wonderful aroma and full flavor. It was an immediate hit with our Test Kitchen staff.
—Kristin Arnett

6 to 8 cups bread flour
2 tablespoons sugar
2 packages (1/4 ounce *each*) active dry yeast
4 teaspoons salt
3 cups warm water (120° to 130°)
1/3 cup olive oil
1 jar (8 ounces) pitted Greek olives, drained and sliced
1/2 cup oil-packed sun-dried tomatoes, chopped

1 In a large mixing bowl, combine 2 cups flour, sugar, yeast and salt. Add water and oil; beat just until moistened. Stir in the olives and tomatoes. Stir in enough of the remaining flour to form a soft dough (dough will be sticky).

2 Turn onto a floured surface; knead until smooth and elastic, about 6-8 minutes. Place in a greased bowl, turning once to grease top. Cover and let rise in a warm place until doubled, about 1 hour.

3 Punch dough down. Turn onto a lightly floured surface; divide into thirds. Shape each portion into a loaf. Place in three greased 9-in. x 5-in. x 3-in. loaf pans. Cover and let rise until doubled, about 45 minutes.

4 Bake at 375° for 30-35 minutes or until golden brown. Remove from pans to wire racks to cool. **Yield:** 3 loaves.

Whole Wheat Honey Rolls

My niece tells me that her son drops the basketball and runs into the house when the aroma of these rolls wafts from their kitchen window. The creamy honey butter adds a little sweetness.
—Karen Johnson

2 packages (1/4 ounce *each*) active dry yeast
2 cups warm buttermilk (110° to 115°)
1/2 cup butter, melted
1/3 cup honey
1 teaspoon salt
1 teaspoon baking soda
3 cups whole wheat flour
1-1/2 to 2-1/2 cups all-purpose flour
Additional melted butter
HONEY BUTTER:
1 cup butter, softened
1/2 cup honey

1 In a large mixing bowl, dissolve yeast in warm buttermilk. Add the butter, honey, salt, baking soda and whole wheat flour. Beat until smooth. Stir in enough all-purpose flour to form a soft dough.

2 Turn onto a floured surface; knead until smooth and elastic, about 6-8 minutes. Place in a greased bowl, turning once to grease top. Cover and let rise in a warm place until doubled, about 1 hour.

3 Punch dough down. Turn onto a lightly floured surface; divide into seven portions. Divide each portion into six pieces; shape each into a ball. Place 2 in. apart on greased baking sheets. Cover and let rise until doubled, about 30 minutes.

4 Brush with melted butter. Bake at 400° for 12-16 minutes or until golden brown. Remove to wire racks to cool. In a small mixing bowl, beat butter and honey until smooth; serve with rolls. **Yield:** 3-1/2 dozen.

EDITOR'S NOTE: Warmed buttermilk will appear curdled.

Amish Onion Cake

This rich, moist bread with an onion-poppy seed topping is great served as an accompaniment to soup and a salad.
—Peggy Fleming

     3 to 4 medium onions, chopped
     2 cups cold butter, *divided*
     1 tablespoon poppy seeds
 1-1/2 teaspoons salt
 1-1/2 teaspoons paprika
     1 teaspoon coarsely ground pepper
     4 cups all-purpose flour
   1/2 cup cornstarch
     1 tablespoon baking powder
     1 tablespoon sugar
     1 tablespoon brown sugar
     5 eggs
   3/4 cup milk
   3/4 cup sour cream

1 In a large skillet, cook onions in 1/2 cup butter over low heat for 10 minutes. Stir in the poppy seeds, salt, paprika and pepper; cook until golden brown, stirring occasionally. Remove from the heat; set aside.

2 In a bowl, combine the flour, cornstarch, baking powder and sugars. Cut in 1-1/4 cups butter until mixture resembles coarse crumbs. Melt the remaining butter. In a bowl, whisk the eggs, milk, sour cream and melted butter. Make a well in dry ingredients; stir in egg mixture just until moistened. Spread into a greased 10-in. springform pan. Spoon onion mixture over the dough. Place pan on a baking sheet.

3 Bake at 350° for 35-40 minutes or until a toothpick inserted near the center comes out clean. Serve warm. **Yield:** 10-12 servings.

Cream Cheese Pumpkin Muffins

I first made this recipe back in 1987 and have since made it many times over the years because it's my children's favorite muffin recipe.
—Wendy Stenman

     1 package (8 ounces) cream cheese, softened
     1 egg
     1 tablespoon sugar
 MUFFIN:
 2-1/4 cups all-purpose flour
     3 teaspoons pumpkin pie spice
     1 teaspoon baking soda
   1/2 teaspoon salt
     2 eggs, lightly beaten
     2 cups sugar
     1 cup canned pumpkin
   1/2 cup canola oil
    24 pecan halves, optional

1 For the filling, in a small mixing bowl, beat the cream cheese, egg and sugar until smooth; set aside. In a large bowl, combine the flour, pumpkin pie spice, baking soda and salt. Beat the eggs, sugar, pumpkin and oil; stir into dry ingredients just until moistened.

2 Divide half of the batter among 24 greased or paper-lined muffin cups. Drop filling by teaspoonfuls over batter. Top with remaining batter. Place a pecan on each muffin if desired.

3 Bake at 350° for 20-22 minutes or until a toothpick comes out clean. Cool for 5 minutes before removing from pans to wire racks. **Yield:** 2 dozen.

Lemon Cheese Braid ✓

This rich and special bread just melts in your mouth. I once made four loaves for my husband's treat day at the office, and they were gone before 10 a.m.! —Coleen Martin

   1 package (1/4 ounce) active dry yeast
   3 tablespoons warm water (110° to 115°)
1/3 cup milk
1/4 cup sugar
1/4 cup butter, melted
   2 eggs
1/2 teaspoon salt
   3 to 3-1/2 cups all-purpose flour
FILLING:
   2 packages (one 8 ounces, one 3 ounces) cream cheese, softened
1/2 cup sugar
   1 egg
   1 teaspoon grated lemon peel
ICING:
1/2 cup confectioners' sugar
1/4 teaspoon vanilla extract
   2 to 3 teaspoons milk

1 In a large mixing bowl, dissolve yeast in warm water. Add the milk, sugar, butter, eggs, salt and 2 cups flour; beat on low speed for 3 minutes. Stir in enough of remaining flour to form a soft dough.

2 Turn onto a floured surface; knead until smooth and elastic, about 6-8 minutes. Place in a greased bowl, turning once to grease top. Cover and let rise in a warm place until doubled, about 1 hour. Meanwhile, in a small mixing bowl, beat all the filling ingredients until fluffy; set aside.

3 Punch dough down. Turn onto a lightly floured surface; roll into a 14-in. x 12-in. rectangle. Place on a greased baking sheet. Spread filling down center third of rectangle. On each long side, cut 1-in.-wide strips, 3 in. into center. Starting at one end, fold alternating strips at an angle across filling. Seal end. Cover and let rise for 30 minutes.

4 Bake at 375° for 25-30 minutes or until golden brown. Cool on a wire rack. Combine confectioners' sugar, vanilla and enough milk to achieve drizzling consistency; drizzle over bread. **Yield:** 12-14 servings.

Blueberry Bread

This is a simple quick bread recipe that I look forward to making when fresh blueberries are in season. It's so good, though, that I end up making it year-round. —Karen Scales

   2 cups plus 2 tablespoons all-purpose flour, *divided*
3/4 cup sugar
   1 teaspoon baking powder
1/2 teaspoon salt

1/4 teaspoon baking soda
   1 egg
2/3 cup orange juice
   2 tablespoons butter, melted
   1 cup fresh *or* frozen blueberries

1 In a large mixing bowl, combine 2 cups flour, sugar, baking powder, salt and baking soda. Beat the egg, orange juice and butter. Add to the dry ingredients; beat just until combined. Toss blueberries with remaining flour; fold into batter.

2 Pour into a greased 8-in. x 4-in. x 2-in. loaf pan. Bake at 325° for 60-65 minutes or until a toothpick inserted near the center comes out clean. Cool in pan for 10 minutes before removing to a wire rack to cool completely. **Yield:** 1 loaf.

Streusel Coffee Cake

(Pictured on page 32)

I like to find fabulous light coffee cake recipes to enjoy with my coffee on relaxing weekend mornings. This one is a favorite. —Peggy Fleming

2/3 cup chopped walnuts
1/3 cup packed brown sugar
1 tablespoon butter, melted
1/2 teaspoon ground cinnamon
COFFEE CAKE:
1/4 cup butter, softened
1-1/4 cups sugar
2 egg yolks
1/4 cup canola oil
1/4 cup unsweetened applesauce
1 teaspoon vanilla extract
3 cups cake flour
2 teaspoons baking powder
1 teaspoon baking soda
1/4 teaspoon salt
1-1/2 cups reduced-fat sour cream
4 egg whites
2 teaspoons confectioners' sugar

1 In a small bowl, combine the nuts, brown sugar, butter and cinnamon; set aside. In a large mixing bowl, beat the butter and sugar until light and crumbly. Beat in the egg yolks, oil, applesauce and vanilla. Combine the dry ingredients; add to sugar mixture alternately with sour cream. In another mixing bowl, beat egg whites on high speed until stiff peaks form. Fold into batter.

2 Pour half of the batter into a 10-in. fluted tube pan coated with nonstick cooking spray and floured; sprinkle with nut mixture. Pour in remaining batter.

3 Bake at 350° for 45-55 minutes or until a toothpick inserted near the center comes out clean. Cool for 10 minutes before removing from pan to a wire rack to cool completely. Sprinkle with confectioners' sugar. **Yield:** 14 servings.

TEST KITCHEN TIP

Make a confectioners' sugar glaze to drizzle over the coffee cake instead of just dusting with confectioners' sugar. (See the cinnamon rolls' icing recipe on page 41.)

Swiss-Onion Bread Ring

This tempting cheesy bread has a pleasant onion flavor that is always a hit with company. It's crisp and golden on the outside, rich and buttery on the inside. —Rita Krajcir

2-1/2 teaspoons poppy seeds, *divided*
2 tubes (11 ounces *each*) refrigerated French bread dough
1 cup (4 ounces) shredded Swiss cheese
3/4 cup sliced green onions
6 tablespoons butter, melted

1 Sprinkle 1/2 teaspoon poppy seeds in a greased 10-in. fluted tube pan. Cut the dough into forty 1-in. pieces; place half in prepared pan. Sprinkle with half of the cheese and onions. Top with 1 teaspoon poppy seeds; drizzle with half of the butter. Repeat layers.

2 Bake at 375° for 30-35 minutes or until golden brown. Immediately invert onto a wire rack. Serve warm. **Yield:** 1 loaf.

Buttermilk Potato Doughnut Holes

My grandmother always used to make these old-fashioned doughnut holes for my sister and me when we were growing up. Now, when I make them myself, I fondly think of her. —Joylyn Trickel

2 cups sugar
3 eggs
1/3 cup shortening
1-1/2 cups hot mashed potatoes (prepared without milk and butter)
1 cup buttermilk
1 teaspoon vanilla extract
5-1/2 cups all-purpose flour
4 teaspoons baking powder
1 teaspoon salt
1 teaspoon ground nutmeg
Oil for deep-fat frying
Additional sugar

1 In a large mixing bowl, beat the sugar, eggs and shortening. Add the potatoes, buttermilk and vanilla. Combine the dry ingredients; add to potato mixture. Cover and refrigerate for 1 hour.

2 In an electric skillet or deep-fat fryer, heat oil to 375°. Drop rounded teaspoonfuls of batter, a few at a time, into hot oil. Fry for 1-1/2 minutes on each side or until golden brown. Drain on paper towels; roll in additional sugar while warm. **Yield:** about 9-1/2 dozen.

EDITOR'S NOTE: One pound of russet potatoes—about 3 medium potatoes—equals about 3-1/2 cups chopped or 2 to 3 cups mashed.

Cherry Chip Scones

Whether served for breakfast or dessert, these flaky scones dotted with dried cherries and vanilla chips are a real treat.
—Julie Ferron

3 cups all-purpose flour
1/2 cup sugar
2-1/2 teaspoons baking powder
1/2 teaspoon baking soda
6 tablespoons cold butter
1 cup (8 ounces) vanilla yogurt
1/4 cup plus 2 tablespoons milk, *divided*
1-1/3 cups dried cherries
2/3 cup vanilla *or* white chips

1 In a large bowl, combine the flour, sugar, baking powder and baking soda. Cut in butter until the mixture resembles coarse crumbs. Combine yogurt and 1/4 cup milk; stir into crumb mixture just until moistened. Knead in the cherries and chips.

2 On a greased baking sheet, pat dough into a 9-in. circle. Cut into eight wedges; separate wedges. Brush with the remaining milk. Bake at 400° for 20-25 minutes or until golden brown. Serve warm. **Yield:** 8 servings.

Mashed Potato Cinnamon Rolls

These rolls are at the core of our Christmas morning, after the gifts from Santa have been opened. The whole family shapes the rolls from the dough that chilled overnight. One year my kids, David and Sara, made one for their daddy as big as a dinner plate!
—Coleen Martin

   1/2 pound russet potatoes, peeled and quartered
     2 packages (1/4 ounce *each*) active dry yeast
     2 tablespoons plus 3/4 cup sugar, *divided*
     2 cups warm water (110° to 115°)
  3/4 cup butter, melted
     2 eggs, beaten
  2/3 cup instant nonfat dry milk powder
     1 tablespoon salt
     2 teaspoons vanilla extract
     8 to 10 cups all-purpose flour

FILLING:
  1/2 cup butter, melted
  3/4 cup packed brown sugar
     3 tablespoons ground cinnamon

ICING:
     2 cups confectioners' sugar
  1/4 cup milk
     2 tablespoons butter, melted
  1/2 teaspoon vanilla extract

1 Place potatoes in a saucepan and cover with water. Bring to a boil. Reduce heat; cover and cook for 15-20 minutes or until tender. Drain, reserving 1/2 cup cooking liquid; set aside. Mash potatoes; set aside 1 cup. (Save remaining potatoes for another use.)

2 Heat reserved potato liquid to 110°-115°. In a large mixing bowl, dissolve yeast and 2 tablespoons sugar in potato liquid; let stand for 5 minutes. Add the warm water, mashed potatoes, butter, eggs, remaining sugar, milk powder, salt, vanilla and 5 cups flour; beat until smooth. Stir in enough remaining flour to form a soft dough.

3 Turn onto a floured surface; knead until smooth and elastic, about 6-8 minutes. Place in a greased bowl, turning once to grease top. Cover and refrigerate overnight.

4 Punch dough down. Turn onto a lightly floured surface; divide into thirds. Roll each portion into a 12-in. x 8-in. rectangle. Spread butter over dough to within 1/2 in. of edges. Combine brown sugar and cinnamon; sprinkle over the dough.

5 Roll up jelly-roll style, starting with a long side; pinch seams to seal. Cut each into 12 slices; place cut side down in three greased 13-in. x 9-in. x 2-in. baking pans. Cover and let rise until almost doubled, about 45 minutes.

6 Bake at 350° for 25-30 minutes. Remove to wire racks to cool. Combine icing ingredients; drizzle over warm rolls. **Yield:** 3 dozen.

Sour Cream Banana Bread

I just love this wonderful, moist banana bread! No one can ever tell it's been "lightened up." —Stephanie Marchese

- 1-1/2 cups all-purpose flour
- 1 cup sugar
- 1 teaspoon baking soda
- 1/2 teaspoon salt
- 1 cup mashed ripe bananas (about 2 medium)
- 1/2 cup egg substitute
- 1/2 cup canola oil
- 1/2 cup fat-free sour cream
- 1 teaspoon vanilla extract

1 Coat a 9-in. x 5-in. x 3-in. loaf pan with non-stick cooking spray and dust with flour; set aside. In a large bowl, combine the flour, sugar, baking soda and salt. Combine the bananas, egg substitute, oil, sour cream and vanilla; stir into the dry ingredients just until moistened.

2 Pour into prepared pan. Bake at 350° for 55-65 minutes or until a toothpick inserted into the center comes out clean. Cool for 10 minutes before removing from pan to a wire rack. **Yield:** 1 loaf.

Christmas Morning Popovers

Popovers have been a Christmas morning tradition in my family for 30 years. I get up early to make the popovers, then wake the family to begin opening our gifts. When the popovers are ready, I serve them with lots of butter and assorted jams. My father-in-law began the tradition.

—Sue A. Jurack

- 1-1/4 cups milk
- 1 tablespoon butter, melted and cooled
- 1 cup all-purpose flour
- 1/4 teaspoon salt
- 2 eggs

1 In a small mixing bowl, beat the milk, butter, flour and salt until blended. Add eggs, one at a time, beating well after each addition. Fill buttered popover pans or large custard cups three-fourths full.

2 Bake at 450° for 15 minutes. Reduce heat to 350°; bake 20 minutes longer or until very firm. Remove from the oven and prick each popover with a sharp knife to allow steam to escape. Serve immediately. **Yield:** 9 servings.

TEST KITCHEN TIP

Let the eggs and milk come to room temperature for about 30 minutes before preparing the recipe. Allowing them to warm up results in greater height.

Rosemary Garlic Bread

(*Pictured on page 32*)

The aroma that fills the house when this savory yeast bread is baking is wonderful. The roasted garlic and rosemary add such an exquisite flavor.
—*Diane Werner*

5 whole garlic bulbs
2 teaspoons olive oil
1/4 cup minced fresh rosemary *or* 4 teaspoons
    dried rosemary, crushed
1 tablespoon chicken broth
9 to 9-1/2 cups bread flour
1/2 cup sugar

3 packages (1/4 ounce *each*) quick-rise yeast
3 teaspoons salt
1-1/2 cups milk
1 cup water
3/4 cup butter, *divided*
1 egg
1-1/2 teaspoons garlic salt

1 Remove papery outer skin from garlic (do not peel or separate cloves). Cut top off garlic heads, leaving root end intact. Place cut side up in a small baking dish. Brush with oil; sprinkle with rosemary. Cover and bake at 425° for 30-35 minutes or until softened. Cool for 10 minutes; squeeze softened garlic into a bowl. Add broth; lightly mash.

2 In a large mixing bowl, combine 3 cups flour, sugar, yeast and salt. In a saucepan, heat the milk, water and 1/2 cup butter to 120°-130°. Add to dry ingredients; beat just until moistened. Beat in egg and garlic paste until smooth. Stir in enough remaining flour to form a soft dough

(dough will be sticky). Turn onto a floured surface; knead until smooth and elastic, about 6-8 minutes. Cover and let rest for 10 minutes.

3 Divide dough into thirds. Divide each portion into three pieces; shape each into an 18-in. rope. Place three ropes on a greased baking sheet and braid; pinch ends to seal and tuck under. Repeat with remaining dough. Cover and let rise in a warm place until doubled, about 30 minutes.

4 Bake at 350° for 15 minutes. Melt remaining butter; add garlic salt. Brush over bread. Bake 10-15 minutes longer or until golden brown. Remove from pans to wire racks to cool. **Yield:** 3 loaves.

Little Texas Corn Bread

I love to serve this cheesy corn bread alongside a bowl of heart-warming chili. The green chilies add a nice little kick.
—*Sarah Thompson*

1 cup cornmeal
1 cup (4 ounces) shredded cheddar cheese
1 tablespoon baking powder
2 eggs
1 can (8-1/2 ounces) cream-style corn
1 cup (8 ounces) sour cream
1/2 cup vegetable oil
1 can (4 ounces) chopped green chilies, drained

1 In a large bowl, combine the cornmeal, cheese and baking powder. In another bowl, combine the eggs, corn, sour cream, oil and chilies. Stir into dry ingredients just until moistened.

2 Pour into a greased 8-in. square baking dish. Bake at 400° for 30-35 minutes or until a tooth-

pick comes out clean. Serve warm. Refrigerate leftovers. **Yield:** 8 servings.

EDITOR'S NOTE: This recipe does not contain flour.

Oat Pancakes

These are my husband's favorite pancakes. I like to add blueberries or raspberries to the batter before cooking them. My kids prefer to add milk chocolate chips. —*Coleen Martin*

1 cup quick-cooking oats	2 eggs, lightly beaten
1 cup all-purpose flour	1-1/2 cups milk
2 tablespoons sugar	1/4 cup vegetable oil
2 teaspoons baking powder	1 teaspoon lemon juice
1 teaspoon salt	

1 In a large bowl, combine the first five ingredients. Combine the egg, milk, oil and lemon juice; add to dry ingredients and stir just until moistened.

2 Pour batter by 1/4 cupfuls onto a lightly greased hot griddle; turn when bubbles form on top of pancakes. Cook until second side is golden brown. **Yield:** 6 servings.

TEST KITCHEN TIP

For a quick breakfast, place all the dry ingredients in a resealable plastic bag and write the additional ingredients on the bag. Then in the morning, just finish mixing it up.

Cranberry Orange Scones

These scones are an "always make" for out-of-town company. When I serve them at breakfast, I hear lots of oohs and aahs! —*Diane Werner*

2 cups all-purpose flour
10 teaspoons sugar, *divided*
1 tablespoon grated orange peel
2 teaspoons baking powder
1/2 teaspoon salt
1/4 teaspoon baking soda
1/3 cup cold butter
1 cup dried cranberries
1/4 cup orange juice
1/4 cup half-and-half cream
1 egg
1 tablespoon milk
GLAZE (optional):
1/2 cup confectioners' sugar
1 tablespoon orange juice
ORANGE BUTTER:
1/2 cup butter, softened
2 to 3 tablespoons orange marmalade

1 In a large bowl, combine flour, 7 teaspoons sugar, orange peel, baking powder, salt and baking soda. Cut in butter until the mixture resembles coarse crumbs; set aside. In a small bowl, combine cranberries, orange juice, cream and egg. Add to flour mixture and stir until a soft dough forms.

2 On a floured surface, gently knead 6-8 times. Pat dough into an 8-in. circle. Cut into 10 wedges.

Separate wedges and place on an ungreased baking sheet. Brush with milk; sprinkle with remaining sugar.

3 Bake at 400° for 12-15 minutes or until lightly browned. Combine glaze ingredients if desired; drizzle over scones. Combine orange butter ingredients; serve with warm scones. **Yield:** 10 scones.

Strawberry Rhubarb Coffee Cake

Rhubarb has always been one of my favorites—and this coffee cake is extra special. Each spring I can't wait for co-worker Diane Werner to share some of her rhubarb patch with me, so I can make this coffee cake. —Sue A. Jurack

2/3 cup sugar
1/3 cup cornstarch
2 cups chopped fresh rhubarb
1 package (10 ounces) frozen sweetened sliced strawberries, thawed
2 tablespoons lemon juice

CAKE:
3 cups all-purpose flour
1 cup sugar
1 teaspoon baking powder
1 teaspoon baking soda
1 cup cold butter
2 eggs
1 cup buttermilk
1 teaspoon vanilla extract

TOPPING:
3/4 cup sugar
1/2 cup all-purpose flour
1/4 cup cold butter

1 In a large saucepan, combine sugar and cornstarch; stir in rhubarb and strawberries. Bring to a boil over medium heat; cook for 2 minutes or until thickened. Remove from the heat; stir in lemon juice. Cool.

2 For cake, in a large bowl, combine flour, sugar, baking powder and baking soda. Cut in butter until mixture resembles coarse crumbs. Beat the eggs, buttermilk and vanilla; stir into crumb mixture just until moistened.

3 Spoon two-thirds of the batter into a greased 13-in. x 9-in. x 2-in. baking pan. Spoon cooled filling over batter. Top with remaining batter.

4 For topping, combine sugar and flour. Cut in butter until mixture resembles coarse crumbs; sprinkle over batter. Bake at 350° for 45-50 minutes or until golden brown. Cool on a wire rack. **Yield:** 12-16 servings.

Garlic Cheese Bread

My kids love this bread, and I am always happy to make it for them since it's so easy. It's a nice change of pace from the more traditional garlic bread. —Sue Megonigle

1 package (8 ounces) cream cheese, softened
1/4 cup sour cream
1/4 cup grated Parmesan cheese
2 tablespoons mayonnaise
2 tablespoons minced fresh parsley
1 tablespoon minced green onions
6 to 8 garlic cloves, minced
1 loaf (1 pound) French bread, cut into 1-inch slices

1 In a small mixing bowl, combine the first seven ingredients. Beat until blended. Spread on one side of each slice of bread.

2 Place on ungreased baking sheets. Broil 4 in. from heat for 3 minutes or until cheese is melted and lightly browned. **Yield:** 8-10 servings.

Irish Soda Bread ✓

Unlike most Irish soda breads, this one is made with yeast. It has a moist texture, and the golden raisins add a wonderful sweetness. This festive loaf is a must for St. Patrick's day!
—*Patricia Schmeling*

        1 package (1/4 ounce) active dry yeast
      1/2 cup warm water (110° to 115°)
        3 tablespoons sugar, *divided*
        1 cup warm buttermilk (110° to 115°)
        2 tablespoons butter, softened
      1/2 teaspoon salt
      1/2 teaspoon baking soda
    3-1/2 to 4 cups all-purpose flour
      3/4 cup golden raisins

1 In a large mixing bowl, dissolve yeast in warm water. Add 1 tablespoon sugar; let stand for 5 minutes. Beat in the buttermilk, butter, salt, baking soda, 1 cup flour and remaining sugar until smooth. Stir in raisins and enough remaining flour to form a soft dough.

2 Turn onto a floured surface; knead until smooth and elastic, about 6-8 minutes. Place in a greased bowl, turning once to grease top. Cover and let rise in a warm place until doubled, about 40 minutes.

3 Punch dough down. Turn onto a lightly floured surface; knead for 2 minutes. Shape into a round loaf. Place on a greased baking sheet. With a sharp knife, cut a 1/4-in.-deep cross on top of loaf. Cover and let rise until doubled, about 30 minutes.

4 Bake at 350° for 30-35 minutes or until golden brown. Remove from pan to a wire rack to cool. **Yield:** 1 loaf.

EDITOR'S NOTE: Warmed buttermilk will appear curdled.

Toffee Streusel Coffee Cake

A delicious reminder of my childhood, this coffee cake was one of the many delightful treats my mom often made.
—*Megan Taylor*

      2 cups all-purpose flour
      1 cup packed brown sugar
    1/2 cup sugar
    1/8 teaspoon salt
    1/2 cup cold butter
      1 teaspoon baking soda

      1 cup buttermilk
      1 egg, beaten
      1 teaspoon vanilla extract
      1 cup milk chocolate toffee bits *or* 4 Heath candy bars (1.4 ounces *each*), chopped

1 In a large bowl, combine the first four ingredients; cut in butter until crumbly. Set aside 1/2 cup for topping. Stir baking soda into remaining flour mixture. Combine the buttermilk, egg and vanilla; stir into flour mixture just until moistened.

2 Pour into a greased 13-in. x 9-in. x 2-in. baking pan. Add the toffee bits to the reserved crumb topping; sprinkle over batter. Cut through batter with a knife to swirl the topping.

3 Bake at 350° for 30-35 minutes or until a toothpick inserted near the center comes out clean. Cool on a wire rack. **Yield:** 12-16 servings.

Frosted Cinnamon-Raisin Biscuits

The frosting adds a touch of sweetness to these easy dropped biscuits that are a great accompaniment to a country-style breakfast.
—Sarah Thompson

2 cups all-purpose flour
1/4 cup sugar
2 teaspoons baking powder
1 teaspoon salt
1/4 teaspoon baking soda
1/3 cup shortening
2/3 cup buttermilk

1/3 cup raisins
1-1/2 teaspoons ground cinnamon
FROSTING:
1-1/2 cups confectioners' sugar
2 tablespoons butter, softened
1-1/2 teaspoons vanilla extract
3 to 5 teaspoons warm water

1 In a large bowl, combine the first five ingredients; cut in shortening until mixture resembles coarse crumbs. Stir in buttermilk just until moistened. Turn onto a floured surface; sprinkle with raisins and cinnamon. Knead 8-10 times (cinnamon will give it a marbled appearance).

2 Drop batter into 12 mounds 2 in. apart on a greased baking sheet. Bake at 425° for 12-16 minutes or until golden brown. Remove from pan to a wire rack.

3 For frosting, combine the sugar, butter, vanilla and enough water to achieve desired consistency. Frost warm biscuits. Serve immediately. **Yield:** 1 dozen.

Coconut Bread

This moist quick bread is bursting with tropical flavor. I've been making it since the first year I joined the company, over 10 years ago!
—Coleen Martin

3 cups all-purpose flour
2 teaspoons baking powder
1/2 teaspoon baking soda
1/2 teaspoon salt
2 cups sugar
1 cup vegetable oil
4 eggs, lightly beaten
2 teaspoons coconut extract
1 cup buttermilk
1 cup flaked coconut
1 cup chopped walnuts

1 Combine the flour, baking powder, baking soda and salt; set aside. In a large bowl, combine the sugar, oil, eggs and coconut extract. Add dry ingredients alternately with buttermilk; stir just until moistened. Fold in coconut and nuts.

2 Pour into two greased 9-in. x 5-in. x 3-in. loaf pans. Bake at 325° for 1 hour or until a toothpick inserted near the center comes out clean. Cool for 10 minutes before removing from pans to wire racks to cool completely. **Yield:** 2 loaves.

Sour Cream 'n' Chive Biscuits

My family thinks these are the most tender biscuits ever to come out of my oven. They're tasty served with beef stew, soups and salads.

—Betty Reuter

2 cups all-purpose flour
1 tablespoon baking powder
1/2 teaspoon salt
1/4 teaspoon baking soda
1/3 cup shortening
3/4 cup sour cream
1/4 cup milk
1/4 cup snipped fresh chives

1 In a bowl, combine the first four ingredients. Cut in shortening until mixture resembles coarse crumbs. With a fork, stir in sour cream, milk and chives until the mixture forms a ball.

2 On a lightly floured surface, knead 5-6 times. Roll out to 3/4-in. thickness; cut with a floured 2-in. biscuit cutter. Place 2 in. apart on an ungreased baking sheet.

3 Bake at 350° for 12-15 minutes or until golden brown. Remove from pan to a wire rack. **Yield:** 12-15 biscuits.

TEST KITCHEN TIP
If you have any shredded cheese in the refrigerator—Swiss, cheddar or Colby—you may add it to the dough.

Strawberries 'n' Cream Bread

I love to make this quick bread using fresh strawberries from the farmers market.

—Kris Lehman

1/2 cup butter, softened
3/4 cup sugar
2 eggs
1/2 cup sour cream
1 teaspoon vanilla extract
1-3/4 cups all-purpose flour
1/2 teaspoon baking powder
1/2 teaspoon baking soda
1/2 teaspoon salt
1/4 teaspoon ground cinnamon
3/4 cup chopped fresh strawberries
3/4 cup chopped walnuts, toasted, *divided*

1 In a large mixing bowl, cream butter and sugar until fluffy. Beat in eggs, one at a time, beating well after each addition. Add sour cream and vanilla; mix well. Combine the flour, baking powder, baking soda, salt and cinnamon. Stir into creamed mixture just until moistened. Fold in strawberries and 1/2 cup nuts.

2 Pour into a greased 8-in. x 4-in. x 2-in. loaf pan. Sprinkle with remaining nuts. Bake at 350° for 65-70 minutes or until a toothpick inserted near the center comes out clean. Cool for 10 minutes before removing from pan to a wire rack to cool completely. **Yield:** 1 loaf.

Almond-Filled Butterhorns

My husband's grandmother was quite the baker. She was known for her tender butterhorns. —Sue Draheim

3-1/4 teaspoons active dry yeast
    1 cup warm milk (110° to 115°)
  1/2 cup sugar, *divided*
    1 cup butter, softened
    4 cups all-purpose flour
  1/8 teaspoon salt
    4 eggs

FILLING:
    5 tablespoons butter, softened, *divided*
    1 cup sugar
    1 cup ground almonds
    1 egg, lightly beaten
    1 teaspoon almond extract
  1/2 teaspoon grated lemon peel

GLAZE:
    1 cup confectioners' sugar
    2 tablespoons milk
  1/4 teaspoon vanilla extract

1 In a small bowl, dissolve yeast in milk. Add 1/4 cup sugar and butter; mix well. In a large mixing bowl, combine the flour, salt and remaining sugar. Add the eggs, one at a time, beating well after each addition. Add yeast mixture; beat until smooth. Do not knead. Cover and refrigerate overnight.

2 Punch dough down. Turn onto a lightly floured surface; divide into thirds. Roll each portion into a 12-in. circle. Melt 3 tablespoons butter; brush 1 tablespoon over each circle. In a bowl, combine the sugar, almonds, egg, extract, lemon peel and remaining butter. Spread a third over each circle of dough. Cut each circle into 12 wedges. Roll up wedges from the wide end and place point side down 2 in. apart on greased baking sheets. Curve ends to form a crescent. Cover and let rise in a warm place until doubled, about 30 minutes.

3 Bake at 375° for 10-12 minutes or until lightly browned. Remove from pan to wire racks. Combine glaze ingredients; brush over warm rolls. **Yield:** 3 dozen.

SUE DRAHEIM

Sue has tried all different types of recipes while working in our Test Kitchen for 7 years, but her favorites to prepare at home are pies, yeast breads and anything grilled. Other than cooking, her most recent interest is upholstery. She has been married for 8 years and is mom to two children—Nicholas, 6, and Megan, 5. She once spent a summer with her own mother at the Libby Hillman Cooking School in Vermont.

SALADS and DRESSINGS

Layered Lettuce Salad

I often just make the dressing for other salads—especially when I have extra basil in my garden. It is so flavorful.
—*Coleen Martin*

1 head lettuce, torn
1 cup minced fresh parsley
4 hard-cooked eggs, sliced
2 large tomatoes, chopped
1 package (10 ounces) frozen peas, thawed
6 bacon strips, cooked and crumbled
1 cup (4 ounces) shredded cheddar cheese
1 small red onion, chopped
DRESSING:
 1-1/2 cups mayonnaise
 1/2 cup sour cream
 1 teaspoon dill weed
 3/4 teaspoon dried basil
 1/2 teaspoon salt
 1/8 teaspoon pepper
Fresh dill sprigs, optional

1 In a large bowl, layer the first eight ingredients in order listed. In a small bowl, combine mayonnaise, sour cream, dill, basil, salt and pepper.

2 Carefully spread over top of salad. Cover and refrigerate for several hours or overnight. Garnish with dill sprigs if desired. **Yield:** 12 servings.

TEST KITCHEN TIP
Coleen uses reduced-fat mayonnaise and sour cream in the dressing with good results.

Autumn Salad

This recipe is a perfect accompaniment to Thanksgiving or Christmas dinner. The vinaigrette adds a wonderfully fresh flavor.
—*Patricia Schmeling*

1/4 cup white wine vinegar
 2 teaspoons Dijon mustard
1/2 teaspoon dill weed
1/2 teaspoon ground nutmeg
1/8 teaspoon kosher salt
1/8 teaspoon pepper
1/2 cup olive oil

3 large unpeeled Red Delicious apples, cored and thinly sliced
1/3 cup crumbled blue cheese
1/4 cup walnut halves, toasted
 1 bunch romaine, torn
 1 bunch watercress, trimmed

1 In a small bowl, whisk the vinegar, mustard, dill, nutmeg, salt and pepper. Slowly add oil while whisking. In a bowl, combine the apples, cheese, walnuts and 3 tablespoons dressing; toss to coat. Cover and refrigerate for up to 4 hours. Cover and refrigerate remaining dressing.

2 Place romaine and watercress in a large salad bowl; drizzle with remaining dressing and toss to coat. Arrange romaine mixture and apple mixture on serving plates. Serve immediately. **Yield:** 8 servings.

Cherry Brie Tossed Salad

(Pictured on page 50)

Draped in a light vinaigrette and dotted with dried cherries and cubes of Brie cheese, this pretty tossed salad is nice for holidays and other special occasions or whenever you need a dish to pass.

—Sue Draheim

1 cup cider vinegar
1/2 cup sugar
1/4 cup olive oil
1 teaspoon ground mustard
1-1/2 teaspoons poppy seeds
SALAD:
2 tablespoons butter

3/4 cup sliced almonds
3 tablespoons sugar
8 cups torn romaine
8 ounces Brie *or* Camembert, rind removed, cubed
1 package (6 ounces) dried cherries

1 In a jar with a tight-fitting lid, combine the first five ingredients; shake until sugar is dissolved.

2 In a heavy skillet, melt butter over medium heat. Add almonds; cook and stir until toasted, about 4 minutes. Sprinkle with sugar; cook and stir until sugar is melted, about 3 minutes. Spread on foil to cool; break apart.

3 In a large salad bowl, combine the romaine, cheese and cherries. Shake dressing; drizzle over salad. Sprinkle with sugared almonds. Toss to coat. **Yield:** 8-10 servings.

TEST KITCHEN TIP

Swiss cheese can be substituted for Brie or Camembert. Sue has made it with feta and dried cranberries as an alternative. You can also add fresh pears.

Blue Cheese Salad Dressing

This thick and creamy dressing makes a great accompaniment to a mix of fresh salad greens. It also makes a great dip for fresh vegetables.

—Anita Bukowski

2 cups mayonnaise
1 cup (8 ounces) sour cream
1/4 cup white wine vinegar
1/4 cup minced fresh parsley
1 garlic clove, crushed
1/2 teaspoon ground mustard
1/2 teaspoon salt
1/4 teaspoon pepper
4 ounces crumbled blue cheese

In a blender or food processor, combine all ingredients; cover and process until smooth. Store in the refrigerator. **Yield:** 3 cups.

Bok Choy Salad

Depending on what I have at home, I sometimes use only the sunflower kernels or almonds in this salad. The recipe makes a big amount, perfect for cookouts or reunions.   —Stephanie Marchese

> 1 head bok choy, finely chopped
> 2 bunches green onions, thinly sliced
> 2 packages (3 ounces *each*) ramen noodles, broken
> 1/4 cup slivered almonds
> 2 tablespoons sunflower kernels
>
> 1/4 cup butter
> DRESSING:
> 1/3 to 1/2 cup sugar
> 1/2 cup vegetable oil
> 2 tablespoons cider vinegar
> 1 tablespoon soy sauce

1 In a large bowl, combine the bok choy and green onions; set aside. Save seasoning packet from ramen noodles for another use. In a large skillet, saute the noodles, almonds and sunflower kernels in butter for 7 minutes or until browned. Remove from the heat; cool to room temperature. Add to bok choy mixture.

2 In a jar with a tight-fitting lid, combine the dressing ingredients; shake well. Just before serving, drizzle over salad and toss to coat. **Yield:** 10 servings.

Wild Rice Salad

Chicken, green grapes and water chestnuts are delicious additions to this rice salad, which makes a great summer lunch. Simply serve with a fresh croissant or slice of bread on the side.   —Janaan Cunningham

> 1 cup uncooked wild rice
> Seasoned salt, optional
> 2 cups diced cooked chicken
> 1-1/2 cups halved green grapes
> 1 cup sliced water chestnuts, drained
> 3/4 cup reduced-fat mayonnaise
> 1 cup cashews, optional
> Lettuce leaves

1 Cook rice according to package directions, omitting salt or substituting seasoned salt if desired. Drain well; cool to room temperature.

2 In a large bowl, combine the rice, chicken, grapes, water chestnuts and mayonnaise. Toss gently with a fork. Cover and chill.

3 Just before serving, add cashews if desired. Serve on lettuce-lined plates or in a lettuce-lined bowl. **Yield:** 6 servings.

Minty Beet Carrot Salad

The bold colors of this unique salad draw you in to give it a try. The unusual combination of ingredients made me a bit nervous before trying it for the first time, but I was very pleased with the delicious results! —*Joylyn Trickel*

- 12 fresh beets (2 inches *each*), trimmed
- 6 large carrots, thinly sliced
- 1 cup crumbled goat cheese *or* feta cheese
- 2 tablespoons minced shallot
- 1/3 cup tarragon vinegar
- 1/3 cup chopped fresh mint
- 1/4 cup olive oil
- 1-1/2 teaspoons sugar
- 1/2 teaspoon salt
- 1/4 teaspoon pepper
- 1/4 cup minced chives

1 Line a baking sheet with foil. Place beets on foil; sprinkle lightly with water. Wrap tightly in foil. Bake at 350° for 40-50 minutes or until tender; cool. Peel and cut beets into thin slices.

2 Place carrots in a steamer basket; place in a saucepan over 1 in. of water. Bring to a boil; cover and steam for 6-8 minutes or until crisp-tender.

3 On salad plates, arrange the beet and carrot slices, overlapping the slices. Sprinkle with cheese and shallot. In a small bowl, whisk the vinegar, mint, oil, sugar, salt and pepper; drizzle over vegetables. Sprinkle with chives. **Yield:** 6 servings.

TEST KITCHEN TIP

Save a step by only using the beets and not the carrots.

Spinach with Hot Bacon Dressing

This dressing is sweet and tangy—well worth the effort for a homemade dressing. You can also serve it over other greens or even potato salad. —*Peggy Fleming*

- 1 cup sugar
- 3 tablespoons cornstarch
- 1-1/2 teaspoons celery seed
- 1 teaspoon salt
- 3/4 teaspoon ground mustard
- 2 cups milk
- 3/4 cup cider vinegar
- 1/2 cup butter, cubed
- 3 eggs, lightly beaten
- 4 bacon strips, cooked and crumbled
- 3 hard-cooked eggs, chopped

Torn fresh spinach

1 In a saucepan, combine the sugar, cornstarch, celery seed, salt and mustard. Gradually stir in milk and vinegar. Add butter. Cook and stir until mixture comes to a boil; cook and stir for 1-2 minutes or until thickened and bubbly.

2 Stir a small amount of hot liquid into beaten eggs; return all to the pan. Bring to a gentle boil; cook and stir 2 minutes longer. Remove from the heat; stir in bacon and hard-cooked eggs. Serve immediately over spinach. **Yield:** about 4 cups.

Swiss Cashew Tossed Salad

I make the dressing for this salad all the time. My family and friends love it. It makes enough to keep in the fridge for several salads—all week long! —Stephanie Marchese

   1/3 cup white vinegar
   3/4 cup sugar
     2 teaspoons prepared mustard
     1 teaspoon grated onion
Dash salt
     1 cup vegetable oil
     1 teaspoon poppy seeds
     1 medium bunch romaine, torn
     1 cup salted cashew halves
     4 ounces Swiss cheese, julienned

1 In a blender, combine the vinegar, sugar, mustard, onion and salt; cover and process until well blended. While processing, gradually add oil in a steady stream. Stir in poppy seeds.

2 In a salad bowl, combine the romaine, cashews and Swiss cheese. Serve with dressing. **Yield:** 8-10 servings.

SUE A. JURACK

Sue's background is as diverse as the food she prepares! She's been a home economist, giving demonstrations in schools and on national TV...worked on radio talk shows...owned a culinary school in Switzerland...and for the last 9 years, has been working in our Test Kitchen. Cooking is her creative outlet, and she loves to entertain. With "so many recipes to try," Sue rarely makes the same thing twice, except for Wiener Schnitzel, her family's traditional birthday dish.

Tomato Basil Couscous Salad

This is a great salad for picnics since the dressing is made with oil and vinegar, not mayonnaise. It's so good, though, that I serve it year-round.
—Karen Scales

     2 cups chicken broth
     1 package (10 ounces) couscous
     1 cup chopped green onions
     1 cup seeded diced plum tomatoes
  1/3 cup thinly sliced fresh basil
  1/3 cup olive oil

  1/3 cup red wine vinegar
  1/4 teaspoon crushed red pepper flakes
  1/2 teaspoon salt
  1/8 teaspoon pepper
     1 cup halved cherry tomatoes

1 In a saucepan, bring broth to a boil; add couscous. Cover and remove from the heat; let stand for 5 minutes. Transfer to a large bowl; fluff with a fork and cool.

2 Add the onions, tomatoes, basil, oil, vinegar, pepper flakes, salt and pepper; mix well. Cover and refrigerate until chilled. Garnish with tomatoes. **Yield:** 8 servings.

Fruit Salad Dressing

(Pictured on page 51)

This smooth and citrusy dressing tastes terrific drizzled over a variety of seasonal fresh fruit—cantaloupe, honeydew melon and strawberries, just to name a few. It makes a cool, colorful salad for breakfast, lunch or picnics in the summer.
—*Janet Briggs*

3 tablespoons all-purpose flour
2 cans (6 ounces *each*) pineapple juice
1 can (6 ounces) frozen orange juice
    concentrate, thawed

1/2 to 1 cup sugar
1/4 cup honey
1/4 cup lemon juice
Assorted fresh fruit

1 In a large saucepan, combine the first six ingredients. Bring to a boil; cook and stir for 2 minutes or until thickened and bubbly. Cool.

2 Serve over fruit. Leftover dressing may be refrigerated for up to 1 week. **Yield:** 2 cups.

Colorful Pepper Salad

This is my husband's favorite summer salad. We love the sweetness of the honey dressing with some heat from the pepper flakes. It is a perfect accompaniment to any barbecue menu. —*Sue A. Jurack*

3 *each* large green, sweet red and yellow peppers,
    thinly sliced
18 cherry tomatoes, halved
DRESSING:
1/4 cup finely chopped red onion
3 tablespoons cider vinegar
3 tablespoons olive oil
3 tablespoons honey
1 tablespoon Dijon mustard
1/4 teaspoon salt
1/4 teaspoon garlic powder
1/4 teaspoon celery seed
1/4 teaspoon pepper
1/8 teaspoon crushed red pepper flakes, optional

In a large bowl, combine the peppers and tomatoes. In a jar with a tight-fitting lid, combine the dressing ingredients; shake well. Pour over vegetables and toss to coat. **Yield:** 16 servings.

Test Kitchen Tip

The salad stays crunchy for up to 3 days in the refrigerator.

Cranberry-Pear Tossed Salad

Using apricot nectar in place of some of the oil is a wonderful way to reduce calories in the dressing and give an excellent flavor boost.
—*Diane Werner*

1/3 cup apricot nectar
1/3 cup red wine vinegar
1/3 cup canola oil
 2 teaspoons Dijon mustard
1/4 teaspoon salt
1/8 teaspoon pepper
 2 tablespoons sugar

1/2 cup chopped walnuts
 12 cups torn mixed salad greens
 3 medium ripe pears, sliced
1/2 cup dried cranberries
3/4 cup crumbled blue cheese

1 For dressing, in a bowl, whisk the first six ingredients; set aside. In a heavy skillet, melt sugar over medium heat, stirring constantly. Add walnuts; stir to coat. Remove from the heat.

2 In a large salad bowl, combine greens, pears and cranberries. Drizzle with dressing. Add sugared nuts and blue cheese; toss. **Yield:** 12 servings.

Roasted Potato Salad

Roasting the red potatoes along with garlic and onion instead of boiling them in water adds a wonderful flavor. This is a great salad to take to a barbecue.
—*Julie Ferron*

1/2 pound fresh green beans, cut into 1-1/2-inch pieces
 1 large whole garlic bulb
 2 pounds small red potatoes, quartered
 2 medium sweet red peppers, cut into large chunks
 2 green onions, sliced
1/4 cup chicken broth
1/4 cup balsamic vinegar
 2 tablespoons olive oil
 2 teaspoons sugar
 1 teaspoon minced fresh rosemary *or* 1/4 teaspoon dried rosemary, crushed
1/2 teaspoon salt

1 In a large saucepan, bring 6 cups water to a boil. Add beans; bring to a boil. Cover and cook for 3 minutes. Drain and immediately place beans in ice water; drain and pat dry.

2 Remove papery outer skin from garlic (do not peel or separate cloves). Cut top off garlic bulb. Place cut side up in a greased 15-in. x 10-in. x 1-in. baking pan. Add the potatoes, red peppers, onions and beans; drizzle with broth. Bake, uncovered, at 400° for 30-40 minutes or until garlic is softened.

3 Remove garlic; set aside. Bake vegetables 30-35 minutes longer or until tender. Cool for 10-15 minutes. Squeeze softened garlic into a large bowl. Stir in the vinegar, oil, sugar, rosemary and salt. Add vegetables; toss to coat. Serve warm or cold. **Yield:** 9 servings.

Cinnamon-Basil Fruit Salad

Each spring, I can't wait to plant my large herb garden with over 25 different herbs and several edible flowers. I usually grow several varieties of basil, one of my favorite herbs. I love the way basil and mint are used in the syrup for this salad. It perks up the flavor of any fruit salad. —Sue A. Jurack

- 2 cups sugar
- 1 cup water
- 1 cup packed fresh basil leaves
- 3 sprigs fresh spearmint *or* mint
- 1 cinnamon stick (3 inches)
- 2 cups fresh raspberries *or* blackberries
- 1 cup cubed cantaloupe
- 1 cup cubed honeydew
- 1 cup fresh blueberries
- 1 medium apple, sliced

1 In a small saucepan, bring the sugar and water to a boil. Remove from the heat. Stir in the basil, spearmint and cinnamon stick. Cover and refrigerate overnight.

2 Discard the herbs and cinnamon stick from syrup. In a serving bowl, combine the fruit. Drizzle with syrup; gently toss to coat. Cover and refrigerate until chilled. Serve with a slotted spoon. **Yield:** 8-10 servings.

TEST KITCHEN TIP:
When basil and mint are plentiful in your garden, make the simple sugar syrup and store it in pint jars in the freezer. In winter, this fruit salad with the basil syrup will remind you of your garden and the warmer days of summer.

Japanese Peanut Salad Dressing

After tasting it just once, this salad dressing quickly became a favorite for my family. It's delicious over a variety of mixed greens. —Wendy Stenman

- 1/2 cup canola oil
- 6 tablespoons rice wine vinegar
- 6 green onions, thinly sliced
- 1/4 cup chopped peanuts
- 1/4 cup sesame seeds, toasted
- 1/4 cup sugar
- 1-1/2 teaspoons salt
- 1/2 teaspoon pepper

In a jar with a tight-fitting lid, combine all ingredients; shake well. Store in the refrigerator. **Yield:** 1-1/2 cups.

EDITOR'S NOTE: Always dress salad greens just before serving so they won't become soggy. Don't overdress salads. Too much dressing will weigh down ingredients and mask their flavor.

Light Honey French Salad Dressing

This version of the classic French salad dressing has all of the flavor, but less calories, fat and sodium. —*Mark Morgan*

1/2 cup ketchup
1/2 cup honey
1/2 cup chopped onion
1/3 cup cider vinegar
1/4 cup apricot nectar
  3 garlic cloves, minced
  1 teaspoon paprika
1/2 teaspoon celery seed
1/4 teaspoon salt
1/3 cup canola oil

1 In a blender or food processor, combine the first nine ingredients; cover and process until well blended.

2 While processing, gradually add oil in a steady stream. Process until thickened. Store in the refrigerator. **Yield:** 2 cups.

Greek Orzo Salad

The herbs and vegetables give this fresh-tasting pasta salad a colorful appearance, while the dressing adds a nice gloss. —*Diane Werner*

  1 cup uncooked orzo pasta
  2 cups frozen corn, thawed
  8 ounces fresh mozzarella cheese, cubed
1/2 cup chopped sweet red pepper
1/2 cup halved grape tomatoes
1/2 cup pitted Greek olives, halved
1/4 cup chopped green onions

1/4 cup minced fresh basil
  2 tablespoons minced fresh parsley
  3 tablespoons balsamic vinegar
  2 tablespoons olive oil
1/4 teaspoon salt
1/4 teaspoon pepper

1 Cook pasta according to package directions; drain and rinse in cold water. Place in a large serving bowl; add the corn, cheese, red pepper, tomatoes, olives, onions, basil and parsley.

2 In a jar with a tight-fitting lid, combine the vinegar, oil, salt and pepper; shake well. Pour over salad and toss to coat. **Yield:** 8 servings.

TEST KITCHEN TIP

Grill extra corn on the cob to use for this salad; it will enhance the flavor. About four ears will give you 2 cups of corn.

Black Bean and Corn Salad

I like to spoon this salad onto flour tortillas with chicken and cheese to make a quesadilla—it's really tasty served this way!
—Tamra Duncan

- 1/3 cup olive oil
- 1 tablespoon red wine vinegar
- 1 teaspoon cider vinegar
- 1 garlic clove, minced
- 1/2 teaspoon ground cumin
- 1/2 teaspoon dried oregano
- 1/2 teaspoon salt, optional
- 1/4 teaspoon sugar
- 1/8 teaspoon cayenne pepper
- 2 cans (15 ounces *each*) black beans, rinsed and drained
- 1 can (8 ounces) whole kernel corn, drained
- 3/4 cup chopped red onion
- 1/2 cup chopped sweet red pepper

In a large bowl, whisk the first nine ingredients until well blended. Add the beans, corn, onion and red pepper; toss well. Cover and refrigerate for 8 hours or overnight. **Yield:** 12 servings.

DIANE WERNER

Her Italian mother, who made everything from scratch, is credited with Diane's appreciation of cooking and the wonderful gratitude one gets from preparing a good meal for family and friends. While her mom tended to cook "on the heavier side," Diane leans toward lighter fare such as well-seasoned stir-fries and grilled foods. Her husband of 30 years also is in the food industry. They have four children.

Cashew Turkey Pasta Salad

This is a great way to use up leftover turkey after the holidays. Grilled chicken is a good substitute. *—Megan Taylor*

- 1-1/2 cups uncooked tricolor spiral pasta
- 3 cups cubed cooked turkey
- 1 celery rib, diced
- 3 green onions, chopped
- 1/4 cup diced green pepper
- 3/4 cup mayonnaise
- 6 tablespoons packed brown sugar
- 1-1/2 teaspoons cider vinegar
- 3/4 teaspoon salt
- 3/4 teaspoon lemon juice
- 1 cup salted cashew halves

1 Cook pasta according to package directions; drain and rinse in cold water. In a large bowl, combine the pasta, turkey, celery, onions and green pepper.

2 In a small bowl, combine the mayonnaise, brown sugar, vinegar, salt and lemon juice; pour over pasta mixture and toss to coat. Cover and refrigerate for at least 2 hours. Just before serving, stir in cashews. **Yield:** 6 servings.

SOUPS *and* SANDWICHES

Mushroom Crab Melts

These open-faced sandwiches are elegant enough for a luncheon party. They're nice to make ahead and just pop in the oven.
　　　　　　　　　　　　　　　　—*Betty Reuter*

　3 bacon strips, diced
　1 cup sliced fresh mushrooms
1/4 cup chopped onion
　1 can (6 ounces) crabmeat, drained, flaked and cartilage removed
　1 cup (4 ounces) shredded Swiss cheese
1/2 cup mayonnaise
1/3 cup grated Parmesan cheese
　2 tablespoons butter, softened
　6 English muffins, split
Dash *each* cayenne pepper and paprika

1 In a skillet, cook bacon over medium heat until crisp. Remove with a slotted spoon to paper towels. Drain, reserving 2 tablespoons drippings. In the drippings, saute mushrooms and onion until tender. In a large bowl, combine the crab, Swiss cheese, mayonnaise, mushroom mixture, Parmesan cheese and bacon.

2 Spread butter over muffin halves. Top with crab mixture; sprinkle with cayenne and paprika. Place on an ungreased baking sheet. Bake at 400° for 10-15 minutes or until lightly browned. **Yield:** 6 servings.

French Onion Soup

I got this savory soup recipe from a co-worker my first year out of college. It's been a family favorite ever since.
　　　　　　　　　　　　　　　　—*Janaan Cunningham*

1/4 cup butter
　2 pounds onions, thinly sliced
　1 tablespoon sugar
　4 tablespoons all-purpose flour
　3 cans (14-1/2 ounces *each*) beef broth
　2 cups water
　1 teaspoon salt

　1 teaspoon dried minced onion
　1 teaspoon beef bouillon granules
1/4 teaspoon garlic salt
1/4 teaspoon pepper
　8 slices French bread, toasted
　1 cup (4 ounces) shredded Swiss cheese

1 In a Dutch oven or soup kettle, melt butter. Add onions and sugar; cook over low heat until lightly browned, about 1 hour.

2 Sprinkle flour over onions and stir until blended. Gradually stir in broth. Add the water, salt, dried onion, bouillon, garlic salt and pepper.

Bring to a boil; cook and stir for 2 minutes. Reduce heat; cover and simmer for 45 minutes.

3 Ladle soup into ovenproof bowls. Top with a slice of toasted bread; sprinkle with cheese. Place on a baking sheet. Bake at 400° for 5 minutes. **Yield:** 8 servings.

TEST KITCHEN TIP
Refrigerate the onions before slicing—your tear ducts won't get as much of a workout!

White Bean and Pasta Soup

(Pictured on page 62)

This is a hearty soup that's delicious accompanied by sourdough bread. When the recipe was photographed for this book, the staff in the photo studio thought it was so good that they ate it for lunch!

—*Karen Johnson*

1-1/2 cups dried great northern beans
   3/4 pound Italian sausage links, casings removed
     1 large onion, chopped
     1 large carrot, chopped
     3 garlic cloves, minced
     6 cups chicken broth
     3 cups water
     2 tablespoons dried currants
     1 teaspoon dried basil
     1 can (14-1/2 ounces) diced tomatoes, undrained
     1 cup uncooked small shell pasta
Shredded Parmesan cheese

1 Place beans in a Dutch oven or soup kettle; add water to cover by 2 in. Bring to a boil; boil for 2 minutes. Remove from the heat; cover and let stand for 1 hour. Drain and rinse beans, discarding liquid.

2 In the same pan, cook the sausage, onion, carrot and garlic over medium heat until meat is no longer pink; drain. Add the broth, water, currants, basil and beans. Bring to a boil. Reduce heat; cover and simmer for 1-1/2 to 2 hours or until beans are tender, stirring occasionally.

3 Add the tomatoes and pasta; bring to a boil. Reduce heat; cover and simmer for 15 minutes or until the pasta is tender. Serve with Parmesan cheese. **Yield:** 12 servings (3 quarts).

Focaccia Sandwich

Slices of this pretty sandwich are great for any casual get-together. Add or change ingredients to your taste.

—*Peggy Fleming*

1/3 cup mayonnaise
  1 can (2-1/4 ounces) chopped ripe olives, drained
  1 focaccia bread (about 12 ounces), halved lengthwise
  4 romaine leaves
1/4 pound shaved deli ham
  1 medium sweet red pepper, thinly sliced into rings
1/4 pound shaved deli turkey
  1 large tomato, thinly sliced
1/4 pound thinly sliced hard salami
  1 jar (7-1/4 ounces) roasted sweet red peppers, drained
  4 to 6 slices provolone cheese

In a small bowl, combine the mayonnaise and olives; spread over the bottom half of bread. Layer with the remaining ingredients; replace bread top. Cut into wedges; secure with toothpicks. **Yield:** 24 servings.

TEST KITCHEN TIP

A rectangular-shaped focaccia bread, measuring about 12 in. x 8 in., works best for this sandwich.

Grilled Portobello Sandwiches

This sandwich is so good, I've actually made one just for myself, and I don't usually do that. The flavor is absolutely wonderful!
—*Diane Werner*

2 tablespoons sesame oil
2 tablespoons balsamic vinegar
1/4 teaspoon salt
1/4 teaspoon pepper
4 to 5 portobello mushrooms (about 1 pound), stems removed
1 large sweet onion, cut into 1/4-inch slices
4 flour tortillas (10 inches)
2-1/2 cups (10 ounces) shredded Monterey Jack cheese
Salsa and sour cream

1 In a shallow bowl, combine the oil, vinegar, salt and pepper. Add the mushrooms and onion; turn to coat.

2 Coat a grill rack with nonstick cooking spray before starting the grill. Grill onion over medium heat for 8-10 minutes or until crisp-tender, turning often. Remove and set aside. Grill mushrooms for 3-4 minutes, turning every minute or until lightly browned. Remove and cut into 1/4-in. slices.

3 Layer mushroom and onion on half of each tortilla; sprinkle with cheese. Fold tortilla over filling. Grill for 1-2 minutes on each side or until browned and cheese is melted. Serve with salsa and sour cream. **Yield:** 4 servings.

TEST KITCHEN TIP

Whole mushroom caps are easier to grill than sliced mushrooms, and they maintain their flavor and texture well. Thinly slice before assembling the sandwich.

Roasted Veggie Sandwiches

The roasted veggies along with the basil yogurt spread taste terrific in these sandwiches.   —*Stephanie Marchese*

3 tablespoons balsamic vinegar
2 teaspoons olive oil
1/4 cup minced fresh basil *or* 1 tablespoon dried basil
1 small eggplant, peeled and sliced lengthwise
1 medium sweet red pepper, sliced
1 small red onion, sliced and separated into rings
1 small zucchini, thinly sliced
1 small yellow summer squash, thinly sliced
BASIL YOGURT SPREAD:
1/4 cup fat-free plain yogurt
2 tablespoons reduced-fat mayonnaise
1 tablespoon minced fresh basil *or* 1 teaspoon dried basil
1 teaspoon lemon juice
4 French rolls, warmed

1 In a large bowl, combine the vinegar, oil and basil. Add the eggplant, red pepper, onion, zucchini and yellow squash; toss to coat. Place vegetables in a single layer in a large roasting pan. Bake, uncovered, at 450° for 20-30 minutes or until tender, stirring occasionally.

2 Meanwhile, in a small bowl, combine the yogurt, mayonnaise, basil and lemon juice. Hollow out rolls if necessary. Serve roasted vegetables on rolls with yogurt spread. **Yield:** 4 servings.

Baked Potato Soup

Here's a great way to use up leftover baked potatoes. The soup has a rich and creamy texture, and the green onions, cheese and bacon add great flavor and color.
—Amy Welk-Thieding

- 4 large baking potatoes (about 2-3/4 pounds)
- 2/3 cup butter
- 2/3 cup all-purpose flour
- 3/4 teaspoon salt
- 1/4 teaspoon white pepper
- 6 cups milk
- 1 cup (8 ounces) sour cream
- 1/4 cup thinly sliced green onions
- 10 bacon strips, cooked and crumbled
- 1 cup (4 ounces) shredded cheddar cheese

1 Bake potatoes at 350° for 65-75 minutes or until tender. Cool completely; peel and cube potatoes.

2 In a large saucepan, melt butter; stir in flour, salt and pepper until smooth. Gradually add milk. Bring to a boil; cook and stir for 2 minutes or until thickened. Reduce heat; add potatoes and heat through. Remove from the heat; whisk in sour cream and green onions. Garnish with bacon and cheese. **Yield:** 10 servings.

TEST KITCHEN TIP

Real bacon bits work great for the garnish if you don't have time to cook bacon.

Sausage Corn Chowder

This hearty soup has been a family favorite since I first acquired the recipe from a popular Wisconsin restaurant. Served with crusty French bread and a tossed salad, it is a great Saturday night supper. I've even served it to a group of 50 at a church luncheon.
—Sue A. Jurack

- 1 pound bulk pork sausage
- 1 cup coarsely chopped onion
- 4 cups cubed peeled potatoes (1/2-inch cubes)
- 2 cups water
- 1 teaspoon salt
- 1/2 teaspoon dried marjoram
- 1/8 teaspoon pepper
- 1 can (15-1/4 ounces) whole kernel corn, drained
- 1 can (14-3/4 ounces) cream-style corn
- 1 can (12 ounces) evaporated milk

1 In a Dutch oven or soup kettle, cook sausage and onion over medium heat until meat is no longer pink; drain. Add the potatoes, water, salt, marjoram and pepper.

2 Bring to a boil. Reduce heat; cover and simmer for 15 minutes or until potatoes are just tender. Add the corn, cream-style corn and milk; heat through. **Yield:** 10 servings.

TEST KITCHEN TIP

Use sage-flavored bulk sausage to perk up this down-home soup.

Broccoli Chicken Braid

I first tried this recipe when it was prepared in the Test Kitchen. I liked it so much, I've been making it at home ever since!
—*Joylyn Trickel*

  2 cups chopped cooked chicken
  1 cup chopped fresh broccoli florets
  1 cup (4 ounces) shredded cheddar cheese
1/4 cup chopped green pepper
1/4 cup chopped sweet red pepper
  1 garlic clove, minced
  1 teaspoon dill weed
1/4 teaspoon salt
1/2 cup mayonnaise
  2 tubes (8 ounces *each*) refrigerated crescent rolls
  1 egg white, lightly beaten
  2 tablespoons slivered almonds

1 In a large bowl, combine the first eight ingredients. Stir in mayonnaise. On an ungreased baking sheet, unroll both tubes of crescent dough into one long rectangle. Roll into a 15-in. x 12-in. rectangle, sealing seams and perforations. Spoon chicken mixture down center third of dough.

2 On each long side, cut eight strips about 3-1/2 in. into the center. Bring one strip from each side over filling and pinch ends to seal; repeat. Brush with egg white. Sprinkle with almonds.

3 Bake at 375° for 15-20 minutes or until filling is heated through and top is golden brown. **Yield:** 8 servings.

Test Kitchen Tip
Use 1 tablespoon of fresh dill instead of dill weed if you want to enhance the dill flavor.

Hearty Beef Barley Soup

A big slice of sourdough bread goes great with a bowl of this heart-warming soup that's brimming with beef and barley.
—*Megan Taylor*

1/4 cup all-purpose flour
  1 teaspoon salt
1/2 teaspoon pepper, *divided*
  2 pounds lean boneless beef sirloin steak, cut into 1/2-inch cubes
  2 tablespoons canola oil
  4 cups sliced fresh mushrooms

  4 cans (14-1/2 ounces *each*) reduced-sodium beef broth
  4 medium carrots, sliced
1/2 teaspoon garlic powder
1/2 teaspoon dried thyme
  1 cup quick-cooking barley

1 In a large resealable plastic bag, combine the flour, salt and 1/4 teaspoon pepper. Add beef and shake to coat. In a Dutch oven, brown beef in oil over medium heat. Remove and set aside.

2 In the same pan, saute mushrooms until tender. Add the broth, carrots, garlic powder, thyme and remaining pepper; bring to a boil. Add barley and beef. Reduce heat; cover and simmer for 20-25 minutes until the meat, vegetables and barley are tender. **Yield:** 8 servings.

Spiral Stromboli

(Pictured on page 62)

You can change the meats and cheeses in this oven-baked sandwich for variety or to suit your liking. The stuffed loaf takes advantage of refrigerated dough, so it's easy to assemble.—Kris Lehman

1 tube (11 ounces) refrigerated crusty French loaf
3/4 to 1 cup shredded mozzarella cheese
3/4 to 1 cup shredded cheddar cheese
1/4 pound thinly sliced salami

1/4 pound thinly sliced deli ham
1/4 cup chopped roasted sweet red peppers
1 tablespoon butter, melted
2 to 3 tablespoons shredded Parmesan cheese

1 Unroll the dough and pat into a 14-in. x 12-in. rectangle. Sprinkle mozzarella and cheddar cheeses to within 1/2 in. of edges; top with salami, ham and red peppers. Roll up jelly-roll style, starting with a short side; seal seam and tuck ends under.

2 Place seam side down on an ungreased baking sheet. Brush with butter; sprinkle with Parmesan cheese. Bake at 375° for 25-30 minutes or until golden brown. Slice with a serrated knife. **Yield:** 4 servings.

KRIS LEHMAN

On those stretches that Kris hasn't been in the office the past 12-1/2 years, co-workers could tell you where she most likely was—Disney World. Her family has been there more than 18 times! Making crafts and getting good bargains at rummage sales are other pastimes she enjoys...along with cooking, of course. Desserts are her favorite to make.

Raspberry Grilled Cheese

When I first heard the ingredients in this recipe, I wouldn't have even given it a second look, let alone make it. But when our Test Kitchen tried it, I tasted a piece and found it was fabulous. I served it as a snack on a camping outing and now have a standing request for these sandwiches.

—Rita Krajcir

2 tablespoons seedless red raspberry preserves
4 slices sourdough bread
2 tablespoons chopped pecans
1 to 2 tablespoons sliced green onion
4 slices Muenster *or* baby Swiss cheese
3 tablespoons butter, softened

1 Spread preserves on two slices of bread; top with the pecans, onion and cheese. Top with remaining bread.

2 Butter outsides of sandwiches. Toast on a hot griddle for 3-4 minutes on each side or until golden brown. **Yield:** 2 servings.

Spicy Chicken Rice Soup

We love Southwestern-type food, so this soup is a favorite. Remember to taste your soup and season it to your family members' liking.
—*Coleen Martin*

- 4 cups chicken broth
- 2 cups cubed cooked chicken
- 2 celery ribs, chopped
- 2 medium carrots, chopped
- 1 medium green pepper, chopped
- 1 medium onion, chopped
- 1/3 cup uncooked long grain rice
- 1/4 cup minced fresh cilantro
- 1/2 teaspoon salt
- 1/2 teaspoon dried oregano
- 1/2 teaspoon pepper
- 1/4 teaspoon ground cumin
- 1/8 to 1/4 teaspoon crushed red pepper flakes

In a large saucepan, combine all ingredients. Bring to a boil. Reduce heat; cover and simmer for 20-25 minutes or until rice and vegetables are tender. **Yield:** 6 servings.

TEST KITCHEN TIP

For additional flavor, add more cumin and a 4-ounce can of chopped green chilies. Coleen always keeps green chilies in her pantry.

Baked Deli Sandwich

Sometimes I substitute pepper Jack cheese for the mozzarella to give it extra zip when assembling this sandwich! It's easy to double for a crowd.
—*Tamra Duncan*

- 1 loaf (1 pound) frozen bread dough, thawed
- 2 tablespoons butter, melted
- 1/4 teaspoon garlic salt
- 1/4 teaspoon dried basil
- 1/4 teaspoon dried oregano
- 1/4 teaspoon pizza seasoning
- 1/4 pound sliced deli ham
- 6 thin slices mozzarella cheese
- 1/4 pound sliced deli smoked turkey breast
- 6 thin slices cheddar cheese

Pizza sauce, warmed, optional

1. On a baking sheet coated with nonstick cooking spray, roll dough into a small rectangle. Let rest for 5-10 minutes. In a small bowl, combine the butter and seasonings. Roll out dough into a 14-in. x 10-in. rectangle. Brush with half of the butter mixture.

2. Layer the ham, mozzarella cheese, turkey and cheddar cheese lengthwise over half of the dough to within 1/2 in. of edges. Fold dough over filling and pinch firmly to seal. Brush with remaining butter mixture.

3. Bake at 400° for 10-12 minutes or until golden brown. Cut into 1-in. slices. Serve with pizza sauce if desired. **Yield:** 4-6 servings.

Basil Turkey Burgers

I often reach for this recipe when I want an alternative to ground beef burgers. I made these for a friend while visiting her in Connecticut, and she had me stock the freezer with them before I could leave!   —Betty Reuter

- 1/4 cup fat-free mayonnaise
- 2 tablespoons minced fresh basil, *divided*
- 1/4 cup fat-free milk
- 2 tablespoons finely chopped onion
- 1 tablespoon dry bread crumbs
- 1/8 teaspoon salt
- 1/8 teaspoon pepper
- 12 ounces lean ground turkey
- 4 hamburger buns, split
- 4 lettuce leaves
- 1 large tomato, sliced

1 In a small bowl, combine mayonnaise and 1 tablespoon basil. Cover and refrigerate until serving. In a large bowl, combine the milk, onion, bread crumbs, salt, pepper and remaining basil. Crumble turkey over mixture and mix well. Shape into four patties.

2 Coat grill rack with nonstick cooking spray before starting the grill for indirect heat. Grill patties, covered, over indirect medium heat for 5-6 minutes on each side or until meat is no longer pink and a thermometer reads 165°. Serve on buns with lettuce, tomato and basil mayonnaise. **Yield:** 4 servings.

TEST KITCHEN TIP

If freezing the patties, omit the basil from the turkey mixture; instead, top each burger with a few fresh basil leaves when serving.

Saucy Barbecue Beef Sandwiches

These tangy beef sandwiches are a big hit with my family. I freeze the meat mixture in individual portions so we can have a quick meal on a hectic day.   —Janet Briggs

- 1 boneless beef chuck roast (3-1/2 to 4 pounds), cut into chunks
- 1-3/4 cups ketchup
- 1 cup chopped onion
- 1/2 cup packed brown sugar
- 1/3 cup cider vinegar
- 1/3 cup Worcestershire sauce
- 3 tablespoons lemon juice
- 4 garlic cloves, minced
- 2 tablespoons ground mustard
- 1 teaspoon paprika
- 1 teaspoon chili powder
- 16 sandwich rolls, split

1 In a Dutch oven, combine the first 11 ingredients. Bring to a boil. Reduce the heat; cover and simmer for 3 hours or until beef is tender, stirring occasionally.

2 Remove beef from sauce and shred; return to the sauce and heat through. Serve on rolls. **Yield:** 16 servings.

Grilled Triple-Decker Club

Don't plan to serve much else when preparing this filling sandwich! I had a Monte Cristo sandwich much like this at a restaurant that was served with raspberry jam, so sometimes I serve it with this sandwich, too. —Joylyn Trickel

   3 slices whole wheat bread
   2 slices mozzarella cheese
   2 thin slices deli ham
   2 thin slices deli turkey
   2 tablespoons mayonnaise
   1 egg
   1 tablespoon milk
   1 tablespoon butter

1 Layer one slice of bread, one slice of cheese, ham, second slice of bread, turkey, mayonnaise, remaining cheese and remaining bread. In a small bowl, whisk egg and milk. Brush over the outsides of sandwich.

2 In a skillet over medium heat, melt butter. Brown sandwich on both sides until cheese is melted. **Yield:** 1 serving.

TEST KITCHEN TIP

Looking for a lighter sandwich? Take out the middle bread layer.

JOYLYN TRICKEL

Joylyn and her husband enjoy doing just about everything outdoors, including taking road trips, mountain biking, fishing, hiking, camping and grilling. Making pizza on the grill is a favorite. Inside, she spends time coming up with new appetizers using whatever is left in the kitchen and makes fancy wedding cakes for friends and family when an occasion presents itself.

Super Italian Sub

This is a great make-ahead sandwich that serves a lot. I've used it for picnics and for a quick lunch on busy days. —Karen Scales

   1 loaf (1 pound) unsliced Italian bread
1/3 cup olive oil
1/4 cup red wine vinegar
   8 garlic cloves, minced
   1 teaspoon dried oregano
1/4 teaspoon pepper
1/2 pound thinly sliced deli ham

1/2 pound thinly sliced deli turkey
1/4 pound thinly sliced salami
1/4 pound sliced provolone cheese
1/4 pound sliced mozzarella cheese
   1 medium green pepper, thinly sliced into rings

1 Cut bread in half lengthwise; hollow out top and bottom, leaving a 1/2-in. shell (discard removed bread or save for another use). Combine the oil, vinegar, garlic, oregano and pepper; brush over cut sides of bread top and bottom.

2 On the bottom half, layer half of the meats, cheeses and green pepper. Repeat layers. Replace bread top. Wrap tightly in plastic wrap; refrigerate for up to 24 hours. **Yield:** 10-12 servings.

Classic Chicken Noodle Soup

(Pictured on page 63 and on front cover)

This brothy soup has lots of vegetables! It's very satisfying on a wintry day. The recipe takes some time to make but is well worth it.
—*Patricia Schmeling*

1 broiler/fryer chicken (3 to 4 pounds), cut up	1/4 teaspoon pepper
10 cups water	**SOUP INGREDIENTS:**
1 large carrot, sliced	2 large carrots, sliced
1 large onion, sliced	2 celery ribs, sliced
1 celery rib, sliced	1 medium onion, chopped
1 garlic clove, minced	2 cups uncooked fine egg noodles
1 bay leaf	1 cup frozen peas
1 teaspoon dried thyme	1/2 cup frozen cut green beans
1 teaspoon salt	

1 In a large soup kettle or Dutch oven, combine the first 10 ingredients. Bring to a boil. Reduce heat; cover and simmer for 1-1/2 to 2 hours or until the meat is tender.

2 Remove chicken; cool. Remove and discard skin and bones. Chop chicken; set aside. Skim fat from broth; strain broth, discarding vegetables and bay leaf. Return broth to the pan; add car- rots, celery and onion. Bring to a boil. Reduce heat; cover and simmer for 10 minutes or until the vegetables are just tender.

3 Add noodles and chicken. Bring to a boil. Reduce heat; cover and simmer for 6 minutes. Stir in peas and beans. Cook for 2-4 minutes or until beans and noodles are tender. **Yield:** 6-8 servings.

Test Kitchen Tip

Patricia cooks the chicken the day before she makes the soup and refrigerates it overnight. Then it's easy to remove the solidified fat from the broth and handle the cooked chicken.

Asparagus Brie Soup

This rich, creamy soup is so special that I often serve it before our Easter dinner. Brie and asparagus are two foods we really enjoy—and this soup combines them in a delicious way.
—*Sue A. Jurack*

1/2 pound fresh asparagus, trimmed and cut into 2-inch pieces
1/2 cup butter
1/4 cup all-purpose flour
  3 cups chicken broth
  1 cup heavy whipping cream
1/2 cup white wine
  4 to 6 ounces Brie, rind removed and cubed
Dash salt and pepper

1 In a large saucepan, saute asparagus in butter until tender. Stir in flour until blended. Cook and stir for 2 minutes or until golden brown. Gradually add the broth, cream and wine. Bring to a boil. Reduce heat; simmer, uncovered, for 10-15 minutes. Cool slightly.

2 In a blender or food processor, process soup in batches until smooth. Return to the pan. Add Brie; simmer, uncovered, for 5 minutes or until cheese is melted. Season with salt and pepper. **Yield:** 4 servings.

Blue Cheese Roast Beef Sandwiches

This recipe is a great way to dress up a roast beef sandwich. The blue cheese spread is simply scrumptious.
—Janet Briggs

1/2 cup crumbled blue cheese
1/3 cup sour cream
3 tablespoons mayonnaise
Salt and pepper to taste

8 slices rye *or* whole wheat bread
3/4 pound thinly sliced deli roast beef
1/3 cup roasted sweet red peppers
Bibb *or* Boston lettuce leaves

1 In a bowl, mash the blue cheese with a fork. Whisk in the sour cream and mayonnaise; season with salt and pepper. Spread over one side of each slice of bread.

2 On four slices; layer roast beef, red peppers and lettuce; top with remaining bread. **Yield:** 4 servings.

Tortilla Soup

The presentation of this soup is so pretty…its zippy taste is even better!
—Julie Ferron

1 medium dried Ancho pepper, seeded and chopped
1 cup water
Oil for deep-fat frying
6 corn tortillas (6 inches), halved and cut into 1/4-inch strips
1 small onion, sliced
4 garlic cloves, peeled
1 can (14-1/2 ounces) whole tomatoes, drained
6 cups vegetable *or* chicken broth
1/4 cup chopped fresh cilantro
1/2 teaspoon salt
1/8 teaspoon cayenne pepper, optional
1-1/2 cups (6 ounces) shredded Monterey Jack cheese
1 large avocado, peeled and diced
1 medium lime, sliced and quartered

1 In a small bowl, combine the Ancho pepper and water; let stand for 20 minutes or until pepper is softened. Drain and discard water; set pepper aside.

2 In a large saucepan, heat 1 in. of oil to 350°. Add half of the tortilla strips; cook and stir until golden brown. Remove with a slotted spoon to paper towels to drain. Repeat with remaining tortilla strips; set aside.

3 Drain saucepan, reserving 2 teaspoons of oil. In reserved oil, cook the onion, garlic and pepper over low heat until onion is golden brown, about 7 minutes. Remove from the heat; cool slightly. Transfer to a food processor; add tomatoes. Cover and process until smooth.

4 Return mixture to the pan. Cook, uncovered, over medium heat for 10 minutes or until mixture has thickened to the consistency of tomato paste. Add broth; bring to a boil. Reduce heat; cover and simmer for 30 minutes.

5 Add cilantro, salt and cayenne if desired. Divide cheese and avocado among six bowls; top with soup, tortilla strips and lime. **Yield:** 6 servings.

Colorful Chicken Croissants ✓

In just about 15 minutes, you can whip up these pleasant chicken sandwiches, which are fabulous for an afternoon luncheon. —*Anita Bukowski*

  2 cups cubed cooked chicken breast
1/4 cup diced celery
1/4 cup golden raisins
1/4 cup dried cranberries
1/4 cup sliced almonds
3/4 cup mayonnaise
  2 tablespoons chopped red onion
1/4 teaspoon salt, optional
1/4 teaspoon pepper
  4 croissants, split

In a bowl, combine the first nine ingredients. Spoon about 1/2 cup onto each croissant. **Yield:** 4 servings.

Grilled Tomato Sandwiches

After having one too many BLT's one summer, I started making these instead. I actually like these sandwiches a lot better! —*Wendy Stenman*

  8 slices tomato (3/4 inch thick)
1/2 teaspoon salt, *divided*
  6 tablespoons mayonnaise
  1 teaspoon lemon juice
  1 garlic clove, minced
  1 round cheese focaccia bread *or* focaccia bread of your choice (12 inches), halved lengthwise

  1 tablespoon balsamic vinegar
1/4 teaspoon pepper
  1 cup chopped artichoke hearts
  3 cups torn romaine *or* spinach

1 Sprinkle one side of tomato slices with 1/8 teaspoon salt. Place salt side down on paper towels for 10 minutes. Repeat with second side. In a small bowl, combine the mayonnaise, lemon juice and garlic; set aside.

2 Coat grill rack with nonstick cooking spray before starting the grill. Place bread cut side down on grill. Place tomatoes on grill. Grill, covered, over medium heat for 2 minutes or until bread is golden brown.

3 Sprinkle tomatoes with vinegar, pepper and remaining salt. Spread mayonnaise mixture over bread. On the bottom half, layer tomatoes, artichokes and romaine; replace bread top. Cut into wedges; serve immediately. **Yield:** 4 servings.

TEST KITCHEN TIP
The tomatoes must be sliced thick and grilled no more than the 2 minutes specified in the recipe.

Butternut Bisque

I've served this wonderful soup to family as well as company. It's especially good to serve in the cooler fall months.
— *Kristin Arnett*

3-1/2 pounds butternut squash, peeled, seeded and cubed
    1 cup sliced carrots
    1 medium tart apple, peeled and chopped
  1/2 cup chopped shallots
    2 tablespoons olive oil
    3 large tomatoes, seeded and chopped
    4 cups chicken broth
1-1/4 cups half-and-half cream
1-1/2 teaspoons salt
  1/4 teaspoon cayenne pepper
  3/4 cup frozen corn, thawed
    2 tablespoons minced chives
Sour cream and additional chives, optional

1 In a large bowl, toss the squash, carrots, apple, shallots and oil. Transfer to a large roasting pan. Bake, uncovered, at 400° for 1 hour or until browned and tender, stirring twice. Cool slightly. Place in a food processor or blender; cover and process until almost smooth.

2 In a Dutch oven or soup kettle, cook tomatoes over medium heat for 5 minutes. Add the pureed vegetables, broth, cream, salt and cayenne; heat through (do not boil). Stir in corn and chives. Garnish servings with sour cream and chives if desired. **Yield:** 10 servings.

Spinach Po' Boy

I like to make this warm and cheesy sandwich for a simple dinner, served with fresh fruit on the side.
— *Janet Briggs*

  1 loaf (8 ounces) unsliced French bread
1/2 cup butter, *divided*
1/3 cup chopped green onions
  6 cups fresh spinach, coarsely chopped

1/2 teaspoon garlic powder
1/8 teaspoon hot pepper sauce
1/2 cup shredded sharp cheddar cheese
1/2 cup shredded mozzarella cheese

1 Cut bread in half lengthwise; spread cut sides with half of the butter. Set aside. In a large skillet, cook onions in remaining butter over medium heat for 4-5 minutes or until tender. Add the spinach, garlic powder and hot pepper sauce; cook and stir 3 minutes longer or until spinach is tender.

2 Spread over bottom half of loaf; sprinkle with cheeses. Replace bread top. Wrap in foil; place on a baking sheet. Bake at 375° for 20 minutes. Open foil; bake 5 minutes longer or until golden brown. **Yield:** 6 servings.

TEST KITCHEN TIP
French bread rolls can be used in place of the loaf of bread.

Florentine Tomato Soup

I had this delicious soup at a gathering with other Food and Nutrition majors when I was in college. I didn't know it was a Taste of Home recipe until I brought in a copy of it and compared it to our recipe database. Of course, the recipe popped right up!
—*Tamra Duncan*

1/2 cup chopped green pepper
1/2 cup chopped onion
1 garlic clove, minced
1 teaspoon olive oil
1 can (14-1/2 ounces) diced tomatoes, undrained
1-1/2 cups water

1 tablespoon minced fresh basil *or* 1 teaspoon dried basil
1 teaspoon chicken bouillon granules
1/4 teaspoon pepper
3/4 cup uncooked medium egg noodles
1 package (10 ounces) frozen chopped spinach, thawed

1 In a saucepan, saute the green pepper, onion and garlic in oil until tender. Add the tomatoes, water, basil, bouillon and pepper; bring to a boil.

2 Stir in noodles; reduce heat. Simmer, uncovered, for 10 minutes. Add spinach; cook until noodles are tender. **Yield:** 5 servings.

Vegetarian Burgers

These do not taste like hamburgers, but they are so good! I made them for my family many years ago when I first became a vegetarian. At that time there were no prepared veggie burgers on the market.
—*Julie Ferron*

3/4 cup unsalted sunflower kernels
1 can (15 ounces) garbanzo beans *or* chickpeas, rinsed and drained
2 cups grated carrots
1 cup chopped onion
1/2 cup whole wheat flour
2 tablespoons vegetable oil
8 hamburger buns, optional
Lettuce and tomato slices, optional

1 Place sunflower kernels in a food processor; cover and process until ground. Remove and set aside. Place beans in food processor; cover and process until ground. In a large bowl, combine the sunflower kernels, beans, carrots, onion, flour and oil. Shape 1/2 cupfuls into patties.

2 In a nonstick skillet coated with nonstick cooking spray, cook the patties over medium heat for 3 minutes on each side or until lightly browned and crisp. Serve on rolls with lettuce and tomato if desired. **Yield:** 8 servings.

BEEF

Flank Steak with Cranberry Sauce

Cranberry sauce doesn't have to be just for poultry. It pairs well with flank steak, as this recipe deliciously proves.
—*Mark Morgan*

2 teaspoons grated orange peel
1/2 teaspoon salt
1/2 teaspoon ground cinnamon
1 beef flank steak (1-1/2 pounds)
CRANBERRY SAUCE:
1/4 cup chopped green onions
1 garlic clove, minced
3/4 cup dried cranberries
1/2 cup reduced-sodium beef broth
1/2 cup red wine
1/2 cup cranberry juice
2 teaspoons cornstarch
2 tablespoons cold water
1/4 teaspoon salt
1/4 teaspoon pepper

1 Combine the orange peel, salt and cinnamon; rub over steak. Cover and refrigerate for 1 hour.

2 In a saucepan coated with nonstick cooking spray, saute onions and garlic until tender. Add cranberries, broth, wine and cranberry juice. Bring to a boil. Reduce heat; simmer, uncovered, 10 minutes. Combine cornstarch and water until smooth; stir into cranberry mixture. Bring to a boil; cook and stir 2 minutes or until thickened. Stir in salt and pepper. Reduce heat; keep warm.

3 Broil steak 3-4 in. from the heat for 7-9 minutes on each side or until meat reaches desired doneness (for medium-rare, a meat thermometer should read 145°; medium, 160°; well-done, 170°). Slice steak across the grain; serve with cranberry sauce. **Yield:** 6 servings.

Razorback Chili

This recipe is perfect to whip up for football season. We serve it over corn chips and top it with sour cream and shredded cheddar cheese. This chili was a game-day favorite back in college after cheering on the Razorbacks.
—*Tamra Duncan*

1 pound lean ground beef
2 cans (15-1/2 ounces *each*) chili beans, undrained
1 can (16 ounces) kidney beans, rinsed and drained
1 can (15 ounces) tomato sauce
1 can (10 ounces) diced tomatoes and green chilies, undrained
1 cup salsa
1 tablespoon chili powder
1 teaspoon ground cumin
1 teaspoon onion powder
1 teaspoon garlic powder
1/2 teaspoon salt
10 cups corn chips, optional
1-1/2 cups (10 ounces) shredded cheddar cheese
3/4 cup sour cream

1 In a large saucepan or Dutch oven, cook beef over medium heat until no longer pink; drain. Add the beans, tomato sauce, tomatoes, salsa and seasonings. Bring to a boil. Reduce heat; cover and simmer for 40-45 minutes or until thickened and heated through.

2 Serve in bowls over corn chips if desired. Top with cheddar cheese and sour cream. **Yield:** 10 servings.

Easy Beef Wellington

(Pictured on page 79)

This very impressive-looking yet easy-to-make dish can be made ahead. Just finish the baking process when your guests arrive.
—*Janaan Cunningham*

1 beef tenderloin (4 to 5 pounds)
MADEIRA SAUCE:
  2 cans (10-1/2 ounces *each*) condensed beef consomme, undiluted
  2 tablespoons tomato paste
1/2 teaspoon beef bouillon granules
  2 tablespoons butter, softened
  2 tablespoons all-purpose flour
1/2 cup Madeira wine

FILLING:
  2 cups chopped fresh mushrooms
  4 shallots, chopped
1/4 pound sliced deli ham, chopped
1/4 cup minced fresh parsley
  1 package (17.3 ounces) frozen puff pastry sheets, thawed
  2 tablespoons milk

1 Place the tenderloin in a greased 15-in. x 10-in. x 1-in. baking pan; fold under ends of meat. Bake, uncovered, at 475° for 20-25 minutes or until browned. Cover and refrigerate for at least 2 hours or until chilled.

2 For sauce, in a large saucepan, combine the consomme, tomato paste and bouillon granules. Bring to a boil. Reduce heat; simmer, uncovered, for 20 minutes or until reduced to 2 cups. Combine butter and flour. Stir into sauce, a teaspoon at a time. Bring to a boil; cook and stir for 2 minutes or until thickened. Remove from the heat; stir in wine and set aside.

3 For the filling, in a large skillet, combine the mushrooms, shallots, ham and 2 tablespoons Madeira sauce. Cook over low heat for 10 minutes, stirring occasionally. Stir in the parsley; cook 10 minutes longer or until liquid has evaporated, stirring occasionally. Set aside.

4 On a lightly floured surface, unfold one puff pastry sheet; cut lengthwise along one fold line, forming two rectangles. Cut smaller rectangle into a 6-in. x 3-in. rectangle; use remaining piece for decorations if desired. Moisten a 6-in. edge of large rectangle with water. Attach smaller rectangle along that edge, pressing lightly to seal. Transfer to an ungreased baking sheet.

5 Spread half of the filling down the center of pastry. Place the tenderloin on the filling. Spread the remaining filling over the top of meat. Roll out remaining puff pastry into a rectangle 8 in. wide and 5 in. longer than the tenderloin; place over the meat. Brush pastry edges with milk; fold edges under meat.

6 Bake, uncovered, at 425° for 40 minutes (meat will be medium); cover lightly with foil if needed. Transfer to a serving platter. Let stand for 15 minutes before slicing. Rewarm Madeira sauce if necessary. Serve with tenderloin. **Yield:** 12-16 servings.

JANAAN CUNNINGHAM

With a teenage son active in sports and school activities as well as her own busy schedule, Janaan finds weeknights to be hectic. That's why she often relies on fast-to-fix dishes like those in *Quick Cooking* magazine. On weekends, however, she can frequently be found in the kitchen preparing more elaborate meals. Cookies are a favorite treat ever since she first made them with her mom at age 7. She's been head of the Test Kitchen for 6 years.

Grilled Chuck Steak

The marinade for this steak is equally delicious brushed on beef kabobs. I like it so much better than store-bought varieties.

—Janet Briggs

4 garlic cloves, minced
1/4 cup olive oil
1 cup red wine vinegar
2/3 cup ketchup
2 tablespoons Worcestershire sauce

2 teaspoons sugar
2 teaspoons dried basil
1 beef chuck steak (about 3 pounds, 1-1/2 inches thick)

1 In a small saucepan, saute garlic in oil for 3-4 minutes or until tender; remove from the heat. In a 4-cup measure, combine the vinegar, ketchup, Worcestershire sauce, sugar, basil and garlic.

2 Pour 1 cup marinade into a large resealable plastic bag; add the meat. Seal bag and turn to coat; refrigerate for at least 6 hours or overnight. Cover and refrigerate remaining marinade.

3 Coat grill rack with nonstick cooking spray before starting the grill. Prepare grill for indirect heat. Drain and discard marinade from steak. Grill steak, uncovered, over medium heat until browned on each side.

4 Move steak to indirect side of grill. Grill, covered, for 45-50 minutes on each side or until meat reaches desired doneness (for medium-rare, a meat thermometer should read 145°; medium, 160°; well-done, 170°), basting occasionally with marinade. **Yield:** 6-8 servings.

Glazed Corned Beef

This roasted corned beef brisket is a wonderful treat for St. Patrick's Day. The tangy sauce is a perfect complement.

—Patricia Schmeling

1 corned beef brisket (3 to 4 pounds), trimmed
1 medium onion, sliced
1 celery rib, sliced
1/4 cup butter
1 cup packed brown sugar
2/3 cup ketchup
1/3 cup white vinegar
2 tablespoons prepared mustard
2 teaspoons prepared horseradish

1 Place corned beef and contents of seasoning packet in a Dutch oven; cover with water. Add onion and celery. Bring to a boil. Reduce heat; cover and simmer for 2-1/2 hours or until meat is tender. Drain and discard liquid and vegetables. Place beef on a rack in a shallow roasting pan; set aside.

2 In a saucepan, melt the butter over medium heat. Stir in the remaining ingredients. Cook and stir until sugar is dissolved. Brush over beef. Bake, uncovered, at 350° for 25 minutes. Let stand for 10 minutes before slicing. **Yield:** 12 servings.

TEST KITCHEN TIP
Slice corned beef against the grain for the most tender slices of meat.

Italian-Style Meat Roll

I also use this meat mixture for meatballs. Either way, it's mouth-watering. —Janaan Cunningham

    1 slice bread, cut into cubes
    1 egg
    2 tablespoons water
    1 small onion, chopped
    1 celery rib, chopped
    1 teaspoon Italian seasoning
  1/2 teaspoon salt
  1/4 teaspoon pepper
    2 pounds lean ground beef
    1 package (2-1/2 ounces) sliced dried beef
1-1/2 cups shredded mozzarella cheese

1 Process bread in a blender or food processor until fine crumbs form; transfer to a bowl. In same blender, combine the egg, water, onion, celery, Italian seasoning, salt and pepper; cover and process until smooth. Stir into the bread crumbs. Crumble beef over mixture and mix well.

2 On a 16-in. x 12-in. piece of waxed paper, shape meat mixture into an 11-in. x 8-in. rectangle. Top with the dried beef and cheese to within 1/2 in. of edge. Roll up jelly-roll style, starting with a short side; pinch to seal edges.

3 Place seam side down in a greased 11-in. x 7-in. x 2-in. baking dish. Bake, uncovered, at 350° for 1-1/4 to 1-1/2 hours or until a meat thermometer reads 160°. Let stand for 10 minutes before serving. **Yield:** 8 servings.

TEST KITCHEN TIP

For meatballs, pat the beef mixture into a square about 1 inch thick. Then cut into 1-inch squares and roll each square into a meatball.

Gone-All-Day Casserole

On those oh-so-busy days, it's great to come home to this savory slow-cooked dish. Wild rice and almonds give the meal a special look and taste. —Rita Krajcir

    1 cup uncooked wild rice, rinsed and drained
    1 cup chopped celery
    1 cup chopped carrots
    2 cans (4 ounces *each*) mushroom stems and pieces, drained
    1 large onion, chopped
    1 garlic clove, minced
  1/2 cup slivered almonds
    3 beef bouillon cubes
2-1/2 teaspoons seasoned salt
    2 pounds boneless beef round steak, cut into 1-inch cubes
    3 cups water

Place ingredients in order listed in a 3-qt. slow cooker (do not stir). Cover and cook on low for 6-8 hours or until rice is tender. Stir before serving. **Yield:** 12 servings.

TEST KITCHEN TIP

Lightly coat the inside of your slow cooker with nonstick cooking spray before filling it with ingredients. This simple tip makes cleanup a breeze.

Norwegian Meatballs

The spices—nutmeg, allspice and ginger—are what gives this dish its authentic Norwegian flavor. —*Sarah Thompson*

          1 egg, beaten
      1/2 cup milk
          1 tablespoon cornstarch
          1 medium onion, finely chopped
          1 teaspoon salt
Dash pepper
      1/4 teaspoon ground nutmeg
      1/4 teaspoon ground allspice
      1/4 teaspoon ground ginger
    1-1/2 pounds lean ground beef
          3 to 4 tablespoons butter
GRAVY:
          1 tablespoon butter
          2 tablespoons all-purpose flour
          1 cup beef broth
      1/2 cup milk
Salt and pepper to taste
Minced fresh parsley, optional

1 In a large mixing bowl, combine the egg, milk, cornstarch, onion, salt, pepper, nutmeg, allspice and ginger. Crumble beef over mixture; mix well. Shape into 1-1/2-in. meatballs. (Mixture will be very soft. For easier shaping, rinse hands in cold water frequently.)

2 In a large skillet, cook the meatballs, half at a time, in butter over medium heat for 10 minutes or until no longer pink. Remove meatballs to paper towels to drain, reserving 1 tablespoon drippings in skillet.

3 For gravy, add butter to drippings. Stir in flour. Add broth and milk. Bring to a boil; cook and stir for 2 minutes or until thickened. Season with salt and pepper. Return meatballs to skillet; heat through. Garnish with parsley if desired. **Yield:** 6 servings.

Oriental Steak

My kids call this steak "skinny meat." It's one of their very favorite meals and I'm happy to make it for them often. —*Coleen Martin*

    1/2 cup soy sauce
      2 tablespoons brown sugar
      2 tablespoons vegetable oil
      2 teaspoons onion powder
      2 teaspoons lemon juice
    1/4 teaspoon ground ginger
      1 beef flank steak (about 3/4 inch thick)

1 In a large resealable plastic bag, combine the first six ingredients; add steak. Seal bag and turn to coat. Cover and refrigerate for at least 4 hours.

2 Drain and discard marinade. Grill steak, uncovered, over medium heat for 3-4 minutes on each side or until meat reaches desired doneness (for medium-rare, a meat thermometer should read 145°). **Yield:** 4 servings.

TEST KITCHEN TIP
Coleen likes to freeze the steak in the marinade. Then she just places the steak in the refrigerator before she goes to work, and they're ready for the grill when she gets home.

Peppered Steaks with Salsa

(Pictured on page 78)

We really enjoy these steaks paired with the refreshing from-scratch salsa. The simple marinade makes the steaks very juicy.

—*Tamra Duncan*

1/2 cup red wine vinegar
2 tablespoons lime juice
2 tablespoons olive oil
2 teaspoons chili powder
1 garlic clove, minced
1 to 2 teaspoons crushed red pepper flakes
1 teaspoon salt
1/2 teaspoon pepper
4 boneless beef chuck eye steaks (about 8 ounces *each*)

SALSA:
1 large tomato, seeded and chopped
1 medium ripe avocado, chopped
2 green onions, thinly sliced
1 tablespoon lime juice
1 tablespoon minced fresh cilantro
1 garlic clove, minced
1/4 to 1/2 teaspoon salt
1/4 teaspoon pepper

1 In a small bowl, combine the first eight ingredients. Pour 1/2 cup into a large resealable plastic bag; add steaks. Seal bag and turn to coat; refrigerate for 8 hours or overnight. Cover and refrigerate remaining marinade for basting. Meanwhile, combine salsa ingredients; cover and chill.

2 Drain and discard marinade from steaks. Grill, covered, over medium heat for 7-8 minutes on each side or until meat reaches desired doneness (for medium-rare, a meat thermometer should read 145°; medium, 160°; well-done, 170°), basting with reserved marinade. Serve with salsa. **Yield:** 4 servings.

Classic Beef Stew

This is a wonderfully comforting dish to serve on a cold, wintry night along with warm buttered biscuits.

—*Karen Johnson*

2 pounds beef stew meat, cut into 1-inch cubes
1 to 2 tablespoons vegetable oil
1-1/2 cups chopped onions
1 can (14-1/2 ounces) diced tomatoes, undrained
1 can (10-1/2 ounces) condensed beef broth, undiluted
3 tablespoons quick-cooking tapioca
1 garlic clove, minced
1 tablespoon dried parsley flakes
1 teaspoon salt
1/4 teaspoon pepper
1 bay leaf
6 medium carrots, cut into 2-inch pieces
3 medium potatoes, peeled and cut into 2-inch pieces
1 cup sliced celery (1-inch pieces)

1 In a Dutch oven, brown the beef, half at a time, in oil. Drain. Return all meat to pan. Add the onions, tomatoes, broth, tapioca, garlic, parsley, salt, pepper and bay leaf. Bring to a boil; remove from the heat.

2 Cover and bake at 350° for 1-1/2 hours. Stir in carrots, potatoes and celery. Bake, covered, 1 hour longer or until meat and vegetables are tender. Discard bay leaf. **Yield:** 6-8 servings.

BETTY REUTER

The love of food runs in Betty's family. Her grandfather owned one of Milwaukee's most-popular bakeries, and he also ran the bakery at the Wisconsin State Fair. The fair still uses his recipes. In fact, people stand in line for hours to get a taste of his cream puffs! Her parents frequently entertained, and Betty was often in the kitchen alongside them, helping prepare for guests. She has three grown sons, who appreciate their mom's fondness for cooking and baking.

Veal Cutlets with Red Peppers

I've made this for many guests over the years, and they all tell me how much they enjoy it. It's very pretty with red bell pepper.
—*Karen Johnson*

1-1/2 pounds veal slices (about 1/4 inch thick)
  1/4 cup lemon juice
    2 tablespoons olive oil
    2 teaspoons grated lemon peel
    2 garlic cloves, minced
    1 teaspoon sugar
    1 teaspoon salt
    1 teaspoon paprika
  1/2 teaspoon ground mustard
  1/2 teaspoon ground nutmeg
  1/2 cup all-purpose flour
    6 tablespoons butter, *divided*
    2 medium onions, sliced
    2 medium sweet red peppers, julienned
  1/2 pound fresh mushrooms, sliced
    1 can (14-1/2 ounces) chicken broth
    2 teaspoons cornstarch
    2 teaspoons water

1 Place veal in a 13-in. x 9-in. x 2-in. dish; set aside. In a medium bowl, combine the lemon juice, oil, lemon peel, garlic, sugar, salt, paprika, mustard and nutmeg; reserve 2 tablespoons. Pour remaining marinade over veal. Let stand for 30 minutes at room temperature.

2 Discard marinade from veal. Place flour in a shallow dish; coat veal with flour, shaking off excess. In a large skillet, brown veal slices, two at a time, in 4 tablespoons butter; set aside. In the same skillet, saute the onions, red peppers and mushrooms in remaining butter until tender, stirring to loosen browned bits. Stir in broth and reserved marinade; cover and simmer 10 minutes.

3 Combine cornstarch and water until smooth. Stir into vegetable mixture. Bring to a boil; cook and stir for 2-3 minutes or until thickened. Add the veal; heat through. **Yield:** 6 servings.

EDITOR'S NOTE: This recipe was tested with a veal cutlet or veal for scallopini, not processed veal cube steak.

Party Beef Casserole

Not only is this casserole a real crowd-pleaser, it's a convenient meal-in-one. —*Coleen Martin*

    3 tablespoons all-purpose flour
    1 teaspoon salt
1/2 teaspoon pepper
    2 pounds boneless round steak, cut into 1/2-inch cubes
    2 tablespoons vegetable oil
    1 cup water
1/2 cup beef broth
    1 garlic clove, minced
    1 tablespoon dried minced onion
1/2 teaspoon dried thyme
1/4 teaspoon dried rosemary, crushed
    2 cups sliced fresh mushrooms
    2 cups frozen peas, thawed
    3 cups mashed potatoes (mashed with milk and butter)
    1 tablespoon butter, melted
Paprika

1 In a large resealable plastic bag, combine flour, salt and pepper; add beef cubes and shake to coat. In a skillet over medium heat, brown beef in oil. Place beef and drippings in a greased shallow 2-1/2-qt. baking dish.

2 To skillet, add water, broth, garlic, onion, thyme and rosemary; bring to a boil. Simmer, uncovered, for 5 minutes; stir in mushrooms. Pour over meat; mix well.

3 Cover and bake at 350° for 1-1/2 to 1-3/4 hours or until beef is tender. Sprinkle peas over meat. Spread potatoes evenly over top. Brush with butter; sprinkle with paprika. Bake 15-20 minutes more. **Yield:** 6-8 servings.

Taco Pie

This is a great recipe to serve for a casual meal! Everybody likes the Mexican-style dish, and it is so easy to prepare. —*Betty Reuter*

    1 pound ground beef
    1 package taco seasoning mix
1/2 cup water
1/3 cup stuffed olives, sliced
    1 tube (8 ounces) refrigerated crescent rolls
1-1/2 cups corn chips, crushed, *divided*

    1 cup (8 ounces) sour cream
3/4 cup shredded cheddar cheese
    1 cup shredded lettuce
    2 medium tomatoes, seeded and chopped

1 In a skillet, cook beef over medium heat until no longer pink; drain. Add the taco seasoning, water and olives. Bring to a boil. Reduce heat; simmer, uncovered, for 5 minutes.

2 Separate crescent dough into eight triangles and place in a 9-in. deep-dish pie plate with points toward the center. Press onto the bottom and up the sides of pan to form a crust; seal perforations. Sprinkle half the corn chips over crust. Spoon beef mixture over chips. Spread sour cream over beef. Sprinkle with cheddar cheese; top with remaining chips.

3 Bake, uncovered, at 375° for 20-25 minutes until golden brown. Serve topped with lettuce and tomatoes. **Yield:** 6 servings.

Steak 'n' Shrimp Kabobs

I like to marinate the kabobs the night before, then I can have dinner on the table in minutes. —*Sarah Thompson*

1 cup teriyaki sauce
1 can (6 ounces) pineapple juice
1/2 cup packed brown sugar
6 garlic cloves, minced
1/4 teaspoon Worcestershire sauce
1/8 teaspoon pepper
1 pound boneless beef sirloin steak, cut into 1-inch cubes
1 pound large uncooked shrimp, peeled and deveined
1 pound whole fresh mushrooms
2 large green peppers, cut into 1-inch pieces
2 medium onions, halved and quartered
1 pint cherry tomatoes
1-1/2 teaspoons cornstarch

1 In a large bowl, combine the first six ingredients; mix well. Pour half of the marinade into a large resealable plastic bag; add beef. Seal bag and turn to coat; refrigerate for 8 hours or overnight, turning occasionally. Cover and refrigerate remaining marinade.

2 Drain and discard marinade from beef. On metal or soaked wooden skewers, alternately thread beef, shrimp, mushrooms, green peppers, onions and tomatoes; set aside. In a small saucepan, combine cornstarch and reserved marinade until smooth. Bring to a boil; cook and stir for 1-2 minutes or until sauce is thickened.

3 Grill kabobs, covered, over indirect medium heat for 6 minutes, turning once. Baste with sauce. Grill 8-10 minutes longer or until shrimp turn pink and beef reaches desired doneness, turning and basting twice. **Yield:** 6-8 servings.

Russian Stroganoff

This is one of my family's favorite recipes, so I make it for them frequently. The tender beef strips in a mushroom sauce taste so good over noodles. —*Wendy Stenman*

1/4 cup all-purpose flour
3/4 teaspoon salt, *divided*
1-1/2 pounds boneless beef sirloin steak, cut into 1/2-inch strips
3 tablespoons olive oil
1 medium onion, chopped
1 garlic clove, minced
2 cups sliced fresh mushrooms

1 can (8 ounces) tomato sauce
3/4 cup water
1 tablespoon beef bouillon granules
1 tablespoon Worcestershire sauce
4 drops hot pepper sauce
1/4 teaspoon pepper
1/2 cup reduced-fat sour cream
Hot cooked noodles

1 Combine flour and 1/4 teaspoon salt in a large resealable plastic bag. Add beef, a few pieces at a time, and shake to coat. In a large skillet, cook beef in batches in oil until no longer pink; remove.

2 Add onion and garlic; saute until tender. Add the mushrooms, tomato sauce, water, bouillon granules, Worcestershire sauce, hot pepper sauce, remaining salt and pepper. Bring to a boil. Reduce heat; cover and simmer for 3-4 minutes or until mushrooms are tender.

3 Return beef to the pan. Stir in sour cream; heat gently (do not boil). Serve immediately over noodles. **Yield:** 4 servings.

Ground Beef 'n' Biscuits

This simple-to-make dish is great to serve for a weeknight dinner. The saucy meal is family-pleasing.
—*Anita Bukowski*

- 1-1/2 pounds ground beef
- 1/2 cup chopped celery
- 1/2 cup chopped onion
- 2 tablespoons all-purpose flour
- 1 teaspoon salt
- 1/4 teaspoon dried oregano
- 1/8 teaspoon pepper
- 2 cans (8 ounces *each*) tomato sauce
- 1 package (10 ounces) frozen peas
- 1 tube (7-1/2 ounces) refrigerated buttermilk biscuits
- 1 cup (4 ounces) shredded cheddar cheese

1 In a large skillet, cook the beef, celery and onion over medium heat until meat is no longer pink and celery is tender; drain. Stir in the flour, salt, oregano and pepper until blended. Add tomato sauce and peas; simmer for 5 minutes.

2 Transfer to a greased 13-in. x 9-in. x 2-in. baking dish. Separate biscuits; arrange over beef mixture. Sprinkle with cheese. Bake, uncovered, at 350° for 20 minutes or until biscuits are golden and cheese is melted. **Yield:** 6 servings.

Italian Veal Pie

Simply delicious describes this meaty main dish! It's like a potpie with flecks of oregano in the flaky crust.
—*Sue Draheim*

- 1-1/2 cups all-purpose flour
- 1/4 cup grated Parmesan cheese
- 1 teaspoon garlic salt
- 1 teaspoon dried oregano
- 1/2 cup cold butter
- 4 to 5 tablespoons cold water

FILLING:
- 1 pound boneless veal sirloin steak, cubed
- 1/2 cup all-purpose flour
- 1/4 cup butter

- 1 can (14-1/2 ounces) diced tomatoes
- 1 can (8 ounces) tomato sauce
- 1/4 cup chopped onion
- 3 tablespoons grated Parmesan cheese
- 1 tablespoon sugar
- 1 teaspoon garlic powder
- 1 teaspoon dried basil
- 1 teaspoon dried oregano
- 1/8 teaspoon pepper
- 4 slices cheddar cheese (1/4 inch thick)

1 In a large bowl, combine the flour, cheese, garlic salt and oregano. Cut in butter until crumbly. Gradually add water, tossing with a fork until dough forms a ball. Divide pastry into thirds; set aside a third.

2 On a floured surface, roll out remaining pastry to fit a 9-in. pie plate. Transfer pastry to pie plate. Trim pastry to 1/2 in. beyond edge of pie plate; flute edges.

3 For filling, coat veal cubes with flour. In a skillet, brown veal on all sides in butter. Add the tomatoes, tomato sauce, onion, cheese, sugar and seasonings. Bring to a boil. Reduce heat; simmer, uncovered for 30 minutes.

4 Transfer into prepared crust. Top with cheese slices. Roll out remaining pastry. Cut into 2-in. circles. Place on top of filling. Bake at 400° for 30-35 minutes or until golden brown and bubbly. **Yield:** 4-6 servings.

Barbecued Brisket

Slow baking not only makes this brisket nice and tender, but allows for the sweet tangy flavor of the barbecue sauce to permeate the meat.
—*Anita Bukowski*

    1 fresh beef brisket (3 to 4 pounds)
1-1/4 cups water, *divided*
  1/2 cup chopped onion
    3 garlic cloves, minced
    1 tablespoon vegetable oil
    1 cup ketchup
    3 tablespoons red wine vinegar
    2 tablespoons lemon juice
    2 tablespoons brown sugar
    1 tablespoon Worcestershire sauce
    2 teaspoons cornstarch
    1 teaspoon paprika
    1 teaspoon chili powder
  1/4 teaspoon salt
  1/4 teaspoon pepper
  1/4 teaspoon Liquid Smoke, optional

1 Place brisket in a large Dutch oven. Add 1/2 cup water. Cover and bake at 325° for 2 hours.

2 Meanwhile, in a medium saucepan, saute onion and garlic in oil until tender. Add ketchup, vinegar, lemon juice, brown sugar, Worcestershire sauce, cornstarch, paprika, chili powder, salt, pepper and remaining water. Simmer, uncovered, for 1 hour, stirring occasionally. Add Liquid Smoke if desired; mix well.

3 Drain drippings from Dutch oven. Pour sauce over meat. Cover and bake 1 hour longer or until meat is tender. **Yield:** 6-8 servings.

EDITOR'S NOTE: This is a fresh beef brisket, not corned beef.

Veal Scallopini

This dish makes a weeknight dinner extra-special. I also often serve it on weekends for company.
—*Sue Myers*

    2 tablespoons all-purpose flour
  1/8 teaspoon salt
  1/8 teaspoon pepper
    1 egg
  1/2 to 3/4 pound veal cutlets *or* boneless skinless chicken breasts, flattened to 1-inch thickness

    2 tablespoons olive oil
    4 ounces fresh mushrooms, halved
    1 cup chicken broth
    2 tablespoons Marsala wine
Hot cooked spaghetti

1 In a small bowl, combine the flour, salt, and pepper. In another bowl, lightly beat the egg. Dip veal in egg, then coat with flour mixture.

2 In a large skillet, brown veal in oil on both sides. Stir in the mushrooms, broth and wine. Bring to a boil. Reduce heat; simmer, uncovered, for 5-10 minutes or until mushrooms are tender. Serve over spaghetti. **Yield:** 2 servings.

Bavarian Pot Roast

The first time I tried this roast, the meat was incredibly tender and flavorful. The sweet apple juice, ginger and cinnamon give the dish a unique and irresistible aroma. —*Joylyn Trickel*

1 boneless beef top round roast (about 4 pounds), halved
1-1/2 cups apple juice
1 can (8 ounces) tomato sauce
1 small onion, chopped
2 tablespoons white vinegar

1 tablespoon salt
2 to 3 teaspoons ground cinnamon
3/4 teaspoon ground ginger *or* 1 tablespoon minced fresh gingerroot
1/4 cup cornstarch
1/2 cup water

1 In a Dutch oven coated with nonstick cooking spray, brown roast on all sides over medium-high heat; drain. Transfer to a 5-qt. slow cooker.

2 In a bowl, combine the juice, tomato sauce, onion, vinegar, salt, cinnamon and ginger; pour over roast. Cover and cook on high for 5-7 hours.

3 Combine cornstarch and water until smooth; stir into cooking juices. Cover and cook 1 hour longer or until the meat is tender and gravy begins to thicken. **Yield:** 12 servings.

Test Kitchen Tip

Sometimes Joylyn makes this pot roast in a Dutch oven instead of the slow cooker. She simmers it over low heat for 4-5 hours.

Baked Spaghetti

This is a great dish to prepare when you need to feed a lot of people. I have even made it ahead of time. The cream of mushroom soup gives this dish a nice, creamy texture. —*Amy Welk-Thieding*

1 pound ground beef
1 cup chopped onion
1 cup chopped green pepper
1 tablespoon butter
1 can (28 ounces) diced tomatoes, undrained
1 can (4 ounces) mushroom stems and pieces, drained
1 can (2-1/4 ounces) sliced ripe olives, drained
2 teaspoons dried oregano
12 ounces spaghetti, cooked and drained
2 cups (8 ounces) shredded cheddar cheese
1 can (10-3/4 ounces) condensed cream of mushroom soup, undiluted
1/4 cup water
1/4 cup grated Parmesan cheese

1 In a large skillet, cook the beef over medium heat until no longer pink; drain and set aside. In same skillet, saute onion and green pepper in butter until tender. Add the tomatoes, mushrooms, olives, oregano and ground beef. Bring to a boil. Reduce heat; simmer, uncovered, for 10 minutes.

2 Place half of the spaghetti in a greased 13-in. x 9-in. x 2-in. baking dish. Top with half of the vegetable mixture. Sprinkle with 1 cup of cheddar cheese. Repeat layers. Mix the soup and water until smooth; pour over casserole. Sprinkle with Parmesan cheese. Bake, uncovered, at 350° for 30-35 minutes or until heated through. **Yield:** 12 servings.

Oven Swiss Steak

My whole family likes this version of Swiss steak because it's not as saucy but is still chock-full of veggies.
—Janet Briggs

1/4 cup all-purpose flour
1/2 teaspoon salt
1-1/2 pounds boneless beef round steak (3/4 inch thick), cut into 6 serving-size pieces
1 tablespoon vegetable oil
1/3 cup white wine
1 can (14-1/2 ounces) whole tomatoes, undrained and chopped
1/2 cup finely chopped celery
1/2 cup sliced fresh mushrooms
1/2 cup finely chopped carrots
1 teaspoon beef bouillon granules
1/2 teaspoon Worcestershire sauce

1 In a small bowl, combine flour and salt. Sprinkle 1/2 teaspoon flour mixture over each piece of meat. Pound into meat, turn over and repeat on other side. In a large skillet, brown meat on both sides in oil.

2 Transfer to an 11-in. x 7-in. x 2-in. baking dish, reserving pan drippings. Stir remaining flour into skillet until smooth. Gradually add wine. Add the remaining ingredients.

3 Bring to a boil; cook and stir for 2 minutes or until thickened. Pour over meat. Cover and bake at 350° for 1-1/2 hours or until meat is tender. **Yield:** 6 servings.

Hearty Beef Enchiladas

My husband loves his food extra-cheesy, so I can never put too much cheese over the top of these enchiladas! You can set out small bowls of diced onions and tomatoes so folks can add their own garnishes.
—Joylyn Trickel

1 pound ground beef
1 medium onion, chopped
1 can (15-1/2 ounces) chili beans, undrained
1 can (10 ounces) enchilada sauce, *divided*
1/2 cup salsa, *divided*
Vegetable oil
7 corn *or* flour tortillas (8 inches)
1 cup (4 ounces) shredded cheddar cheese
2 tablespoons sliced ripe olives

1 In a large saucepan, cook beef and onion over medium heat until meat is no longer pink; drain. Stir in the beans, 2/3 cup enchilada sauce and 2 tablespoons salsa; set aside.

2 In a skillet, heat 1/4 in. of oil. Dip each tortilla in hot oil for 3 seconds on each side or just until limp; drain on paper towels.

3 Top each tortilla with 2/3 cup beef mixture. Roll up and place seam side down in an 11-in. x 7-in. x 2-in. baking dish. Drizzle with remaining enchilada sauce and salsa. Sprinkle with cheese and olives. Bake, uncovered, at 350° for 20-25 minutes or until bubbly. **Yield:** 7 enchiladas.

KRISTIN ARNETT

Since she was a little girl with an Easy-Bake Oven, Kristin has been interested in baking and cooking. She has a passion for food that is simply prepared and beautifully presented, so it's no surprise she enjoys entertaining family and friends. Her six children especially love to eat what she creates! Before joining our Test Kitchen staff 6 years ago, she owned her own catering company for 13 years.

Garlic Rosemary Steak with Potato Cakes

This recipe is a favorite with my family. The potato cakes make it fun and different, and the kids love to help make them.

—Kristin Arnett

3/4 cup olive oil
3/4 cup soy sauce
1/3 cup balsamic vinegar
12 large garlic cloves, minced
6 teaspoons dried rosemary, crushed
1 boneless beef top sirloin steak (about 3-1/2 pounds, 2 inches thick)
Salt and pepper to taste
POTATO CAKES:
3 pounds white potatoes (about 6 large)
12 green onions, chopped
2 eggs
2 teaspoons ground cumin
1 teaspoon salt
1/4 teaspoon pepper
3 tablespoons olive oil, *divided*
ONIONS AND PEPPERS:
2 large onions, cut into 1-inch pieces
1/4 cup olive oil
2 medium sweet red peppers, cut into 1-inch pieces
1 medium green pepper, cut into 1-inch pieces
3/4 teaspoon dried marjoram
1/8 teaspoon dried red pepper flakes
1 teaspoon salt
1/4 teaspoon pepper

1 In a small bowl, combine the first five ingredients. Pour half of the marinade into a large resealable plastic bag. Season steak with salt and pepper; add to bag. Seal bag and turn to coat; refrigerate overnight, turning occasionally. Cover and refrigerate remaining marinade for serving.

2 For potato cakes, place potatoes in a Dutch oven and cover with water. Bring to a boil. Reduce heat; cover and cook until just tender, about 20 minutes. Drain and refrigerate until chilled. Peel and shred potatoes. Transfer to a large bowl; add green onions. In a small bowl, beat the eggs, cumin, salt and pepper; gently mix into potatoes. Form into round patties (about 2-1/2 in. diameter). Cover and refrigerate up to 6 hours.

3 In a large skillet over medium-high heat, fry cakes in batches in 2 tablespoons oil for 8 minutes per side or until golden brown. Add remaining oil as needed.

4 For onions and peppers, in a large skillet, saute onions in oil for 4 minutes. Add peppers; saute for about 5 minutes or until peppers begin to soften. Add marjoram and red pepper flakes. Season with salt and pepper; cook and stir 2 minutes longer. Remove from the heat and keep warm.

5 Let steak stand at room temperature for 30 minutes. Discard marinade; pat steak dry. Broil steak 6 in. from the heat for 12 minutes on each side or until steak reaches desired doneness (for medium-rare, a meat thermometer should read 145°; medium, 160°; well-done, 170°).

6 Let stand for 10 minutes. Thinly slice steak across the grain; arrange on a serving platter with onions and peppers and potato cakes. Heat the reserved marinade and serve with steak. **Yield:** 8-12 servings.

Bacon Cheeseburger Pizza

The flavor of cheeseburgers and pizza come together in this fantastic recipe. I love the addition of bacon and dill pickles. What's not to like about this quick-to-fix pizza?

—*Sue A. Jurack*

      1/2 pound ground beef
        1 small onion, chopped
        1 prebaked Italian bread shell crust (1 pound)
        1 can (8 ounces) pizza sauce
        6 bacon strips, cooked and crumbled
      20 dill pickle coin slices
        2 cups (8 ounces) shredded mozzarella cheese
        2 cups (8 ounces) shredded cheddar cheese
        1 teaspoon pizza *or* Italian seasoning

1 In a skillet, cook beef and onion over medium heat until meat is no longer pink; drain and set aside.

2 Place crust on an ungreased 12-in. pizza pan. Spread with pizza sauce. Top with beef mixture, bacon, pickles and cheeses. Sprinkle with pizza seasoning. Bake at 450° for 8-10 minutes or until cheese is melted. **Yield:** 8 slices.

Test Kitchen Tip

Cook the ground beef and onion in advance to shorten the prep time. The prebaked Italian bread shell crust makes this a snap to put together for supper on a busy weeknight.

Beef Barley Stew

This is a very hearty stew, but the subtle wine with portobello mushrooms, thyme and bay leaves make it special enough to serve to company.

—*Diane Werner*

      1 pound beef stew meat, cut into 1/2-inch pieces
      1 tablespoon olive oil
      2 cups sliced carrots
      1 cup chopped onion
      1 cup sliced celery
      2 to 3 garlic cloves, minced
      2 cups sliced baby portobello mushrooms
      1 can (14-1/2 ounces) stewed tomatoes
      1 cup water
      1 cup dry red wine
      1 cup beef broth
      2 bay leaves
      1 teaspoon salt
      3/4 teaspoon dried thyme
      1/4 teaspoon pepper
      1/3 cup uncooked medium pearl barley
      1/4 cup all-purpose flour
      1/3 cup cold water
      1 to 2 tablespoons balsamic vinegar
   Minced fresh parsley, optional

1 In a Dutch oven, cook beef in oil until meat is no longer pink. Add the carrots, onion, celery and garlic; cook for 5 minutes. Add the mushrooms, stewed tomatoes, water, wine, broth, bay leaves, salt, thyme, and pepper.

2 Bring to a boil. Reduce heat; cover and simmer for 1 hour. Add barley; cover and simmer 45 minutes longer or until barley and meat are tender.

3 Combine flour and cold water until smooth. Gradually stir into pan. Bring to a boil; cook and stir for 2 minutes or until thickened. Remove from the heat. Discard bay leaves. Stir in balsamic vinegar just before serving. Sprinkle each serving with parsley if desired. **Yield:** 6-8 servings.

Beef Sirloin Tip Roast

With only five ingredients, this dish is quickly put together. As it bakes, I can prepare the other components of the meal.
—Amy Welk-Thieding

1 boneless beef sirloin tip roast (about 3 pounds)
1-1/4 cups water, *divided*
1 can (8 ounces) mushroom stems and pieces, drained
1 envelope onion soup mix
3 tablespoons cornstarch

1 Place a large piece of heavy-duty foil (21 in. x 17 in.) in a shallow roasting pan. Place roast on foil. Pour 1 cup water and mushrooms over roast. Sprinkle with soup mix. Wrap foil around roast; seal tightly.

2 Bake at 350° for 2-1/2 to 3 hours or until meat reaches desired doneness (for medium-rare, a meat thermometer should read 145°; medium, 160°; well-done, 170°).

3 Remove roast to a serving platter and keep warm. Pour drippings and mushrooms into a saucepan. Combine cornstarch and remaining water until smooth; gradually stir into drippings. Bring to a boil; cook and stir for 2 minutes or until thickened. Serve with sliced beef. **Yield:** 10-12 servings.

Traditional Lasagna

I make batches of this lasagna every year to give our neighbors as gifts at Christmastime. They're always well received!
—Megan Taylor

1 pound ground beef
3/4 pound bulk pork sausage
3 cans (8 ounces *each*) tomato sauce
2 cans (6 ounces *each*) tomato paste
2 garlic cloves, minced
2 teaspoons sugar
1 teaspoon Italian seasoning
1 teaspoon salt
1/2 teaspoon pepper
3 eggs
3 cups (24 ounces) small-curd cottage cheese
1 carton (8 ounces) ricotta cheese
1/2 cup grated Parmesan cheese
3 tablespoons minced fresh parsley
9 lasagna noodles, cooked and drained
6 slices provolone cheese
3 cups (12 ounces) shredded mozzarella cheese, *divided*

1 In a large skillet, cook beef and sausage over medium heat until no longer pink; drain. Add the tomato sauce, tomato paste and seasonings. Bring to a boil. Reduce heat; simmer, uncovered, for 1 hour, stirring occasionally. In a bowl, combine the eggs, cottage cheese, ricotta, Parmesan cheese and parsley.

2 Spread 1 cup of meat sauce in an ungreased 13-in. x 9-in. x 2-in. baking dish. Layer with three noodles, provolone cheese, 2 cups cottage cheese mixture, 1 cup mozzarella, three noodles, 2 cups meat sauce, remaining cottage cheese mixture and 1 cup mozzarella. Top with the remaining noodles, meat sauce and mozzarella (dish will be full).

3 Cover and bake at 375° for 50 minutes. Uncover; bake 20 minutes longer. Let stand for 15 minutes before cutting. **Yield:** 12 servings.

PORK

Greek Pork Wraps

The creamy cucumber dressing makes these wraps reminiscent of a gyro.
—*Sue Myers*

        1/4 cup lemon juice
          2 tablespoons olive oil
          1 tablespoon prepared mustard
    1-3/4 teaspoons minced garlic, *divided*
          1 teaspoon dried oregano
          1 pork tenderloin (1 pound)
          1 cup chopped peeled cucumber
          1 cup reduced-fat plain yogurt
        1/4 teaspoon salt
        1/4 teaspoon dill weed
          8 flour tortillas (6 inches)
        1/2 cup chopped green onions

1 In a large resealable plastic bag, combine the lemon juice, oil, mustard, 1-1/4 teaspoons garlic and oregano; add the pork. Seal bag and turn to coat; refrigerate for 2 hours.

2 In a bowl, combine the cucumber, yogurt, salt, dill and remaining garlic; cover and refrigerate until serving.

3 Drain and discard marinade. Coat grill rack with nonstick cooking spray before starting the grill for indirect medium-hot heat. Grill pork, un- covered, over direct-heated area for 5 minutes, turning once. Move to indirect-heated area; cover and cook 10-15 minutes longer or until a meat thermometer reads 160°. Let stand for 5 minutes.

4 Meanwhile, wrap tortillas in foil; place on grill for 2-3 minutes or until warmed, turning once. Slice pork into strips; place on tortillas. Top each with 3 tablespoons yogurt sauce and 1 tablespoon green onions. **Yield:** 4 servings.

Creamy Dijon Pork Chops

The mustard cream adds a nice touch to this speedy skillet supper. My family prefers them to plain pork chops.
—*Janet Briggs*

        4 bone-in pork rib *or* loin chops (1/4 to 1/2 inch thick)
        1 tablespoon olive oil
        1 medium onion, thinly sliced
        1 teaspoon paprika
      1/4 teaspoon salt
      1/8 teaspoon pepper
      1/2 cup dry white wine
      1/2 cup heavy whipping cream
        1 tablespoon Dijon mustard

1 In a large skillet, cook pork chops in oil over medium heat for 5 minutes on each side. Add onion; cook for 5 minutes or until onion is light- ly browned and meat juices run clear. Sprinkle with paprika, salt and pepper. Remove pork and onions; keep warm.

2 In the same skillet, cook wine over high heat until reduced to 1-2 tablespoons, stirring con- stantly. Reduce heat to low; add cream. Cook for 4-5 minutes or until thickened, stirring con- stantly. Remove from the heat; stir in mustard. Serve over pork and onions. **Yield:** 4 servings.

Molasses-Peanut Butter Glazed Ribs

(Pictured on page 98)

Nothing says summer better than these ribs sizzling on the grill. Serve them with fresh corn on the cob, and neighbors will flock to this delightful backyard barbecue fiesta! —Diane Werner

4 pounds pork baby back ribs, cut into
    serving-size pieces
1/2 cup finely chopped onion
2 garlic cloves, minced
1 tablespoon cornstarch
1/2 cup plus 1 tablespoon maple syrup
1/2 cup water

1/4 cup reduced-sodium soy sauce
1/4 cup light molasses
3 tablespoons cider vinegar
1 teaspoon minced fresh gingerroot
1 teaspoon crushed red pepper flakes
1/4 cup creamy peanut butter

1 Prepare grill for indirect medium-low heat. Grill ribs, covered, over indirect medium-low heat for 1 hour, turning occasionally.

2 In a saucepan coated with nonstick cooking spray, saute onion and garlic over medium heat until tender. In a bowl, combine the cornstarch, syrup, water, soy sauce, molasses, vinegar, ginger and red pepper flakes until blended. Stir into onion mixture. Bring to a boil; cook for 2-3 minutes or until thickened. Add peanut butter; cook for 2 minutes or until peanut butter is melted, stirring constantly. Set aside.

3 Add 10 briquettes to coals. Grill 20-30 minutes longer or until meat is tender, basting ribs with sauce several times. **Yield:** 6 servings.

TEST KITCHEN TIP
You can make the sauce the day before you need it; store in the refrigerator.

Cran-Apple Ham Slice

Don't care for the leftovers after preparing a whole ham? Try this recipe that uses a ham slice. Cranberry juice gives the sauce a pretty pink color. —Kris Lehman

1 tablespoon brown sugar
2 teaspoons cornstarch
Dash ground allspice
1/2 cup cranberry juice
1 small apple, peeled and chopped
1/2 cup fresh *or* frozen cranberries
1 fully cooked ham slice (about 1 pound)

1 In a microwave-safe bowl, combine the brown sugar, cornstarch and allspice. Stir in cranberry juice until smooth. Add apple and cranberries; mix well. Microwave, uncovered, on high for 2-4 minutes or until thickened, stirring every minute. Keep warm.

2 Place the ham slice in a shallow 3-qt. microwave-safe dish. Cover and microwave at 70% power for 3-5 minutes or until heated through. Top with fruit mixture. **Yield:** 4 servings.

EDITOR'S NOTE: This recipe was tested in a 1,100-watt microwave.

Orange-Glazed Canadian Bacon

Instead of serving the usual bacon, I like to prepare this recipe that calls for Canadian bacon instead. It's a special brunch recipe that's always well liked. —*Sue Draheim*

1-1/4 pounds Canadian bacon
1-1/2 cups orange juice
   6 tablespoons brown sugar, *divided*
  1/2 teaspoon ground mustard

1/2 teaspoon ground cardamom
1/4 teaspoon coarsely ground pepper
  3 bay leaves

1 In an 11-in. x 7-in. x 2-in. baking pan coated with nonstick cooking spray, arrange bacon in two rows, overlapping the slices.

2 In a saucepan, combine the orange juice, 4 tablespoons brown sugar, mustard, cardamom and pepper until blended. Bring to a boil over medium heat, stirring frequently. Boil for 1 minute. Pour over bacon; arrange bay leaves on top.

3 Bake, uncovered, at 325° for 20-25 minutes. Discard bay leaves and all but 1/4 cup pan juices. Sprinkle remaining brown sugar over bacon.

4 Broil 4 in. from the heat for 3-5 minutes or until bacon is glazed and bubbly. Serve immediately. **Yield:** 6-8 servings.

Roasted Pork Tenderloin And Vegetables

My mother-in-law served this recipe at a family gathering. She didn't know I submitted it to Light & Tasty magazine until she saw the recipe in print! She was very excited. The roasted vegetables are so good…it's a great way to get kids to eat more veggies. —*Coleen Martin*

  2 pork tenderloins (3/4 pound *each*)
  2 pounds red potatoes, quartered
  1 pound carrots, halved and cut into 2-inch pieces
  1 medium onion, cut into wedges
  1 tablespoon olive oil
  2 teaspoons dried rosemary, crushed
  1 teaspoon rubbed sage
1/2 teaspoon salt
1/4 teaspoon pepper

1 Place the pork in a shallow roasting pan coated with nonstick cooking spray; arrange the potatoes, carrots and onion around pork. Drizzle with oil. Combine the seasonings; sprinkle over meat and vegetables.

2 Bake, uncovered, at 450° for 30-40 minutes or until a meat thermometer reads 160°, stirring vegetables occasionally. **Yield:** 6 servings.

Sweet-and-Sour Pork

Taking just minutes to make, this tangy stir-fry is a satisfying weeknight dinner. —*Anita Bukowski*

  1 can (14 ounces) pineapple tidbits
  2 tablespoons cornstarch
  2 tablespoons brown sugar
3/4 teaspoon salt
1/4 teaspoon ground ginger
1/4 teaspoon pepper
1/3 cup water
1/3 cup ketchup
  2 tablespoons white vinegar
  2 tablespoons soy sauce
  1 pound pork tenderloin, cut into 1-1/2-inch x 1/4-inch strips
  1 medium onion, chopped
  2 tablespoons vegetable oil
  1 medium green pepper, cut into thin strips
Hot cooked rice

1 Drain pineapple, reserving juice; set aside. In a small bowl, combine the cornstarch, brown sugar, salt, ginger and pepper. Stir in the water, ketchup, vinegar, soy sauce and reserved juice until smooth.

2 In a large skillet or wok, stir-fry pork and onion in oil for 5-7 minutes or until meat is no longer pink.

Stir pineapple juice mixture; add to skillet. Bring to a boil; cook and stir for 1-2 minutes or until thickened.

3 Add green pepper and reserved pineapple. Reduce heat; cover and cook for 5 minutes. Serve over rice. **Yield:** 4 servings.

Cranberry Pork Chops

(*Pictured on front cover*)

My family loves pork chops, and this is such an easy way to make them a bit special. Dried cranberries add a touch of sweetness. —*Karen Johnson*

  4 bone-in pork loin chops (1/2 inch thick)
  2 tablespoons butter
  1 cup chicken broth, *divided*
1/2 teaspoon dried rosemary, crushed
1/4 cup sliced green onions

1/4 cup dried cranberries
1/8 teaspoon pepper
  3 teaspoons cornstarch
Hot cooked rice

1 In a large skillet, brown the pork chops in butter for 3 minutes on each side. Add 1/2 cup broth and rosemary. Reduce heat; cover and simmer for 5 minutes or until meat juices run clear. Remove chops and keep warm.

2 Add the onions, cranberries and pepper to skillet. Combine cornstarch and remaining broth until smooth; gradually add to skillet. Bring to a boil; cook and stir for 2 minutes or until thickened. Serve over pork and rice. **Yield:** 4 servings.

Test Kitchen Tip

Dried cherries are a nice substitute for the cranberries.

Pepperoni Pizza Chili

My husband won first place in a chili cook-off at work for this Italian version of chili. —*Suzanne Kern*

 1 pound ground beef
 1 can (16 ounces) kidney beans, rinsed and drained
 1 can (15 ounces) pizza sauce
 1 can (14-1/2 ounces) Italian stewed tomatoes
 1 can (8 ounces) tomato sauce
1-1/2 cups water
 1 package (3-1/2 ounces) sliced pepperoni
 1/2 cup chopped green pepper
 1 teaspoon Italian seasoning
 1 teaspoon salt
Shredded mozzarella cheese, optional

1 In a large saucepan, cook beef over medium heat until no longer pink; drain. Stir in beans, pizza sauce, tomatoes, tomato sauce, water, pepperoni, green pepper, Italian seasoning and salt.

2 Bring to a boil. Reduce heat; simmer, uncovered, for 30 minutes or until chili reaches desired thickness. Garnish with cheese if desired. **Yield:** 8 servings.

RITA KRAJCIR

Rita loves to bake, but cooking comes in a very close second. It doesn't matter what...she loves to try her hand at "anything and everything!" Taking a home economics class in high school first sparked her interest. Scrapbooking and other fun craft projects are a few more pastimes. She has worked at Reiman Publications for 15 years now.

Peachy Pork Steaks

With its fresh fruity flavor, this recipe is great anytime—summer or winter! No one can resist the succulent steaks. —*Rita Krajcir*

 4 pork steaks (1/2 inch thick), trimmed
 2 tablespoons olive oil
 3/4 teaspoon dried basil
 1/4 teaspoon salt, optional
Dash pepper
 1 can (15-1/4 ounces) reduced-sugar sliced peaches

 2 tablespoons white vinegar
 1 tablespoon beef bouillon granules
 2 tablespoons cornstarch
 1/4 cup cold water
Hot cooked rice

1 In a large skillet, brown pork steaks on both sides in oil. Sprinkle with basil, salt if desired and pepper. Drain peaches, reserving juice.

2 Place peaches in a slow cooker; top with pork. Combine the vinegar, bouillon and reserved peach juice; pour over pork. Cover and cook on high for 1 hour. Reduce heat to low; cook 4 hours longer or until meat is tender.

3 Remove pork and peaches; keep warm. Skim fat from cooking liquid; pour into a saucepan. Combine cornstarch and cold water until smooth; stir into cooking liquid. Bring to a boil; cook and stir for 2 minutes or until thickened. Serve over pork, peaches and rice. **Yield:** 4 servings.

Cherry-Stuffed Pork Loin

(Pictured on page 99)

This easy pork roast is moist and has a wonderful stuffing. It's impressive when I serve it to guests. The gravy is a great complement.
—Patricia Schmeling

1 cup dried cherries
1/2 cup water
1/2 cup minced fresh parsley
1 medium onion, chopped
1 celery rib, diced
1/4 cup shredded carrot
1 tablespoon rubbed sage
1 garlic clove, minced
1 teaspoon minced fresh rosemary
3 tablespoons butter
2-1/2 cups salad croutons
1 cup chicken broth
1/2 teaspoon pepper, *divided*
1/4 teaspoon ground nutmeg
1/4 teaspoon almond extract
1 boneless whole pork loin roast (about 3 pounds)

GRAVY:
1-3/4 cups chicken broth
1/2 cup water
1/2 cup heavy whipping cream
1/2 teaspoon minced fresh rosemary

1 In a small saucepan, bring cherries and water to a boil. Remove from the heat; set aside (do not drain). In a skillet, saute the parsley, vegetables and seasonings in butter until tender. Remove from the heat. Stir in the croutons, broth, 1/4 teaspoon pepper, nutmeg, almond extract and cherries. Let stand until the liquid is absorbed.

2 Cut a lengthwise slit down the center of the roast to within 1/2 in. of bottom. Open roast so it lies flat; flatten to 3/4-in. thickness. Spread stuffing over meat to within 1 in. of edges. Close roast; tie at 1-in. intervals with kitchen string. Place on a rack in a shallow roasting pan. Sprinkle with remaining pepper.

3 Bake, uncovered, at 350° for 1-1/2 to 2 hours or until a meat thermometer reads 160°. Let stand for 10-15 minutes before slicing.

4 For gravy, add broth and water to roasting pan; stir to loosen browned bits. Pour into a saucepan. Bring to a boil over medium-high heat; cook until reduced by half. Stir in cream and rosemary. Simmer, uncovered, until thickened. Serve with the roast. **Yield:** 10-12 servings.

Sunday Boiled Dinner

The root vegetables make this a hearty dish that's perfect on a cold winter's night.
—Kris Lehman

1 smoked boneless ham *or* pork shoulder (about 2 pounds)
1 medium onion, quartered
2 pounds carrots, halved
2 pounds red potatoes, quartered
2 pounds rutabagas, peeled and cut into 1-1/2-inch cubes
1 teaspoon salt
1/2 teaspoon pepper
1 medium cabbage, halved
Prepared horseradish, optional

1 In a large Dutch oven or soup kettle, place the ham, onion, carrots, potatoes, rutabagas, salt and pepper. Add water just to cover; bring to a boil. Place cabbage on top of vegetables. Reduce heat; cover and simmer for 1 hour or until the vegetables are tender. Drain.

2 Cut cabbage into wedges; remove core. Serve meat and vegetables with horseradish if desired. **Yield:** 8 servings.

Orange Pork Tenderloin

This is one of my favorite recipes to serve to company. It's simple to prepare and is pretty presented on a bed of rice.

—Janaan Cunningham

1 pork tenderloin (1 pound), cut into slices	1 cup orange juice, *divided*
1 tablespoon butter, softened	1 tablespoon all-purpose flour
1/4 teaspoon dried thyme	1-1/2 teaspoons sugar
Dash cayenne pepper	

1 Place pork in an ungreased 13-in. x 9-in. x 2-in. baking dish. Combine the butter, thyme and cayenne; spread over pork. Pour 3/4 cup orange juice over meat. Bake, uncovered, at 425° for 25-30 minutes or until meat juices run clear, basting occasionally.

2 Remove pork and keep warm. Pour pan drippings into a measuring cup; add enough remaining orange juice to measure 3/4 cup. Pour into a saucepan. Stir in flour and sugar until smooth.

3 Bring to a boil over medium heat; cook and stir for 2 minutes or until thickened. Serve with pork. **Yield:** 3 servings.

Pork Lo Mein

This full-flavored stir-fry is sure to bring rave reviews from your family. Ginger, sesame oil, red pepper flakes and soy sauce jazz up the snow pea, sweet pepper and pork combination. You could serve it with rice as an alternative to the pasta.

—Erin Frakes

- 1 pork tenderloin (1 pound)
- 1/4 cup reduced-sodium soy sauce
- 3 garlic cloves, minced
- 1 teaspoon minced fresh gingerroot
- 1/4 teaspoon crushed red pepper flakes
- 2 cups fresh snow peas
- 1 medium sweet red pepper, julienned
- 3 cups cooked thin spaghetti
- 1/3 cup reduced-sodium chicken broth
- 2 teaspoons sesame oil

1 Cut tenderloin in half lengthwise. Cut each half widthwise into 1/4-in. slices; set aside. In a large resealable plastic bag, combine the soy sauce, garlic, ginger and pepper flakes; add pork. Seal bag and turn to coat; refrigerate for 20 minutes.

2 In a large nonstick skillet or wok coated with nonstick cooking spray, stir-fry pork with marinade for 4-5 minutes or until meat is no longer pink. Add peas and red pepper; stir-fry for 1 minute. Stir in spaghetti and broth; cook 1 minute longer. Remove from the heat; stir in sesame oil. **Yield:** 4 servings.

Pork Roast with Apple-Mushroom Sauce

I turn to this recipe when I'm hosting a dinner party. Guests always request second helpings! —*Betty Reuter*

- 1 teaspoon dried thyme
- 1/4 teaspoon pepper
- 1 boneless pork loin roast (3 pounds)
- 3 small tart apples, cored and cut into eighths
- 3 tablespoons butter
- 3/4 pound fresh mushrooms, sliced
- 1/4 teaspoon salt, *divided*
- 1/2 cup apple cider *or* juice
- 1 cup chicken broth
- 1 cup heavy whipping cream
- 1 teaspoon brown sugar
- 2 tablespoons cornstarch
- 1/4 cup cold water

Fresh thyme sprigs, optional

1 Rub thyme and pepper over roast. Place in a greased 13-in. x 9-in. x 2-in. baking pan. Bake, uncovered, at 450° for 20 minutes. Reduce heat to 325°; bake 1-1/4 hours longer or until a meat thermometer reads 160°.

2 In a skillet, saute apples in butter until tender. Remove with a slotted spoon; keep warm. In the same skillet, saute mushrooms until tender; set aside.

3 Sprinkle 1/8 teaspoon salt over roast. Cover and let stand for 10-15 minutes before slicing. Pour cider into baking pan; stir to loosen browned bits. Transfer to a saucepan; add the broth, cream, brown sugar and remaining salt. Combine cornstarch and water until smooth; stir into broth mixture. Bring to a boil; cook and stir for 2 minutes or until thickened. Add mushrooms and heat through.

4 Garnish roast with apples and thyme sprigs if desired. Serve with mushroom sauce. **Yield:** 8-10 servings.

Jambalaya

A marvelous Southern dish of sausage, shrimp and rice, this is also an easy cleanup since it cooks in one pot. —*Wendy Stenman*

- 3/4 pound bulk Italian sausage
- 1/2 cup chopped onion
- 1/2 cup chopped green pepper
- 1 garlic clove, minced
- 2 cups diced fully cooked ham
- 1 can (14-1/2 ounces) chicken broth
- 1 can (14-1/2 ounces) diced tomatoes, undrained
- 3/4 cup uncooked long grain rice
- 1 bay leaf
- 1/4 teaspoon dried thyme
- 1 pound uncooked medium shrimp, peeled and deveined

1 Crumble sausage into a large skillet. Cook over medium heat until no longer pink; drain. Stir in the onion, green pepper and garlic; cook until vegetables are tender.

2 Add the ham, broth, tomatoes, rice, bay leaf and thyme; cover and simmer for 20-25 minutes or until rice is tender. Stir in shrimp; cover and cook for 3-4 minutes or until shrimp turn pink. Discard bay leaf. **Yield:** 6-8 servings.

Honey-Mustard Pork Scallopini

This quick entree has loads of flavor from the honey-mustard blend. The cracker crumb coating seals in the juices and keeps the meat moist and tender. —*Sue A. Jurack*

  4 boneless pork chops (about 4 ounces *each*), trimmed
  2 tablespoons honey
  2 tablespoons spicy brown mustard
1/3 cup crushed butter-flavored crackers (about 8 crackers)
1/3 cup dry bread crumbs
  1 tablespoon vegetable oil
  1 tablespoon butter

1 Flatten pork to 1/8-in. thickness. Combine honey and mustard; brush over both sides of pork. In a shallow bowl, combine cracker and bread crumbs; add pork and turn to coat.

2 In a skillet, heat oil and butter. Fry pork for 2-3 minutes on each side or until crisp and juices run clear. **Yield:** 4 servings.

TEST KITCHEN TIP

Flatten the pork chops in advance and substitute prepared honey-mustard if you are really in a hurry.

Sunday Chops and Stuffing

A nice meal-in-one for autumn, this recipes goes together in a snap. The apples and seasonings really complement the pork. —*Amy Welk-Thieding*

  2 cups water
  2 celery ribs, chopped
  7 tablespoons butter, *divided*
1/4 cup dried minced onion
  6 cups seasoned stuffing croutons
  6 bone-in pork loin chops (3/4 inch thick)

  1 tablespoon vegetable oil
1/4 teaspoon salt
1/4 teaspoon pepper
  2 medium tart apples, sliced
1/4 cup packed brown sugar
1/8 teaspoon pumpkin pie spice

1 In a large saucepan, combine the water, celery, 6 tablespoons butter and onion. Bring to a boil. Remove from the heat; stir in croutons. Spoon into a greased 13-in. x 9-in. x 2-in. baking dish; set aside.

2 In a large skillet, brown pork chops on both sides in oil. Arrange over the stuffing. Sprinkle with salt and pepper. Combine the apples, brown sugar and pumpkin pie spice; spoon over pork chops. Dot with remaining butter.

3 Bake, uncovered, at 350° for 30-35 minutes or until a meat thermometer reads 160° and meat juices run clear. **Yield:** 6 servings.

TEST KITCHEN TIP

When preparing this recipe, toss the apples with 1/2 teaspoon lemon juice to prevent them from turning brown.

Sliced Ham with Roasted Vegetables

(*Pictured on page 98*)

This baked ham with roasted vegetables is perfect for a fall day. The vegetables can be purchased fresh from a farmers market. —*Patricia Schmeling*

6 medium potatoes, peeled and cubed
5 medium carrots, julienned
1 medium turnip, peeled and cubed
1 large onion, cut into thin wedges
6 slices (4 to 6 ounces *each*) fully cooked
   ham, halved

1/4 cup orange juice concentrate
2 tablespoons brown sugar
1 teaspoon prepared horseradish
1 teaspoon grated orange peel

1 Line two 15-in. x 10-in. x 1-in. baking pans with foil and coat with nonstick cooking spray. Place potatoes, carrots, turnip and onion in pan; generously coat with nonstick cooking spray. Bake, uncovered, at 425° for 25-30 minutes or until tender.

2 Arrange ham slices over the vegetables. Combine the remaining ingredients; spoon over ham and vegetables. Cover and bake 10 minutes longer or until the ham is heated through. **Yield:** 6 servings.

Apricot-Filled Pork Tenderloin

This pretty stuffed pork tenderloin makes a fabulous company entree. It tastes wonderful and looks so nice when it's sliced to reveal a golden apricot center. —*Karen Scales*

2 pork tenderloins (1 pound *each*)
1 package (6 ounces) dried apricots
1/3 cup sweet-and-sour salad dressing
1/4 cup packed brown sugar
3 tablespoons teriyaki sauce
2 tablespoons ketchup
1 teaspoon Dijon mustard
1 onion slice, separated into rings
1 garlic clove, minced
2 teaspoons minced fresh gingerroot
1/4 teaspoon pepper
1/8 teaspoon pumpkin pie spice

1 Make a lengthwise cut three-quarters of the way through each tenderloin; pound to flatten evenly. Set aside three apricots for marinade. Stuff remaining apricots into pork to within 1/2 in. of ends; secure with toothpicks or kitchen string.

2 In a blender, combine the remaining ingredients and reserved apricots; cover and process until smooth. Set aside 1/3 cup. Pour remaining marinade into a large resealable plastic bag; add tenderloins. Seal bag and turn to coat. Refrigerate for at least 2 hours, turning often.

3 Drain and discard marinade. Place pork in a greased 13-in. x 9-in. x 2-in. baking dish. Drizzle with reserved marinade. Bake, uncovered, at 400° for 30-35 minutes or until a meat thermometer reads 160°. **Yield:** 6 servings.

Pork and Chicken Roulade

This is a very popular recipe with the Test Kitchen staff. I received it from co-worker Kristin Arnett and know several others who have made it.

—Janet Briggs

  4 garlic cloves, peeled
  1 teaspoon pepper
  2 cups chopped fresh parsley
  1/2 cup chopped fresh basil
  4 tablespoons olive oil, *divided*
  1 pork tenderloin (1 pound)
  2 boneless skinless chicken breast halves

  3 ounces prosciutto *or* thinly sliced deli ham
Salt and additional pepper
  3 cups reduced-sodium chicken broth
  3/4 cup heavy whipping cream
  1 tablespoon butter, softened
  1 tablespoon all-purpose flour

1 In a food processor, finely chop garlic. Add the pepper, parsley and basil; cover and process until finely chopped. While processing, gradually add 3 tablespoons oil in a steady stream. Set aside.

2 Starting about a third in from one side, make a lengthwise slit in the tenderloin to within 1/2 in. of bottom. Turn tenderloin over and make another lengthwise slit, starting from about a third in from the opposite side. Open tenderloin so it lies flat; flatten to about 1/3-in. thickness. Cut chicken breast halves horizontally in half; flatten to 1/4-in. thickness.

3 Spread 3 tablespoons garlic mixture over one side of pork. Arrange chicken over pork. Spread with 3 tablespoons garlic mixture. Top with prosciutto; spread with remaining garlic mixture. Roll up tightly jelly-roll style, starting with a long side. Tie at 2-in. intervals with kitchen string. Cover and refrigerate for at least 1 hour.

4 Place a large piece of heavy-duty foil (18 in. x 16 in.) on a baking sheet. Lightly sprinkle tenderloin with salt and additional pepper. In a large skillet, brown tenderloin on all sides in remaining oil. Transfer to prepared pan; wrap foil around pork, keeping the seam side of foil up. Bake at 400° for 40-45 minutes or until a meat thermometer reads 170°.

5 Meanwhile, discard drippings from skillet. Add broth and cream. Bring to a boil, scraping up browned bits. Boil until sauce is reduced to 1-1/2 cups, about 20 minutes. Let pork stand for 10 minutes; carefully remove foil. Add any juices to sauce. Mix butter and flour until blended; whisk into sauce. Bring to a boil; cook and whisk until slightly thickened, about 5 minutes. Strain sauce; season with pepper. Serve with pork. **Yield:** 3-4 servings.

Orange-Glazed Ham

Ham is an Easter favorite at my house, especially when prepared this way.

—Janaan Cunningham

  1 fully cooked bone-in ham (6 to 8 pounds)
  1 tablespoon ground mustard
  1 teaspoon ground allspice
  3/4 cup orange marmalade
Kumquats and kale, optional

1 Score the ham. Combine mustard and allspice; rub over ham. Place on a rack in a shallow baking pan. Bake, uncovered, at 325° for 2 to 2-1/2 hours or until a meat thermometer reads 140° and ham is heated through.

2 Spread top of ham with marmalade during the last hour of baking. Baste occasionally with pan drippings. Garnish with kumquats and kale if desired. **Yield:** 12-16 servings.

Sausage Bean Burritos

These burritos are such an easy and satisfying dish! I often serve them for lunch to my daughter and her friends.
—*Patricia Schmeling*

 3/4 pound bulk pork sausage
 1/2 cup chopped green pepper
 1/3 cup chopped onion
   1 can (15 ounces) black beans, rinsed and drained
1-1/2 cups cooked long grain rice
1-1/2 cups salsa, *divided*
  10 flour tortillas (7 inches)
   1 cup (4 ounces) shredded cheddar cheese, *divided*

1 In a large saucepan, cook sausage, green pepper and onion over medium heat until meat is no longer pink; drain. Stir in the beans, rice and 1 cup salsa; mix well.

2 Spread about 1/2 cup down the center of each tortilla; sprinkle with 1 tablespoon cheese. Roll up. Place seam side down in a greased 13-in. x 9-in. x 2-in. baking dish. Top with remaining salsa.

3 Cover and bake at 350° for 30 minutes. Uncover; sprinkle with remaining cheese. Bake 5-10 minutes longer or until cheese is melted. **Yield:** 10 burritos.

TEST KITCHEN TIP
The level of heat can be regulated by using hot or mild sausage.

Holiday Pork Roast

When this recipe was tested in our Test Kitchen, it had everyone's mouth watering. It tasted as good as the aroma promised.
—*Peggy Fleming*

1/2 cup Dijon mustard
  2 tablespoons soy sauce
  1 tablespoon olive oil
  4 garlic cloves, minced
  1 teaspoon dried thyme
  1 boneless rolled pork loin roast (about 4 pounds)

  1 teaspoon salt
1/4 teaspoon pepper
1-1/2 cups white wine

1 In a small bowl, combine the mustard, soy sauce, oil, garlic and thyme; rub over roast. Place in a large resealable bag; seal and refrigerate overnight, turning occasionally.

2 Place roast on a rack in a shallow roasting pan. Sprinkle with salt and pepper; pour wine into the pan. Bake, uncovered, at 325° for 2-1/2 hours or until a meat thermometer reads 160°, basting with pan juices every 30 minutes. Let stand for 10 minutes before slicing. **Yield:** 12-15 servings.

Chicago-Style Deep-Dish Pizza

It wasn't until I moved away from the Chicago suburbs, where I grew up, that I realized how fabulous and unique Chicago-style pizza really is! Whenever I am craving pizza from the Windy City, I turn to this recipe. —*Peggy Fleming*

3-1/2 cups all-purpose flour
1/4 cup cornmeal
1 package (1/4 ounce) quick-rise yeast
1-1/2 teaspoons sugar
1/2 teaspoon salt
1 cup water
1/3 cup olive oil

TOPPINGS:
6 cups (24 ounces) shredded mozzarella cheese, *divided*
1 can (28 ounces) diced tomatoes, well drained
1 can (8 ounces) tomato sauce
1 can (6 ounces) tomato paste
1/2 teaspoon salt
1/4 teaspoon *each* garlic powder, dried oregano, dried basil and pepper
1 pound bulk Italian sausage, cooked and crumbled
48 slices pepperoni
1/2 pound sliced fresh mushrooms
1/4 cup grated Parmesan cheese

1 In a large mixing bowl, combine 1-1/2 cups flour, cornmeal, yeast, sugar and salt. In a small saucepan, heat water and oil to 120°-130°. Add to dry ingredients; beat just until moistened. Add remaining flour to form a stiff dough.

2 Turn onto a floured surface; knead until smooth and elastic, about 6-8 minutes. Place in a greased bowl, turning once to grease top. Cover and let rise in a warm place until doubled, about 30 minutes.

3 Punch dough down; divide in half. Roll each portion into an 11-in. circle. Press dough onto the bottom and up the sides of two greased 10-in. ovenproof skillets. Sprinkle each with 2 cups mozzarella cheese.

4 In a bowl, combine the tomatoes, tomato sauce, tomato paste and seasonings. Spoon 1-1/2 cups over each pizza. Layer each with half of the sausage, pepperoni, mushrooms, 1 cup mozzarella and 2 tablespoons Parmesan cheese. Cover and bake at 450° for 35 minutes. Uncover; bake 5-8 minutes longer or until lightly browned. **Yield:** 2 pizzas (8 slices each).

TEST KITCHEN TIP

Two 9-in. springform pans may be used in place of the skillets. Place pans on baking sheets. Run a knife around edge of pan to loosen crust before removing sides of pan.

PEGGY FLEMING

During college, Peggy worked part-time catering and as a teacher's assistant for a large-quantity foods class, learning to cook from the planning stage to preparation. She has put that background to great use in our Test Kitchen for the past 4-1/2 years, but generally she prefers baking to cooking. When time allows, yeast breads are a favorite. For fun, she enjoys taking evening classes on topics such as pottery or Italian.

Ham with Pineapple Sauce

The tangy-sweet pineapple sauce adds a nice flavor and color to this ham. Leftovers make great sandwiches!
—*Amy Welk-Thieding*

1 boneless fully cooked ham (4 to 6 pounds)	4-1/2 teaspoons ketchup
3/4 cup water, *divided*	1-1/2 teaspoons ground mustard
1 cup packed brown sugar	1-1/2 cups undrained crushed pineapple
4-1/2 teaspoons soy sauce	2 tablespoons plus 1 teaspoon cornstarch

1 Place ham on a rack in a shallow roasting pan. Bake at 325° for 1-1/4 to 2 hours or until a meat thermometer reads 140° and ham is heated through.

2 Meanwhile, in a saucepan, combine 1/4 cup water, brown sugar, soy sauce, ketchup, mustard and pineapple. Bring to a boil. Reduce heat; cover and simmer for 10 minutes. Combine cornstarch and remaining water until smooth; stir into pineapple sauce. Bring to a boil; cook and stir for 2 minutes or until thickened. Serve with the ham. **Yield:** 16-24 servings (3 cups sauce).

TEST KITCHEN TIP

Sometimes Amy cuts the sauce in half and only serves half of the ham, leaving the remainder of the ham for leftovers.

Sweet 'n' Sour Sausage

Carrots, green pepper and pineapple lend gorgeous color to this slow-cooked sausage supper that's scrumptious over either rice or chow mein noodles. —*Nancy Fridirici*

1 pound smoked kielbasa *or* Polish sausage, sliced
1 can (20 ounces) unsweetened pineapple chunks, undrained
1-1/2 cups baby carrots, quartered lengthwise
1 large green pepper, cut into 1-inch pieces
1 medium onion, cut into chunks
1/3 cup packed brown sugar
1 tablespoon soy sauce
1/2 teaspoon chicken bouillon granules
1/4 teaspoon garlic powder
1/4 teaspoon ground ginger
2 tablespoons cornstarch
1/4 cup cold water
Hot cooked rice *or* chow mein noodles

1 In a 3-qt. slow cooker, combine the first 10 ingredients. Cover and cook on low for 4-5 hours.

2 Combine cornstarch and water until smooth; stir into the sausage mixture. Cover and cook on high for 30 minutes or until thickened. Serve over rice. **Yield:** 6 servings.

Barbecued Pork Potpie

When I make this recipe, it is always well received by my family. They even argue over who gets the leftovers!
—Wendy Stenman

1 cup chopped onion
1 cup chopped sweet red pepper
1 large Anaheim pepper, seeded and chopped
3/4 cup finely chopped celery
2 garlic cloves, minced
1 tablespoon canola oil
1 teaspoon ground cumin
1 teaspoon ground coriander
1/4 cup white wine vinegar
1 can (14-1/2 ounces) reduced-sodium chicken broth
1 bottle (12 ounces) chili sauce
3 tablespoons brown sugar
1 square (1 ounce) unsweetened chocolate, grated
1 tablespoon Worcestershire sauce
2 tablespoons cornstarch
6 cups cubed cooked pork loin roast (2 pounds)
1 tube (11-1/2 ounces) refrigerated corn bread twists

1 In a large nonstick skillet, saute the onion, peppers, celery and garlic in oil until tender. Add cumin and coriander; cook and stir over medium heat for 2 minutes. Add vinegar and cook for 2 minutes.

2 Set aside 1/2 cup broth. Add the chili sauce, brown sugar, chocolate, Worcestershire sauce and remaining broth to vegetable mixture. Bring to a boil. Reduce heat; simmer, uncovered, for 10-15 minutes, stirring occasionally.

3 Combine cornstarch and reserved broth until smooth; stir into vegetable mixture. Bring to a boil; cook and stir for 1-2 minutes or until slightly thickened. Stir in pork. Transfer to a 13-in. x 9-in. x 2-in. baking dish coated with nonstick cooking spray.

4 Roll out corn bread dough and cut into strips; twist and place over filling in a lattice design. Bake, uncovered, at 375° for 10-15 minutes or until golden brown. Let stand for 15 minutes before serving. **Yield:** 12 servings.

EDITOR'S NOTE: When cutting or seeding hot peppers, use rubber or plastic gloves to protect your hands. Avoid touching your face.

Smoked Sausage Skillet

Fully cooked sausage and quick-cooking cabbage make this meal-in-one a true time-saver when the clock is ticking closer to dinnertime.
—Karen Scales

1 pound smoked kielbasa *or* Polish sausage, sliced
3 cups shredded cabbage
1 celery rib, finely chopped
1 tablespoon vegetable oil

2 tablespoons Dijon mustard
1/2 teaspoon garlic salt
1/4 teaspoon rubbed sage
2 cups cooked noodles

1 In a large skillet, saute the sausage, cabbage and celery in oil for 5 minutes. Add the mustard, garlic salt and sage.

2 Cook and stir over medium heat for 4-6 minutes or until vegetables are tender. Stir in noodles and heat through. **Yield:** 4 servings.

Pork Tenderloin with Pineapple Salsa

The fresh salsa makes this dish perfect for a hot summer night or picnic. It's great the rest of the year, though, too.
—Patricia Schmeling

 2 pork tenderloins (1 pound *each*)
 3 tablespoons brown sugar
 3 tablespoons Dijon mustard
 3/4 teaspoon minced fresh gingerroot
SALSA:
 2 cups chopped fresh pineapple
 1/3 cup chopped sweet red pepper
 1 small jalapeno pepper, seeded and chopped
 2 green onions, chopped
 1 tablespoon minced fresh cilantro
 1 tablespoon brown sugar

1 Place pork on a greased rack in a foil-lined shallow roasting pan. Combine the brown sugar, mustard and ginger; spread over pork. Bake, uncovered, at 425° for 35-40 minutes or until a meat thermometer reads 160°. Let stand for 5-10 minutes before slicing.

2 In a bowl, combine the salsa ingredients. Serve with pork. **Yield:** 6 servings.

EDITOR'S NOTE: When cutting or seeding hot peppers, use rubber or plastic gloves to protect your hands. Avoid touching your face.

Pennsylvania-Style Pork Roast

This is a different way to dress up a pork roast. My family enjoys the combination of pork and sauerkraut.
—Janet Briggs

 1 teaspoon onion powder
 1 teaspoon garlic powder
 1 teaspoon celery seed, crushed
 1 teaspoon Worcestershire sauce
 1/4 teaspoon pepper
 1 boneless rolled pork loin roast (4 to 5 pounds)
 2 cans (14 ounces *each*) sauerkraut, undrained
 1 teaspoon sugar, optional
 8 ounces smoked kielbasa *or* Polish sausage, cut into 1/2-inch pieces

1 In a small bowl, combine the first five ingredients; rub over roast. Place fat side up in a Dutch oven. Combine sauerkraut and sugar if desired. Spoon sauerkraut and sausage over and around the roast.

2 Cover and bake at 350° for 2-1/4 to 2-3/4 hours or until a meat thermometer reads 160°. Let stand for 15 minutes before slicing. **Yield:** 12-16 servings.

Italian Sausage and Peppers

I find this is a great recipe to make when serving a crowd. If you know your guests like a little zip, use hot Italian sausage.
—*Janet Briggs*

3 pounds Italian sausage links, cut into 3/4-inch slices
4 medium green peppers, cut into thin strips
1 medium onion, thinly sliced and quartered
1 tablespoon butter
1 tablespoon olive oil
3 tablespoons chicken broth
6 plum tomatoes, coarsely chopped
1 tablespoon minced fresh parsley
1/2 teaspoon salt
1/4 teaspoon pepper
1/2 teaspoon lemon juice

1 In a Dutch oven, cook the sausage over medium heat until no longer pink; drain. Add the remaining ingredients.

2 Cover and cook for 30 minutes or until vegetables are tender, stirring occasionally. Serve with a slotted spoon. *Yield:* 12 servings.

Pork and Pear Stir-Fry

This is a very special stir-fry with pork tenderloin, fresh pears and snow peas. Not only does it look fabulous, the flavors are dynamic together.
—*Diane Werner*

1/2 cup plum preserves
3 tablespoons soy sauce
2 tablespoons lemon juice
1 tablespoon prepared horseradish
2 teaspoons cornstarch
1/4 teaspoon crushed red pepper flakes
1 medium sweet yellow *or* green pepper, julienned
1/2 to 1 teaspoon minced fresh gingerroot
1 tablespoon vegetable oil
3 medium ripe pears, peeled and sliced
1 pound pork tenderloin, cut into 1/4-inch strips
1 can (8 ounces) sliced water chestnuts, drained
1-1/2 cups fresh *or* frozen snow peas, thawed
1 tablespoon sliced almonds, toasted
Hot cooked rice

1 In a small bowl, combine the first six ingredients; set aside. In a large skillet or wok, stir-fry yellow pepper and ginger in oil for 2 minutes. Add pears; stir-fry for 1 minute or until pepper is crisp-tender. Remove and keep warm.

2 Stir-fry pork in batches for 1-2 minutes or until meat is no longer pink. Return pear mixture and all of the pork to pan. Add water chestnuts and reserved plum sauce. Bring to a boil; cook and stir for 2 minutes or until slightly thickened. Add peas; heat through. Sprinkle with almonds. Serve over rice. *Yield:* 4 servings.

TEST KITCHEN TIP

This recipe is quick to fix. Just shop for the pork, pears and vegetables—the other ingredients are pantry staples.

Calgary Stampede Ribs

You'll need to hand out extra napkins when serving these yummy, saucy pork ribs! —*Tamra Duncan*

  4 pounds pork baby back ribs, cut into serving-size pieces
  3 garlic cloves, minced
  1 tablespoon sugar
  1 tablespoon paprika
  2 teaspoons *each* salt, pepper, chili powder and ground cumin
BARBECUE SAUCE:
  1 small onion, finely chopped
  2 tablespoons butter
  1 cup ketchup
  1/4 cup packed brown sugar
  3 tablespoons lemon juice
  3 tablespoons Worcestershire sauce
  2 tablespoons white vinegar
1-1/2 teaspoons ground mustard
  1 teaspoon celery seed
  1/8 teaspoon cayenne pepper

1 Rub ribs with garlic; place in a shallow roasting pan. Cover and bake at 325° for 2 hours. Cool slightly. Combine the seasonings and rub over ribs. Cover and refrigerate for 8 hours or overnight.

2 In a saucepan, saute onion in butter until tender. Stir in the remaining sauce ingredients. Bring to a boil. Reduce heat; cook and stir until thickened, about 10 minutes. Remove from the heat; set aside 3/4 cup for serving.

3 Brush ribs with some of the remaining sauce. Grill, covered, over medium heat for 12 minutes, turning and basting with sauce. Serve with reserved sauce. **Yield:** 4 servings.

Pork Chops and Sweet Potatoes

Sweet potatoes go so well with pork that I even serve this easy dish to company. It never fails to please! —*Sarah Thompson*

  4 cups cooked sliced sweet potatoes
  2 tablespoons all-purpose flour
1/2 teaspoon salt
1/4 teaspoon pepper
  4 pork chops (1/2 inch thick)
  2 tablespoons butter
1/2 cup orange juice
1/2 cup currant jelly
  1 tablespoon lemon juice
  1 teaspoon ground mustard
  1 teaspoon paprika
  1 teaspoon grated lemon peel
1/2 teaspoon ground ginger

1 Place sweet potatoes in a greased 13-in. x 9-in. x 2-in. baking pan. In a shallow dish, combine the flour, salt and pepper; coat pork chops. In a large skillet, brown chops in butter over medium heat for 4-5 minutes on each side. Place over sweet potatoes.

2 Drain drippings from skillet. Add remaining ingredients; cook and stir until smooth and bubbly. Pour 3/4 cup sauce over pork chops. Bake, uncovered, at 350° for 30-40 minutes or until pork is tender. Brush chops with remaining sauce. **Yield:** 4 servings.

LAMB

Rack of Lamb

Dijon mustard is a natural complement to this tender and juicy rack of lamb. —*Patricia Schmeling*

4 racks of lamb (about 1-1/2 pounds *each*), trimmed
2 tablespoons Dijon mustard
1 cup soft bread crumbs
1/4 cup minced fresh parsley
1/4 teaspoon salt
1/4 teaspoon pepper
1/4 cup butter, melted
1 garlic clove, minced

1 Place lamb on a rack in a greased large roasting pan; brush with mustard. In a small bowl, combine the bread crumbs, parsley, salt and pepper. Press onto the meat. Combine butter and garlic; drizzle over meat.

2 Bake, uncovered, at 350° for 35-40 minutes or until meat reaches desired doneness (for medium-rare, a meat thermometer should read 145°; medium, 160°; well-done, 170°). Let stand for 5-10 minutes before slicing. **Yield:** 8 servings.

Stuffed Lamb Chops

The mushroom stuffing nicely complements the flavor of the lamb chops in this recipe. I like to serve mint jelly on the side. —*Sarah Thompson*

1/2 cup chopped fresh mushrooms
1/2 cup finely chopped celery
1 tablespoon finely chopped onion
2 tablespoons butter
1-1/4 cups dry bread crumbs, *divided*
1 tablespoon minced fresh parsley
3/4 teaspoon salt, *divided*
2 eggs, lightly beaten
2 tablespoons milk
Dash paprika
6 bone-in lamb loin chops (1-1/2 inches thick)
Mint jelly

1 In a large skillet, saute the mushrooms, celery and onion in butter until tender. Stir in 1/2 cup bread crumbs, parsley and 1/4 teaspoon salt; set aside.

2 In a shallow bowl, combine the eggs and milk. In another shallow bowl, combine paprika and remaining bread crumbs and salt. Cut a pocket in each chop by slicing almost to the bone; stuff with mushroom mixture. Dip chops in egg mixture, then coat with crumb mixture. Let stand for 5 minutes.

3 Place in an ungreased 9-in. square baking pan. Bake, uncovered, at 400° for 30 minutes. Turn chops over; bake 15 minutes longer or until meat reaches desired doneness (for rare, a meat thermometer should read 140°; medium, 160°; well-done, 170°). Serve with mint jelly. **Yield:** 3 servings.

Lamb with Mint Salsa

(Pictured on page 118)

I grow fresh mint—one of those out-of-control crops. The salsa accompanying the lamb is a great way to put it to use.
—Diane Werner

　5 teaspoons olive oil
　2 garlic cloves, minced
　1 teaspoon *each* dried basil, thyme
　　and rosemary, crushed
1/2 teaspoon salt
1/4 teaspoon pepper
　2 racks of lamb (about 1-1/2 pounds *each*),
　　trimmed
SALSA:
　1 cup minced fresh mint

　1 small cucumber, peeled, seeded and
　　chopped
1/2 cup seeded chopped tomato
1/3 cup finely chopped onion
1/3 cup chopped sweet yellow pepper
　1 jalapeno pepper, seeded and chopped
　3 tablespoons lemon juice
　2 tablespoons sugar
　2 garlic cloves, minced
3/4 teaspoon ground ginger
1/4 teaspoon salt

1 In a small bowl, combine the oil, garlic and seasonings. Rub over lamb. Place in a roasting pan; cover and refrigerate for 1 hour. In a bowl, combine the salsa ingredients; cover and refrigerate until serving.

2 Bake lamb, uncovered, at 425° for 20-30 minutes or until meat reaches desired doneness (for medium-rare, a meat thermometer should read 145°; medium, 160°; well-done, 170°). Cover loosely with foil and let stand for 5-10 minutes before slicing. Serve with salsa. **Yield:** 4 servings.

EDITOR'S NOTE: When cutting or seeding hot peppers, use rubber gloves to protect your hands. Avoid touching your face.

Rosemary Leg of Lamb

Roasting the leg of lamb with the bone in ensures a wonderfully rich flavor. This is such a special entree.
—Karen Johnson

　4 garlic cloves, minced
　1 to 2 tablespoons minced fresh rosemary *or* 1 teaspoon
　　dried rosemary, crushed
　1 teaspoon salt
1/2 teaspoon pepper
　1 bone-in leg of lamb (7 to 9 pounds), trimmed
　1 teaspoon cornstarch
1/4 cup beef broth

1 In a small bowl, combine the garlic, rosemary, salt and pepper; rub over meat. Place on a rack in a large shallow roasting pan. Bake, uncovered, at 350° for 1-1/2 to 2-1/2 hours or until meat reaches desired doneness (for rare, a meat thermometer should read 140°; medium, 160°; well-done, 170°). Let stand for 10 minutes before slicing.

2 Meanwhile, pour pan drippings into a small saucepan, scraping browned bits. Skim fat. Combine cornstarch and broth until smooth; whisk into drippings. Bring to a boil; cook and stir for 1 minute or until thickened. Serve with lamb. **Yield:** 10-12 servings.

Lamb Shanks Deluxe

I got this recipe from my mom. The lamb shanks are so tender and make a deliciously flavored gravy.
—*Sue Draheim*

1/2 medium lemon
1/4 teaspoon garlic powder
  4 lamb shanks (about 12 ounces *each*)
  1 cup all-purpose flour, *divided*
  2 teaspoons salt
1/2 teaspoon pepper
  3 tablespoons olive oil

  2 cups beef consomme
  1 cup water
1/2 cup dry vermouth
  1 medium onion, chopped
  4 medium carrots, cut into chunks
  4 celery ribs, cut into chunks

1 Rub lemon and garlic over the lamb shanks; let stand for 10 minutes. In a large resealable plastic bag, combine 3/4 cup flour, salt and pepper. Add shanks, one at a time, and shake to coat.

2 In a large skillet, brown lamb in oil over medium-high heat. Transfer to a shallow roasting pan. Stir the remaining flour into the skillet; cook and stir until browned. Stir in the consomme, water and vermouth until blended. Bring to a boil; cook and stir for 2-3 minutes or until thickened.

3 Stir in the onion. Pour over lamb. Bake, uncovered, at 350° for 1-1/2 hours. Turn shanks; add the carrots and celery. Cover and bake 1 hour longer or until meat and vegetables are tender. **Yield:** 4 servings.

TEST KITCHEN TIP

Trim the fat from the shanks before cooking. Thicken juices for gravy if desired.

Greek Lamb Kabobs

I marinate the lamb overnight so I can quickly have a meal on the table the following evening. —*Sue Myers*

1/2 cup lemon juice
  4 teaspoons olive oil
  2 tablespoons dried oregano
  6 garlic cloves, minced
  1 pound boneless lean lamb, cut into 1-inch cubes
16 cherry tomatoes
  1 large green pepper, cut into 1-inch pieces
  1 large onion, cut into 1-inch wedges

1 In a small bowl, combine the lemon juice, oil, oregano and garlic; mix well. Remove 1/4 cup for basting; cover and refrigerate. Pour the remaining marinade into a large resealable plastic bag; add lamb. Seal bag and turn to coat; refrigerate for at least 8 hours or overnight, turning occasionally.

2 Coat grill rack with nonstick cooking spray before starting the grill. Drain and discard marinade from lamb. On eight metal or soaked wooden skewers, alternately thread lamb, tomatoes, green pepper and onion.

3 Grill kabobs, uncovered, over medium heat for 3 minutes on each side. Baste with reserved marinade. Grill 8-10 minutes longer or until meat reaches desired doneness, turning and basting frequently. **Yield:** 4 servings.

Southwestern Lamb Chops

Whether grilled or cooked on the stovetop, these lamb chops are loaded with flavor. A not-too-spicy sauce accompanies the tender chops. —*Sue A. Jurack*

- 1 cup orange juice
- 2 jalapeno peppers, seeded and finely chopped
- 1 teaspoon ground cumin
- 1/2 teaspoon salt, optional
- Dash pepper
- 3/4 cup halved sliced sweet onion
- 4 teaspoons cornstarch
- 1/4 cup cold water
- 1 cup fresh orange sections
- 2 tablespoons minced fresh cilantro
- 8 bone-in lamb loin chops (1 inch thick)

1 In a saucepan, combine the orange juice, jalapeno, cumin, salt if desired and pepper. Cook over medium-high heat until mixture begins to simmer. Stir in onion.

2 Combine cornstarch and water until smooth; add to the sauce. Bring to a boil over medium heat; cook and stir for 1 minute or until thickened. Remove from the heat. Stir in oranges and cilantro; keep warm.

3 Grill the lamb chops, covered, over medium-hot heat for 6-7 minutes on each side or until meat reaches desired doneness (for rare, a meat thermometer should read 140°; medium, 160°; well-done, 170°). Serve with orange sauce. **Yield:** 4 servings.

EDITOR'S NOTE: When cutting or seeding hot peppers, use rubber or plastic gloves to protect your hands. Avoid touching your face.

TEST KITCHEN TIP

Mandarin oranges could be substituted for orange segments to hurry along this entree. Gently fold into the sauce so they don't break apart.

Roast Lamb with Plum Sauce

You'll find the plum sauce in this recipe to be a nice change of pace from the mint sauce or jelly often served with lamb. —*Tamra Duncan*

- 1 leg of lamb (5 to 6 pounds), trimmed
- 3 garlic cloves, peeled
- 1/2 cup thinly sliced green onions
- 1/4 cup butter
- 1 jar (12 ounces) plum jam
- 1/2 cup chili sauce
- 1/4 cup white wine
- 1 tablespoon lemon juice
- 1/2 teaspoon ground allspice
- 1 tablespoon dried parsley flakes

1 With a sharp knife, make three deep cuts in meat; insert a garlic clove in each. Place on a rack in a large roasting pan. Bake, uncovered, at 325° for 1-1/2 hours.

2 Meanwhile, in a medium saucepan, saute onions in butter until tender but not brown. Add the jam, chili sauce, wine, lemon juice and allspice; bring to a boil, stirring occasionally. Simmer, uncovered, for 10 minutes.

3 Baste lamb with some of the plum sauce. Bake 1 hour longer or until a meat thermometer reads 160°, basting occasionally. Let stand for 10 minutes before slicing. Bring the remaining sauce to a boil; stir in parsley. Serve with lamb. **Yield:** 10-12 servings.

Spinach-Stuffed Lamb

This meaty entree is great for the holidays. A stuffing made with spinach, garlic and goat cheese makes it extra-special.
—Peggy Fleming

3 tablespoons minced garlic
1 tablespoon olive oil
2 packages (10 ounces *each*) frozen chopped spinach, thawed and squeezed dry
8 ounces crumbled goat cheese *or* feta cheese

3/4 teaspoon salt, *divided*
1/4 teaspoon pepper, *divided*
1 boneless butterflied leg of lamb (4 to 5 pounds), trimmed
3 garlic cloves, slivered
3 tablespoons minced fresh rosemary

1 In a small skillet, saute minced garlic in oil for 2-3 minutes. Remove from the heat; stir in the spinach, cheese, 1/2 teaspoon salt and 1/8 teaspoon pepper.

2 Untie lamb and open so it lies flat; flatten to 3/4-in. thickness. Spread spinach mixture over meat to within 1 in. of edges. Starting with a short side, roll up lamb and tuck ends in; tie with kitchen string at 2-in. intervals. With a sharp knife, make slits on the outside of meat; insert garlic slivers. Sprinkle with rosemary and remaining salt and pepper.

3 Place seam side down on a rack in a shallow roasting pan. Cover and bake at 425° for 1 hour. Uncover; bake 15-30 minutes longer or until browned and a meat thermometer reads 160°, basting occasionally with pan juices. Let stand for 10-15 minutes before slicing. **Yield:** 8-10 servings.

Apricot Lamb Chops

While we enjoy these fruity lamb chops, we like to reserve them for special-occasion dinners.
—Betty Reuter

12 bone-in lamb loin chops (1 inch thick)
1/4 teaspoon salt
1/4 teaspoon garlic powder
2 tablespoons Dijon-mayonnaise blend
2 tablespoons brown sugar
1/2 cup apricot nectar
2 tablespoons minced fresh mint
2/3 cup dried apricot halves, cut into 1/4-inch strips

1 Sprinkle lamb chops with salt and garlic powder. Rub each side of chops with Dijon-mayonnaise blend and sprinkle with brown sugar. In a large nonstick skillet coated with nonstick cooking spray, brown chops on both sides over medium-high heat.

2 Add apricot nectar and mint. Reduce heat; cover and simmer for 12-15 minutes. Add apricots. Simmer, uncovered, 5 minutes longer or until meat reaches desired doneness and sauce is slightly thickened. Serve sauce over lamb. **Yield:** 6 servings.

TEST KITCHEN TIP
Betty likes to use regular dried apricots, which are not as sweet as Mediterranean apricots. Use kitchen shears to cut the apricots into strips.

Lamb Fajitas

*(**Pictured on page 119**)*

My family enjoys lamb, especially these fajitas, which are a popular change of pace from grilled or roasted lamb. —*Mark Morgan*

1 boneless leg of lamb *or* lamb shoulder (3 to 4 pounds)
1/2 cup vegetable oil
1/2 cup lemon juice
1/3 cup packed brown sugar
1/3 cup soy sauce
1/4 cup cider vinegar
3 tablespoons Worcestershire sauce
1 tablespoon ground mustard
1/2 teaspoon pepper
1 large sweet red pepper, sliced
1 large green pepper, sliced
1 large onion, sliced
16 flour tortillas (7 inches), warmed
Chopped tomato and cucumber, optional

1 Cut lamb into thin bite-size strips. In a bowl, combine the oil, lemon juice, brown sugar, soy sauce, vinegar, Worcestershire sauce, mustard and pepper. Pour into a large resealable plastic bag; add lamb. Seal bag and turn to coat; refrigerate for 3 hours, turning occasionally.

2 Place the lamb and marinade in a Dutch oven or large saucepan; bring to a boil. Reduce heat; cover and simmer for 8-10 minutes or until meat is tender. Add the peppers and onion; cook for 4 minutes or until vegetables are crisp-tender.

3 Using a slotted spoon, place meat and vegetables on tortillas; top with tomato and cucumber if desired. Fold in sides of tortilla and serve immediately. **Yield:** 8 servings.

Hot 'n' Spicy Lamb Shanks

The first time I made this dish, I was planning a special evening with my boyfriend. I was completely unaware that he, too, had special plans for that evening—a proposal! —*Joylyn Trickel*

4 lamb shanks (about 12 ounces *each*)
5 tablespoons olive oil, *divided*
2 cups chopped onions
3 tablespoons minced garlic
1 jalapeno pepper, seeded and minced
1 can (14-1/2 ounces) crushed tomatoes in puree
1 can (14-1/2 ounces) reduced-sodium beef broth
1 cup dry red wine
1/2 cup ketchup
1/4 cup packed brown sugar
2 tablespoons prepared mustard
2 tablespoons cider vinegar
2 tablespoons Worcestershire sauce
2 teaspoons minced fresh rosemary
1 teaspoon ground cumin
2 bay leaves
GLAZE:
1/4 cup honey
1 to 3 tablespoons chipotle peppers in adobo sauce, chopped
2 tablespoons lime juice
2 teaspoons grated lime peel

1 In a large Dutch oven or soup kettle, brown lamb shanks, two at a time, in 3 tablespoons oil. Remove meat and discard drippings. In same pan, saute onions, garlic and jalapeno in remaining oil until tender, scraping up any browned bits.

2 Add the tomatoes, broth, wine, ketchup, brown sugar, mustard, vinegar, Worcestershire sauce, rosemary, cumin and bay leaves. Add lamb. Cover and bring to a boil. Reduce heat; simmer for 1 hour. Rearrange shanks so the top ones are on the bottom. Simmer 1 hour longer. Meanwhile, combine the glaze ingredients.

3 Transfer shanks to a foil-lined 15-in. x 10-in. x 1-in. baking pan. Brush with some of the glaze. Bake at 400° for 5 minutes. Turn and brush with glaze; bake 5 minutes longer.

4 Meanwhile, skim and discard any fat from the cooking juices. Discard bay leaves. Bring to a boil; cook and stir for 5 minutes to reduce slightly. Serve with shanks. **Yield:** 4 servings.

EDITOR'S NOTE: When cutting or seeding hot peppers, use rubber gloves to protect your hands. Avoid touching your face.

Greek Burgers

My stepdad's parents were born in Greece, so when I served these to him, he really enjoyed the flavor.
—Coleen Martin

1 pound ground lamb
1 tablespoon Dijon mustard
1 tablespoon lemon juice
1 tablespoon minced onion
1 garlic clove, minced
1/2 teaspoon dried rosemary, crushed
1/2 teaspoon salt
1/4 teaspoon pepper
4 hamburger buns *or* hard rolls, split
Sliced cucumber and tomato, optional
Ranch salad dressing, optional

1 In a medium bowl, combine the first eight ingredients; mix well. Shape into four patties.

2 Pan-fry, grill or broil until meat is no longer pink. Serve on buns with cucumber, tomato and ranch dressing if desired. **Yield:** 4 servings.

TEST KITCHEN TIP

You can serve these burgers in pita bread instead of buns. For a little added Greek flavor, stir some crumbled feta cheese into the ranch dressing.

Traditional Lamb Stew

I like to make this stew over the weekend, then reheat it for Monday night's dinner. I think the flavor gets even better when it keeps for a day.
—Megan Taylor

1-1/2 pounds lamb stew meat
2 tablespoons olive oil, *divided*
3 large onions, quartered
3 medium carrots, cut into 1-inch pieces
4 small potatoes, peeled and cubed
1 can (14-1/2 ounces) beef broth
1 teaspoon salt
1/4 teaspoon pepper
1 tablespoon butter
1 tablespoon all-purpose flour
1-1/2 teaspoons minced fresh parsley
1-1/2 teaspoons minced chives
1/2 teaspoon minced fresh thyme

1 In a Dutch oven, brown meat in 1 tablespoon oil over medium heat. Remove with a slotted spoon; set aside. In the same pan, cook onions and carrots in remaining oil for 5 minutes or until onions are tender, stirring occasionally. Add the meat, potatoes, broth, salt and pepper. Bring to a boil. Remove from the heat.

2 Cover and bake at 350° for 50-60 minutes or until meat and vegetables are tender. With a slotted spoon, remove meat and vegetables to a large bowl; keep warm. Pour pan juices into another bowl; set aside.

3 In the Dutch oven, melt butter over medium heat. Stir in flour until smooth. Gradually whisk in pan juices. Bring to a boil; cook and stir for 2 minutes or until thickened. Stir in the parsley, chives, thyme, meat and vegetables and heat through. **Yield:** 4 servings.

Herbed Marinated Lamb Chops

I also use the flavorful marinade from this recipe on pork chops with equally delicious results. —*Janet Briggs*

- 1/4 cup dry red wine
- 2 tablespoons reduced-sodium soy sauce
- 1-1/2 teaspoons minced fresh mint *or* 1/2 teaspoon dried mint
- 1 teaspoon minced fresh basil *or* 1/4 teaspoon dried basil
- 1/2 teaspoon pepper
- 1 garlic clove, minced
- 4 bone-in lamb loin chops (1 inch thick)

1 In a large resealable plastic bag, combine the wine, soy sauce, mint, basil, pepper and garlic; add the lamb chops. Seal bag and turn to coat; refrigerate for 8 hours or overnight.

2 Drain and discard marinade. Grill lamb, uncovered, over medium heat or broil 4-6 in. from the heat for 5-7 minutes on each side or until meat reaches desired doneness (for medium, a meat thermometer should read 160°; well-done, 170°). **Yield:** 4 servings.

Grilled Rack of Lamb

This rack of lamb makes a great company entree. The marinade keeps the meat juicy and tender while grilling. —*Nancy Fridirici*

- 2 cups apple cider *or* juice
- 2/3 cup cider vinegar
- 2/3 cup thinly sliced green onions
- 1/2 cup vegetable oil
- 1/3 cup honey
- 1/4 cup steak sauce
- 2 teaspoons dried tarragon
- 2 teaspoons salt
- 1/2 teaspoon pepper
- 4 racks of lamb (about 1-1/2 pounds *each*), trimmed

1 In a saucepan, combine the first nine ingredients. Bring to a boil. Reduce heat; simmer, uncovered, for 20 minutes. Remove 1 cup for basting; cover and refrigerate. Pour the remaining marinade into a large resealable plastic bag; add lamb. Seal bag and turn to coat; refrigerate for 2-3 hours or overnight, turning once or twice.

2 Coat grill rack with nonstick cooking spray before starting the grill. Drain and discard marinade from lamb. Cover rib ends of lamb with foil. Grill, covered, over medium heat for 15 minutes.

3 Baste with reserved marinade. Grill 5-10 minutes longer, basting occasionally, or until meat reaches desired doneness (for medium-rare, a meat thermometer should read 145°; medium, 160°; well-done, 170°). Let stand for 5-10 minutes before slicing. **Yield:** 4-6 servings.

POULTRY

Chicken Fajitas

This recipe goes together in a snap and is very popular at my house. If you don't like your food hot, just leave out the red pepper flakes. —Sue Megonigle

　　4 tablespoons vegetable oil, *divided*
　　2 tablespoons lemon juice
1-1/2 teaspoons seasoned salt
1-1/2 teaspoons dried oregano
1-1/2 teaspoons ground cumin
　　1 teaspoon garlic powder
　1/2 teaspoon chili powder
　1/2 teaspoon paprika
　1/2 teaspoon crushed red pepper flakes, optional
1-1/2 pounds boneless skinless chicken breasts, cut into thin strips
　1/2 medium sweet red pepper, julienned
　1/2 medium green pepper, julienned
　　4 green onions, thinly sliced
　1/2 cup chopped onion
　　6 flour tortillas (8 inches), warmed
Shredded cheddar cheese, taco sauce, salsa, guacamole *and/or* sour cream

1 In a large resealable plastic bag, combine 2 tablespoons oil, lemon juice and seasonings; add chicken. Seal bag and turn to coat; refrigerate for 1-4 hours.

2 In a large skillet, saute peppers and onions in remaining oil until crisp-tender. Remove and keep warm. In the same skillet, cook chicken with marinade over medium-high heat for 5-6 minutes or until no longer pink. Return pepper mixture to the pan; heat through.

3 Spoon filling down the center of tortillas; fold in sides. Serve with cheese, taco sauce, salsa, guacamole and/or sour cream. **Yield:** 6 servings.

Cornflake Crunch Tenders

The cornflakes give a nice crunch to these oven-baked chicken tenders, which are great for a meal or snacking. —Kris Lehman

　　1 cup finely crushed cornflakes
　1/2 teaspoon Italian seasoning
　1/2 teaspoon salt
　1/4 teaspoon pepper
　　1 egg

　16 chicken tenders (about 1-3/4 pounds)
　1/4 cup butter, melted
Marinara sauce, warmed

1 In a shallow bowl, combine the cornflakes, Italian seasoning, salt and pepper. In another shallow bowl, lightly beat egg. Dip chicken in egg, then in cornflake mixture.

2 Line a 15-in. x 10-in. x 1-in. baking pan with foil; coat the foil with nonstick cooking spray. Arrange chicken in prepared pan. Drizzle with butter. Bake, uncovered, at 400° for 20 minutes or until juices run clear. Serve with marinara sauce. **Yield:** 4 servings.

Cider Marinated Turkey

Marinating the turkey gives it a wonderful flavor. This recipe quickly became a favorite with my family. —*Wendy Stenman*

8 cups apple cider *or* unsweetened apple juice
1/2 cup kosher salt
2 bay leaves
2 sprigs fresh thyme
8 whole cloves
5 garlic cloves
1 teaspoon whole allspice, crushed
2 medium navel oranges, quartered
3 quarts cold water
1 turkey (12 pounds)
1 medium onion, quartered
2 medium carrots, halved and quartered
2 sprigs fresh sage *or* 1 tablespoon rubbed sage
1 tablespoon canola oil

1 In a large kettle, combine the first seven ingredients. Bring to a boil; cook and stir until salt is dissolved. Stir in oranges. Remove from the heat. Add water; cool to room temperature.

2 Remove giblets from turkey; discard. Place a turkey-size oven roasting bag inside a second roasting bag; add turkey. Place in a roasting pan. Carefully pour cooled marinade into the bag. Squeeze out as much air as possible; seal bag and turn to coat. Refrigerate for 12-24 hours, turning several times.

3 Drain and discard marinade. Rinse turkey under cold water; pat dry. Place onion, carrots and sage in cavity. Rub oil over skin. Skewer turkey openings; tie drumsticks together.

4 If grilling turkey, coat grill rack with nonstick cooking spray before starting the grill. Prepare grill for indirect heat, using a drip pan. Place turkey over drip pan; grill, covered, over indirect medium heat for 2 to 2-1/2 hours or until a meat thermometer inserted into a thigh reads 180°, tenting turkey with foil after about 1 hour.

5 If baking turkey, place breast side up on a rack in a roasting pan. Bake, uncovered, at 325° for 3 hours or until a meat thermometer reads 180°.

6 If desired, thicken pan juices for gravy. Remove and discard skin and vegetables in cavity before carving turkey. **Yield:** 12 servings plus leftovers.

TEST KITCHEN TIP

It is best not to use a prebasted turkey for this recipe. However, if you do, omit the salt in the recipe.

WENDY STENMAN

Most of Wendy's work experience has been in the food industry. Before joining our Test Kitchen staff 7 years ago, she taught high school home economics and was a nutrition educator...did some catering...and ran taste-testing panels that critiqued new salad dressings and sauces. She says that preparing meals for her husband and four children is an expression of her love for them.

Creamy White Chili

I make this often during football season. Family and friends love the flavors—it's so different from other tomato-based chili recipes. —*Patricia Schmeling*

1 pound boneless skinless chicken breasts, cut into 1/2-inch cubes
1 medium onion, chopped
1-1/2 teaspoons garlic powder
1 tablespoon vegetable oil
2 cans (15-1/2 ounces *each*) great northern beans, rinsed and drained
1 can (14-1/2 ounces) chicken broth
2 cans (4 ounces *each*) chopped green chilies
1 teaspoon salt
1 teaspoon ground cumin
1 teaspoon dried oregano
1/2 teaspoon pepper
1/4 teaspoon cayenne pepper
1 cup (8 ounces) sour cream
1/2 cup heavy whipping cream

1 In a large saucepan, saute the chicken, onion and garlic powder in oil until chicken is no longer pink. Add the beans, broth, chilies and seasonings.

2 Bring to a boil. Reduce heat; simmer, uncovered, for 30 minutes. Remove from the heat; stir in sour cream and heavy cream. Serve immediately. **Yield:** 7 servings.

TEST KITCHEN TIP
You can make this using half-and-half cream instead of heavy cream with great success.

Chicken Tortilla Casserole

My aunt in California shared this zesty chicken casserole recipe with me. It's easy, filling and feeds a big group. —*Sarah Thompson*

5 to 6 corn tortillas (6 inches), cut into strips
8 cups cubed cooked chicken breast
1 can (4 ounces) chopped green chilies
1 can (10-3/4 ounces) condensed cream of mushroom soup, undiluted
1 can (10-3/4 ounces) condensed cream of chicken soup, undiluted
1 cup (8 ounces) sour cream
3 cups (12 ounces) shredded Monterey Jack cheese

1 In a greased 13-in. x 9-in. x 2-in. baking dish, layer half of the tortilla strips, chicken and chilies. In a bowl, combine the soups and sour cream; spread half over the chicken. Sprinkle with half of the cheese. Repeat layers.

2 Bake, uncovered, at 350° for 45 minutes or until bubbly and golden brown. Let stand for 10 minutes before serving. **Yield:** 8-10 servings.

Bacon-Feta Chicken Rolls

(Pictured on page 128)

These pretty roll-ups are festive enough to serve for company. They're a tasty change from plain chicken breasts. —Tamra Duncan

4 boneless skinless chicken breast halves
8 bacon strips, cooked and drained
1 cup (4 ounces) crumbled feta cheese
4 roasted red pepper halves, patted dry
1/2 teaspoon salt
1/4 teaspoon pepper
1 tablespoon olive oil
1/2 teaspoon Italian seasoning

1 Flatten chicken to 1/4-in. thickness. Top each with two strips of bacon, 1/4 cup feta cheese and a red pepper half; sprinkle with salt and pepper. Roll up, starting with a short side, bringing the ends to meet. Tie at 1-1/2-in. intervals with kitchen string.

2 In a skillet over medium heat, brown chicken on all sides in oil. Transfer to an ungreased 8-in. square baking dish. Sprinkle with Italian seasoning. Bake, uncovered, at 350° for 35-40 minutes or until chicken juices run clear. **Yield:** 4 servings.

Stuffed Turkey Spirals

The basil sauce drizzled over the top of the turkey really makes this a special dish. —Peggy Fleming

2 boneless skinless turkey breast halves (1 pound *each*)
1/4 cup olive oil, *divided*
4 teaspoons dried basil, *divided*
1 pound thinly sliced deli ham
1 pound thinly sliced Swiss cheese
1 teaspoon salt
1 teaspoon pepper
BASIL SAUCE:
2 cups mayonnaise
1/2 cup milk
1 to 2 tablespoons dried basil
1 teaspoon sugar

1 Cut each turkey breast horizontally from the long side to within 1/2 in. of opposite side. Open flat; cover with plastic wrap. Flatten into 12-in. x 10-in. rectangles.

2 Remove plastic; top each with 1 teaspoon oil and 1 teaspoon basil. Layer with ham and cheese to within 1 in. of edges. Roll up jelly-roll style, starting with a long side; tie with kitchen string. Place on a rack in a roasting pan.

3 In a small bowl, combine salt, pepper and remaining oil and basil; spoon some over turkey. Bake at 325° for 75-90 minutes or until a meat thermometer reads 170°, basting occasionally with remaining oil mixture.

4 In a blender or food processor, combine the sauce ingredients; cover and process until blended. Let turkey stand for 5 minutes before slicing; serve with basil sauce. **Yield:** about 30 servings.

TEST KITCHEN TIP
If you have an abundance of fresh basil from your garden, substitute 3 to 6 tablespoons fresh basil for the dried basil.

Slow-Cooked Herbed Turkey

When herbs are plentiful in my garden, I prepare this recipe. The turkey stays moist in the slow cooker and is bursting with herb flavors. When I served this to our Bible study potluck group, everyone wanted the recipe!
—*Sue A. Jurack*

1 can (14-1/2 ounces) chicken broth
1/2 cup lemon juice
1/4 cup packed brown sugar
1/4 cup minced fresh sage
1/4 cup minced fresh thyme
1/4 cup lime juice
1/4 cup cider vinegar
1/4 cup olive oil

1 envelope onion soup mix
2 tablespoons Dijon mustard
1 tablespoon minced fresh marjoram
1-1/2 teaspoons paprika
1 teaspoon garlic powder
1 teaspoon pepper
1/2 teaspoon salt
2 boneless turkey breasts (2 pounds *each*)

1 In a blender, combine the first 15 ingredients; cover and process until blended. Place the turkey breasts in a gallon-size resealable plastic bag; add marinade. Seal bag and turn to coat; seal and refrigerate overnight.

2 Transfer turkey breasts to a 5-qt. slow cooker. Pour marinade into a large saucepan; bring to a rolling boil for 1 minute. Pour over turkey. Cover and cook on high for 3-1/2 to 4 hours or until juices run clear and a meat thermometer reads 170°. Let stand for 10 minutes before slicing. **Yield:** 14-16 servings.

Garlic Lover's Chicken

The garlic and lemon are great together on this breaded chicken. I've served this several times for special-occasion dinners.
—*Karen Scales*

1/2 cup dry bread crumbs
1/3 cup grated Parmesan cheese
2 tablespoons minced fresh parsley
1/2 teaspoon salt, optional
1/8 teaspoon pepper
1/4 cup milk
6 boneless skinless chicken breast halves
1/4 cup butter, melted
1 to 2 garlic cloves, minced
2 tablespoons lemon juice
Paprika

1 In a large resealable plastic bag, combine the bread crumbs, Parmesan cheese, parsley, salt if desired and pepper. Place milk in a shallow bowl. Dip chicken in milk, then place in bag and shake to coat.

2 Place chicken in a greased 13-in. x 9-in. x 2-in. baking dish. Combine the butter, garlic and lemon juice; drizzle over chicken. Sprinkle with paprika. Bake, uncovered, at 350° for 25-30 minutes or until juices run clear. **Yield:** 6 servings.

TEST KITCHEN TIP
Store dry bread crumbs in the freezer so they don't get stale.

Citrus Grilled Turkey Breast

Drippings from the grilled meat make an outstanding gravy. Leftovers of this turkey are perfect for salads or open-faced sandwiches the next day. —*Mark Morgan*

　1 bone-in turkey breast (4 to 5 pounds)
1/4 cup fresh parsley sprigs
1/4 cup fresh basil leaves
　3 tablespoons butter
　4 garlic cloves, halved
1/2 teaspoon salt
　1 medium lemon, thinly sliced
　1 medium orange, thinly sliced
　1 tablespoon cornstarch
　2 tablespoons water
　1 cup orange juice
　1 teaspoon grated orange peel
　1 teaspoon grated lemon peel
1/4 teaspoon pepper

1 Using fingers, carefully loosen the skin from both sides of turkey breast. In a food processor or blender, combine the parsley, basil, butter, garlic and salt; cover and process until smooth. Spread under turkey skin; arrange lemon and orange slices over herb mixture. Secure skin to underside of breast with toothpicks.

2 Coat grill rack with nonstick cooking spray before starting the grill. Prepare grill for indirect heat, using a drip pan; place turkey over drip pan. Grill, covered, over indirect medium heat for 1-3/4 to 2-1/4 hours or until a meat thermometer reads 170° and juices run clear. Cover and let stand for 10 minutes.

3 Meanwhile, pour pan drippings into a measuring cup; skim fat. In a saucepan, combine the cornstarch and water until smooth. Add the orange juice and peel, lemon peel, pepper and pan drippings. Bring to a boil; cook and stir for 2 minutes or until thickened.

4 Discard the skin, lemon and orange slices from turkey breast. Remove herb mixture from turkey; stir into gravy. Slice turkey and serve with gravy. **Yield:** 10-12 servings.

TEST KITCHEN TIP

Allow 2-3 days for a frozen turkey breast to thaw in the refrigerator. Place the packaged turkey breast in two plastic grocery bags to avoid any dripping or leaking from the package during defrosting.

MARK MORGAN

Whatever the season, Mark loves to fire up the grill to prepare supper for his wife and three kids—most days of the week! He also is an avid fisherman. Every few years he takes an extended vacation in Alaska to go fishing for salmon, which he grills, smokes or cans. Mark's interest in cooking began at age 11 when, after complaining about dinner, his mother told him he could cook the next week's meals. He did, and he's been active in the kitchen ever since.

Turkey Biscuit Potpie

This recipe is a great way to use up leftover turkey. I like mushrooms, so I usually add 1-1/2 cups and cook them with the onion and garlic. We love the herb flavors. —Mark Morgan

1	large onion, chopped
1	garlic clove, minced
1-1/2	cups cubed peeled potatoes
1-1/2	cups sliced carrots
1	cup frozen cut green beans, thawed
1	cup reduced-sodium chicken broth
4-1/2	teaspoons all-purpose flour
1	can (10-3/4 ounces) reduced-fat condensed cream of mushroom soup, undiluted
2	cups cubed cooked turkey
2	tablespoons minced fresh parsley
1/2	teaspoon dried basil
1/2	teaspoon dried thyme
1/4	teaspoon pepper

BISCUITS:
1	cup all-purpose flour
2	teaspoons baking powder
1/2	teaspoon dried oregano
2	tablespoons cold butter
7	tablespoons 1% milk

1 In a large saucepan coated with nonstick cooking spray, cook onion and garlic over medium heat until tender. Add potatoes, carrots, beans and broth; bring to a boil. Reduce heat; cover and simmer for 15-20 minutes or until potatoes are tender.

2 Remove from the heat. Combine the flour and mushroom soup; stir into vegetable mixture. Add the turkey and seasonings. Transfer to a 2-qt. baking dish coated with nonstick cooking spray.

3 In a bowl, combine the flour, baking powder and oregano. Cut in butter until evenly distributed. Stir in milk. Drop batter in six mounds onto hot turkey mixture.

4 Bake, uncovered, at 400° for 20-25 minutes or until a toothpick inserted in center of biscuits comes out clean and biscuits are golden brown. **Yield:** 6 servings.

Savory Roast Chicken

This chicken is so effortless that you can get a million other things done while it bakes in the oven. Fresh savory is a great herb for poultry.
—Suzanne Kern

1	broiler/fryer chicken (2-1/2 to 3 pounds)
2	tablespoons butter, melted
3	tablespoons lemon juice

1	tablespoon minced fresh savory *or* 1 teaspoon dried savory

1 Place chicken breast side up on a rack in a shallow roasting pan. Combine the butter, lemon juice and savory; brush over chicken.

2 Bake, uncovered, at 375° for 1-1/2 hours or until juices run clear, basting occasionally with the pan drippings. **Yield:** 4 servings.

Jalapeno-Lime Marinated Chicken

(Pictured on page 129)

The marinade adds a zesty taste and makes the chicken very tender. I think this is a perfect recipe for a summer picnic.
—Coleen Martin

1 cup orange juice concentrate	2 teaspoons ground cumin
2/3 cup chopped onion	2 teaspoons grated lime peel
1/2 cup lime juice	1/2 teaspoon garlic salt
1/2 cup honey	2 garlic cloves, minced
1 jalapeno pepper, seeded and diced	10 boneless skinless chicken breast halves

1 In a 4-cup measuring cup, combine the first nine ingredients. Pour 2 cups into a large resealable plastic bag; add chicken. Seal bag and turn to coat; refrigerate for 2-4 hours. Cover and refrigerate remaining marinade for basting.

2 Coat grill rack with nonstick cooking spray before starting the grill. Drain and discard marinade from chicken. Grill chicken, covered, over medium heat for 4-6 minutes on each side or until juices run clear, basting frequently with the reserved marinade. **Yield:** 10 servings.

EDITOR'S NOTE: When cutting or seeding hot peppers, use rubber or plastic gloves to protect your hands. Avoid touching your face.

TEST KITCHEN TIP
Cut chicken breast halves in half again if serving a buffet with more than one entree choice. Guests are more likely to try different items.

Fruited Chicken

My family just loves the flavor of this chicken. The tang of the cranberries and orange peel add just the right zip for a more flavorful dish.
—Rita Krajcir

    1 large onion, sliced
    6 boneless skinless chicken breast halves
  1/3 cup orange juice
    2 tablespoons soy sauce
    2 tablespoons Worcestershire sauce
    2 tablespoons Dijon mustard
    1 tablespoon grated orange peel
    2 garlic cloves, minced
  1/2 cup chopped dried apricots
  1/2 cup dried cranberries
Hot cooked rice

1 Place onion and chicken in a 5-qt. slow cooker. Combine the orange juice, soy sauce, Worcestershire sauce, mustard, orange peel and garlic; pour over chicken. Sprinkle with apricots and cranberries.

2 Cover and cook on low for 7-8 hours or until chicken juices run clear. Serve over rice. **Yield:** 6 servings.

Turkey Drumsticks

The aroma of these drumsticks is awesome while cooking! The turkey is so tender, it just falls off the bones.

—*Sue Draheim*

- 4 turkey drumsticks
- 1 medium onion, sliced and separated into rings
- 1 can (14-1/2 ounces) stewed tomatoes
- 1/2 cup boiling water
- 2 teaspoons chicken bouillon granules
- 1/2 teaspoon garlic salt
- 1/2 teaspoon dried oregano
- 1/2 teaspoon dried basil
- 2 tablespoons minced fresh parsley

1 Place drumsticks in a 13-in. x 9-in. x 2-in. baking dish. Arrange onion over drumsticks. Pour tomatoes on top. Combine the water, bouillon, garlic salt, oregano and basil; pour over onion. Sprinkle with parsley.

2 Cover and bake at 325° for 2 hours or until tender and a meat thermometer reads 180°. **Yield:** 4 servings.

Orange Walnut Chicken

Orange and lemon juice along with orange marmalade make a pretty and flavorful sauce for this mouth-watering chicken.

—*Diane Werner*

- 1/3 cup orange juice concentrate
- 5 tablespoons vegetable oil, *divided*
- 2 tablespoons soy sauce
- 2 garlic cloves, minced
- 4 boneless skinless chicken breast halves
- 1/2 cup coarsely chopped walnuts
- 1 tablespoon butter
- 4 green onions, thinly sliced
- 1/2 cup orange marmalade
- 1/2 cup orange juice
- 1/4 cup lemon juice
- 2 tablespoons honey
- 1 to 2 tablespoons grated orange peel
- 2 to 3 teaspoons grated lemon peel
- 1/2 teaspoon salt
- 1/8 teaspoon pepper
- Hot cooked rice

1 In a small bowl, combine the orange juice concentrate, 4 tablespoons oil, soy sauce and garlic. Pour half of the marinade into a large resealable plastic bag; add chicken. Seal bag and turn to coat; refrigerate for 2-3 hours. Cover and refrigerate remaining marinade.

2 Discard marinade from chicken. In a large skillet, cook chicken in remaining oil until juices run clear. Meanwhile, in a small saucepan, saute walnuts in butter until lightly browned; remove and set aside.

3 Set aside 1/4 cup onions for garnish. Add remaining onions to the saucepan; saute until tender. Add the marmalade, juices, honey, orange and lemon peel, salt, pepper and reserved marinade. Bring to a boil.

4 Reduce heat; simmer, uncovered, for 5-10 minutes or until sauce reaches desired consistency. Serve chicken over rice; top with sauce, toasted walnuts and reserved onions. **Yield:** 4 servings.

Parmesan Chicken Pasta

I developed this recipe one Saturday night when I wanted to make something a little nicer but spend minimal time in the kitchen. I'd tried something similar at a restaurant a few weeks earlier. It's a great way to use leftover grilled chicken...or you can use purchased grilled chicken strips.   —*Tamra Duncan*

      8 ounces uncooked penne *or* medium tube pasta
      1 cup cubed fully cooked ham
      2 garlic cloves, minced
      2 tablespoons olive oil
      2 cups grilled chicken breast strips
      1 package (10 ounces) frozen chopped spinach, thawed and squeezed dry
      1 jar (7-1/2 ounces) marinated artichoke hearts, drained and chopped
    1/4 cup chopped seeded plum tomato
      1 jar (17 ounces) Alfredo sauce
      1 cup milk
    1/2 cup shredded Parmesan cheese

1 Cook pasta according to package directions. Meanwhile, in a large skillet, saute the ham and garlic in oil until garlic is tender. Add the chicken, spinach, artichokes and tomato; cook and stir until heated through.

2 Stir in the Alfredo sauce and milk; bring to boil. Reduce heat. Drain pasta; stir into chicken mixture and heat through. Sprinkle with Parmesan cheese. **Yield:** 4-6 servings.

Mexican-Style Chicken Kiev

I like to prepare this dish the night before. That way I can just pop the chicken in the oven when I come home from work.
—*Janet Briggs*

      4 large boneless skinless chicken breast halves
      1 can (4 ounces) chopped green chilies, drained
      2 ounces Monterey Jack cheese, cut into 4 strips
    1/4 cup fine dry bread crumbs
      2 tablespoons grated Parmesan cheese

    3-1/2 teaspoons chili powder
      1/4 teaspoon salt
      1/8 teaspoon ground cumin
        4 tablespoons butter, melted, *divided*
        1 cup picante sauce
      1/2 cup cold water
        2 teaspoons cornstarch
      1/2 teaspoon chicken bouillon granules

1 Flatten chicken to 1/4-in. thickness. Place 2 tablespoons of chilies and one strip of Monterey Jack cheese on long end of each. Fold in sides and ends of chicken; secure with a toothpick.

2 In a shallow bowl, combine the bread crumbs, Parmesan cheese, chili powder, salt and cumin. Dip chicken in 3 tablespoons butter, then roll in crumb mixture.

3 Place seam side down in an ungreased 11-in. x 7-in. x 2-in. baking dish. Drizzle with remaining butter. Cover and refrigerate for at least 4 hours.

4 Bake, uncovered, at 400° for 20-25 minutes or until chicken is tender. In a small saucepan, combine picante sauce, water, cornstarch and bouillon. Bring to a boil over medium heat; cook and stir for 1 minute. Remove toothpicks from chicken; serve with sauce. **Yield:** 4 servings.

Chicken Cheese Lasagna

I like to make a double batch of this lasagna and freeze one for another day. The filling can also be stuffed in man- icotti shells. —Coleen Martin

  1 medium onion, chopped
  1 garlic clove, minced
1/2 cup butter
1/2 cup all-purpose flour
  1 teaspoon salt
  2 cups chicken broth
1-1/2 cups milk
  4 cups (16 ounces) shredded mozzarella cheese, *divided*
  1 cup grated Parmesan cheese, *divided*
  2 teaspoons dried basil
  2 teaspoons dried oregano
1/2 teaspoon white pepper
  1 carton (15 ounces) ricotta cheese
  1 tablespoon minced fresh parsley
  9 lasagna noodles (8 ounces), cooked and drained
  2 packages (10 ounces *each*) frozen chopped spinach, thawed and squeezed dry
  2 cups cubed cooked chicken

1 In a large saucepan, saute onion and garlic in but- ter until tender. Stir in the flour and salt. Gradu- ally stir in broth and milk. Bring to a boil; cook and stir for 2 minutes or until thickened. Reduce heat; stir in 2 cups mozzarella cheese, 1/2 cup Parme- san cheese, basil, oregano and pepper; set aside.

2 In a large bowl, combine the ricotta cheese, parsley and remaining mozzarella; set aside.

3 Spread a fourth of the cheese sauce in a greased 13-in. x 9-in. x 2-in. baking dish; top with three noodles. Layer with half of the ricotta mixture, spinach and chicken. Repeat. Top with a fourth of the cheese sauce, three noodles and remain- ing cheese sauce. Sprinkle with remaining Parmesan cheese.

4 Bake, uncovered, at 350° for 35-40 minutes. Let stand for 15 minutes before cutting. **Yield:** 12 servings.

TEST KITCHEN TIP

For a change, substitute cooked bulk Italian sausage for the chicken. Using 1% milk and reduced-fat cheeses will help cut the calories. You can also use no-cook lasagna noodles without making any adjustment to the liquid or cooking time.

Chicken Quesadillas

For a fun, easy and tasty way to "recycle" leftover chicken, give this recipe a try! The quesadillas have an impressive look and taste with little preparation.
—*Anita Bukowski*

2-1/2 cups shredded cooked chicken
2/3 cup salsa
1/3 cup sliced green onions
3/4 to 1 teaspoon ground cumin
1/2 teaspoon salt
1/2 teaspoon dried oregano

6 flour tortillas (8 inches)
1/4 cup butter, melted
2 cups (8 ounces) shredded Monterey Jack cheese
Sour cream and guacamole

1 In a large skillet, combine the first six ingredients. Cook, uncovered, over medium heat for 10 minutes or until heated through, stirring occasionally.

2 Brush one side of each tortilla with butter; place buttered side down on a lightly greased baking sheet. Spoon 1/3 cup chicken mixture over half of each tortilla; sprinkle with 1/3 cup cheese. Fold plain side of tortilla over cheese.

3 Bake at 475° for 10 minutes or until crisp and golden brown. Cut into wedges; serve with sour cream and guacamole. **Yield:** 4-6 servings.

Cornish Hens with Orange Stuffing

Since it is just the two of us, my husband and I enjoy it when we can find special recipes just for two. This one is perfect.
—*Joylyn Trickel*

1 medium navel orange
1/4 cup sliced green onions
1/4 cup chopped celery
1 tablespoon vegetable oil
1-1/2 cups seasoned stuffing mix
1/4 teaspoon grated orange peel
4 to 5 tablespoons orange juice
1 Cornish game hen (20 ounces), halved
1 tablespoon honey, warmed
1 tablespoon water

1 Peel and section the orange; cut each section into quarters and set aside. In a skillet, saute onions and celery in oil until crisp-tender. In a bowl, combine the onion mixture, stuffing mix, orange peel and reserved orange sections. Stir in just enough orange juice to moisten stuffing mixture.

2 Arrange stuffing in two mounds in a greased shallow 2-qt. baking dish. Place Cornish hen halves skin side up over stuffing. Cover and bake at 375° for 30 minutes.

3 Uncover; bake for 15 minutes. Combine honey and water; brush over hens. Bake 10-15 minutes longer or until juices run clear. **Yield:** 2 servings.

Tasty Baked Chicken

Tarragon and paprika add a nice flavor to this chicken, which bakes up golden brown in the oven.

—*Betty Reuter*

1 broiler/fryer chicken (3 to 4 pounds), cut up
1 teaspoon salt
1/2 teaspoon dried tarragon
1/4 teaspoon paprika
1/4 teaspoon pepper

1/4 cup dry sherry
3 tablespoons lemon juice
2 teaspoons soy sauce
2 shallots, chopped

1 Place the chicken in a greased 13-in. x 9-in. x 2-in. baking dish. Sprinkle with salt, tarragon, paprika and pepper. Combine the sherry, lemon juice and soy sauce; drizzle over chicken. Top with shallots.

2 Bake, uncovered, at 425° for 20 minutes. Reduce heat to 375°. Cover and bake for 30 minutes, basting occasionally. Uncover; bake 15-20 minutes longer or until a meat thermometer reads 180°. **Yield:** 4-6 servings.

Turkey Breast Florentine

A lovely dish for guests, this spinach-stuffed turkey breast looks beautiful when you slice it for serving.

—*Anita Bukowski*

1 turkey breast half (3 to 4 pounds), bone removed
5 bacon strips
3/4 cup chopped onion
3 tablespoons all-purpose flour
3/4 teaspoon dried tarragon
1/2 teaspoon salt
1/4 teaspoon pepper
1-1/2 cups milk
1 package (10 ounces) frozen chopped spinach, thawed and squeezed dry
1 jar (4-1/2 ounces) sliced mushrooms, drained
1 tablespoon butter, melted
1/3 cup cubed process cheese (Velveeta)

1 Cut a lengthwise slit in turkey breast to within 1/2 in. of opposite side; open meat so it lies flat. Cover with plastic wrap and flatten to 1/2-in. thickness. Remove plastic wrap; set aside.

2 In a skillet, cook two bacon strips until crisp. Drain, reserving 2 tablespoons drippings. Crumble bacon; set aside. In the drippings, saute onion until tender. Stir in flour, tarragon, salt and pepper until blended. Gradually stir in milk. Bring to a boil; cook and stir for 2 minutes or until thickened. Remove from heat. Refrigerate 1/2 cup sauce.

3 Add the spinach, mushrooms and crumbled bacon to the remaining sauce; spread over turkey breast. Starting at a short end, roll up and tuck in ends; tie with kitchen string. Place on a rack in a greased roasting pan. Brush with butter. Cover loosely with foil. Bake at 350° for 1 hour.

4 Remove foil. Cut remaining bacon strips in half; place over the turkey. Bake 25-35 minutes longer or until a meat thermometer reads 170°. Discard string. Let turkey stand for 10 minutes before slicing.

5 Meanwhile, heat the reserved sauce; stir in cheese until melted. Serve with the turkey. **Yield:** 6-8 servings.

Chicken Tostadas

If you like Mexican fare, you're going to love these piled-high tostadas! They make a quick-to-fix weekday dinner.

—Janet Briggs

   6 flour tortillas (8 inches)
   1 can (15 ounces) black beans, rinsed and drained
   2 teaspoons chili powder, *divided*
   1 teaspoon ground cumin, *divided*
 1/2 cup salsa
 3/4 pound boneless skinless chicken breasts, cut into strips
   2 cups finely chopped seeded tomatoes
   1 cup chopped onion
1-1/2 cups (6 ounces) shredded cheddar cheese
   2 cups torn romaine
Sour cream, optional

1 Spritz both sides of tortillas with nonstick cooking spray. Place on ungreased baking sheets. Bake at 350° for 7 minutes; turn and bake 3 minutes longer or until crisp. Set aside.

2 In a food processor, process the beans until smooth. In a saucepan, combine the beans, 1 teaspoon chili powder, 1/2 teaspoon cumin and salsa; bring to a boil. Remove from the heat; set aside. Sprinkle chicken with remaining chili powder and cumin. In a skillet coated with nonstick cooking spray, cook chicken over medium heat for 5 minutes or until juices run clear, stirring constantly.

3 Spread bean mixture over tortillas to within 1/2 in. of edges. Top with chicken, tomatoes, onion and cheese. Bake at 350° for 2 minutes or until cheese is melted. Top with romaine. Serve with sour cream if desired. **Yield:** 6 servings.

Turkey Schnitzel

Our family was fortunate to have lived in Europe for 11 years. This is by far our two sons' all-time favorite recipe. Typically in Germany and Austria, schnitzel is served with French fries and lemon wedges—the lemon is for squeezing lemon juice onto the breaded cutlets. In Europe I used veal, but now that we are back home, I find that turkey slices are a great substitute.   —Sue A. Jurack

1/4 cup milk
1/2 cup all-purpose flour
  2 eggs, beaten
3/4 cup seasoned bread crumbs

1 pound turkey slices (1/4 inch thick)
2 tablespoons butter
2 tablespoons canola oil

1 Place the milk, flour, eggs and bread crumbs in four separate shallow bowls. Dip turkey slices into milk, then coat with flour. Dip into eggs and coat with bread crumbs. Place on waxed paper; let stand for 5-10 minutes.

2 In a large skillet, heat butter and oil over medium-high heat. Brown turkey slices for 2 minutes on each side or until juices run clear. **Yield:** 4 servings.

TEST KITCHEN TIP

Letting the breaded cutlets stand for 5-10 minutes helps the coating stay on during cooking.

Roasted Chicken with Rosemary

I've found no better way to serve a special Sunday dinner than with this well-seasoned roasted chicken. —*Karen Johnson*

1/2 cup butter, melted
2 tablespoons dried rosemary, crushed
2 tablespoons minced fresh parsley
3 garlic cloves, minced
1 teaspoon salt
1/2 teaspoon pepper
1 whole roasting chicken (5 to 7 pounds)
8 small red potatoes, halved
6 carrots, cut into 2-inch pieces and halved lengthwise
2 medium onions, quartered

1 In a small bowl, combine the butter, rosemary, parsley, garlic, salt and pepper. Place chicken breast side up on a rack in a roasting pan. Spoon half of the butter mixture over chicken. Place the potatoes, carrots and onions around chicken; drizzle with remaining butter mixture.

2 Cover and bake at 350° for 1-1/4 hours, basting every 30 minutes. Uncover; bake 1 hour longer or until juices run clear and a meat thermometer inserted into thigh reads 180°, basting frequently. Cover and let stand for 10 minutes before carving. If desired, thicken pan drippings for gravy. **Yield:** 6 servings.

Chicken and Rice Dinner

This is one of my husband's favorite dishes—it's hearty, filling and tastes fantastic. The chicken bakes to a beautiful golden brown.
—*Megan Taylor*

4 boneless skinless chicken breast halves
1/4 to 1/3 cup all-purpose flour
2 tablespoons vegetable oil
2-1/3 cups water
1-1/2 cups uncooked long grain rice
1 cup milk
1 teaspoon poultry seasoning
1 teaspoon salt
1/2 teaspoon pepper
Minced fresh parsley

1 Coat chicken pieces with flour. In a large skillet, brown chicken in oil on both sides. In a bowl, combine the water, rice, milk, poultry seasoning, salt and pepper. Pour into a greased 13-in. x 9-in. x 2-in. baking dish. Top with chicken.

2 Cover tightly with foil. Bake at 350° for 35-45 minutes or until rice and chicken are tender. Sprinkle with parsley. **Yield:** 4-6 servings.

TEST KITCHEN TIP
Keep a package of frozen cubed cooked chicken on hand for those days when you're in a hurry to put together a casserole. Or use cans of boneless chunk chicken.

Phyllo Chicken Packets

I used to make this special recipe when I ran my own catering company years ago. It was often requested.
—Kristin Arnett

3/4 cup chopped green onions
3/4 cup mayonnaise
3 tablespoons lemon juice
1-1/2 teaspoons minced garlic, *divided*
1/2 teaspooon dried tarragon
2/3 cup butter, melted
12 sheets phyllo dough (18 inches x 14 inches)
6 boneless skinless chicken breast halves
Salt and pepper to taste
2 tablespoons grated Parmesan cheese

1 In a small bowl, combine the onions, mayonnaise, lemon juice, 1 teaspoon garlic and tarragon; set aside. In another small bowl, combine the butter and remaining garlic.

2 Place one sheet of phyllo dough on a work surface with a short edge facing you. Evenly brush with 2 teaspoons garlic butter. Top with a second sheet of phyllo, brushing with another 2 teaspoons garlic butter. (Keep remaining phyllo dough covered with plastic wrap and a damp towel to prevent drying out.)

3 Lightly sprinkle chicken with salt and pepper. Center one chicken breast half on the lower third of prepared phyllo. Spread about 3 tablespoons mayonnaise mixture over chicken. Fold bottom edge of dough over chicken, then fold in sides. Roll up jelly-roll style; cover with plastic wrap and set aside. Repeat, making five more chicken packets.

4 Place in an ungreased 15-in. x 10-in. x 1-in. baking pan. Brush tops with remaining garlic butter; sprinkle with cheese. Bake, uncovered, at 375° for 25-30 minutes or until a meat thermometer reads 170°. Serve warm. **Yield:** 6 servings.

EDITOR'S NOTE: Reduced-fat or fat-free mayonnaise is not recommended for this recipe.

Chicken Broccoli Casserole

This warm and inviting casserole is real comfort food. Chicken and broccoli are such a pleasing combination.
—Sue Megonigle

3 cups fresh broccoli florets (about 1-1/4 pounds)
2 cups cubed cooked chicken *or* turkey
1 can (10-3/4 ounces) condensed cream of chicken soup, undiluted
1/2 cup mayonnaise
1/2 cup grated Parmesan cheese
1/2 teaspoon curry powder
1 cup cubed fresh bread
2 tablespoons butter, melted

1 Place broccoli and 1 in. of water in a large saucepan. Bring to a boil. Reduce heat; cover and simmer for 5-8 minutes or until crisp-tender. Drain and place in a greased 11-in. x 7-in. x 2-in. baking dish.

2 Combine the chicken, soup, mayonnaise, Parmesan cheese and curry powder; spoon over broccoli. Top with bread cubes and butter. Bake, uncovered, at 350° for 25-30 minutes or until heated through. **Yield:** 6 servings.

EDITOR'S NOTE: Reduced-fat or fat-free mayonnaise is not recommended for this recipe.

Leek and Turkey Pizza

My family enjoys this hearty pizza. I like to make it in the summer when I have leftover grilled sausage. I just dice the grilled sausage and add it to the pizza. —Megan Taylor

2 medium leeks (white portion only), sliced
2 teaspoons olive oil
2 turkey Italian sausage links, casings removed

1 prebaked Italian bread shell crust
1/2 cup pizza sauce
1/4 cup thinly sliced red onion
1/2 cup shredded mozzarella cheese

1 In a large nonstick skillet, cook the leeks in oil over medium heat for 4-5 minutes or until lightly browned, stirring constantly. Remove and set aside. Crumble sausage into the same skillet. Cook over medium heat until no longer pink; drain.

2 Place the crust on an ungreased baking sheet or 12-in. pizza pan. Spread with pizza sauce; top with leeks, sausage, onion and cheese. Bake at 450° for 10 minutes or until cheese just begins to brown. **Yield:** 6 servings.

Skillet Chicken and Vegetables

Red wine vinegar gives this comforting dish a little tang. It's a complete meal made in one skillet. —Janet Briggs

6 cups water
8 pearl onions
2 bacon strips, diced
2 bone-in chicken breast halves (12 ounces *each*), skin removed
2 tablespoons olive oil
1/2 cup quartered fresh mushrooms
1 garlic clove, minced
1 cup plus 2 tablespoons reduced-sodium chicken broth, *divided*
2 tablespoons red wine vinegar
4 small red potatoes, halved
1/2 teaspoon salt, optional
1/8 teaspoon pepper
1 tablespoon all-purpose flour
Minced fresh parsley, optional

1 In a Dutch oven, bring water to a boil. Add onions; boil for 3 minutes. Drain and rinse in cold water; peel and set aside.

2 In a large skillet, cook bacon over medium heat until crisp. Remove to paper towels with a slotted spoon. Discard drippings. In the same skillet, brown chicken on all sides in oil. Remove and set aside.

3 Add mushrooms and garlic; saute until tender. Add 1 cup broth, vinegar, potatoes, salt if desired, pepper and onions. Return chicken to the pan. Bring to a boil. Reduce heat; cover and simmer for 35 minutes or until potatoes are tender and chicken juices run clear.

4 Remove chicken and vegetables and keep warm. Combine flour and remaining broth until smooth; add to cooking juices. Bring to a boil; cook and stir for 2 minutes or until thickened. Pour over chicken and vegetables. Sprinkle with bacon. Garnish with parsley if desired. **Yield:** 2 servings.

Duck a la Orange

My mother-in-law prepared this duck for holidays and other special occasions. My husband loves duck, so I prepare this entree each year for his birthday dinner. The orange concentrate provides great flavor to the serving sauce. I have tried this recipe on wild duck, but we prefer the flavor of domestic ducklings. —Sue A. Jurack

- 1 package (6.2 ounces) fast-cooking long grain and wild rice mix
- 1 domestic duckling (5 to 6 pounds)
- 1/4 cup orange juice concentrate
- 3 tablespoons honey
- 2 tablespoons butter, melted
- 2 tablespoons soy sauce

ORANGE SAUCE:
- 1/4 cup orange juice concentrate
- 1 cup water
- 1 tablespoon cornstarch
- 1 tablespoon cold water
- 1/8 teaspoon salt

1 Prepare rice mix according to package directions. Prick duck skin all over with a fork. Loosely stuff duck with rice. Skewer neck opening; tie drumsticks together with kitchen string. Place breast side up on a rack in a roasting pan Bake, uncovered, at 350° for 1 hour.

2 Combine the orange juice concentrate, honey, butter and soy sauce; baste about 1/4 cup over duck. Bake 1-1/2 to 2 hours longer or until a meat thermometer reads 180° for the duck and 165° for the stuffing, basting occasionally with remaining orange juice mixture.

3 Drain fat from pan as it accumulates. Cover loosely with foil if duck browns too quickly. Cover and let stand for 20 minutes before removing stuffing and carving. Discard any remaining basting sauce.

4 For orange sauce, in a saucepan, combine the orange juice concentrate and water; bring to a boil. Combine cornstarch and cold water until smooth; stir into orange sauce. Cook and stir for 2 minutes or until thickened. Season with salt. Serve with duck. **Yield:** 4-6 servings.

TEST KITCHEN TIP
Piercing the skin with a fork helps to release the fat that is found under the skin.

Caribbean Chicken

Both family and friends love this recipe, so I make it often for them in the warm summer months for a taste of the tropics!
—Wendy Stenman

1/2 cup lemon juice
1/3 cup honey
3 tablespoons canola oil
6 green onions, sliced
3 jalapeno peppers, seeded and chopped
3 teaspoons dried thyme
3/4 teaspoon salt
1/4 teaspoon ground allspice
1/4 teaspoon ground nutmeg
6 boneless skinless chicken breast halves

1 Place the first nine ingredients in a blender or food processor; cover and process until smooth. Reserve 1/2 cup for basting; cover and refrigerate. Pour remaining marinade into a large resealable plastic bag; add chicken. Seal bag and turn to coat; refrigerate for 6 hours or overnight.

2 Coat grill rack with nonstick cooking spray before starting the grill. Drain and discard marinade from chicken. Grill, covered, over medium heat for 4-6 minutes on each side or until juices run clear, basting frequently with reserved marinade. **Yield:** 6 servings.

EDITOR'S NOTE: When cutting or seeding hot peppers, use rubber or plastic gloves to protect your hands. Avoid touching your face.

Chicken with Black Bean Salsa

I like to serve the grilled chicken and salsa with a long grain and wild rice mix on the side. Use a kitchen shears to easily mince the cilantro.
—Karen Scales

1 cup lime juice
2 tablespoons olive oil
2 teaspoons ground cumin
1 teaspoon salt
1 teaspoon dried oregano
1/2 teaspoon pepper
5 boneless skinless chicken breast halves
BLACK BEAN SALSA:
1 can (15 ounces) black beans, rinsed and drained
1 mango, peeled and cubed
1/4 cup minced fresh cilantro
3 tablespoons lime juice
1 tablespoon olive oil
2 teaspoons brown sugar
1 teaspoon chopped jalapeno pepper
Sour cream and lime wedges, optional

1 In a small bowl, combine the first six ingredients; mix well. Pour 2/3 cup marinade into a large resealable plastic bag; add the chicken. Seal bag and turn to coat; refrigerate for 1-2 hours. Cover and refrigerate remaining marinade for basting.

2 For salsa, in a bowl, combine the beans, mango, cilantro, lime juice, oil, brown sugar and jalapeno. Cover and refrigerate.

3 Drain and discard marinade from chicken. Grill, covered, over medium heat 7-8 minutes on each side or until juices run clear, basting occasionally with reserved marinade. Serve with salsa. Garnish with sour cream and lime if desired. **Yield:** 5 servings.

EDITOR'S NOTE: When cutting or seeding hot peppers, use rubber or plastic gloves to protect your hands. Avoid touching your face.

Tender Chicken Nuggets

My kids love these chicken nuggets so much better than the fast food variety! Other parents often ask me for the recipe.
—*Sue Draheim*

1 cup crushed cornflakes
1/2 cup grated Parmesan cheese
1/2 teaspoon salt
1/4 teaspoon pepper
1/8 teaspoon garlic powder

1/4 cup prepared ranch salad dressing
1 pound boneless skinless chicken breasts, cut into 1-inch cubes
Additional ranch dressing

1 In a shallow bowl, combine the first five ingredients. Place dressing in another bowl. Toss chicken cubes in dressing, then roll in cornflake mixture. Place in a greased 11-in. x 7-in. x 2-in. baking pan.

2 Bake, uncovered, at 400° for 12-15 minutes or until juices run clear. Serve with additional dressing for dipping. **Yield:** 4 servings.

Turkey with Cherry Stuffing

If you're tired of the traditional roast turkey, give this recipe a try! Cherries add a bright festive color and flavor that everyone in my family just loves.
—*Rita Krajcir*

3/4 cup chopped celery
1/3 cup chopped onion
2 tablespoons butter
3/4 teaspoon dried thyme
1/4 teaspoon poultry seasoning
5 cups seasoned stuffing cubes
3/4 cup golden raisins
3/4 cup chicken broth
1 can (14-1/2 ounces) pitted tart cherries, drained
1 turkey (10 to 12 pounds)
2 tablespoons vegetable oil

1 In a saucepan, saute celery and onion in butter until tender. Stir in thyme and poultry seasoning. In a large bowl, combine the stuffing, raisins and celery mixture. Add broth and cherries; toss to mix. Loosely stuff turkey just before baking. Skewer openings; tie drumsticks together. Place breast side up on a rack in a roasting pan. Brush with oil.

2 Bake, uncovered, at 325° for 4 to 4-1/2 hours or until a meat thermometer inserted into the thigh reads 180° and into the stuffing reads 165°.

Baste occasionally with pan drippings. Cover loosely with foil if turkey browns too quickly. Cover and let stand for 20 minutes before removing stuffing and carving. If desired, thicken pan drippings for gravy. **Yield:** 10-12 servings (6 cups stuffing).

EDITOR'S NOTE: The stuffing may be prepared as directed and baked separately in a greased 2-qt. baking dish. Cover and bake at 325° for 50-60 minutes. Uncover; bake 10 minutes longer or until lightly browned.

SEAFOOD

Lime Fish Tacos

A quick and easy way to serve fish, these tacos have a wonderful lime flavor.
    —Wendy Stenman

> 1 pound red snapper *or* orange roughy fillets
> 1 garlic clove, minced
> 2 tablespoons butter
> 7 teaspoons lime juice, *divided*
> 1/4 teaspoon white pepper
> 2 tablespoons reduced-fat sour cream
> 2 tablespoons fat-free mayonnaise
> Dash hot pepper sauce
> 7 flour tortillas (8 inches), warmed
> 1 cup shredded lettuce
> 1 cup chopped fresh tomato

1 Remove skin from fish and cut fish into 1-in. cubes. In a nonstick skillet, saute garlic in butter and 5 teaspoons lime juice for 30 seconds. Add fish and pepper. Cook for 6-8 minutes over medium heat until fish flakes easily with a fork.

2 Meanwhile, combine the sour cream, mayonnaise, hot pepper sauce and remaining lime juice. Place a spoonful of fish on each tortilla. Top each with lettuce, tomato and sour cream sauce; fold over. **Yield:** 7 servings.

Seafood Jambalaya

My neighbor always gave me a container of this jambalaya when he made it. My family fought over it. I even made him make it for a Kentucky Derby party I had, and everyone raved.
    —Kristin Arnett

> 1/2 pound fresh mushrooms, sliced
> 3 medium onions, chopped
> 2 medium green peppers, chopped
> 3 celery ribs
> 3 garlic cloves, minced
> 2 tablespoons olive oil
> 1 package (16 ounces) fully cooked smoked sausage, cubed
> 1 pound cooked large shrimp, peeled and deveined
>
> 1 pound frozen cooked crawfish tail meat, thawed
> 1 can (14-1/2 ounces) chicken broth
> 1 can (14-1/2 ounces) diced tomatoes
> 2 tablespoons Worcestershire sauce
> 2 tablespoons Cajun seasoning
> 1 to 3 teaspoons hot pepper sauce
> 1/4 teaspoon white pepper
> 4 cups cooked long grain white rice

1 In a large Dutch oven, saute the mushrooms, onions, pepper, celery and garlic in oil. Add the sausage, shrimp, crawfish, broth, tomatoes, seasonings and rice.

2 Bake, uncovered, at 325° for 45 minutes or until heated through, stirring after 20 minutes. **Yield:** 8-10 servings.

TEST KITCHEN TIP
You can use cooked chicken, crab and ham in place of the crawfish and shrimp.

Seafood Pizza

(Pictured on page 152)

This fun pizza has a white sauce versus a red pizza sauce. It's creamy and saucy. The seafood is a different twist for a pizza topping. —Amy Welk-Thieding

1 package (6-1/2 ounces) pizza crust mix
3 tablespoons butter, *divided*
2 tablespoons all-purpose flour
3/4 cup milk
1/4 cup chicken broth
1/4 cup shredded Monterey Jack cheese
1/4 cup shredded Swiss cheese
1/4 pound uncooked bay scallops, left whole *or* chopped

1/4 pound cooked shrimp, peeled, deveined and left whole *or* chopped
1/4 pound imitation crabmeat, chopped
2 cups (8 ounces) shredded mozzarella cheese
Minced fresh basil *or* paprika, optional

1 Prepare pizza dough according to package directions. Press onto a lightly greased 12-in. pizza pan; build up edges slightly. Prick dough thoroughly with a fork. Bake at 400° for 5-6 minutes or until crust is firm and begins to brown.

2 Meanwhile, in a saucepan, melt 2 tablespoons butter over medium heat. Stir in flour until smooth. Gradually stir in milk and broth. Bring to a boil; cook and stir for 2 minutes or until thickened. Reduce heat; add Monterey Jack and Swiss cheese, stirring until melted. Remove from the heat.

3 In a skillet, melt the remaining butter over medium heat. Add scallops; cook and stir for 3-4 minutes or until firm and opaque. Stir in the shrimp, crab and 3 tablespoons cheese sauce. Remove from the heat.

4 Spread remaining cheese sauce over the crust. Top with the seafood mixture; sprinkle with mozzarella cheese and basil or paprika if desired. Bake at 400° for 13-16 minutes or until golden brown. Let stand for 5-10 minutes before cutting. **Yield:** 8 slices.

Crab-Topped Fish Fillets

In just a few minutes, this fish can be ready for the oven, which makes it a great dish for weeknights. However, it's so elegant and delicious that it is also special enough for company. —Erin Frakes

1 pound sole, orange roughy *or* cod fillets
1 can (6 ounces) crabmeat, drained, flaked and cartilage removed *or* 1 cup imitation crabmeat, chopped
1/2 cup grated Parmesan cheese
1/2 cup mayonnaise
1 teaspoon lemon juice
Paprika, optional
1/3 cup slivered almonds, toasted

1 Place fillets in a greased 8-in. square baking dish. Bake, uncovered, at 350° for 18-22 minutes or until fish flakes easily with a fork. Meanwhile, in a bowl, combine the crab, Parmesan cheese, mayonnaise and lemon juice.

2 Drain cooking juices from baking dish; spoon crab mixture over fillets. Broil 5 in. from the heat for 5 minutes or until topping is lightly browned. Sprinkle with paprika if desired and almonds. **Yield:** 4 servings.

Lemon Herbed Salmon

This salmon dish makes a wonderful weekday dinner. While the salmon bakes, I can make the rest of the meal.
—Diane Werner

2-1/2 cups soft bread crumbs
4 garlic cloves, minced
1/2 cup chopped fresh parsley
6 tablespoons grated Parmesan cheese
1/4 cup chopped fresh thyme *or* 1 tablespoon dried thyme

2 teaspoons grated lemon peel
1/2 teaspoon salt
6 tablespoons butter, melted, *divided*
1 salmon fillet (3 to 4 pounds)

1 In a shallow bowl, combine the bread crumbs, garlic, parsley, cheese, thyme, lemon peel and salt. Add 4 tablespoons butter and toss lightly to coat; set aside.

2 Pat salmon dry. Place skin side down in a greased baking dish. Brush with remaining butter; cover with crumb mixture. Bake at 350° for 20-25 minutes or until salmon flakes easily with a fork. **Yield:** 8 servings.

Crawfish Etoufee

This is a fun and interesting dish to serve when entertaining. For some, it's an introduction to crawfish and Cajun food. Our favorite seafood restaurant features this dish on their menu and it's fabulous!
—Tamra Duncan

1/2 cup butter
1/2 cup plus 2 tablespoons all-purpose flour
1-1/4 cups chopped celery
1 cup chopped green pepper
1/2 cup chopped green onions
1 can (14-1/2 ounces) chicken broth
1 cup water
1/4 cup minced fresh parsley
1 tablespoon tomato paste
1 bay leaf
1/2 teaspoon salt
1/4 teaspoon pepper
1/4 teaspoon cayenne pepper
2 pounds frozen cooked crawfish tail meat, thawed
Hot cooked rice

1 In a heavy skillet or Dutch oven, melt butter; stir in flour. Cook and stir over low heat for about 20 minutes until mixture is a caramel-colored paste. Add the celery, pepper and onions; stir until coated. Add the broth, water, parsley, tomato paste, bay leaf, salt, pepper and cayenne pepper. Bring to a boil.

2 Reduce heat; cover and simmer for 30 minutes, stirring occasionally. Discard bay leaf. Add crawfish and heat through. Serve over rice. **Yield:** 6-8 servings.

TEST KITCHEN TIP:
Sometimes Tamra serves this with cooked penne pasta instead of rice. You can mix it all together or just serve it over the pasta. Also, you can add a bit more tomato paste for a deeper color and more cayenne pepper to raise the heat level.

Catfish Po' Boys

A zesty cornmeal mixture coats catfish strips in these filling sandwiches. —Kris Lehman

2 tablespoons fat-free mayonnaise
1 tablespoon fat-free sour cream
1 tablespoon white wine vinegar
1 teaspoon sugar
2 cups broccoli coleslaw mix
1 pound catfish fillets, cut into 2-1/2-inch strips
2 tablespoons fat-free milk
1/4 cup cornmeal
2 teaspoons Cajun seasoning
1/2 teaspoon salt
1/8 teaspoon cayenne pepper
2 teaspoons olive oil
4 kaiser rolls, split

1 In a small bowl, whisk the mayonnaise, sour cream, vinegar and sugar until smooth. Add coleslaw mix; toss. Set aside.

2 In a shallow bowl, toss the catfish with milk. In a large resealable plastic bag, combine cornmeal, Cajun seasoning, salt and cayenne. Add catfish, a few pieces at a time, and shake to coat.

3 In a large nonstick skillet, heat oil over medium heat. Cook catfish for 4-5 minutes on each side or until fish flakes easily with a fork and coating is golden brown. Spoon coleslaw onto rolls; top with catfish. **Yield:** 4 servings.

Basil Parmesan Shrimp

This recipe is a nice and light way to serve shrimp. The basil adds a sweet taste, while the vinegar gives it just a little tang. —Rita Krajcir

1/2 cup olive oil, *divided*
1/4 cup minced fresh basil
1 tablespoon white vinegar
1 tablespoon plus 1/2 cup grated Parmesan cheese, *divided*
1/2 teaspoon sugar
1 pound large uncooked shrimp, peeled and deveined
1/4 cup butter
Lettuce leaves

1 For dressing, combine 1/4 cup oil, basil, vinegar, 1 tablespoon Parmesan and sugar in a saucepan over low heat. Meanwhile, combine shrimp and remaining Parmesan.

2 In a skillet, heat butter and remaining oil. Add shrimp and saute until shrimp turn pink, about 4 minutes. Drain on paper towels. Serve on lettuce; drizzle with warm dressing. **Yield:** 4-6 servings.

Crawfish Pizza

After they tested this in the Test Kitchen, I took the recipe home to make for a Packer football party. I cut the pizza into wedges to serve as an appetizer. —Megan Taylor

1/2 cup *each* chopped green pepper, onion and green onions
  3 garlic cloves, minced
1/3 cup butter
  1 pound process cheese (Velveeta), cubed
  4 ounces cream cheese, cubed
1/4 cup mayonnaise
  1 tablespoon Worcestershire sauce
  1 teaspoon dried parsley flakes
1/2 to 1 teaspoon hot pepper sauce
1/2 teaspoon *each* cayenne pepper, pepper and Cajun seasoning
  2 pounds frozen cooked crawfish tail meat, thawed
Vegetable oil for frying
 10 flour tortillas (8 inches)
  2 cups (8 ounces) shredded Mexican cheese blend *or* cheddar cheese

1 In a large skillet, saute green pepper, onions and garlic in butter until tender. Reduce heat to low. Add the process cheese, cream cheese and mayonnaise; cook and stir until melted. Stir in the Worcestershire sauce, parsley, hot pepper sauce and seasonings. Cook until slightly thickened. Add crawfish. Bring to a boil. Reduce heat; simmer, uncovered, for 10-15 minutes until heated through.

2 Meanwhile, heat oil in a skillet. Fry each tortilla for 1-2 minutes on each side or until browned. Drain on paper towels. Spread 1/2 cup crawfish mixture on each tortilla. Sprinkle with cheese. Place on ungreased baking sheets. Bake at 350° for 4-5 minutes or until cheese is melted. **Yield:** 10 servings.

EDITOR'S NOTE: Reduced-fat or fat-free mayonnaise may not be substituted for regular mayonnaise in this recipe.

TEST KITCHEN TIP
Two pounds of frozen salad shrimp can be substituted for the crawfish.

Cajun Baked Catfish

This is our favorite way to serve catfish. I've made this with half of the spices at first. When my family got older, I doubled the spices. —Wendy Stenman

  2 tablespoons canola oil
  2 teaspoons garlic salt
  2 teaspoons dried thyme
  2 teaspoons paprika
1/2 teaspoon cayenne pepper
1/2 teaspoon hot pepper sauce
1/4 teaspoon pepper
  4 catfish fillets (about 8 ounces *each*)

1 In a small bowl, combine the first seven ingredients; brush over both sides of fish.

2 Place fish in a 13-in x 9-in x 2-in. baking dish coated with nonstick cooking spray. Bake at 450° for 10-13 minutes or until fish flakes easily with a fork. **Yield:** 4 servings.

Firecracker Salmon Steaks

(Pictured on page 153)

As a salmon fisherman, this is one of the recipes I recommend to my fishing buddies and family. Fillets can be easily substituted for the steaks. —Mark Morgan

1/4 cup balsamic vinegar
1/4 cup chili sauce
1/4 cup packed brown sugar
3 garlic cloves, minced
2 teaspoons minced fresh parsley

1 teaspoon minced fresh gingerroot
1/4 to 1/2 teaspoon cayenne pepper
1/4 to 1/2 teaspoon crushed red pepper flakes, optional
4 salmon steaks (about 8 ounces *each*)

1 In a small bowl, combine the first eight ingredients. If grilling the salmon, coat the grill rack with nonstick cooking spray before starting the grill.

2 Grill salmon, uncovered, over medium heat or broil 4-6 in. from the heat for 4-5 minutes on each side or until fish flakes easily with a fork, brushing occasionally with sauce. **Yield:** 4 servings.

Seafood Lasagna

A different way to serve seafood, this lasagna is rich, creamy and very satisfying. —Janaan Cunningham

1 green onion, finely chopped
2 tablespoons vegetable oil
2 tablespoons plus 1/2 cup butter, *divided*
1/2 cup chicken broth
1 bottle (8 ounces) clam juice
1 pound bay scallops
1 pound uncooked small shrimp, peeled and deveined
1 package (8 ounces) imitation crabmeat, chopped
1/4 teaspoon white pepper, *divided*
1/2 cup all-purpose flour
1-1/2 cups milk
1/2 teaspoon salt
1 cup heavy whipping cream
1/2 cup shredded Parmesan cheese, *divided*
9 lasagna noodles, cooked and drained

1 In a large skillet, saute onion in oil and 2 tablespoons butter until tender. Stir in broth and clam juice; bring to a boil. Add the scallops, shrimp, crab and 1/8 teaspoon pepper; return to a boil. Reduce heat; simmer, uncovered, for 4-5 minutes or until shrimp turn pink and scallops are firm and opaque, stirring gently. Drain, reserving cooking liquid; set seafood mixture aside.

2 In a saucepan, melt the remaining butter; stir in flour until smooth. Combine milk and reserved cooking liquid; gradually add to the saucepan. Add salt and remaining pepper. Bring to a boil; cook and stir for 2 minutes or until thickened. Remove from the heat; stir in cream and 1/4 cup Parmesan cheese. Stir 3/4 cup white sauce into the seafood mixture.

3 Spread 1/2 cup white sauce in a greased 13-in. x 9-in. x 2-in. baking dish. Top with three noodles; spread with half of the seafood mixture and 1-1/4 cups sauce. Repeat layers. Top with remaining noodles, sauce and Parmesan. Bake, uncovered, at 350° for 35-40 minutes or until golden brown. Let stand for 15 minutes before cutting. **Yield:** 12 servings.

Crumb-Topped Scallops

The scallops are so moist and tender cooked in the microwave oven. A pretty crumb topping blankets this tasty seafood entree.
—*Karen Scales*

1/4 cup dry bread crumbs
1 tablespoon butter, melted
1 to 2 teaspoons dried parsley flakes
1 pound sea scallops
6 fresh mushrooms, quartered
1 tablespoon white wine
1-1/2 teaspoons lemon juice
1/4 teaspoon dried thyme
1/8 teaspoon garlic powder
1/8 teaspoon seasoned salt
1/8 teaspoon pepper
Lemon wedges, optional

1 In a small bowl, combine the bread crumbs, butter and parsley; set aside. Place scallops and mushrooms in a 9-in. microwave-safe pie plate. Combine the wine, lemon juice and seasonings; pour over scallop mixture.

2 Cover and microwave at 50% power for 2 minutes; drain. Sprinkle with crumb mixture. Cover and microwave at 50% power 3-4 minutes longer or until scallops are opaque, stirring once. Serve with lemon if desired. **Yield:** 4 servings.

EDITOR'S NOTE: This recipe was tested in a 1,100-watt microwave.

Spicy Shrimp Wraps

This is a very different way to serve shrimp, but one that my family loves. The recipe is quick and easy. Coated with taco seasoning, the cooked shrimp are tucked inside a tortilla wrap, along with coleslaw and dressed-up bottled salsa.
—*Wendy Stenman*

1 cup salsa
1 medium ripe mango, peeled, pitted and diced
1 tablespoon ketchup
1 envelope reduced-sodium taco seasoning
1 tablespoon olive oil
1 pound uncooked medium shrimp, peeled and deveined
6 flour tortillas (8 inches), warmed
1-1/2 cups coleslaw mix
6 tablespoons reduced-fat sour cream

1 In a small bowl, combine the salsa, mango and ketchup; set aside. In a large resealable plastic bag, combine taco seasoning and oil; add shrimp. Seal bag and shake to coat. In a nonstick skillet or wok, cook shrimp over medium-high heat for 2-3 minutes or until shrimp turn pink.

2 Top tortillas with coleslaw mix, salsa mixture and shrimp. Fold bottom third of tortilla up over filling; fold sides over. Serve with sour cream. **Yield:** 6 servings.

TEST KITCHEN TIP
Save a little money by shredding cabbage and carrots yourself instead of buying coleslaw mix.

Coconut Fried Shrimp

I surprised my husband with this flavorful crisp dish on his birthday a number of years ago. He now requests it often.
—*Patricia Schmeling*

1-1/4 cups all-purpose flour
1-1/4 cups cornstarch
6-1/2 teaspoons baking powder
  1/2 teaspoon salt
  1/4 teaspoon Cajun seasoning
1-1/2 cups cold water
  1/2 teaspoon vegetable oil
    1 pound uncooked large shrimp, peeled and deveined
2-1/2 cups flaked coconut
Additional oil for deep-fat frying
    1 cup orange marmalade
  1/4 cup honey

1 In a small bowl, combine the first five ingredients. Stir in water and oil until smooth. Dip shrimp into batter, then coat with coconut.

2 In an electric skillet or deep-fat fryer, heat oil to 375°. Fry shrimp, a few at a time, for 3 minutes or until golden brown. Drain on paper towels.

3 In a saucepan, heat marmalade and honey; stir until blended. Serve as a dipping sauce for the shrimp. **Yield:** 3-4 servings.

TEST KITCHEN TIP
Only fry two to three shrimp at a time or the temperature of the oil will lower and the shrimp will not be crisp.

Asparagus Crab Quiche

This easy-to-make dish gets compliments—and recipe requests—every time I serve it. It makes such a pretty presentation.
—*Sarah Thompson*

3/4 pound fresh asparagus, cut into 2-inch pieces
  1 unbaked pastry shell (9 inches)
  1 can (6 ounces) crabmeat, drained, flaked and cartilage removed
  1 cup (4 ounces) shredded Swiss cheese
  1 tablespoon all-purpose flour
  3 eggs, beaten
1-1/2 cups half-and-half cream
  1/2 teaspoon salt
  3 drops hot pepper sauce
  2 tablespoons grated Parmesan cheese
  8 fresh asparagus spears for garnish

1 Place asparagus in a large saucepan with enough water to cover; bring to a boil. Reduce heat; cover and simmer for 3-5 minutes or until crisp-tender. Drain well and pat dry. Arrange cooked asparagus over bottom of pastry. Top with crab. Combine Swiss cheese and flour; sprinkle over crab.

2 In a small bowl, combine the eggs, cream, salt and hot pepper sauce. Pour into pastry. Sprinkle with Parmesan cheese. Arrange asparagus spears in a spoke fashion on top of quiche. Bake at 350° for 35-40 minutes. Let stand for 5 minutes before cutting. **Yield:** 6 servings.

Crab Cakes with Red Pepper Sauce

Don't forget to have lemons on hand so you and your guests can squeeze some fresh lemon juice over these succulent crab cakes.
—*Joylyn Trickel*

  1/4 cup mayonnaise
  1/4 cup chopped fresh chives
    2 tablespoons minced fresh parsley
    1 tablespoon lemon juice
  1/2 teaspoon seafood seasoning
  1/8 teaspoon cayenne pepper
Dash pepper
    1 pound lump crabmeat, cartilage removed
    4 to 5 slices French bread (1 inch thick), crust removed
RED PEPPER SAUCE:
  1/2 cup chopped sweet red pepper
  1/4 cup chopped green onions
  1/4 cup Dijon mustard
  1/4 cup mayonnaise
    2 tablespoons minced shallots
    2 tablespoons minced fresh parsley
    2 tablespoons honey
    1 tablespoon lemon juice
Salt and pepper to taste
    2 tablespoons butter
    1 tablespoon olive oil
Lemon wedges

1 In a large bowl, combine the first seven ingredients; stir in crab. In a food processor or blender, process bread slices, a few at a time, until fine crumbs form (total volume should be 2-1/2 cups). Add 1 cup to the crab mixture; mix well.

2 Shape 1/4 cupfuls of crab mixture into patties. Coat both sides of patties with remaining bread crumbs, pressing to adhere. Place on a baking sheet; cover and refrigerate for up to 6 hours.

3 Meanwhile, for sauce, in a blender or food processor, combine the red pepper, onions, mustard, mayonnaise, shallots, parsley, honey, lemon juice, salt and pepper; cover and process until finely chopped. Refrigerate until serving.

4 In a large skillet, melt half of butter and half of oil. Place half of the crab cakes in skillet. Cook over medium heat for 5 minutes on each side or until lightly browned (carefully turn the delicate cakes over). Repeat with remaining butter, oil and crab cakes. Serve with sauce and lemon wedges. **Yield:** 10 servings.

TEST KITCHEN TIP
Chilling these delicate crab cakes makes them less fragile during frying.

Zippy Coconut Baked Fish

This fish dish bakes in minutes. The flavors blend well, and the chutney adds a zest to the dipping sauce.
—*Patricia Schmeling*

1/3 cup butter, melted
3 tablespoons orange juice
2 tablespoons lemon juice
2 teaspoons garlic powder
2 teaspoons ground ginger
1 to 2 teaspoons crushed red pepper flakes
1/2 teaspoon salt
1/2 teaspoon pepper
1-1/2 cups flaked coconut

1 cup dry bread crumbs
8 fresh red snapper, bass *or* turbot fillets
(6 ounces *each*)
CHUTNEY SAUCE:
1/2 cup mayonnaise
1/4 cup mango chutney
1 tablespoon lemon juice
1 teaspoon curry powder

1 In a shallow bowl, combine the first eight ingredients. In another shallow bowl, combine coconut and bread crumbs. Dip fillets in butter mixture, then coat with coconut mixture. Transfer to 15-in. x 10-in. x 1-in. baking pan coated with nonstick cooking spray.

2 Bake at 425° for 15-20 minutes or until fish flakes easily with a fork. Meanwhile, in a small bowl, combine the sauce ingredients. Serve with fish. **Yield:** 8 servings.

TEST KITCHEN TIP
Because fish fillets vary in thickness, the baking time may vary depending on what type of fish you use.

Clam Fritters

We like clams, so these fritters are a special treat at our house. They're even more delicious when dipped in tartar sauce.
—*Janaan Cunningham*

2/3 cup all-purpose flour
1 teaspoon baking powder
1/4 teaspoon salt
1/8 teaspoon pepper
1 can (6-1/2 ounces) minced clams
1 egg
3 tablespoons milk
1/3 cup diced onion
Vegetable oil for deep-fat frying
Tartar sauce *and/or* lemon wedges, optional

1 In a small bowl, combine the flour, baking powder, salt and pepper; set aside. Drain clams, reserving 2 tablespoons juice; set clams aside. In another small bowl, beat the egg, milk and reserved clam juice; stir into dry ingredients just until moistened. Add the clams and onion.

2 In an electric skillet or deep-fat fryer, heat oil to 375°. Drop batter by tablespoonfuls into oil. Fry for 2-3 minutes, turning occasionally, until golden brown. Drain on paper towels. Serve with tartar sauce and/or lemon if desired. **Yield:** 14-16 fritters.

Stir-Fried Scallops

Scallops cook up quickly in this colorful one-skillet dish, which is ideal to make on a hectic week-night. Try serving the saucy mixture over angel hair pasta or rice. —Sue Myers

1 small onion, chopped
3 garlic cloves, minced
1 tablespoon olive oil
3/4 pound sea scallops, halved
2 medium plum tomatoes, chopped

2 tablespoons lemon juice
1/4 teaspoon salt
1/8 teaspoon pepper
Hot cooked pasta *or* rice, optional

1 In a nonstick skillet or wok, stir-fry onion and garlic in hot oil until tender. Add scallops; stir-fry until scallops turn opaque. Add tomatoes; cook and stir 1-2 minutes longer until heated through.

2 Stir in the lemon juice, salt and pepper. Serve over pasta or rice if desired. **Yield:** 2 servings.

SUE MYERS

A Reiman Publications employee for 14 years, Sue brings a creative flair to whatever she does—whether it's fixing one of her favorite foods (salads and cookies) or putting together a quick dinner so she and her husband can get outdoors with their three dogs or do some gardening. When Sue is not managing her busy schedule at work, she enjoys tackling a remodeling project at home.

Salmon Loaf

Folding the beaten egg whites into the salmon mixture makes the meat loaf texture light and airy. —Janet Briggs

1 small onion, finely chopped
1 can (14-3/4 ounces) salmon, drained, bones and skin removed
1/2 cup soft bread crumbs
1/4 cup butter, melted
3 eggs, *separated*
2 teaspoons lemon juice
1 teaspoon minced fresh parsley
1/2 teaspoon salt
1/8 teaspoon pepper
OLIVE CREAM SAUCE:
2 tablespoons butter
2 tablespoons all-purpose flour
1-1/2 cups milk
1/4 cup chopped stuffed olives

1 In a large bowl, combine the first four ingredients. Stir in the egg yolks, lemon juice, parsley, salt and pepper. In a small mixing bowl, beat the egg whites on high speed until stiff peaks form. Fold into salmon mixture. Pour into a greased 8-in. x 4-in. x 2-in. loaf pan. Place loaf pan in a larger baking pan. Add 1 in. of hot water to larger pan.

2 Bake at 350° for 40-45 minutes or until a knife inserted near the center comes out clean. Let stand for 10 minutes before slicing.

3 Meanwhile, in a saucepan, melt the butter. Stir in flour until smooth; gradually add the milk. Bring to a boil; cook and stir for 1 minute or until thickened. Stir in olives. Serve over the salmon loaf. **Yield:** 4 servings.

Bayou Country Seafood Casserole

The rich flavor and abundance of seafood make this a very special casserole, which is suitable for company.
—Sue Draheim

1 medium onion, chopped
1 medium green pepper, chopped
1 celery rib, chopped
1 garlic clove, minced
6 tablespoons butter
1 can (10-3/4 ounces) condensed cream of mushroom soup, undiluted
1 pound uncooked shrimp, peeled and deveined
1-1/2 cups cooked rice
2 cans (6 ounces *each*) crabmeat, drained, flaked and cartilage removed

4 slices day-old bread, cubed
3/4 cup half-and-half cream
1/4 cup chopped green onion tops
1/2 teaspoon salt
1/4 teaspoon pepper
Dash cayenne pepper
TOPPING:
2 tablespoons butter, melted
1/3 cup dry bread crumbs
2 tablespoons fresh parsley, minced

1 In a large skillet, saute the onion, green pepper, celery and garlic in butter until tender. Add soup and shrimp. Cook and stir over medium heat for 10 minutes or until shrimp turn pink. Stir in the rice, crab, bread cubes, cream, onion tops and seasonings.

2 Spoon into a greased 2-qt. baking dish. Combine topping ingredients; sprinkle over top. Bake, uncovered, at 375° for 25-30 minutes or until heated through. **Yield:** 8 servings.

Fish Italiano

The tomatoes, olives and parsley really dress up the mild flavored cod in this Italian-style dish.
—Janet Briggs

2 tablespoons chopped onion
1 garlic clove, minced
1 tablespoon olive oil
1 cup canned Italian diced tomatoes, drained
1/4 cup white wine
1/4 cup sliced ripe olives
1-1/2 teaspoons minced fresh parsley
1/4 teaspoon salt
1/2 pound cod, haddock *or* orange roughy fillets

1 In a skillet, saute the onion and garlic in oil until tender. Stir in the tomatoes, wine, olives, parsley and salt. Bring to a boil. Cook, uncovered, for 5 minutes.

2 Add fillets. Reduce heat; cover and simmer for 12-15 minutes or until fish flakes easily with a fork. Remove fish to serving plates; keep warm. Simmer sauce, uncovered, for about 4 minutes or until it reaches desired thickness. **Yield:** 2 servings.

Eggs *and* & Cheese

Sausage Garden Quiche

Additional veggies can be added in place of the sausage to make this a hearty vegetarian quiche. —*Megan Taylor*

Pastry for single-crust pie (9 inches)
    5 eggs
    3/4 cup milk
    1/2 cup chopped fresh spinach *or* Swiss chard
    1/3 cup shredded cheddar cheese
    1 tablespoon dried minced onion
    1 tablespoon minced chives
    1/8 teaspoon salt
    1/8 teaspoon garlic powder
Dash pepper
    6 brown-and-serve sausage links
    3 slices fresh tomato, halved

1 Line a 9-in. pie plate with pastry. Trim to 1/2 in. beyond edge of plate; flute edges. Line unpricked pastry shell with a double thickness of heavy-duty foil. Bake at 450° for 8 minutes. Remove foil; bake 5 minutes longer. Cool on a wire rack.

2 In a bowl, whisk eggs and milk. Stir in the spinach, cheese, onion, chives, salt, garlic powder and pepper. Carefully pour into crust. Cook sausage according to package directions. Arrange sausage in a spoke pattern in egg mixture; place tomato slices between links.

3 Bake, uncovered, at 350° for 30-35 minutes or until a knife inserted near the center comes out clean. Let stand for 10 minutes before cutting. **Yield:** 6 servings.

Strawberry French Toast

I served this one year to friends for Easter brunch and everyone loved it, so I've made it year-round since then! —*Patricia Schmeling*

    1 loaf (1 pound) unsliced French bread
    1 carton (8 ounces) spreadable strawberry cream cheese
    4 eggs
    1 cup milk
    3/4 cup sugar, *divided*

    1/4 teaspoon salt
    1/4 teaspoon ground cinnamon
    4 cups fresh strawberries, *divided*
    2 tablespoons amaretto *or* 1/4 teaspoon almond extract
    2 tablespoons butter, melted

1 Cut bread into 3/4-in. slices; spread 12 slices with about 1 tablespoon cream cheese. Top with another 12 slices to form sandwiches. Place in a greased 13-in. x 9-in. x 2-in. baking dish.

2 In a bowl, whisk eggs, milk, 1/4 cup sugar and salt; pour over sandwiches. Sprinkle with cinnamon. Cover and refrigerate for 8 hours or overnight.

3 Chop 1 cup strawberries; place in a small bowl. Stir in amaretto or extract and remaining sugar. Cover and refrigerate until serving.

4 Remove French toast from the refrigerator 30 minutes before baking. Brush bread with butter. Bake, uncovered, at 400° for 25-30 minutes or until golden brown.

5 Meanwhile, slice remaining strawberries; stir into chilled strawberry mixture. Serve over French toast. **Yield:** 6 servings.

Ham 'n' Cheese Omelet Roll

(Pictured on page 168)

This is an impressive-looking and great-tasting egg dish. It has wonderful ingredients all rolled up into one delicious omelet.
—*Peggy Fleming*

4 ounces cream cheese, softened	2 tablespoons Dijon mustard
3/4 cup milk	2-1/4 cups shredded cheddar *or* Swiss cheese, *divided*
2 tablespoons all-purpose flour	
1/4 teaspoon salt	2 cups finely chopped fully cooked ham
12 eggs	1/2 cup thinly sliced green onions

1 Line the bottom and sides of a greased 15-in. x 10-in. x 1-in. baking pan with parchment paper; grease the paper and set aside. In a small mixing bowl, beat cream cheese and milk until smooth. Add flour and salt; mix until combined. In a large mixing bowl, beat the eggs until blended. Add cream cheese mixture; mix well. Pour into prepared pan.

2 Bake at 375° for 30-35 minutes or until eggs are puffed and set. Remove from the oven. Immediately spread with mustard and sprinkle with 1 cup cheese. Sprinkle with ham, onions and 1 cup cheese.

3 Roll up from a short side, peeling parchment paper away while rolling. Sprinkle top of roll with the remaining cheese; bake 3-4 minutes longer or until cheese is melted. **Yield:** 12 servings.

TEST KITCHEN TIP

Grease the parchment paper well and be patient when rolling the cooked egg and peeling off the parchment. You'll be left with a great-looking pinwheel.

Pepperoni Cheese Bake

My husband requests this all the time! Often I bake one on the weekend and use it for a quick breakfast during the week. It calls for just a handful of ingredients and is so quick to make.
—*Suzanne Kern*

2 cups (8 ounces) shredded mozzarella cheese
1/2 cup diced pepperoni
5 eggs
3/4 cup milk
1/4 teaspoon dried basil

1 In a greased 9-in. pie plate, layer the mozzarella cheese and pepperoni. In a bowl, whisk the eggs, milk and basil; pour over the top.

2 Bake at 400° for 20-25 minutes or until a knife inserted near the center comes out clean. Let stand for 10 minutes before cutting. **Yield:** 6-8 servings.

Hearty Egg Casserole

The name of this recipe says it all! The stick-to-your-ribs country breakfast keeps you going all morning long. —*Sarah Thompson*

- 1 pound bulk pork sausage
- 1/2 cup chopped onion
- 1-1/2 cups (6 ounces) shredded cheddar cheese, *divided*
- 1 package (10 ounces) frozen chopped spinach, thawed and well drained
- 1 jar (4-1/2 ounces) sliced mushrooms, drained
- 12 eggs
- 2 cups heavy whipping cream
- 1/4 teaspoon ground nutmeg

1 In a large skillet, cook sausage and onion over medium heat until meat is no longer pink; drain. Remove from the heat; stir in 1 cup cheese, spinach and mushrooms. Pour into a greased 13-in. x 9-in. x 2-in. baking dish. In a bowl, beat the eggs. Add cream and nutmeg; mix well. Pour over sausage mixture.

2 Bake, uncovered, at 350° for 35-40 minutes or until a knife inserted near the center comes out clean. Sprinkle with remaining cheese. Let stand for 5 minutes before cutting. **Yield:** 12 servings.

ANITA BUKOWSKI

With five grown children out of the house, cooking for two has become the order of the day for this empty-nester...but she still loves to prepare crowd-pleasing appetizers and other party foods. Speaking of crowd-pleasers, Anita spent 3 years at our company's Visitor Center baking thousands of cookies for guests to critique for our "Cookie of All Cookies Contest!" She now works part-time and enjoys time off with her seven grandkids.

Asparagus Eggs Benedict

This is a favorite springtime Sunday brunch item in our house. If I'm not in a time crunch, I will make a Hollandaise sauce from scratch. —*Mark Morgan*

- 12 fresh asparagus spears, trimmed and halved
- 1 envelope Hollandaise sauce mix
- 6 eggs
- 3 English muffins, split and toasted
- 1/2 cup shredded Swiss cheese

Paprika

1 Place asparagus in a steamer basket in a large saucepan over 1 in. of water. Bring to a boil; cover and steam for 3-4 minutes or until crisp-tender.

2 Prepare Hollandaise sauce according to package directions. Meanwhile, in a large skillet, bring 2-3 in. of water to a boil. Reduce heat; simmer gently. Break cold eggs, one at a time, into a custard cup or saucer. Holding the dish close to the surface of the water, slip the eggs, one at a time, into the water. Cook, uncovered, for 3-5 minutes or until whites are completely set and yolks begin to thicken. With a slotted spoon, lift each egg out of the water.

3 To assemble, place four pieces of asparagus on each muffin half; top with a poached egg and sprinkle with cheese. Top each with about 3 tablespoons Hollandaise sauce; garnish with paprika. Serve immediately. **Yield:** 6 servings.

Broccoli Quiche Crepe Cups

When I was very young and just learning to cook, this was one of the first recipes I made. I still make these, and my children do, too!
—*Kristin Arnett*

1-1/2 cups milk
   3 eggs
   1 cup all-purpose flour
 1/4 teaspoon salt
   1 to 2 tablespoons butter, melted
FILLING:
   1 package (10 ounces) frozen broccoli with cheese sauce
   3 bacon strips, diced
 1/2 cup chopped onion
   2 eggs
 1/4 cup milk

1 In a blender, combine the milk, eggs, flour and salt; cover and process until smooth. Let stand for 30 minutes.

2 Heat an 8-in. nonstick skillet; brush with butter. Pour 2-3 tablespoons batter into the center of skillet. Lift and tilt pan to evenly coat bottom. Cook until top appears dry; turn and cook 15-20 seconds longer. Remove to a wire rack. Repeat with remaining batter, adding butter to skillet as needed. When cool, stack crepes with waxed paper in between.

3 Line each of four 6-oz. custard cups with a crepe; set aside. Freeze remaining crepes in a freezer bag, leaving waxed paper between each crepe, for up to 3 months.

4 For filling, cook broccoli according to package directions. Cut up any larger pieces of broccoli. In a microwave-safe bowl, microwave bacon on high for 2 minutes; drain. Add the onion; microwave on high for 3 minutes or until tender. Beat eggs and milk; stir in broccoli mixture and bacon mixture. Spoon into prepared crepe cups.

5 Bake, uncovered, at 350° for 30-35 minutes or until a knife inserted near the center comes out clean. Remove from custard cups and serve immediately. **Yield:** 4 servings.

Corned Beef 'n' Cheese Strata

If you like Reuben sandwiches, you'll love the flavor of this easy-to-prepare strata that's good for any meal of the day.
—*Anita Bukowski*

  10 slices rye bread, cut into 3/4-inch cubes
1-1/2 pounds cooked corned beef, shredded
2-1/2 cups (10 ounces) shredded Swiss cheese
   6 eggs
   3 cups milk
 1/4 teaspoon pepper

1 Place bread cubes in a greased 13-in. x 9-in. x 2-in. baking dish. Sprinkle with the corned beef and cheese. Whisk the eggs, milk and pepper; pour over the top. Cover and refrigerate overnight.

2 Remove strata from the refrigerator 30 minutes before baking. Cover and bake at 350° for 40 minutes. Uncover; bake 10 minutes longer or until a thermometer reads 160°. Let stand for 5-10 minutes before cutting. **Yield:** 9-12 servings.

Bacon Quiche Tarts

This is a fun way to make quiche that people of all ages enjoy. The tarts are a great addition to breakfast or brunch.
—*Karen Scales*

2 packages (3 ounces *each*) cream cheese, softened
5 teaspoons milk
2 eggs
1/2 cup shredded Colby cheese
2 tablespoons chopped green pepper
1 tablespoon finely chopped onion
1 tube (8 ounces) refrigerated crescent rolls
5 bacon strips, cooked and crumbled

1 In a small mixing bowl, beat cream cheese and milk until smooth. Add the eggs, cheese, green pepper and onion; mix well.

2 Separate dough into eight triangles; press onto the bottom and up the sides of greased muffin cups. Sprinkle half of the bacon into cups. Pour egg mixture over bacon; top with remaining bacon. Bake at 375° for 18-22 minutes or until a knife comes out clean. Serve warm. **Yield:** 8 servings.

Sausage 'n' Spinach Eggs

This recipe is also nice prepared with chorizo and cilantro in place of the Italian sausage and oregano.
—*Karen Johnson*

1 pound bulk hot Italian sausage
2 large onions, finely chopped
1/2 pound sliced fresh mushrooms
2 garlic cloves, minced
1/4 teaspoon salt
1/4 teaspoon ground nutmeg
1/4 teaspoon dried oregano
1/4 teaspoon pepper
2 tablespoons olive oil
8 cups torn fresh spinach (about 1/2 pound)
8 eggs
1/4 teaspoon hot pepper sauce
1 cup (4 ounces) shredded Monterey Jack cheese

1 Crumble sausage into a 10-in. ovenproof skillet; cook over medium heat until no longer pink. Drain and set aside. In the same skillet, saute the onions, mushrooms, garlic and seasonings in oil until vegetables are tender. Add spinach in batches; cook over medium-low heat for 3-4 minutes or until spinach begins to wilt.

2 In a large bowl, whisk eggs and hot pepper sauce. Return sausage to skillet; add egg mixture. As eggs set, lift edges, letting uncooked portion flow underneath. Cook until eggs are nearly set, about 8-10 minutes.

3 Meanwhile, preheat broiler. Broil egg mixture 6 in. from the heat for 30-60 seconds or until set. Sprinkle with cheese; broil 30 seconds longer or until melted. Cut into wedges. Serve immediately. **Yield:** 8 servings.

Rich 'n' Cheesy Macaroni

(Pictured on page 169)

The flavors of the three different cheeses blend nicely and put a flavorful twist on traditional macaroni and cheese.
— *Erin Frakes*

2-1/2 cups uncooked elbow macaroni
6 tablespoons butter, *divided*
1/4 cup all-purpose flour
1 teaspoon salt
1 teaspoon sugar
2 cups milk

8 ounces process American cheese, cubed
1-1/3 cups small-curd cottage cheese
2/3 cup sour cream
2 cups (8 ounces) shredded sharp cheddar cheese
1-1/2 cups soft bread crumbs

1 Cook macaroni according to package directions; drain. Place in a greased 2-1/2-qt. baking dish. In a saucepan, melt 4 tablespoons butter. Stir in the flour, salt and sugar until smooth. Gradually stir in milk. Bring to a boil; cook and stir for 2 minutes or until thickened.

2 Reduce heat; add American cheese and stir until melted. Stir in cottage cheese and sour cream. Pour over macaroni. Sprinkle with cheddar cheese. Melt remaining butter and toss with bread crumbs; sprinkle over top. Bake, uncovered, at 350° for 30 minutes or until golden brown. **Yield:** 6-8 servings.

Three-Cheese Souffles

Brunch guests are delighted to see these individual souffles on the table.
— *Coleen Martin*

1/3 cup butter
1/3 cup all-purpose flour
2 cups milk
1 teaspoon Dijon mustard
1/4 teaspoon salt
Dash hot pepper sauce
1-1/2 cups (6 ounces) shredded Swiss cheese
1 cup (4 ounces) shredded cheddar cheese
1/4 cup shredded Parmesan cheese
6 eggs, *separated*
1/2 teaspoon cream of tartar

1 Melt butter in a medium saucepan. Stir in flour. Gradually add the milk, mustard, salt and hot pepper sauce. Bring to a boil; cook and stir for 2 minutes or until thickened. Reduce heat; add cheeses and stir until melted. Remove from the heat and set aside.

2 In a small mixing bowl, beat egg yolks until thick and lemon-colored, about 3-4 minutes. Add 1/3 cup cheese mixture and mix well. Return all to the saucepan; return to the heat and cook for 1-2 minutes. Cool completely, about 30-40 minutes.

3 In another mixing bowl, beat egg whites until soft peaks form. Add cream of tartar; beat until stiff peaks form. Fold into cheese mixture. Pour into ungreased 1-cup souffle dishes or custard cups. Place in a shallow pan. Pour warm water into larger pan to a depth of 1 in. Bake, uncovered, at 325° for 40-45 minutes or until tops are golden brown. Serve immediately. **Yield:** 8 servings.

TEST KITCHEN TIP Unbaked souffles can be made ahead and frozen. Cover each dish or cup with foil and freeze. To bake, remove foil and place frozen souffles in a shallow pan; add warm water to a depth of 1 in. Bake at 325° for 60-65 minutes or until tops are golden brown.

Overnight Caramel French Toast

We often serve this recipe for holiday brunches. It really tastes like fresh caramel rolls. Once you taste it, I bet you'll never serve plain French toast again!
—*Coleen Martin*

1 cup packed brown sugar
1/2 cup butter
2 tablespoons light corn syrup
12 slices bread
1/4 cup sugar

1 teaspoon ground cinnamon, *divided*
6 eggs
1-1/2 cups milk
1 teaspoon vanilla extract

1 In a small saucepan, bring the brown sugar, butter and corn syrup to a boil over medium heat, stirring constantly. Remove from the heat. Pour into a greased 13-in. x 9-in. x 2-in. baking dish. Top with six slices of bread.

2 Combine sugar and 1/2 teaspoon cinnamon; sprinkle half over the bread. Place remaining bread on top. Sprinkle with remaining cinnamon-sugar. In a bowl, whisk the eggs, milk, vanilla and remaining cinnamon; pour over bread. Cover and refrigerate for 8 hours or overnight.

3 Remove French toast from the refrigerator 30 minutes before baking. Bake, uncovered, at 350° for 30-35 minutes. Let stand for 5 minutes before inverting onto a serving plate. **Yield:** 4-6 servings.

TEST KITCHEN TIP
Coleen likes to add 1/2 cup chopped pecans to the brown sugar mixture.

Zucchini Egg Bake

Loaded with zucchini, herbs and cheese, this makes a wonderful brunch dish with slices of toast served on the side.
—*Julie Ferron*

3 cups chopped peeled zucchini
1 large onion, chopped
2 garlic cloves, minced
1/4 cup butter
4 eggs
1/2 cup grated Parmesan cheese
1/4 cup minced fresh parsley
1-1/2 teaspoons minced fresh basil *or* 1/2 teaspoon dried basil
1-1/2 teaspoons minced fresh marjoram *or* 1/2 teaspoon dried marjoram
1/2 teaspoon salt
1/2 cup shredded Monterey Jack cheese

1 In a large skillet, saute the zucchini, onion and garlic in butter until tender; set aside. In a bowl, whisk the eggs, Parmesan cheese, parsley, basil, marjoram and salt. Stir in zucchini mixture and Monterey Jack cheese.

2 Pour into a greased 1-qt. baking dish. Bake at 350° for 20-25 minutes or until a knife inserted near the center comes out clean. Let stand for 5 minutes before serving. **Yield:** 6 servings.

Scrambled Egg Brunch Bread

I like this recipe because it's easy to do and impressive, too—a great combination in a recipe. —*Peggy Fleming*

  2 tubes (8 ounces *each*) refrigerated crescent rolls
  4 ounces thinly sliced deli ham, julienned
  4 ounces cream cheese, softened
1/2 cup milk
  8 eggs
1/4 teaspoon salt
Dash pepper
1/4 cup chopped sweet red pepper
  2 tablespoons chopped green onion
  1 teaspoon butter
1/2 cup shredded cheddar cheese

1 Unroll each tube of crescent dough (do not separate rectangles). Place side by side on a greased baking sheet with long sides touching; seal seams and perforations. Arrange ham lengthwise down center third of rectangle.

2 In a small mixing bowl, beat cream cheese and milk. Separate one egg; set egg white aside. Add the egg yolk, remaining eggs, salt and pepper to cream cheese mixture; mix well. Add red pepper and onion.

3 In a large skillet, melt butter; add egg mixture. Cook and stir over medium heat just until set. Remove from the heat. Spoon scrambled eggs over ham. Sprinkle with cheese.

4 On each long side of dough, cut 1-in.-wide strips to the center to within 1/2 in. of filling. Starting at one end, fold alternating strips at an angle across filling. Pinch ends to seal and tuck under. Beat reserved egg white; brush over dough. Bake at 375° for 25-28 minutes or until golden brown. **Yield:** 6 servings.

Swiss Cheese 'n' Onion Quiche

You can add ham cubes, crumbled cooked bacon or cooked medium shrimp to this quiche if you'd like. They're all delicious additions. —*Janet Briggs*

  3 tablespoons butter, softened, *divided*
  1 unbaked pastry shell (9 inches)
  1 large onion, chopped
  2 cups (8 ounces) shredded Swiss cheese
  1 tablespoon all-purpose flour
  3 eggs
  1 cup half-and-half cream
1/4 teaspoon salt

1 Spread 1 tablespoon butter over bottom of pastry shell; set aside. In a skillet, saute onion in remaining butter until tender. Spread in pastry shell. Toss Swiss cheese with flour; sprinkle over onion. In a bowl, whisk the eggs, cream and salt. Pour evenly over cheese.

2 Bake, uncovered, at 400° for 10 minutes. Reduce heat to 325°; bake 30-35 minutes longer or until a knife inserted near the center comes out clean. Let stand for 10 minutes before cutting. **Yield:** 6-8 servings.

Three-Cheese Pesto Pizza

I like to serve this pizza as either a main dish or appetizer. Either way, folks go back for more! The pesto, cheese and olive topping makes a delicious statement. —*Julie Ferron*

1/2 cup chopped red onion
1/2 cup chopped sweet red pepper
  1 tablespoon olive oil
  1 prebaked Italian bread shell crust (14 ounces)
1/2 cup prepared pesto sauce
1/2 cup chopped ripe olives
  1 cup crumbled feta cheese
  1 cup (4 ounces) shredded mozzarella cheese
  1 cup shredded Parmesan cheese
  2 plum tomatoes, thinly sliced

1 In a large skillet, saute onion and red pepper in oil until tender. Place crust on an ungreased 12-in. pizza pan; spread with pesto. Top with the onion mixture, olives, cheeses and tomatoes.

2 Bake at 400° for 15-20 minutes or until cheese is melted. **Yield:** 4 servings.

Julie Ferron

For Julie, dessert is the "fun" part of a meal, so it's no surprise that all kinds of sweet treats are what she spends most of her time in the kitchen preparing. When her two grown children were young and lived at home, they were "hard to cook for." Julie's own mother, who liked to use canned soup in lots of recipes, could've probably said the same thing about her!

Swiss Cheese Fondue

Our family lived in Switzerland for 8 years, so cheese fondue is not only a Swiss national favorite but ours, too. The Swiss bring slices of French bread to the table, which they break into cubes. Tradition says that the first one to lose his or her bread in the fondue pot buys the first bottle of wine.
—*Sue A. Jurack*

  1 garlic clove, halved
  2 cups dry white wine, *divided*
1/4 teaspoon ground nutmeg

7 cups (28 ounces) shredded Swiss cheese
2 tablespoon cornstarch
Cubed French bread

1 Rub garlic clove over the bottom and sides of a fondue pot; discard garlic and set pot aside. In a large saucepan, bring 1-3/4 cups wine and nutmeg to a simmer over medium-low heat. Gradually add cheese, stirring after each addition until cheese is melted (cheese will separate from wine).

2 Combine cornstarch and remaining wine until smooth; gradually stir into cheese mixture. Cook and stir until mixture comes to a boil. Cook and stir for 1-2 minutes or until thickened and mixture is blended and smooth. Transfer to prepared fondue pot and keep warm. Serve with bread cubes. **Yield:** about 4 cups.

Cheesy Leek Strata

The leeks and sourdough bread cubes make this a delectable variation of strata. —Janet Briggs

- 1 loaf (1 pound) sourdough bread, cut into 1/2-inch cubes
- 2 small leeks (white portion only), chopped
- 1 medium sweet red pepper, chopped
- 1-1/2 cups (6 ounces) shredded Swiss cheese, *divided*
- 1-1/2 cups (6 ounces) shredded cheddar cheese, *divided*
- 8 eggs
- 2 cups milk
- 1/2 cup beer
- 2 garlic cloves, minced
- 1/4 teaspoon salt
- 1/4 teaspoon pepper

1 In a 13-in. x 9-in. x 2-in. baking dish coated with nonstick cooking spray, layer half of the bread cubes, half of the leeks and half of the red pepper, 3/4 cup Swiss cheese and 3/4 cup cheddar cheese. Repeat layers once.

2 In a bowl, whisk the eggs, milk, beer, garlic, salt and pepper. Pour over cheese. Cover with plastic wrap. Weigh strata down with a slightly smaller baking dish. Refrigerate for at least 2 hours or overnight.

3 Remove strata from the refrigerator 30 minutes before baking. Bake, uncovered, at 350° for 40-45 minutes or until center is set and a thermometer reads 160°. Let stand for 5-10 minutes before cutting. **Yield:** 9-12 servings.

Croissant French Toast

This French toast is crisp and served with both vanilla and raspberry sauce. I served this to friends one Easter for brunch and sent a copy of the recipe home with them.
—Patricia Schmeling

- 1/2 cup sugar
- 1 tablespoon all-purpose flour
- 2 cups heavy whipping cream
- 4 egg yolks
- 1 tablespoon vanilla extract
- 1 cup vanilla ice cream

BERRY SAUCE:
- 2 cups unsweetened raspberries
- 2 tablespoons sugar

FRENCH TOAST:
- 3 eggs
- 4 croissants, split
- 2 tablespoons butter

1 In a large saucepan, combine the sugar and flour. Stir in cream until smooth. Cook and stir over medium-high heat until thickened and bubbly. Reduce heat; cook and stir 2 minutes longer. Remove from the heat. Stir a small amount of hot filling into egg yolks; return all to the pan, stirring constantly. Cook and stir until mixture reaches 160°.

2 Remove from the heat. Gently stir in vanilla and ice cream until the ice cream is melted. Place plastic wrap over the surface of the sauce; cool.

3 For berry sauce, combine raspberries and sugar in a saucepan. Simmer, uncovered, for 2-3 minutes. Remove from the heat; set aside.

4 In a shallow bowl, beat eggs. Dip both sides of croissants in egg mixture. On a griddle, brown croissants on both sides in butter. Serve with sauces. **Yield:** 4 servings.

Pasta, Grains *and* Beans

Minty Orzo and Peas

I enjoyed this recipe so much at taste testing that I started making it at home even before it was published in one of the magazines. With its fresh mint taste, it also makes a nice salad served chilled.
—*Janet Briggs*

    1 cup uncooked orzo pasta
    1 small onion, finely chopped
    1 garlic clove, minced
    2 tablespoons butter
    2 cups frozen peas
    1 teaspoon grated lemon peel
1/4 teaspoon salt
1/8 teaspoon pepper
    2 tablespoons finely chopped fresh mint

1 Cook orzo according to package directions; drain and set aside.

2 In a large skillet, saute onion and garlic in butter until tender. Add peas; cook for 2 minutes or until tender. Add the lemon peel, salt, pepper and orzo; heat through. Stir in mint. Serve immediately. **Yield:** 6 servings.

Asian Noodles with Chicken

My family likes to try and use chopsticks when they eat this pasta and chicken stir-fry. It's one of their favorites.
—*Kristin Arnett*

    8 ounces uncooked angel hair pasta
1/3 cup stir-fry sauce
    2 tablespoons honey
1/4 teaspoon crushed red pepper flakes
    1 pound boneless skinless chicken breasts, cut into strips
    1 tablespoon vegetable oil
    1 medium sweet red pepper, julienned
    1 medium onion, cut into thin wedges
    1 tablespoon minced fresh cilantro
    1 to 2 teaspoons sesame oil
    1 tablespoon sesame seeds

1 Cook pasta according to package directions. Meanwhile, in a small bowl, combine the stir-fry sauce, honey and red pepper flakes; set aside.

2 In a large skillet, saute chicken in oil until browned. Add red pepper and onion; cook for 2 minutes or until vegetables are crisp-tender. Stir in sauce mixture. Add cilantro and cook for 1 minute.

3 Drain pasta and toss with sesame oil. Serve chicken mixture over pasta; sprinkle with sesame seeds. **Yield:** 4 servings.

TEST KITCHEN TIP

Kristin sprinkles the pasta with chopped peanuts, too, and occasionally uses Asian egg noodles.

Black Bean Enchiladas

(Pictured on page 180)

My family loves this recipe and so do I. It's quick and easy, so it's great for busy schedules. You can heat up the enchiladas as kids come and go.
—*Wendy Stenman*

1/2 cup chopped onion
1/2 cup chopped green pepper
1 tablespoon olive oil
1 can (16 ounces) vegetarian refried beans
1 can (15 ounces) black beans, rinsed and drained
1-1/2 cups picante sauce, *divided*

12 flour tortillas (6 inches)
2 medium tomatoes, chopped
1/2 cup shredded reduced-fat cheddar cheese
1/2 cup shredded reduced-fat Mexican cheese blend
3 cups shredded lettuce
6 tablespoons fat-free sour cream, optional

1 In a nonstick skillet, saute the onion and green pepper in oil for 2-3 minutes or until tender. Add the refried beans, black beans and 3/4 cup picante sauce; heat through.

2 Spoon 1/4 cupful down the center of each tortilla. Roll up and place seam side down in a 13-in. x 9-in. x 2-in. baking dish coated with nonstick cooking spray. Combine tomatoes and remaining picante sauce; spoon over enchiladas.

3 Cover and bake at 350° for 15 minutes. Uncover; sprinkle with cheeses. Bake 5 minutes longer. Place 1/2 cup lettuce on each plate; top with two enchiladas. Serve with sour cream if desired. **Yield:** 6 servings.

Angel Hair Alfredo

Your family won't believe that this tasty dish takes less than 30 minutes to make.
—*Sue Megonigle*

8 to 12 ounces uncooked angel hair pasta
2 garlic cloves, minced
2 tablespoons olive oil
2 tablespoons all-purpose flour
1 tablespoon cornstarch
1/4 teaspoon garlic salt
1/4 teaspoon pepper
1/4 teaspoon dried basil
1-1/2 cups milk
4 ounces cream cheese, cubed
1/4 cup grated Parmesan cheese
1/3 to 1/2 cup diced fully cooked ham, optional

1 Cook pasta according to package directions. Meanwhile, in a large skillet, saute garlic in oil until lightly browned. Stir in the flour, cornstarch, garlic salt, pepper and basil until blended. Gradually stir in milk. Bring to a boil; cook and stir for 2 minutes or until thickened.

2 Reduce heat; whisk in cream cheese and Parmesan cheese until smooth. Add ham if desired; heat through. Drain pasta; add to sauce and toss to coat. **Yield:** 4-6 servings.

Creamy Cheesy Grits

Rich and creamy, these grits make a great side dish for a Southern-style meal. I make these at my annual Kentucky Derby party.
—Kristin Arnett

- 3 cups reduced-sodium chicken broth
- 2 cups milk
- 1/2 teaspoon salt
- 1 cup quick-cooking grits
- 1 cup (4 ounces) shredded cheddar cheese
- 1/2 cup grated Parmesan cheese
- 1/8 teaspoon white pepper
- 1/8 teaspoon cayenne pepper
- 1/8 teaspoon ground nutmeg, optional

In a large saucepan, bring the broth, milk and salt to a boil. Gradually whisk in grits. Reduce heat to low; cook, uncovered, for 25 minutes or until grits become thick, stirring frequently. Stir in the cheeses, white pepper, cayenne and nutmeg if desired. Serve hot. **Yield:** 8 servings.

Black Bean Lasagna

You won't miss the meat in this flavor-packed black bean lasagna!
—Julie Ferron

- 1 can (15 ounces) black beans, rinsed and drained, *divided*
- 5 tablespoons olive oil, *divided*
- 1 teaspoon salt, *divided*
- 1/2 teaspoon pepper, *divided*
- 1 small onion, chopped
- 4 garlic cloves, minced
- 3/4 cup dry red wine
- 2 cups tomato puree
- 2 cups canned crushed tomatoes
- 1 teaspoon sugar
- 1 teaspoon dried oregano
- 1 bay leaf
- 1 carton (15 ounces) part-skim ricotta cheese
- 1 egg, beaten
- 1/4 cup minced fresh cilantro
- 1 cup grated Parmesan cheese, *divided*
- 9 lasagna noodles, cooked and drained
- 1 pound part-skim mozzarella cheese, thinly sliced

1 In a food processor, puree 1 cup of beans with 2 tablespoons oil, 1/2 teaspoon salt and 1/4 teaspoon pepper; set aside. In a saucepan, cook onion and garlic in remaining oil until tender. Add wine; simmer, uncovered, until most of the liquid has evaporated.

2 Stir in the tomato puree, tomatoes, sugar, oregano, bay leaf, and the remaining black beans, salt and pepper. Simmer, uncovered, for 1 hour, stirring occasionally (do not boil). Discard bay leaf.

3 In a small bowl, combine the ricotta cheese, egg, cilantro and 1/2 cup Parmesan cheese. In a greased 13-in. x 9-in. x 2-in. baking dish, layer three noodles, half of the ricotta mixture and a third of the tomato-bean sauce. Top with a third of the mozzarella; sprinkle with a third of the remaining Parmesan.

4 Top with three noodles; layer with pureed bean mixture and a third each of the tomato-bean sauce, mozzarella and Parmesan. Top with remaining noodles, ricotta mixture, tomato-bean sauce, mozzarella and Parmesan. Bake, uncovered, at 375° for 30-35 minutes or until heated through. Let stand for 10 minutes before cutting. **Yield:** 8 servings.

Confetti Barley Pilaf

This colorful pilaf is a tasty accompaniment to poultry as well as other types of meat. The slightly chewy texture of the barley, the tender vegetables and lively spices make it special enough for company. —Mark Morgan

- 1 large onion, finely chopped
- 1 garlic clove, minced
- 1 tablespoon vegetable oil
- 1 cup medium pearl barley
- 1 cup sliced fresh mushrooms
- 1/2 cup shredded carrot
- 1/2 cup coarsely shredded cabbage
- 1/2 cup chopped sweet red pepper
- 1 teaspoon dried basil
- 1 teaspoon dried oregano
- 2-1/2 cups chicken broth *or* vegetable broth

1 In a large nonstick skillet, saute onion and garlic in oil until tender. Add barley; saute for 3-5 minutes or until lightly browned. Add the mushrooms, carrot, cabbage, red pepper, basil and oregano. Cook and stir until the vegetables are crisp-tender, about 3 minutes.

2 Stir in broth; bring to a boil. Reduce heat; cover and simmer for 40-45 minutes or until the liquid is absorbed and the barley is tender. **Yield:** 6 servings.

Risotto with Asparagus

This is a rich-tasting, elegant dish! It gets great flavor from the onion and wine combination. —Stephanie Marchese

- 1 pound asparagus, trimmed and cut into 2-inch pieces
- 7-1/2 cups chicken broth
- 1/2 cup finely chopped onion
- 1/4 cup olive oil
- 3 cups uncooked arborio rice
- 1 cup dry white wine
- 1 tablespoon butter
- 1/4 cup grated Parmesan cheese
- Salt and pepper to taste

1 Place asparagus in a large saucepan; add 1/2 in. of water. Bring to a boil. Reduce heat; cover and simmer for 3 minutes or until crisp-tender. Drain and set aside.

2 In a large saucepan, bring broth to a boil. Reduce heat; cover and maintain at a simmer. In a large heavy skillet, cook onion in oil over medium heat until tender. Add rice and stir to coat well; cook 3 minutes longer. Add wine and cook until absorbed.

3 Stir in 1 cup simmering broth. Cook until broth is almost completely absorbed, stirring frequently, then add another cup of simmering broth. Repeat until only about 1/4 cup of broth remains (discard remaining broth); the process should take about 20 minutes. Rice should be slightly firm in center and look creamy.

4 Add asparagus; heat through. Remove from the heat; add the butter, Parmesan cheese, salt and pepper. Serve immediately. **Yield:** 12 servings.

Breakfast Rice Pudding

My husband makes this rice pudding quite often for our breakfast.
—*Sue Draheim*

1-1/3 cups uncooked long grain *or* basmati rice
   1 can (16 ounces) peaches, drained and chopped
   1 cup canned *or* frozen pitted tart cherries, drained
   1 cup heavy whipping cream
1/2 cup packed brown sugar, *divided*
1/4 cup old-fashioned oats
1/4 cup flaked coconut
1/4 cup chopped pecans
1/4 cup butter, melted

1 Cook rice according to package directions. In a large bowl, combine the rice, peaches, cherries, cream and 1/4 cup brown sugar. Transfer to a greased 1-1/2-qt. baking dish.

2 Combine the oats, coconut, pecans, butter and remaining brown sugar; sprinkle over rice. Bake, uncovered, at 375° for 25-30 minutes or until golden brown. **Yield:** 8 servings.

Test Kitchen Tip
This recipe is equally good with fresh blueberries instead of the cherries.

Smoked Sausage and Beans

Although this simmers for an hour, it only takes minutes to put together. That hour gives me time to take care of other chores while dinner is cooking. Kielbasa gives the dish a hearty flavor.
—*Kris Lehman*

2 medium onions, chopped
2 garlic cloves, minced
1 tablespoon olive oil
1 pound fully cooked smoked sausage, cut into 1/4-inch slices
3 to 4 cups chicken broth
1 can (16 ounces) kidney beans, rinsed and drained
1 can (15-1/2 ounces) great northern beans, rinsed and drained
1 can (15 ounces) garbanzo beans *or* chickpeas, rinsed and drained
5 to 6 bay leaves
1 teaspoon minced fresh parsley
1 teaspoon ground cumin
Dash hot pepper sauce
Hot cooked rice *or* pasta

1 In a large skillet, saute onions and garlic in oil until tender. Add sausage; cook and stir until lightly browned. Add the broth, beans and seasonings. Bring to a boil.

2 Reduce heat; cover and simmer for 1 hour, stirring occasionally. Discard bay leaves. Serve in a bowl over rice. **Yield:** 8 servings.

Pasta Primavera

(Pictured on page 181)

This works well as either a side dish or a main course. It's my mom's recipe, but I don't know where she got it.
—*Stephanie Marchese*

8 ounces uncooked linguine
1 cup thinly sliced fresh broccoli
1 medium carrot, thinly sliced
1/2 cup sliced green onions
1 garlic clove, minced
1/4 cup butter
1-1/2 cups sliced fresh mushrooms

1 teaspoon dried basil
1/2 teaspoon salt
1/4 teaspoon pepper
6 ounces fresh *or* frozen snow peas (about 2 cups), thawed
1/4 cup dry white wine
1/4 cup shredded Parmesan cheese

1 Cook linguine according to package directions. Meanwhile, in a large skillet, cook the broccoli, carrot, onions and garlic in butter for 3 minutes. Add the mushrooms, basil, salt and pepper; cook for 1 minute. Add snow peas and wine. Cover and cook for 2 minutes or until peas are crisp-tender.

2 Drain linguine; add to skillet and toss to coat. Sprinkle with Parmesan cheese. **Yield:** 4 servings.

Curried Couscous

I serve this both as a side dish and a meatless entree. Either way, people love the combination of ingredients.
—*Diane Werner*

1 cup uncooked couscous
2 cups small fresh broccoli florets
1 cup julienned carrots
1 tablespoon water
1/4 cup sliced green onions
2 tablespoons balsamic vinegar
4-1/2 teaspoons olive oil
1-1/2 teaspoons sugar
1-1/2 teaspoons curry powder
1 teaspoon minced fresh gingerroot
1/2 teaspoon salt
3/4 cup dry roasted cashews, chopped
1 can (15 ounces) garbanzo beans *or* chickpeas, rinsed and drained
3/4 cup crumbled feta cheese, optional

1 Cook couscous according to package directions. Meanwhile, in a microwave-safe bowl, cook the broccoli, carrots and water on high for 1 minute; drain. Transfer to a large bowl. Add the couscous and onions.

2 Combine the vinegar, oil, sugar, curry, ginger and salt; pour over couscous mixture and stir gently to coat. Stir in cashews and garbanzo beans. Gently fold in feta if desired. **Yield:** 8 servings.

Tabouli Primavera

Tabouli is a Middle Eastern vegetarian salad, primarily made with bulgur, lemon juice, tomato and herbs. This version is delicious!
—*Kristin Arnett*

1 cup bulgur
3 cups boiling water
1 cup chopped tomatoes
1 cup shredded carrots
1 package (4 ounces) crumbled feta cheese

2 cans (2-1/4 ounces *each*) sliced ripe olives, drained
1/4 cup minced fresh basil
2 tablespoons lemon juice
1 tablespoon olive oil
1/2 teaspoon salt

1 Place bulgur in a large bowl; stir in boiling water. Cover and let stand for 30 minutes or until most of the liquid is absorbed. Drain and squeeze dry.

2 In another large bowl, combine tomatoes, carrots, feta cheese, olives, basil, lemon juice, oil and salt. Add bulgur and toss to coat. **Yield:** 10 servings.

Four-Cheese Spinach Lasagna

This is a great vegetarian alternative to a traditional red sauce lasagna. My family loves it!
—*Coleen Martin*

2 cups chopped fresh broccoli
1-1/2 cups julienned carrots
1 cup sliced green onions
1/2 cup chopped sweet red pepper
3 garlic cloves, minced
2 teaspoons vegetable oil
1/2 cup all-purpose flour
3 cups milk
1/2 cup grated Parmesan cheese, *divided*
1/2 teaspoon salt
1/4 teaspoon pepper
1 package (10 ounces) frozen chopped spinach, thawed and well drained
1-1/2 cups small-curd cottage cheese
1 cup (4 ounces) shredded mozzarella cheese
1/2 cup shredded Swiss cheese
12 lasagna noodles, cooked and drained

1 In a large skillet, saute the vegetables and garlic in oil until crisp-tender. Remove from the heat; set aside. In a heavy saucepan, whisk flour and milk until smooth. Bring to a boil; cook and stir for 2 minutes. Reduce heat; add 1/4 cup Parmesan cheese, salt and pepper. Cook 1 minute longer or until cheese is melted. Remove from the heat; stir in spinach. Set 1 cup aside.

2 In a bowl, combine the cottage cheese, mozzarella and Swiss. Spread 1/2 cup of spinach mixture in a greased 13-in. x 9-in. x 2-in. baking dish. Layer with four noodles, half of the cheese mixture and vegetables and 3/4 cup spinach mixture. Repeat layers. Top with remaining noodles, reserved spinach mixture and remaining Parmesan.

3 Cover and bake at 375° for 35 minutes. Uncover; bake 15 minutes longer or until bubbly. Let stand for 15 minutes before cutting. **Yield:** 12 servings.

Barley Corn Salad

In the summer, I use fresh corn cut from the cob for this salad. If you like food with a little zest, add a chopped jalapeno pepper. I usually just use a whole sweet red pepper instead of the combination of red and green. —Mark Morgan

   2 cups cooked medium pearl barley
   2 cups frozen corn, thawed
 1/2 cup chopped sweet red pepper
 1/2 cup chopped green pepper
   3 green onions, chopped
   1 tablespoon minced fresh cilantro
   2 tablespoons lemon juice
   2 tablespoons canola oil
 1/2 teaspoon salt
 1/2 teaspoon dried thyme
 1/8 teaspoon pepper

1 In a large bowl, combine the first six ingredients. In a jar with a tight-fitting lid, combine the lemon juice, oil, salt, thyme and pepper; shake well. Pour over salad and toss to coat.

2 Cover and refrigerate for at least 2 hours before serving. **Yield:** 6 servings.

TEST KITCHEN TIP
Cook a large batch of barley and keep it in the freezer in 1-cup amounts for use in salads, soups or stews.

Savory Wheat and Grain Dressing

This dressing is a very aromatic side dish. It is great for the holidays either stuffed in a turkey or served on the side. —Peggy Fleming

 3/4 cup sliced green onions
 3/4 cup sliced celery
 1/2 cup chopped dried apricots
 1/2 cup golden raisins
   3 tablespoons sherry
   2 tablespoons butter
   1 cup uncooked long grain rice

   1 cup bulgur
 1/2 cup quick-cooking barley
   4 cups chicken broth
   2 teaspoons poultry seasoning
   1 teaspoon dried savory
 1/2 teaspoon salt
 1/4 cup minced fresh parsley

1 In a large saucepan or Dutch oven, saute the onions, celery, apricots and raisins in sherry and butter for 2 minutes or until liquid has evaporated. Stir in the rice, bulgur and barley; saute for 3 minutes. Add the broth, poultry seasoning, savory and salt. Bring to a boil.

2 Reduce heat; cover and simmer for 20-25 minutes or until rice is tender. Stir in parsley. **Yield:** 8 servings.

TEST KITCHEN TIP
If you like, substitute dried apples and cranberries for the dried apricots and raisins.

Calico Beans

I made this once for my dad, and now my mom has to make it often since it's one of his favorites. The beans are also perfect to take along to a potluck dinner or picnic. They're a real crowd-pleaser. —Suzanne Kern

        5 bacon strips, diced
        1 pound lean ground beef
    1/2 cup chopped onion
        1 can (21 ounces) pork and beans
        1 can (16 ounces) kidney beans, rinsed and drained
        1 can (15 ounces) butter beans, rinsed and drained
    1/2 cup packed brown sugar
    1/2 cup ketchup
        1 tablespoon white vinegar
        1 teaspoon salt
        1 teaspoon prepared mustard

1 In a large skillet, cook bacon over medium heat until crisp. Remove with a slotted spoon to paper towels to drain. Discard drippings.

2 In the same skillet, cook beef and onion over medium heat until meat is no longer pink; drain. Add the bacon, beans, brown sugar, ketchup, vinegar, salt and mustard.

3 Spoon into a greased 2-qt. baking dish. Bake, uncovered, at 325° for 45 minutes or until the beans are as thick as desired. **Yield:** 8-10 servings.

SUZANNE KERN

Suzanne and her husband have recently adopted a low-carb lifestyle, and that's reflected in the types of food she likes to prepare—grilled meats and refreshingly different salads are tops on her list. She came to the company 16 years ago, but it wasn't until she joined the Test Kitchen staff 8 years ago that she became interested in cooking. Scoping out flea markets and antique shops are other favorite pastimes.

Mostaccioli

We just love this pasta dish! It tastes like lasagna but is so much easier to make. Try it...I'm sure it'll become one of your family's favorites, too. —Sue Draheim

        1 pound uncooked mostaccioli *or* large tube pasta
    1-1/2 pounds bulk Italian sausage
        1 jar (28 ounces) meatless spaghetti sauce
        1 egg, beaten
        1 carton (15 ounces) ricotta cheese
        2 cups (8 ounces) shredded mozzarella cheese
    1/2 cup grated Romano cheese

1 Cook pasta according to package directions; drain. Crumble sausage into a Dutch oven. Cook over medium heat until no longer pink; drain. Stir in the spaghetti sauce and pasta. In a bowl, combine the egg, ricotta cheese and mozzarella cheese.

2 Spoon half of the pasta mixture into a greased shallow 3-qt. baking dish; layer with the cheese mixture and remaining pasta mixture. Cover and bake at 375° for 40 minutes. Uncover; top with Romano cheese. Bake 5 minutes longer or until heated through. **Yield:** 10-12 servings.

Cherry Almond Granola

(Pictured on page 180)

You can eat this granola out of hand for a crunchy snack or serve it in a bowl with milk for a delicious breakfast. Either way, it's delicious.
—Sue Myers

1 cup packed brown sugar	3 teaspoons almond extract
1/2 cup nonfat dry milk powder	6 cups old-fashioned oats
1/2 cup honey	1-1/2 cups dried cherries *or* cranberries
1/3 cup unsweetened apple juice concentrate	1 cup slivered almonds
2 tablespoons canola oil	Fat-free vanilla yogurt, optional

1 In a saucepan, combine the brown sugar, milk powder, honey, apple juice concentrate and oil. Cook and stir over medium heat until sugar is dissolved; stir in extract. In a large bowl, combine the oats, cherries and almonds. Drizzle with sugar mixture and mix well.

2 Spread in a thin layer in two 15-in. x 10-in. x 1-in. baking pans coated with nonstick cooking spray. Bake at 375° for 15-20 minutes or until golden brown, stirring occasionally. Cool completely. Serve with yogurt if desired. Store in an airtight container. **Yield:** 3 quarts.

Three-Rice Pilaf

Sometimes I like to toss a handful of dried cranberries into the rice mixture when I'm whipping up this recipe.
—Karen Johnson

1/2 cup uncooked brown rice
1/2 cup finely chopped carrots
1/2 cup chopped onion
1/2 cup sliced fresh mushrooms
2 tablespoons vegetable oil
1/2 cup uncooked wild rice
3 cups chicken broth
1/4 teaspoon dried thyme
1/4 teaspoon dried rosemary, crushed
1/2 cup uncooked long grain rice
1/3 cup chopped dried apricots
2 tablespoons minced green onion
1/4 teaspoon salt
1/8 teaspoon pepper
1/2 cup chopped pecans, toasted

1 In a large saucepan, saute the brown rice, carrots, onion and mushrooms in oil for 10 minutes or until rice is golden. Add the wild rice, broth, thyme and rosemary; bring to a boil. Reduce heat; cover and simmer for 25 minutes.

2 Stir in long grain rice; cover and simmer for 25 minutes or until liquid is absorbed and wild rice is tender. Remove from the heat; stir in the apricots, green onion, salt and pepper. Cover and let stand for 5 minutes. Sprinkle with pecans. **Yield:** 8-10 servings.

TEST KITCHEN TIP
If you don't have wild rice on hand, increase the brown rice to 1 cup.

Onion Bulgur Salad

Onion, tomato and cucumber blend beautifully with the chewy texture of bulgur. The refreshing salad is perked up even more by the addition of lemon juice and herbs. —*Mark Morgan*

3/4 cup bulgur	1 cup diced seeded tomatoes
2 cups boiling water	1/2 cup minced fresh basil
3/4 cup finely chopped red onion	1/2 cup minced fresh parsley
1 teaspoon salt	1/2 cup chopped green onions
1/2 teaspoon ground allspice	1/4 cup minced fresh mint
1 cup diced seeded cucumber	1/4 cup lemon juice

1 Place bulgur in a bowl; stir in the boiling water. Cover and let stand for 1 hour or until liquid is absorbed. Meanwhile, in another bowl, combine the onion, salt and allspice; let stand for 30 minutes.

2 Drain bulgur and squeeze dry; add bulgur and remaining ingredients to onion mixture. Toss gently to combine. Serve immediately or refrigerate. **Yield:** 8 servings.

TEST KITCHEN TIP

Keep bulgur in its original package until you open it, then transfer it to a canister, jar or other container with a tight lid. It can be stored at room temperature for up to one month.

Spicy Rice Pilaf

I serve this as a spicy and hearty side dish or as a vegetarian entree. The recipe yields a lot, so it's great to prepare for a hungry crowd. —*Tamra Duncan*

1/2 cup chopped onion
2 tablespoons olive oil
2 cups chicken broth
1/4 cup dry lentils, rinsed
1 can (16 ounces) kidney beans, rinsed and drained
1 cup salsa
1 cup uncooked long grain rice
1 cup frozen corn
1 jar (2 ounces) diced pimientos, drained
1 teaspoon chili powder

1 In a saucepan over medium heat, cook onion in oil until tender. Add broth and lentils; bring to a boil. Reduce heat; cover and simmer for 15 minutes.

2 Stir in the remaining ingredients; bring to a boil. Reduce heat; cover and simmer 20-25 minutes longer or until lentils and rice are tender. **Yield:** 12 servings.

Sweet 'n' Sour Beans

I like to take these beans to potlucks. I use a slow cooker for a serving dish and it keeps the beans warm.
                                        —*Janaan Cunningham*

  8 bacon strips, diced
  2 medium onions, halved and thinly sliced
  1 cup packed brown sugar
1/2 cup cider vinegar
  1 teaspoon salt
  1 teaspoon ground mustard
1/2 teaspoon garlic powder
  1 can (28 ounces) baked beans, undrained
  1 can (16 ounces) kidney beans, rinsed and drained
  1 can (15-1/2 ounces) pinto beans, rinsed and drained
  1 can (15 ounces) lima beans, rinsed and drained
  1 can (15-1/2 ounces) black-eyed peas, rinsed and drained

1 In a large skillet, cook bacon over medium heat until crisp. Remove with a slotted spoon to paper towels. Drain, reserving 2 tablespoons drippings. Saute onions in the drippings until tender. Add the brown sugar, vinegar, salt, mustard and garlic powder. Bring to a boil.

2 In a 5-qt. slow cooker, combine the beans and peas. Add onion mixture and bacon; mix well. Cover and cook on high for 3-4 hours or until heated through. **Yield:** 15-20 servings.

Couscous Salad with Dried Cherries

When I read this recipe, it sounded so delicious that I wanted it for my recipe file at home. It has a good combination of textures.
                                        —*Betty Reuter*

  1 cup chicken broth
3/4 cup uncooked couscous
1/2 cup dried cherries
1/2 cup chopped carrot
1/2 cup chopped unpeeled cucumber
1/4 cup sliced green onions

1/4 cup pine nuts, toasted
  3 tablespoons balsamic vinegar
  1 tablespoon olive oil
  1 tablespoon Dijon mustard
Salt and pepper to taste

1 In a large saucepan, bring broth to a boil. Stir in couscous. Cover and remove from the heat; let stand for 5 minutes. Fluff with a fork; cool.

2 In a bowl, combine the couscous, cherries, carrot, cucumber, onions and pine nuts. In a jar with a tight-fitting lid, combine the remaining ingredients; shake well. Pour over salad and toss to coat. Serve immediately. **Yield:** 6 servings.

TEST KITCHEN TIP
Betty likes to plump the dried cherries before adding them to the couscous. Simply cover with boiling water and let stand for 30 minutes, then drain.

Amish Baked Oatmeal

My children love this recipe. My daughter Maggie even made it for the family she worked for in Germany! It is like eating a soft oatmeal cookie for breakfast.

—*Wendy Stenman*

1-1/2	cups quick-cooking oats
1/2	cup sugar
1/2	cup milk
1/4	cup butter, melted
1	egg
1	teaspoon baking powder
3/4	teaspoon salt
1	teaspoon vanilla extract

Warm milk
Fresh fruit *and/or* brown sugar, optional

1 In a large bowl, combine the first eight ingredients; mix well. Spread evenly in a greased 13-in. x 9-in. x 2-in. baking pan. Bake, uncovered, at 350° for 25-30 minutes or until edges are golden brown.

2 Immediately spoon into bowls; add milk. Top with fruit and/or brown sugar if desired. **Yield:** 6 servings.

TEST KITCHEN TIP

Wendy measures all the dry ingredients the night before to save time in the morning.

Beans and Barley Chili

This hearty chili has a flavorful combination of beans, barley and seasonings. The barley adds a ground meat-like texture.

—*Janet Briggs*

1	cup uncooked medium pearl barley
2	cups chopped onions
2	cups chopped sweet red peppers
1	tablespoon vegetable oil
1	can (16 ounces) kidney beans, rinsed and drained
1	can (15-1/2 ounces) black-eyed peas, rinsed and drained
1	can (15 ounces) black beans, rinsed and drained

1	can (14-1/2 ounces) reduced-sodium chicken broth
1	can (14-1/2 ounces) stewed tomatoes
2	tablespoons chili powder
1	tablespoon minced garlic
1-1/2	teaspoons ground cumin
1/8	teaspoon cayenne pepper

Cook barley according to package directions; drain. In a large saucepan, saute onions and red peppers in oil for 5 minutes. Add barley and remaining ingredients; bring to a boil. Reduce heat; simmer, uncovered, for 20 minutes. **Yield:** 12 servings.

Pizza Roll-Ups

A nice alternative to traditional lasagna, these roll-ups are easier to serve, so they're great for entertaining. If there are any left over, I like them for the next day's lunch. —Kris Lehman

8 uncooked lasagna noodles
1/2 pound ground beef *or* turkey
1 small onion, chopped
3/4 teaspoon garlic salt
1/4 teaspoon crushed red pepper flakes
1 jar (26 ounces) spaghetti sauce with mushrooms, *divided*
2 cups (8 ounces) shredded mozzarella cheese, *divided*

1 Cook noodles according to package directions; drain and rinse in cold water. In a large skillet, cook beef and onion over medium heat until meat is no longer pink; drain. Sprinkle with garlic salt and pepper flakes. Remove from heat; stir in 1/2 cup spaghetti sauce. Add 1-1/2 cups cheese; mix well.

2 Spoon 1 cup spaghetti sauce into an 11-in. x 7-in. x 2-in. baking dish. Spoon about 1/4 cup meat mixture down the center of each noodle; roll up and place seam side down in baking dish. Spoon remaining spaghetti sauce evenly over roll-ups.

3 Cover and bake at 375° for 30-35 minutes or until heated through. Uncover; sprinkle with remaining cheese. Let stand for 5 minutes or until cheese is melted. **Yield:** 8 servings.

Apple-Cranberry Wild Rice

The leeks, cranberries and apples really add flair to this wild rice dish. —Peggy Fleming

2-3/4 cups water
1/4 teaspoon salt
2/3 cup uncooked wild rice
1 teaspoon dried savory
1 small leek (white portion only), coarsely chopped
1 teaspoon olive oil
1/3 cup dried cranberries
1/4 cup chopped dried apples
6 tablespoons chicken broth, *divided*
1/2 teaspoon onion salt
1/2 teaspoon lemon-pepper seasoning

1 In a large saucepan, bring water and salt to a boil. Stir in the rice. Reduce heat; cover and simmer for 1 hour or until rice is tender. Drain. Stir in savory; set aside.

2 In a nonstick skillet, saute leek in oil for 1 minute. Stir in the cranberries, apples and 3 tablespoons broth. Cover and simmer for 6-8 minutes or until fruit is tender, stirring occasionally.

3 Add the rice, onion salt, lemon-pepper and remaining broth. Cook and stir for 1-2 minutes or until liquid is absorbed. **Yield:** 6 servings.

TEST KITCHEN TIP

Allow yourself ample time to cook the wild rice. It takes about an hour until it is tender.

Red Beans and Rice

Even my kids like this hearty, stick-to-the-ribs dish. I like to add cubed leftover ham to make it a main dish.
—*Megan Taylor*

1-1/3 cups uncooked rice
2-1/2 cups chopped green peppers
  2 cups chopped onions
  4 garlic cloves, minced
  1 tablespoon olive oil
  1 to 2 tablespoons Cajun seasoning
1/2 teaspoon salt
1/4 teaspoon pepper
  2 cans (16 ounces *each*) kidney beans, rinsed and drained
  1 can (10 ounces) diced tomatoes and green chilies
  1 cup water

1 Cook rice according to package directions. Meanwhile, in a large saucepan, saute the green peppers, onions and garlic in oil until tender. Add the Cajun seasoning, salt and pepper. Cook and stir for 3 minutes.

2 Stir in the beans, tomatoes and water. Bring to a boil. Reduce heat; cover and simmer for 10 minutes. Uncover; cook for 5 minutes. Serve over rice. **Yield:** 4 servings.

Ravioli with Shrimp And Tomato Sauce

The addition of shrimp makes this rich and creamy sauce even more special.
—*Karen Scales*

1/2 cup chopped onion
  2 tablespoons butter
  2 tablespoons all-purpose flour
  1 can (14-1/2 ounces) Italian stewed tomatoes
  1 tablespoon brown sugar
  1 bay leaf
  1 whole clove
1/2 teaspoon dried basil
1/2 teaspoon salt
1/8 to 1/4 teaspoon pepper
  2 packages (9 ounces *each*) refrigerated small cheese ravioli
1-1/2 cups heavy whipping cream, warmed
1/2 pound cooked medium shrimp, peeled and deveined
  1 tablespoon grated Parmesan cheese
  1 tablespoon minced chives

1 In a large skillet, saute onion in butter until tender. Stir in flour until blended. Bring to a boil; cook and stir until thickened. Puree the tomatoes in a blender or food processor; add to onion mixture. Stir in the brown sugar, bay leaf, clove, basil, salt and pepper. Bring to a boil. Reduce heat; cover and simmer for 10 minutes.

2 Meanwhile, cook ravioli according to package directions. Remove and discard bay leaf and clove from the sauce. Reduce heat; gradually stir in cream. Add shrimp; heat through. Drain ravioli; top with sauce, Parmesan cheese and chives. **Yield:** 5 servings.

Fried Rice

Instead of reheating leftover cooked rice, turn it into this tasty new side dish. It's great paired with egg rolls and a green salad. I also like to add chopped cooked shrimp to the rice.
—*Janaan Cunningham*

    1/2 cup chopped green pepper
    1/2 cup egg substitute
      4 cups cold cooked rice
      2 tablespoons reduced-sodium soy sauce

In a large skillet coated with nonstick cooking spray, saute green pepper until crisp-tender. Add egg substitute; cook and stir until egg is completely set. Chop egg into small pieces. Add rice and soy sauce; heat through. **Yield:** 9 servings.

JANET BRIGGS

This mother of two daughters has worked in a test kitchen setting for over 20 years, coming to Reiman Publications 6 years ago. The first thing she learned to make as a child was from-scratch brownies. Today, cookies, soups and appetizers top her list of favorite foods. Janet edits hundreds of recipes each day at work. At home, she most often relies on dishes that can be made in 30 minutes or less but are still full of homemade flavor.

Pasta with Tomatoes and White Beans

When time is short, try this delicious vegetarian main dish. You can vary the recipe by using chickpeas instead of cannellini beans and grated Romano cheese in place of feta. —*Janet Briggs*

      3 cups uncooked penne *or* medium tube pasta
      2 cans (14-1/2 ounces *each*) Italian diced tomatoes
      1 can (15 ounces) white kidney *or* cannellini beans, rinsed and drained
      1 package (10 ounces) fresh spinach, chopped
    1/2 cup finely crumbled feta cheese

1 Cook pasta according to package directions. Meanwhile, in a large skillet, bring the tomatoes and beans to a boil. Reduce heat; simmer, uncovered, for 10 minutes.

2 Add spinach; simmer for 2 minutes or until wilted, stirring occasionally. Drain pasta; top with tomato mixture and cheese. **Yield:** 4 servings.

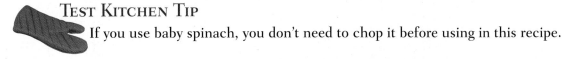

TEST KITCHEN TIP

If you use baby spinach, you don't need to chop it before using in this recipe.

SIDE DISHES

Roasted Cajun Potatoes

These nicely seasoned potatoes pair especially well with grilled pork chops or ribs. —*Tamra Duncan*

2-1/2 pounds medium red potatoes
1/4 cup olive oil
2 shallots, chopped
1 garlic clove, minced
1 teaspoon salt
1/2 teaspoon paprika
1/2 teaspoon cayenne pepper
1/2 teaspoon pepper
2 tablespoons minced fresh parsley

1 Cut each potato lengthwise into eight wedges. In a large bowl, combine the oil, shallots, garlic, salt, paprika, cayenne and pepper; add potatoes and toss to coat. Place in a greased roasting pan.

2 Bake, uncovered, at 450° for 45-50 minutes or until tender and golden brown, turning every 15 minutes. Sprinkle with parsley. **Yield:** 6-8 servings.

TEST KITCHEN TIP
You can substitute russet potatoes for red potatoes in this recipe if you prefer.

Cauliflower Au Gratin

Instead of serving plain cauliflower, I make this dressed-up version featuring cheese and bacon. It's a family favorite. —*Janaan Cunningham*

1 medium head cauliflower (about 1-1/2 pounds), broken into florets
2 garlic cloves, minced
6 tablespoons butter
2 tablespoons all-purpose flour
1-1/2 cups milk
4 bacon strips, cooked and crumbled
1/4 teaspoon salt
1/8 teaspoon pepper
Dash cayenne pepper
1 cup (4 ounces) shredded Swiss cheese

1 Place cauliflower in a large saucepan; add 1 in. of water. Bring to a boil. Reduce heat; cover and cook for 6-7 minutes or until crisp-tender. Drain well; set aside.

2 In another saucepan, saute garlic in butter for 1 minute. Stir in flour until blended; gradually add milk. Bring to a boil; cook and stir for 2 minutes or until thickened. Remove from the heat; stir in cauliflower, bacon, salt, pepper and cayenne.

3 Pour into a greased 1-1/2-qt. baking dish. Sprinkle with cheese. Bake, uncovered, at 400° for 15-20 minutes or until cheese is melted. **Yield:** 5-7 servings.

Southwest Skillet Corn

(Pictured on page 198)

Southwest flavor wins in our house. This stir-fried side dish complements any Mexican menu and grilled foods.
—*Mark Morgan*

1 medium sweet red pepper, chopped
1 tablespoon finely chopped seeded
   jalapeno pepper
1 tablespoon butter

1-1/2 teaspoons ground cumin
1 package (16 ounces) frozen corn, thawed
1/3 cup minced fresh cilantro

In a large nonstick skillet, saute red pepper and jalapeno in butter until tender. Add cumin; cook for 30 seconds. Add corn and cilantro; saute 2 minutes longer or until heated through. **Yield:** 4 servings.

EDITOR'S NOTE: When cutting or seeding hot peppers, use rubber or plastic gloves to protect your hands. Avoid touching your face.

TEST KITCHEN TIP

The heat level of jalapenos varies significantly. Taste a small piece to check the heat level. If the pepper is too mild, include the seeds and veins in what you're cooking.

Fresh Tomato Tart

This tart is best with fresh-from-the-garden tomatoes. It's so pretty to the eye and tastes fabulous!
—*Julie Ferron*

1-1/4 cups all-purpose flour
  2 tablespoons grated Parmesan cheese
1/2 teaspoon pepper
1/4 teaspoon salt
  6 tablespoons cold butter
  2 tablespoons shortening
  2 to 4 tablespoons ice water
FILLING:
3/4 pound fresh mozzarella cheese, thinly sliced
1/3 cup prepared pesto
  2 medium ripe tomatoes, thinly sliced
Salt and pepper to taste

1 In a large bowl, combine flour, Parmesan cheese, pepper and salt; cut in the butter and shortening until crumbly. Gradually add water, tossing with a fork until dough forms a ball. Cover and refrigerate for 1 hour or until easy to handle.

2 On a lightly floured surface, roll out pastry to fit a 9-in. fluted tart pan with removable bottom. Transfer pastry to tart pan; trim pastry even with edge. Line unpricked pastry shell with a double thickness of heavy-duty foil. Bake at 375° for 20 minutes. Remove foil; bake 15 minutes longer. Cool on a wire rack.

3 Remove sides of tart pan. Place crust on a serving plate. Arrange mozzarella over crust with slices overlapping. Spread with pesto. Arrange tomato slices in an overlapping pattern on top. Season with salt and pepper. **Yield:** 6-8 servings.

Roasted Beet Wedges

This recipe makes ordinary beets taste delicious. They come out of the oven sweet and tender.

—Wendy Stenman

1 pound medium fresh beets, peeled
4 teaspoons olive oil
1/2 teaspoon kosher salt
3 to 5 fresh rosemary sprigs

1 Cut each beet into six wedges; place in a large resealable plastic bag. Add olive oil and salt; seal and shake to coat.

2 Place a piece of heavy-duty foil (about 12 in. long) in a 15-in. x 10-in. x 1-in. baking pan.

Arrange beets on foil and top with rosemary. Fold foil around beet mixture and seal tightly.

3 Bake at 400° for 1-1/4 to 1-1/2 hours or until beets are tender. Discard rosemary sprigs. **Yield:** 4 servings.

TEST KITCHEN TIP

For a milder herb flavor, try using fresh thyme instead of rosemary. You may make the beets a day ahead, then slice and serve cold in a salad.

Carrot Casserole

This homey carrot dish makes a nice side for a roast beef dinner. Even those who say they don't normally care for carrots love them prepared this way.

—Kris Lehman

8 cups sliced carrots
2 medium onions, sliced
5 tablespoons butter, *divided*
1 can (10-3/4 ounces) condensed cream of celery soup, undiluted
1/2 teaspoon salt
1/4 teaspoon pepper
1 cup (4 ounces) shredded cheddar cheese
1 cup seasoned croutons

1 Place carrots in a saucepan and cover with water; bring to a boil. Cook until crisp-tender. Meanwhile, in a skillet, saute onions in 3 tablespoons butter until tender. Stir in the soup, salt, pepper and cheese. Drain the carrots; add to the onion mixture.

2 Transfer to a greased 13-in. x 9-in. x 2-in. baking dish. Sprinkle with croutons. Melt remaining butter; drizzle over croutons. Bake, uncovered, at 350° for 20-25 minutes until heated through. **Yield:** 10-12 servings.

Garden Vegetable Medley

Fresh, tasty and colorful, this side dish rounds out most any meal. I like to serve it in the summer along with grilled steaks or pork chops. —Tamra Duncan

- 1 medium yellow summer squash
- 1 medium zucchini
- 1 medium onion, halved
- 1 medium green pepper
- 3 garlic cloves, minced
- 1-1/2 teaspoons minced fresh oregano *or* 1/2 teaspoon dried oregano
- 1-1/2 teaspoons minced fresh basil *or* 1/2 teaspoon dried basil
- 1/2 cup reduced-sodium chicken broth
- 2 cups cherry tomatoes, halved

Cut the yellow squash, zucchini, onion and green pepper into 2-in. x 1/2-in. strips. In a large skillet or wok, simmer vegetables, garlic, oregano and basil in broth over medium heat. Stir constantly until crisp-tender, about 7 minutes. Add tomatoes; heat through. **Yield:** 8 servings.

Amy Welk-Thieding

Time spent in the kitchen is a creative outlet for this registered dietitian, who enjoys experimenting with new cooking techniques and flavors. Since joining the Reiman Publications Test Kitchen staff 3 years ago, she has had even more opportunities to try a variety of foods—though Italian dishes like spaghetti and lasagna are still her favorites. Amy and her husband of 1 year enjoy spending their spare time with family and friends.

Green Beans Italiano

The tomatoes and green beans make a pretty combo in this vegetable dish. Eliminate the salt if you prefer. —Amy Welk-Thieding

- 1 pound fresh green beans, trimmed
- 1/4 cup chopped onion
- 2 teaspoons minced garlic
- 1 teaspoon dried oregano
- 1/2 teaspoon dried basil
- 1/4 teaspoon salt, optional
- 1/4 teaspoon pepper
- 1 tablespoon olive oil
- 2 cups chopped fresh tomatoes

1 Place green beans in a large saucepan and cover with water. Bring to a boil. Cook, uncovered, for 8-10 minutes or until crisp-tender; drain.

2 In a large skillet, saute the onion, garlic, oregano, basil, salt if desired and pepper in oil until onion is tender. Add beans and tomatoes; heat through. **Yield:** 4-6 servings.

Flavorful Sugar Snap Peas

My family likes their vegetables cooked crisp and lightly seasoned. This recipe lets the natural goodness of the sugar snap peas shine through. —*Janet Briggs*

1 pound fresh sugar snap *or* snow peas
1 tablespoon vegetable oil
1/2 cup finely chopped fully cooked ham
1 garlic clove, minced
1/2 teaspoon dried thyme
1/8 teaspoon salt
1/8 teaspoon pepper

1 In a saucepan, cook peas in a small amount of water until crisp-tender, about 3-4 minutes. Heat oil in a large skillet; add ham, garlic and thyme.

2 Cook and stir for 2 minutes. Drain peas; add to skillet and saute for 2 minutes. Season with salt and pepper. **Yield:** 8 servings.

Leek Tart

New and different side dishes are always hard to find, which is why I like this leek tart so well. It's very flavorful and unique. —*Peggy Fleming*

2 cups all-purpose flour
1/4 teaspoon salt
1/4 teaspoon sugar
1/2 cup cold butter
9 to 11 tablespoons cold water
FILLING:
1 pound thick-sliced bacon, diced

3-1/2 pounds leeks (white portion only), sliced
2 tablespoons all-purpose flour
4 eggs
1 cup half-and-half cream
1/2 teaspoon salt
1/4 teaspoon pepper
1/8 teaspoon ground nutmeg

1 In a bowl, combine the flour, salt and sugar; cut in butter until crumbly. Gradually add water, tossing with a fork until dough forms a ball. Cover and refrigerate for 30 minutes.

2 In a large skillet, cook bacon over medium heat until crisp. Remove to paper towels with a slotted spoon. Drain, reserving 2 tablespoons drippings. Saute leeks in the drippings until tender. Stir in the bacon. Stir in flour until blended; set aside.

3 On a floured surface, roll out dough to 1/8-in. thickness. Transfer to an ungreased 10-in. springform pan, draping pastry edge over edge of pan. Spoon leek mixture into crust. Trim pastry to 1/4 in. above filling; press pastry against sides of pan. Bake at 400° for 10 minutes.

4 Meanwhile, in a bowl, beat the eggs, cream, salt, pepper and nutmeg. Pour over leek mixture. Bake 20-25 minutes longer or until a knife inserted near the center comes out clean. Serve warm. **Yield:** 10-12 servings.

TEST KITCHEN TIP

Use kitchen scissors to cut the bacon into small pieces directly into the pan before cooking it.

Pleasing Peas and Asparagus

(Pictured on page 198)

Springtime brings deliciously fresh asparagus. This recipe is a great way to enjoy it. —*Sue Draheim*

1/2 cup water	3 tablespoons butter
2 packages (10 ounces *each*) frozen peas	1 tablespoon minced fresh parsley
3/4 pound fresh asparagus, trimmed and cut into 1-inch pieces *or* frozen asparagus tips	3/4 teaspoon garlic salt, optional
	Dash pepper

1 In a large saucepan, bring water to a boil. Add the peas, asparagus, butter, parsley, garlic salt if desired and pepper. Return to a boil.

2 Reduce heat; cover and simmer for 8-10 minutes or until asparagus is crisp-tender. Drain; serve immediately. **Yield:** 6 servings.

Broccoli Timbales with Lemon Sauce

A unique and special presentation for broccoli, these timbales are real crowd-pleasers. —*Kristin Arnett*

1-1/2 cups heavy whipping cream, *divided*
   2 tablespoons lemon juice
   3 eggs
   3 egg yolks
   2 packages (3 ounces *each*) cream cheese, softened
   5 tablespoons butter, softened, *divided*
   2 to 3 tablespoons grated Parmesan cheese
   4 cups chopped fresh broccoli (about 1-1/4 pounds)
1/2 teaspoon salt, *divided*
1/4 teaspoon white pepper, *divided*
   1 tablespoon all-purpose flour
   1 teaspoon chicken bouillon granules
   3 tablespoons minced fresh dill
Fresh dill sprigs, optional

1 In a small bowl, combine 1 cup cream and lemon juice; let stand for 1 hour at room temperature. Place the remaining cream in a blender or food processor. Add the eggs, egg yolks, cream cheese, 4 tablespoons butter and Parmesan cheese; cover and process until blended. Transfer to a large bowl; fold in the broccoli, 1/4 teaspoon salt and 1/8 teaspoon pepper.

2 Spoon broccoli mixture into six greased 6-oz. ramekins. Place in a baking pan. Add 1 in. of boiling water to larger pan. Bake, uncovered, at 350° for 25-30 minutes or until a knife inserted near the center comes out clean.

3 For sauce, combine flour and remaining butter to form a paste. In a large heavy saucepan, combine the lemon-cream mixture, bouillon and remaining salt and pepper. Bring to boil. Whisk in butter mixture until smooth and thickened. Add dill. Remove from the heat.

4 Carefully run a knife around the edge of the ramekins to loosen. Place on serving plates, top side up. Spoon sauce around timbales. Garnish with dill sprigs if desired. **Yield:** 6 servings.

TEST KITCHEN TIP

Custard cups or muffin cups may be substituted for the ramekins.

Company Brussels Sprouts

Bacon nicely complements the sprouts in this side dish recipe, which is nice to serve to guests. My family prefers them to plain brussels sprouts.
                                                                    —*Betty Reuter*

4 bacon strips, diced	1/2 teaspoon dried basil
12 brussels sprouts, trimmed and halved	1/3 cup chicken broth
1 medium onion, chopped	1 teaspoon olive oil
2 tablespoons minced chives	1/2 teaspoon pepper
1 carrot, thinly sliced	Dash salt
10 stuffed olives, sliced	

1 In a large skillet, cook bacon over medium heat until crisp. Remove to paper towels with a slotted spoon. Drain, reserving 2 tablespoons of the drippings.

2 Add remaining ingredients to the drippings; cook and stir over medium-high heat for 10-15 minutes or until brussels sprouts are crisp-tender. Sprinkle with bacon. **Yield:** 3-4 servings.

TEST KITCHEN TIP
To keep the brussels sprouts bright green, avoid overcooking them.

Roasted Asparagus with Thyme

This good-for-you springtime side dish is easy to prepare, yet the simply seasoned spears look so appealing. I often serve them to guests.
                                                                    —*Julie Ferron*

3 pounds fresh asparagus, trimmed
3 tablespoons olive oil
2 teaspoons minced fresh thyme *or* 3/4 teaspoon dried thyme
1/2 teaspoon salt
1/4 teaspoon pepper

1 Place asparagus in a roasting pan or baking pan lined with heavy-duty foil. Drizzle with oil and toss to coat. Sprinkle with thyme, salt and pepper.

2 Bake, uncovered, at 425° for 10-15 minutes or until asparagus is crisp-tender. **Yield:** 12 servings.

Spring Vegetable Bundles

Founder Roy Reiman always wants readers to say "Wow" when they see or taste a Reiman Publications recipe. This is certainly one of those! —*Coleen Martin*

4 to 6 green onions
1 cup water
1 pound thin asparagus, trimmed
1 medium sweet red pepper, julienned
1 medium sweet yellow pepper, julienned
2 medium carrots, julienned
12 thyme sprigs
1-1/3 cups white wine
3 tablespoons butter

1 Trim both ends of onions; cut the green tops into 7-in. lengths. In a saucepan, bring water to a boil. Add onion tops; boil for 1 minute or until softened. Drain and immediately place in ice water. Drain and pat dry. Chop white portion of onions and set aside.

2 Divide asparagus, peppers and carrots into 12 bundles. Top each with a thyme sprig. Tie each bundle with a blanched onion top.

3 In a large skillet, combine the wine and chopped onions. Add vegetable bundles. Bring to a boil; cook, uncovered, for 5-7 minutes or until vegetables are tender and liquid is reduced by two-thirds.

4 Carefully remove bundles with a slotted spoon. Add butter to skillet; cook and stir until melted. Spoon over bundles. **Yield:** 12 bundles.

TEST KITCHEN TIP
Use asparagus spears that are 1/4 inch in diameter. Larger asparagus should be cut lengthwise in half.

Parmesan Mushrooms

This easy-to-make side dish showcasing mushrooms goes well with your favorite beef, pork or chicken entree. —*Stephanie Marchese*

1 pound sliced fresh mushrooms
1 tablespoon butter
1/2 cup sour cream
1 tablespoon all-purpose flour
1/4 teaspoon salt
Dash pepper
1/3 cup grated Parmesan cheese
1/4 cup minced fresh parsley

1 In a large skillet, saute the mushrooms in butter for 2 minutes. In a small bowl, combine the sour cream, flour, salt and pepper; stir into mushrooms. Cook just until bubbly, stirring frequently.

2 Spoon into a greased 8-in. square baking dish. Sprinkle with cheese. Bake, uncovered, at 425° for 10-15 minutes or until golden brown. Sprinkle with parsley. **Yield:** 4 servings.

Hush Puppies

We serve these hush puppies with Southern-fried catfish and coleslaw. If you like spicy food, add one or two finely chopped jalapeno peppers to the batter. —*Tamra Duncan*

> 1 cup yellow cornmeal
> 1/4 cup all-purpose flour
> 1-1/2 teaspoons baking powder
> 1/2 teaspoon salt
> 1 egg, beaten
> 3/4 cup milk
> 1 small onion, finely chopped
> Oil for deep-fat frying

1 In a medium bowl, combine the cornmeal, flour, baking powder and salt. Add the egg, milk and onion; stir just until mixed.

2 In a deep-fat fryer or electric skillet, heat oil to 375°. Drop batter by teaspoonfuls into oil. Fry for 2 to 2-1/2 minutes or until golden brown. Drain on paper towels. Serve warm. **Yield:** 4-6 servings.

TEST KITCHEN TIP

Use a small ice cream scoop to drop the hush puppy batter into the hot oil. This will help you work more quickly and allow the batches to cook evenly.

Cabbage Saute

This mildly sweet cabbage makes a great side to chicken, turkey or pork. It's a nice change of pace from a plain tossed salad.
—*Karen Scales*

> 1 medium onion, chopped
> 2 tablespoons butter
> 4 medium carrots, thinly sliced
> 6 cups chopped cabbage

> 1/2 cup chicken broth
> 1 teaspoon salt
> 1 teaspoon sugar

1 In a large skillet, saute onion in butter until tender. Add carrots; cook and stir for 2-3 minutes. Stir in the cabbage, broth, salt and sugar; bring to a boil.

2 Reduce heat; cover and simmer for 5-7 minutes or until vegetables are tender. Serve with a slotted spoon. **Yield:** 8 servings.

Swiss Potato Pancake

(Pictured on page 199)

This is the classic Swiss mountain dish called Rosti. The big potato pancake is cut into wedges and usually served with bratwurst, but I have also prepared this cheesy potato dish as a meatless main course. We love the nutty flavor that the Gruyere cheese provides. —Sue A. Jurack

2 tablespoons butter, *divided*
2 tablespoons vegetable oil, *divided*
1 package (30 ounces) frozen shredded hash brown potatoes, thawed
1 teaspoon salt, *divided*

1/4 teaspoon pepper, *divided*
1-1/2 cups (6 ounces) shredded Gruyere *or* Swiss cheese
Minced fresh parsley

1 In a large nonstick skillet, melt 1 tablespoon butter with 1 tablespoon oil over medium-high heat. Spread half of the potatoes in an even layer in skillet. Sprinkle with 1/2 teaspoon salt and 1/8 teaspoon pepper. Top with cheese, and remaining potatoes, salt and pepper. Press mixture gently into skillet. Cook for about 7 minutes or until bottom is browned.

2 Remove from the heat. Loosen pancake from sides of skillet. Invert pancake onto a plate. Return skillet to heat; heat remaining butter and oil.

3 Slide potato pancake brown side up into skillet. Cook about 7 minutes longer or until bottom is browned and cheese is melted. Slide onto a plate. Sprinkle with parsley. Cut into wedges. **Yield:** 6 servings.

TEST KITCHEN TIP

A nonstick skillet is a must so the pancake comes out easily.

Herbed Corn

This wonderful grilled corn is the perfect side for a summer dinner. The thyme and cayenne pepper are unusual but delicious seasonings for the corn. —Patricia Schmeling

1/2 cup butter, softened
2 tablespoons minced fresh parsley
2 tablespoons minced fresh chives
1 teaspoon dried thyme
1/2 teaspoon salt
1/4 teaspoon cayenne pepper
8 medium ears sweet corn, husked

1 In a small bowl, combine the butter and seasonings. Spread 1 tablespoon over each ear of corn. Wrap each ear individually in heavy-duty foil.

2 Grill, covered, over medium heat for 10-15 minutes or until corn is tender, turning frequently. **Yield:** 8 servings.

Simple Oven Fries

These lightly seasoned potato wedges are a nice accompaniment to grilled meat. Plus, they're much lower in fat than their deep-fried cousins.
—*Janet Briggs*

3 large baking potatoes
1 to 2 tablespoons olive oil
1/2 teaspoon salt
1/4 teaspoon paprika
1/8 teaspoon pepper

1 Cut each potato lengthwise into eight wedges. In a large bowl, combine the oil, salt, paprika and pepper; add potato wedges and toss to coat.

2 Place in a single layer on a greased baking sheet. Bake at 450° for 20 minutes. Turn potatoes; bake 10 minutes longer or until golden brown. **Yield:** 4 servings.

Stuffed Zucchini Boats

These are good enough to make a meal...great for late summer when garden-fresh zucchini is plentiful.
—*Diane Werner*

4 medium zucchini
1 egg, beaten
1 cup chopped fresh spinach
3/4 cup dry bread crumbs
1/2 cup tomato sauce
1/3 cup grated Parmesan cheese
1/3 cup finely chopped onion
1 garlic clove, minced
1/4 teaspoon salt
1/8 teaspoon pepper
1 can (14-1/2 ounces) diced tomatoes, drained and finely chopped
1 cup (4 ounces) shredded reduced-fat Swiss cheese

1 Trim ends of zucchini; place in a steamer basket. Place in a large saucepan over 1 in. of water. Bring to a boil; cover and steam for 5 minutes. When cool enough to handle, cut zucchini in half lengthwise; scoop out pulp, leaving a 1/4-in. shell. Set pulp aside.

2 In a bowl, combine the egg, spinach, bread crumbs, tomato sauce, Parmesan cheese, onion, garlic, salt, pepper and zucchini pulp. Spoon into zucchini boats.

3 Place in an ungreased 13-in. x 9-in. x 2-in. baking dish. Bake, uncovered, at 350° for 20 minutes. Top with tomatoes and Swiss cheese. Bake 5-10 minutes longer or until cheese is melted. **Yield:** 8 servings.

TEST KITCHEN TIP
To add a little zip, use pepper Jack cheese in place of the Swiss.

Cheesy Corn Casserole

This dish is a staple for every Thanksgiving dinner. You'd think that this recipe is more important than the turkey the way my family gobbles it up! —*Joylyn Trickel*

　3 eggs, beaten
　1 cup (8 ounces) sour cream
1/2 cup cornmeal
1/2 cup butter, melted
　1 can (8-3/4 ounces) cream-style corn
　1 can (7 ounces) whole kernel corn, drained
　1 can (4 ounces) chopped green chilies
　1 cup cubed Monterey Jack cheese
　1 cup cubed cheddar cheese
1/2 teaspoon salt
1/4 teaspoon Worcestershire sauce

In a large bowl, combine all of the ingredients. Transfer to a greased shallow 2-qt. baking dish. Bake, uncovered, at 350° for 45-55 minutes or until a knife inserted near the center comes out clean. Let stand for 5-10 minutes before serving. **Yield:** 6 servings.

TEST KITCHEN TIP

For a crunchy topping, toss some crushed crackers with melted butter and sprinkle over the casserole before baking.

Herbed New Potatoes

Dill and chives complement the delicate flavor of tiny new potatoes in this recipe. They're so easy to prepare, I make them often. —*Karen Johnson*

3/4 pound small red potatoes, quartered
　1 tablespoon butter, softened
　1 tablespoon sour cream
　2 teaspoons minced fresh dill *or* 1/2 teaspoon dill weed
　2 teaspoons minced chives
1/4 teaspoon salt
1/8 teaspoon pepper
Dash lemon juice

1 Remove a strip of peel from the middle of each potato. Place potatoes in a saucepan and cover with water. Bring to a boil over medium heat. Reduce heat; cover and simmer for 20 minutes or until tender.

2 In small bowl, combine the remaining ingredients. Drain potatoes; add butter mixture and toss gently. **Yield:** 2 servings.

TEST KITCHEN TIP

To easily snip the dill and chives, use a kitchen shears instead of a knife and cutting board.

Broiled Tomatoes Parmesan

I love to make this recipe when tomatoes are at their peak—the tomatoes almost melt in your mouth. —*Joylyn Trickel*

  3 large tomatoes
  1 tablespoon olive oil
  1 garlic clove, minced
  1/4 teaspoon coarsely ground pepper
  1 tablespoon minced fresh basil *or* 1 teaspoon dried basil
  3/4 cup soft bread crumbs
  2 tablespoons grated Parmesan cheese

1 Cut tomatoes in half; remove seeds. Place tomato halves on a broiler pan coated with nonstick cooking spray.

2 Combine the oil, garlic and pepper; brush over tomatoes. Sprinkle with basil. Broil about 6 in. from the heat for 3-4 minutes or until heated through.

3 In a small bowl, combine bread crumbs and Parmesan cheese. Sprinkle over tomatoes. Broil 1-2 minutes longer or until topping is lightly browned. Serve immediately. **Yield:** 6 servings.

Creamy Smashed Potatoes

These potatoes are so good that I serve them at Christmas. My family prefers these to any other mashed potato recipes. —*Megan Taylor*

2-1/2 pounds potatoes, peeled and quartered
  4 ounces reduced-fat cream cheese
  1/2 cup reduced-fat sour cream
  1/2 teaspoon onion salt
  1/2 teaspoon salt
Dash pepper

1 Place potatoes in a saucepan and cover with water. Bring to a boil. Reduce heat; cover and cook for 15-20 minutes or until tender. Drain and place in a large bowl; mash the potatoes. Add the remaining ingredients; mix well.

2 Transfer to a greased 8-in. square baking dish. Bake, uncovered, at 350° for 30-35 minutes or until lightly browned. **Yield:** 4-6 servings.

TEST KITCHEN TIP

Instead of baking the mashed potatoes in the oven, you can spoon them into a slow cooker and keep them warm on low.

Garlicky Baked Butternut Squash

The mild garlic flavor in this dish makes for a deliciously different treatment for butternut squash.
—*Anita Bukowski*

2 tablespoons minced fresh parsley
2 tablespoons olive oil
2 garlic cloves, minced
1 teaspoon salt

1/2 teaspoon pepper
1 large butternut squash (3-1/2 pounds), peeled and cut into 1-inch cubes
1/3 cup grated Parmesan cheese

1 In a large bowl, combine the parsley, oil, garlic, salt and pepper. Add squash and toss to coat.

2 Transfer to an ungreased shallow 2-qt. baking dish. Bake, uncovered, at 400° for 50-55 minutes or until squash is just tender. ***Yield:*** 6 servings.

Broccoli with Roasted Red Peppers

My daughters always request this side dish for all of our holiday dinners. It's an easy and appetizing way to dress up broccoli. The colorful combination tastes so good, you won't believe it's good for you, too!
—*Janet Briggs*

5 cups fresh broccoli florets (about 1 large bunch)
1 to 2 garlic cloves, minced
1 tablespoon butter
1/4 cup diced roasted sweet red peppers
1 tablespoon minced fresh parsley
1/2 teaspoon salt
1/8 teaspoon pepper

1 Place the broccoli in a steamer basket; place in a saucepan over 1 in. of water. Bring to a boil; cover and steam for 5-8 minutes or until crisp-tender.

2 Meanwhile, in a nonstick skillet, saute garlic in butter. Stir in the red peppers, parsley, salt and pepper. Transfer broccoli to a large bowl; add red pepper mixture and toss to coat. ***Yield:*** 6 servings.

TEST KITCHEN TIP
If the stovetop is crowded, you can always cook the broccoli for a few minutes in the microwave.

Sweet Potato Souffle

I've seen many variations of this recipe, but this is the one my family enjoys every Thanksgiving.

—Karen Scales

4 cups mashed cooked sweet potatoes
3/4 cup sugar
2 tablespoons butter, softened
1/3 cup milk
1 teaspoon vanilla extract
1/2 teaspoon salt

TOPPING:
2/3 cup packed brown sugar
2/3 cup chopped pecans
2/3 cup flaked coconut
2 tablespoons butter, melted

1 In a large bowl, combine the sweet potatoes, sugar, butter, milk, vanilla and salt; beat until smooth. Spoon into a greased 2-1/2-qt. baking dish. Combine the topping ingredients; sprinkle over potato mixture.

2 Bake, uncovered, at 350° for 40-45 minutes or until heated through and topping is browned. **Yield:** 8 servings.

TEST KITCHEN TIP

The potato mixture can be prepared ahead of time and refrigerated. Remove from the refrigerator 20 minutes before baking, then sprinkle with the topping just before putting it in the oven.

Creamed Fresh Spinach

I've found that this flavorful, no-fuss side dish is a great way to incorporate spinach into a meal. It's a nice part of a holiday menu.

—Patricia Schmeling

6 packages (6 ounces *each*) fresh baby spinach
1/4 cup butter, cubed
1/4 cup all-purpose flour
1 cup heavy whipping cream
1 cup milk
2 tablespoons finely chopped onion
Salt and white pepper to taste

1 Wash spinach, leaving the water that clings to the leaves. Place in a Dutch oven. Bring to a boil. Reduce heat; steam just until wilted, about 4 minutes. Drain and chop; set aside.

2 Melt butter in a large saucepan over medium heat. Whisk in the flour until smooth. Gradually add cream and milk. Bring to a boil; cook and stir for 2 minutes or until thickened. Stir in the onion, salt and pepper. Fold in spinach; heat through. **Yield:** 8 servings.

Glazed Carrots

Brown sugar and lemon juice enhance the natural sweetness of carrots. This recipe is unique because the carrots are left whole lengthwise. If you like, the carrots can be cut diagonally into 2-inch pieces or on the bias for easier eating at buffets. —*Sarah Thompson*

9 to 12 medium carrots (about 1-1/2 pounds)
4 tablespoons butter
1 to 2 tablespoons lemon juice
2 tablespoons brown sugar

Peel carrots and cut in half lengthwise. Boil in salted water until tender; drain well. Melt butter in a heavy skillet; add lemon juice and brown sugar. Stir until thickened. Add carrots; stir until well glazed and heated through. **Yield:** 6 servings.

Escalloped Potato Casserole

It's a family tradition to have this potato casserole at Christmas, Easter, birthday parties…anytime our family gets together. Mom always makes it, and we all look forward to it. A family gathering without it would not be complete. —*Janaan Cunningham*

1 can (10-3/4 ounces) condensed cream of celery soup, undiluted
1 can (10-3/4 ounces) condensed cream of potato soup, undiluted
1 cup (8 ounces) sour cream
1/2 cup chopped green pepper
1/4 cup chopped onion
1/2 teaspoon salt
1/4 teaspoon pepper
1 package (30 ounces) frozen hash brown potatoes, thawed
1 tablespoon minced fresh parsley
Paprika
1/2 cup shredded cheddar cheese

1 In a large bowl, combine the first seven ingredients; stir in potatoes. Transfer to a greased 13-in. x 9-in. x 2-in. baking dish. Sprinkle with parsley, paprika and cheese.

2 Cover and bake at 350° for 1 hour. Uncover; bake 5-10 minutes longer or until bubbly and golden brown. **Yield:** 10 servings.

TEST KITCHEN TIP
Try substituting O'Brien potatoes for a little kick.

Cider Baked Squash

Cutting the acorn squash into rings creates such a pretty presentation. —*Sarah Thompson*

> 2 medium acorn squash
> 1/2 cup apple cider *or* juice
> 1/4 cup packed brown sugar
> 1/8 teaspoon ground cinnamon
> 1/8 teaspoon ground mace

1 Slice squash into 1-in.-thick rings and remove seeds. Place in a 15-in. x 10-in. x 1-in. baking pan. Pour cider over squash.

2 Combine the brown sugar, cinnamon and mace; sprinkle over squash. Cover and bake at 325° for 45 minutes or until tender. **Yield:** 6 servings.

TEST KITCHEN TIP

To make cutting the squash easier, Sarah pierces the skin several times with a long-handled fork. Then she microwaves it for 1-2 minutes.

Dried Fruit and Sausage Dressing

This recipe was developed by one of our freelance food stylists, Suzanne Breckenridge. I make it every Thanksgiving, and my husband always hopes for leftovers! —*Stephanie Marchese*

> 1/2 pound bulk Italian sausage
> 1 cup chopped onion
> 1/2 cup chopped celery
> 2 tablespoons butter
> 1/4 cup port wine
> 8 ounces coarse-textured white bread
> 3/4 cup chicken broth
> 1 egg, beaten
> 3/4 cup dried cranberries

> 1 medium tart apple, cut into 1/2-inch cubes
> 2 tablespoons golden raisins
> 2 tablespoons chopped dried apricots
> 2 tablespoons minced fresh parsley
> 3 to 4 teaspoons minced fresh rosemary
> 3/4 teaspoon salt
> 3/4 teaspoon pepper

1 Crumble sausage into a small skillet; cook over medium heat until no longer pink. Drain and set aside. In the same skillet, saute onion and celery in butter until tender. Add wine; simmer for 2 minutes.

2 Cut crusts from the bread if desired; tear bread into small pieces. Place in a bowl; add the sausage, onion mixture and remaining ingredients. Mix lightly. Transfer to a greased shallow 1-1/2-qt. baking dish.

3 Cover and bake at 325° for 40 minutes. Uncover; bake 10 minutes longer or until lightly browned. **Yield:** 6 cups.

TEST KITCHEN TIP

If you'd like to use this dressing to stuff a turkey, use 1/4 cup egg substitute in place of the egg.

Roasted Veggie Chili

Roasting the vegetables really intensifies their flavors. This is a great, hearty chili.
—*Peggy Fleming*

   2 cups fresh *or* frozen corn
   2 cups *each* cubed zucchini, yellow summer squash and eggplant
   2 *each* medium green and sweet red peppers, cut into 1-inch pieces
   2 large onions, chopped
1/2 cup garlic cloves, peeled
1/4 cup olive oil
   4 quarts chicken broth
   2 cans (14-1/2 ounces *each*) stewed tomatoes
   2 cans (14-1/2 ounces *each*) tomato puree
1/4 cup lime juice
   4 teaspoons chili powder
1-1/4 teaspoons cayenne pepper
   1 teaspoon ground cumin
1/2 cup butter
1/2 cup all-purpose flour
   3 cans (15 ounces *each*) white kidney *or* cannellini beans, rinsed and drained
1/2 cup minced fresh cilantro
Sour cream and chopped green onions, optional

1 Place the vegetables and garlic in a large roasting pan. Drizzle with oil; toss to coat. Cover and bake at 400° for 20-30 minutes or until vegetables are tender; cool slightly. Remove and chop garlic cloves.

2 In a Dutch oven or soup kettle, combine the broth, tomatoes, tomato puree, lime juice, chili powder, cayenne and cumin. Bring to a boil. Reduce heat; simmer, uncovered, for 25-35 minutes or until mixture is reduced by a fourth.

3 In a saucepan, melt butter; stir in flour until smooth. Cook and stir until bubbly and starting to brown. Slowly whisk into tomato mixture. Add roasted vegetables, garlic, beans and cilantro; mix well. Cook until thickened. Garnish with sour cream and green onions if desired. **Yield:** 24 servings (6 quarts).

TEST KITCHEN TIP

A flat whisk works great when blending the flour into the butter. Since it is flat, you can easily get to the flour around the edge of the saucepan.

SARAH THOMPSON

As a young girl, Sarah would go straight home after school and head to the kitchen to "create" new recipes—most were disasters! Watching Julia Child with her mom was also great fun. They loved how messy she was! Sarah's "cleaned up" her own act to work in our Test Kitchen for a little over a year now. She has a 2-year-old daughter, and loves getting together with her parents and sister for family dinners every couple of weeks.

Broiled French Onion Casserole

Sweet and saucy onions are a perfect companion to roast beef or pork. This recipe is a nice way to make the ordinary onion special.

—Anita Bukowski

2-1/2 pounds sweet onions, halved and thinly sliced
5 tablespoons butter, *divided*
2 tablespoons all-purpose flour
Dash pepper

3/4 cup chicken broth
1/4 cup sherry
1-1/2 cups bread cubes, toasted
1/2 cup shredded Swiss cheese
3 tablespoons grated Parmesan cheese

1 In a large skillet, saute onions in 3 tablespoons butter until tender, about 25 minutes. In a small bowl, combine flour and pepper. Gradually add broth, stirring until smooth. Add sherry. Stir into onion mixture. Bring to a boil; cook and stir for 2 minutes or until thickened.

2 Transfer to a greased 1-1/2-qt. baking dish. Melt remaining butter and toss with bread cubes; sprinkle over the onion mixture. Sprinkle with cheeses. Broil 6 in. from the heat until cheese is melted and lightly browned. **Yield:** 6 servings.

Ginger-Roasted Green Beans

My husband and I like these beans so much that we tend to nibble away at them if they are out of the oven before the rest of the meal is ready.

—Joylyn Trickel

1 tablespoon olive oil
1 teaspoon sesame oil
3/4 teaspoon salt
1 garlic clove, minced
1/4 teaspoon minced fresh thyme *or* dash dried thyme
1 pound fresh green beans
1 tablespoon minced fresh gingerroot

1 In a large bowl, combine the first five ingredients. Add beans; toss to coat. Transfer to a 15-in. x 10-in. x 1-in. baking pan coated with nonstick cooking spray.

2 Bake, uncovered, at 400° for 16-20 minutes or until beans are crisp-tender, stirring occasionally. Sprinkle with ginger. **Yield:** 4 servings.

TEST KITCHEN TIP

Finely grating the ginger will help the flavor come through better than mincing it with a knife.

Pesto-Corn Grilled Peppers

I was raised in Iowa and love fresh sweet corn. This pesto-flavored corn is so beautifully presented in pepper cups that it really adds to the appeal of the recipe.
—Sue A. Jurack

1/2 cup plus 2 teaspoons olive oil, *divided*
3/4 cup grated Parmesan cheese
2 cups tightly packed fresh basil
2 tablespoons sunflower kernels *or* walnuts
4 garlic cloves
1/2 cup finely chopped sweet red pepper
4 cups whole kernel corn
4 medium sweet red, yellow *or* green peppers
1/4 cup shredded Parmesan cheese, optional

1 For pesto, combine 1/2 cup oil, grated Parmesan cheese, basil, sunflower kernels and garlic in a blender or food processor; cover and process until blended. In a skillet, saute red pepper in remaining oil until tender. Add corn and pesto; heat through.

2 Halve peppers lengthwise; remove seeds. Place cut side down on grill; cover and grill over medium heat for 8 minutes. Turn; fill with corn mixture. Grill 4-6 minutes longer or until tender. Sprinkle with shredded Parmesan cheese if desired. **Yield:** 8 servings.

TEST KITCHEN TIP
Use various colored sweet peppers—red, yellow, orange, green or purple—for a beautiful presentation for any summer barbecue party.

Marinated Fresh Vegetables

The sweetness in the poppy seed dressing makes these marinated vegetables a hit wherever I take them.
—Erin Frakes

4 cups fresh broccoli florets
2 cups fresh cauliflowerets
1-1/2 cups sliced fresh mushrooms
1 cup cherry tomatoes, halved
1 cup chopped celery
3/4 cup chopped green pepper
1 cup vegetable oil

3/4 cup sugar
1/3 cup white vinegar
3 tablespoons grated onion
1 tablespoon poppy seeds
1-1/2 teaspoons ground mustard
3/4 teaspoon salt

1 In a large bowl, combine the broccoli, cauliflower, mushrooms, tomatoes, celery and green pepper.

2 In a jar with a tight-fitting lid, combine the remaining ingredients; shake well. Pour over vegetables and toss to coat. Cover and refrigerate for at least 3 hours. Serve with a slotted spoon. **Yield:** 16 servings.

CONDIMENTS

Basil Butter

I make this tasty butter during the growing season and freeze it for later use. When veggies are sauteed in the butter, they taste as fresh as the herbs do when they just come out of my garden. —Coleen Martin

1-1/2 cups loosely packed fresh basil leaves
1/2 pound butter, softened
1 teaspoon lemon juice
1 teaspoon seasoned pepper
1/2 teaspoon garlic salt

1 In a food processor, chop basil. Add the butter, lemon juice, pepper and garlic salt; blend until smooth. Drop by half-tablespoons onto a baking sheet; freeze.

2 Remove from baking sheet and store in freezer bags. Use to flavor chicken, fish or vegetables. **Yield:** 4 dozen butter balls.

TEST KITCHEN TIP
Before the first freeze, Coleen harvests all her herbs from the garden and makes herb butters. They make great hostess gifts. Substitute parsley for half of the basil for a nice fresh flavor. Add a little oregano for a great Italian blend.

Strawberry-Rhubarb Jam

I consider this sweet and flavorful jam to be summer in a jar! The fruity concoction is simply scrumptious spread on toast, English muffins and more. —Peggy Fleming

4 cups fresh strawberries, crushed
2 cups chopped fresh rhubarb
1/4 cup lemon juice
1 package (1-3/4 ounces) powdered fruit pectin
5-1/2 cups sugar

1 In a large kettle, combine the strawberries, rhubarb, lemon juice and pectin. Bring to a full rolling boil over high heat, stirring constantly. Stir in sugar; return to a full rolling boil. Boil for 1 minute, stirring constantly. Remove from the heat; skim off foam.

2 Pour hot mixture into hot jars, leaving 1/4-in. headspace. Adjust caps. Process for 10 minutes in a boiling-water bath. **Yield:** about 6 pints.

TEST KITCHEN TIP
When Peggy starts a canning recipe, the first thing she does is fill the canner with water and start heating the water. It takes quite a while for the large amount of water to come to a boil.

Four-Tomato Salsa

(Pictured on page 221)

Four types of tomatoes, onions and peppers deliciously combine in this salsa, which tastes great served with tortilla chips or spooned over fish or chicken, too. —Janaan Cunningham

7 plum tomatoes, chopped
7 medium tomatoes, chopped
3 medium yellow tomatoes, chopped
3 medium orange tomatoes, chopped
1 teaspoon salt
2 tablespoons lime juice
2 tablespoons olive oil
1 medium white onion, chopped
2/3 cup chopped red onion
2 green onions, chopped
1/2 cup *each* chopped sweet red, orange, yellow and green pepper
3 pepperoncinis, chopped
3 pickled sweet banana wax peppers, chopped
1/2 cup minced fresh parsley
2 tablespoons minced fresh cilantro
1 tablespoon dried chervil
Tortilla chips

In a colander, combine the tomatoes and salt. Let drain for 10 minutes. Transfer to a large bowl. Stir in the lime juice, oil, onions, peppers, parsley, cilantro and chervil. Serve with tortilla chips. Refrigerate or freeze leftovers. **Yield:** 14 cups.

EDITOR'S NOTE: Look for pepperoncinis (pickled peppers) and pickled banana peppers in the pickle and olive aisle of your grocery store.

Cherry Sauce for Ham

I made this sauce for my family years ago, then the recipe got misplaced in my recipe file. I was making a ham for company and my husband requested the cherry sauce because it was so good. It took a little hunting, but I finally found the recipe and we had this deliciously spiced sauce over ham. —Sue A. Jurack

1 jar (12 ounces) cherry preserves
1/4 cup red wine vinegar
2 tablespoons light corn syrup
1/4 teaspoon *each* ground cloves, cinnamon and nutmeg
3 tablespoons slivered almonds

1 In a saucepan, combine the preserves, vinegar, corn syrup, cloves, cinnamon and nutmeg. Bring to a boil, stirring often.

2 Reduce heat; simmer, uncovered, for 2 minutes. Remove from the heat; stir in almonds. Serve with ham. **Yield:** 1-1/2 cups.

Pesto Sauce

I like to serve this pesto sauce over buttered gnocchi with an extra sprinkle of Parmesan cheese. Gnocchi are light little Italian potato dumplings, which are available in Italian grocery stores and cook up in mere minutes. The pesto is also delicious tossed with penne or other types of pasta.

—Sue A. Jurack

- 2/3 cup packed coarsely chopped fresh basil
- 1/3 cup grated Parmesan cheese
- 1/3 cup olive oil
- 2 tablespoons sunflower kernels *or* pine nuts
- 1/2 teaspoon salt
- 1/8 teaspoon pepper
- 1 garlic clove, peeled

In a food processor or blender, combine all of the ingredients; cover and process until blended. Cover and freeze for up to 3 months. **Yield:** 1/2 cup.

TEST KITCHEN TIP

When freezing the pesto sauce, Sue leaves about 3/4 inch in the top of the container, then covers the top with a thin layer of olive oil so the pesto doesn't brown during freezing.

Cherry Almond Preserves

These preserves are great on fresh bread, muffins, pancakes and even ice cream—the consistency's similar to a topping. The recipe yields 11 jars, but they always disappear fast. Friends and family often request them. —Tamra Duncan

- 8 cups pitted sour cherries (about 4 pounds)
- 1-1/2 cups water
- 10 cups sugar
- 2 pouches (3 ounces *each*) liquid fruit pectin
- 1 teaspoon almond extract

1 In a large kettle, bring the cherries and water to a boil; boil for 15 minutes. Add sugar; bring to a full rolling boil, stirring constantly. Boil for 4 minutes. Stir in pectin; return to a full rolling boil. Boil for 1 minute, stirring constantly. Remove from the heat; stir in extract. Skim off foam.

2 Pour hot mixture into hot jars, leaving 1/4-in. headspace. Adjust caps. Process for 15 minutes in a boiling-water bath. **Yield:** 11 half-pints.

Horseradish Spread

(Pictured on page 220)

I like to serve this spread with beef tenderloin or rib roast. The light-textured spread also tastes terrific on sandwiches.
—*Mark Morgan*

1/2 cup heavy whipping cream
1/4 cup freshly grated horseradish root

1/2 teaspoon Dijon mustard
1/4 teaspoon salt

In a small mixing bowl, beat cream until stiff peaks form. Fold in the horseradish, mustard and salt. Cover and refrigerate for 15 minutes before serving. **Yield:** 6 servings.

TEST KITCHEN TIP

Store fresh horseradish root in a sealed plastic bag in the refrigerator, and it should keep for up to 3 months. Take care when grating horseradish because it can sting the eyes even more than onions. Use a vegetable peeler or paring knife to remove the outer skin from the root.

Jamaican Barbecue Sauce

Zesty and spicy, this from-scratch barbecue sauce gives a lot of zip to ribs and chicken, whether grilled or baked in the oven.
—*Erin Frakes*

1 bacon strip, halved
1/2 cup chopped onion
2 tablespoons chopped green onion
1 tablespoon chopped jalapeno pepper
1 cup ketchup
1/2 cup chicken broth
1/2 cup molasses
2 tablespoons lemon juice
2 tablespoons cider vinegar
1 tablespoon minced fresh thyme
1 tablespoon prepared mustard
1 tablespoon soy sauce
1 tablespoon Worcestershire sauce
1 teaspoon salt
1/2 teaspoon pepper
1/4 to 1/2 teaspoon ground cinnamon
1/4 to 1/2 teaspoon ground nutmeg

1 In a saucepan, cook bacon over medium heat until crisp. Discard bacon or save for another use.

2 In the drippings, saute the onions and jalapeno until tender. Stir in the remaining ingredients. Bring to a boil. Remove from the heat; cool. **Yield:** 2 cups.

EDITOR'S NOTE: When cutting or seeding hot peppers, use rubber or plastic gloves to protect your hands. Avoid touching your face.

Habanero Apricot Jam

This jam is excellent warmed and brushed over a baking pork roast. It has an appealing spicy-sweet taste.
—*Megan Taylor*

3-1/2 pounds fresh apricots
  6 tablespoons lemon juice
  2 to 4 habanero peppers, seeded

1 package (1-3/4 ounces) powdered fruit pectin
7 cups sugar

1 Pit and chop apricots; place in a Dutch oven or soup kettle. Stir in lemon juice. Place habaneros in a blender; add a small amount of apricot mixture. Cover and process until smooth. Return to the pan. Stir in pectin. Bring to a full rolling boil. Quickly stir in sugar. Return to a full rolling boil; boil and stir for 1 minute.

2 Pour hot mixture into hot sterilized jars, leaving 1/4-in. headspace. Adjust caps. Process for 10 minutes in a boiling-water bath. For best results, let processed jam stand at room temperature for 2 weeks to set up. **Yield:** 11 half-pints.

EDITOR'S NOTE: When cutting or seeding hot peppers, use rubber or plastic gloves to protect your hands. Avoid touching your face.

MEGAN TAYLOR

When she was younger, Megan used to help her mom fix dinner, but it wasn't until she started working in the Test Kitchen 5 years ago that she seriously got into cooking. Preparing dinner is a special time spent with her family. Abby, age 3, always comes running to help, while Donevan, 10, does his homework at the table and talks about his day. Megan's husband is her official taste-tester...he'll try anything she makes!

Dijon Tartar Sauce ✓

A few years ago, I was looking for a low-calorie sauce to serve with fish. This one really fits the bill. It's so flavorful, you don't even know it's low in calories. —*Diane Werner*

1/2 cup fat-free mayonnaise
  3 tablespoons sweet pickle relish
  3 tablespoons chopped onion
  4 teaspoons Dijon mustard
  2 teaspoons lemon juice
1/4 teaspoon sugar
1/4 teaspoon salt
1/8 teaspoon pepper

In a bowl, combine all ingredients. Store in the refrigerator for up to 1 week. **Yield:** 3/4 cup.

Two Quick Deli Spreads

These easy condiments have lots of flavor and are a great way to jazz up a variety of deli meats. Simply pick up some rolls, and you have a build-your-own sandwich bar that's sure to please. —*Amy Welk-Thieding*

1/3 cup mayonnaise
1/2 to 1 teaspoon prepared horseradish
1/2 teaspoon minced chives
1/4 to 1/2 teaspoon garlic powder
1/3 cup honey mustard
1/2 teaspoon dried tarragon
1/8 teaspoon ground ginger

1 In a small bowl, combine the mayonnaise, horseradish, chives and garlic powder.

2 In another small bowl, combine the mustard, tarragon and ginger. **Yield:** about 1/3 cup of each spread.

Orange-Blueberry Freezer Jam

I buy blueberries by the flat from a local produce supplier who trucks berries from Michigan the day they are picked. While my children can eat them by the pint, this quick jam allows me to savor the berries year-round. —*Mark Morgan*

2-1/2 cups sugar
1 medium navel orange

1-1/2 cups fresh blueberries, mashed
1 pouch (3 ounces) liquid fruit pectin

1 Place sugar in a shallow baking dish. Bake at 250° for 15 minutes. Meanwhile, grate 1 tablespoon peel from the orange. Peel, segment and chop orange.

2 In a large bowl, combine the peel, chopped orange, blueberries and sugar; let stand for 10 minutes, stirring occasionally. Stir in pectin. Stir constantly for 3 minutes.

3 Ladle into clean jars or freezer containers. Let stand for 24 hours at room temperature. Refrigerate for up to 3 weeks or freeze for longer storage. **Yield:** 4 cups.

TEST KITCHEN TIP
When grating citrus fruits, be sure to grate only the outside of the peel—the white pith makes the peel bitter.

Peachy Dessert Sauce

This fruity sauce is lovely over ice cream, pound cake or waffles with whipped cream—a perfect dessert for my husband and me. —Tamra Duncan

  1-1/2 teaspoons sugar
      1 teaspoon cornstarch
    1/4 cup water
      2 tablespoons apricot jam *or* preserves
    1/2 teaspoon lemon juice
    3/4 cup sliced fresh *or* canned peaches
Vanilla ice cream

1 In a small saucepan, combine sugar and cornstarch; stir in water until smooth. Add jam and lemon juice; bring to a boil.

2 Cook and stir for 1-2 minutes; reduce heat. Add peaches and heat through. Serve warm over ice cream. **Yield:** 3/4 cup.

Dried Cherry Cranberry Sauce

This recipe is a great change of pace from the more common orange-cranberry sauce combinations. We especially like it around the holidays served alongside a roast turkey. It's so much better than canned cranberry sauce. —Janet Briggs

    1/4 pound dried cherries
  1-1/2 cups sugar
      2 cups water

      1 package (12 ounces) fresh *or* frozen cranberries, thawed

1 Place cherries in a bowl and cover with warm water. Let stand for 10 minutes or until plumped. Drain cherries, discarding water.

2 In a saucepan, combine the sugar, water, cranberries and cherries. Cook and stir over medium heat until the berries pop, about 15 minutes. Remove from the heat; skim foam. Cool to room temperature. Cover and store in the refrigerator. **Yield:** 5 cups.

TEST KITCHEN TIP
You can also plump the cherries in warmed orange juice instead of water.

Butter Pecan Sauce

(Pictured on page 220)

Buttery, smooth and full of pecans, this sauce is just sensational over ice cream. It's hard to beat its homemade goodness.
—Patricia Schmeling

1/2 cup plus 2 tablespoons packed brown sugar
2 tablespoons sugar
4 teaspoons cornstarch
3/4 cup heavy whipping cream

1 tablespoon butter
1/2 cup chopped pecans, toasted
Vanilla ice cream *or* flavor of your choice

1 In a heavy saucepan, combine the sugars and cornstarch. Gradually stir in cream until smooth. Bring to a boil over medium heat, stirring constantly; cook and stir for 2-3 minutes or until slightly thickened.

2 Remove from the heat; stir in butter until melted. Add the pecans. Serve warm over ice cream. **Yield:** 1-1/2 cups.

Spicy Plum Sauce

Pepper gives this mouth-watering sauce a little kick. Use it with egg rolls, pork or poultry.
—Nancy Fridirici

4 pounds fresh plums, pitted and quartered
1 small onion, quartered
1 garlic clove, peeled
3-1/2 cups sugar
2 cups cider vinegar
1 tablespoon ground ginger
1 tablespoon ground mustard
1 teaspoon ground cinnamon
1 teaspoon crushed red pepper flakes
1/2 teaspoon ground cloves

1 In a blender or food processor, process the plums, onion and garlic in batches until smooth. Transfer to a large saucepan or Dutch oven. Stir in the remaining ingredients. Bring to a boil. Reduce heat; simmer, uncovered, for 60-90 minutes or until reduced by a third.

2 Ladle hot mixture into hot jars, leaving 1/4-in. headspace. Adjust caps. Process for 15 minutes in a boiling-water bath. Remove jars to wire racks to cool completely. **Yield:** 9 half-pints.

Desserts

Frozen Mocha Torte

This frozen torte is often my choice to make and take to potluck suppers. It's fast, easy and delicious!

—Betty Reuter

1-1/4 cups chocolate wafer crumbs (about 24 wafers),
    divided
  1/4 cup sugar
  1/4 cup butter, melted
    1 package (8 ounces) cream cheese, softened
    1 can (14 ounces) sweetened condensed milk
  2/3 cup chocolate syrup
    2 tablespoons instant coffee granules
    1 tablespoon hot water
    1 cup heavy whipping cream, whipped
Chocolate-covered coffee beans, optional

1 In a bowl, combine 1 cup wafer crumbs, sugar and butter. Press onto the bottom and 1 in. up the sides of a greased 9-in. springform pan; set aside.

2 In a mixing bowl, beat cream cheese, milk and syrup until smooth. Dissolve coffee granules in hot water; add to cream cheese. Fold in whipped cream. Pour over crust. Sprinkle with remaining crumbs. Cover; freeze for 8 hours or overnight.

3 Remove from the freezer 15 minutes before serving. Carefully run a knife around edge of pan to loosen. Remove sides of pan. Garnish with coffee beans if desired. **Yield:** 10-12 servings.

KAREN SCALES

Taking home economics in junior high school sparked Karen's interest in cooking. It even inspired her to enter all sorts of baked goods in a county youth fair. She won grand champion, a couple reserve champion, an honorable mention and many blue ribbons over the years. For a while, she wanted to be a family and consumer education teacher; instead, she came to Reiman Publications 7 years ago. Newlywed Karen and her husband are currently enjoying their new home with their two cats.

Layered Banana Chocolate Pudding

Anyone who likes bananas will love this layered pudding treat that gets its start with a convenient boxed pudding mix.

—Kris Lehman

1-3/4 cups cold milk
    1 package (3.9 ounces) instant chocolate
      pudding mix
  24 vanilla wafers

    2 large firm bananas
    1 carton (8 ounces) frozen whipped topping,
      thawed
Grated chocolate, optional

1 In a large mixing bowl, whisk the milk and pudding mix for 2 minutes; let stand for 2 minutes or until soft-set. Arrange half of the vanilla wafers in a 1-qt. bowl.

2 Top with half of the pudding, bananas and whipped topping. Repeat layers. Cover and refrigerate for 3 hours. Garnish with grated chocolate if desired. **Yield:** 6 servings.

Blueberry Cheesecake Ice Cream

(Pictured on page 232)

The Test Kitchen staff went wild when we tested this recipe. It is so creamy and luscious! Every one of us requested a copy of the recipe.
—Tamra Duncan

1/2 cup sugar
1 tablespoon cornstarch
1/2 cup water
1-1/4 cups fresh *or* frozen blueberries
1 tablespoon lemon juice
GRAHAM CRACKER MIXTURE:
2-1/4 cups graham cracker crumbs
2 tablespoons sugar
1/2 teaspoon ground cinnamon

1/2 cup butter, melted
ICE CREAM:
1-1/2 cups sugar
1 package (3.4 ounces) instant cheesecake *or* vanilla pudding mix
1 quart heavy whipping cream
2 cups milk
2 teaspoons vanilla extract

1 In a small saucepan, combine sugar and cornstarch. Gradually stir in water until smooth. Stir in blueberries and lemon juice. Bring to a boil. Reduce heat; simmer, uncovered, for 5 minutes or until slightly thickened, stirring occasionally. Cover and refrigerate until chilled.

2 In a small bowl, combine cracker crumbs, sugar and cinnamon. Stir in butter. Pat into an ungreased 15-in. x 10-in. x 1-in. baking pan. Bake at 350° for 10-15 minutes or until lightly browned. Cool completely on a wire rack.

3 In a large bowl, whisk the ice cream ingredients. Fill ice cream freezer cylinder two-thirds full; freeze according to manufacturer's directions. Refrigerate remaining mixture until ready to freeze. Whisk before adding to ice cream freezer (mixture will have some lumps).

4 Crumble the graham cracker mixture. In a large container, layer the ice cream, graham cracker mixture and blueberry sauce three times; swirl. Freeze. **Yield:** 2 quarts.

Simple Lime Mousse

This is a light and fluffy mousse with just the right amount of tart lime flavor. It's especially good after a Mexican meal that's left your taste buds tingling.
—Karen Scales

1 cup heavy whipping cream
1/4 cup sugar
2 tablespoons lime juice
1 tablespoon grated lime peel
1 teaspoon vanilla extract
Lime slices and fresh mint, optional

1 In a small mixing bowl, combine the cream, sugar, lime juice, peel and vanilla. Beat on high speed until soft peaks form, about 4 minutes.

2 Spoon into dessert dishes. Garnish with lime and mint if desired. **Yield:** 4 servings.

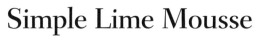

TEST KITCHEN TIP
Karen uses clear vanilla extract for a nicer color.

Lemon Poppy Seed Cheesecake

This fresh and creamy cheesecake has won awards over the years. It's that good! —Kristin Arnett

1-1/2 cups graham cracker crumbs
   3 tablespoons butter, melted
   4 packages (8 ounces *each*) cream cheese,
     softened
   1 cup sugar
   2 tablespoons all-purpose flour

2-1/2 teaspoons vanilla extract
   5 eggs, lightly beaten
1/2 cup heavy whipping cream
1/4 cup lemon juice
   1 tablespoon grated lemon peel
1/3 cup poppy seeds

1 In a small bowl, combine the graham cracker crumbs and butter. Press onto the bottom and 1 in. up the sides of a greased 9-in. springform pan. Set aside.

2 In a large mixing bowl, beat the cream cheese, sugar, flour and vanilla until smooth. Add the eggs, cream, lemon juice, peel and poppy seeds. Beat on low speed just until combined. Pour into prepared crust.

3 Place pan on a baking sheet. Bake at 350° for 55-60 minutes or until the center is almost set. Cool on a wire rack for 10 minutes. Carefully run a knife around edge of pan to loosen; cool 1 hour longer. Refrigerate overnight. Remove sides of pan. Refrigerate leftovers. **Yield:** 12-14 servings.

Cranberry Ice

My granddaughter smacked her lips when she first tasted this tangy treat. She loved the cold tartness—and wanted seconds. I was first served this ruby-red ice by a Swedish-American neighbor one Thanksgiving when I was a child. While this recipe is similar to hers, the addition of unflavored gelatin gives some smoothness to the usual icy texture.
—Sue A. Jurack

   3 cups fresh *or* frozen cranberries
   2 cups water
   1 teaspoon unflavored gelatin
1/2 cup cold water
1-1/2 cups sugar
1/2 cup lemon juice

1 In a large saucepan, bring cranberries and water to a boil. Cook over medium heat until the berries pop, about 10 minutes. Remove from the heat; cool slightly. Press mixture through a sieve or food mill, reserving juice and discarding skins and seeds.

2 In a small bowl, sprinkle gelatin over cold water; set aside. In a saucepan, combine cranberry mixture and sugar; cook and stir until sugar is dissolved and mixture just begins to boil. Remove from the heat. Stir in gelatin mixture until dissolved. Add lemon juice.

3 Transfer to a shallow 1-qt. freezer container. Cover and freeze until ice begins to form around the edges of container, about 1 hour. Freeze until slushy, stirring occasionally. **Yield:** 8 servings.

TEST KITCHEN TIP
You can make the cranberry ice up to a month ahead before serving.

Macadamia Berry Dessert

The crunchy macadamia nut texture in the crust is delightful with the melt-in-your-mouth raspberry filling.
—*Amy Welk-Thieding*

  1 cup crushed vanilla wafers (about 32 wafers)
1/2 cup finely chopped macadamia nuts
1/4 cup butter, melted
  1 can (14 ounces) sweetened condensed milk
  3 tablespoons orange juice
  3 tablespoons lemon juice
  1 package (10 ounces) frozen sweetened raspberries, thawed
  1 carton (8 ounces) frozen whipped topping, thawed
Fresh raspberries and additional whipped topping, optional

1 Combine wafer crumbs, nuts and butter. Press onto bottom of a greased 9-in. springform pan. Place on a baking sheet. Bake at 375° for 8-10 minutes or until golden brown. Cool on a wire rack.

2 In a large mixing bowl, beat the milk, orange juice and lemon juice on low speed until well blended. Add raspberries; beat on low until blended.

Fold in whipped topping. Pour over crust. Cover and freeze for 3 hours or until firm.

3 Remove from the freezer 15 minutes before serving. Carefully run a knife around edge of pan to loosen. Remove sides of pan. Garnish with fresh berries and whipped topping if desired. **Yield:** 12 servings.

Old-Fashioned Whoopie Pies

These are so fun—kids of all ages will love them. I remember taking a batch of these down to the beach when one of my kids was a lifeguard. Everyone loved them!
—*Diane Werner*

1/2 cup baking cocoa
1/2 cup hot water
1/2 cup shortening
1-1/2 cups sugar
  2 eggs
  1 teaspoon vanilla extract
2-2/3 cups all-purpose flour
  1 teaspoon baking powder
  1 teaspoon baking soda

1/4 teaspoon salt
1/2 cup buttermilk
FILLING:
  3 tablespoons all-purpose flour
Dash salt
  1 cup milk
3/4 cup shortening
1-1/2 cups confectioners' sugar
  2 teaspoons vanilla extract

1 In a small bowl, combine cocoa and water; mix well. Cool for 5 minutes. In a large mixing bowl, cream shortening and sugar. Add cocoa mixture, eggs and vanilla; mix well. Combine dry ingredients. Add to creamed mixture alternately with buttermilk; mix well.

2 Drop by rounded tablespoonfuls 2 in. apart onto greased baking sheets. Flatten slightly with a spoon. Bake at 350° for 10-12 minutes or until firm to the touch. Remove to wire racks to cool.

3 For filling, in a saucepan, combine flour and salt. Gradually whisk in milk until smooth; cook and stir over medium-high heat until mixture comes to a boil and has thickened, about 5-7 minutes. Remove from heat. Cover and refrigerate until cool.

4 In a large mixing bowl, cream the shortening, confectioners' sugar and vanilla. Add chilled milk mixture; beat for 7 minutes or until fluffy. Spread filling on half of the cookies; top with remaining cookies. Store in the refrigerator. **Yield:** 2 dozen.

Mocha Truffle Cheesecake

A brownie-like crust with a rich mocha filling makes this heavenly cheesecake very popular with my family.
— *Julie Ferron*

   1 package (18-1/4 ounces) devil's food cake mix
   6 tablespoons butter, melted
   1 egg
   1 to 3 tablespoons instant coffee granules
FILLING/TOPPING:
   2 packages (8 ounces *each*) cream cheese, softened
   1 can (14 ounces) sweetened condensed milk
   2 cups (12 ounces) semisweet chocolate chips, melted
   3 to 6 tablespoons instant coffee granules
1/4 cup hot water
   3 eggs, lightly beaten
   1 cup heavy whipping cream
1/4 cup confectioners' sugar
1/2 teaspoon almond extract

1 In a large mixing bowl, combine the cake mix, butter, egg and coffee granules. Press onto the bottom and 2 in. up the sides of a greased 10-in. springform pan.

2 In another large mixing bowl, beat cream cheese until smooth. Beat in milk and melted chips. Dissolve coffee granules in water. Add coffee and eggs to cream cheese mixture; beat on low speed just until combined.

3 Pour into crust. Place pan on a baking sheet. Bake at 325° for 50-55 minutes or until center is almost set. Cool on a wire rack for 10 minutes. Carefully run a knife around edge of pan to loosen; cool 1 hour longer. Refrigerate overnight.

4 Remove sides of pan. Just before serving, in a small mixing bowl, beat cream until it begins to thicken. Add confectioners' sugar and extract; beat until stiff peaks form. Spread over top of cheesecake. Refrigerate leftovers. **Yield:** 12-16 servings.

Pumpkin Pie Squares

This dessert, a nice change from pumpkin pie, is a great hit everywhere I bring it. I'm always asked for the recipe.
— *Sue Draheim*

   1 can (29 ounces) solid-pack pumpkin
   1 can (12 ounces) evaporated milk
1-1/2 cups sugar
   4 eggs
   2 teaspoons ground cinnamon
   1 teaspoon ground ginger

1/2 teaspoon ground nutmeg
   1 package (18-1/2 ounces) butter recipe golden *or* yellow cake mix
   1 cup butter, melted
   1 cup chopped pecans
Whipped topping, optional

1 In a large mixing bowl, combine the first seven ingredients; beat on medium speed until smooth. Pour into an ungreased 13-in. x 9-in. x 2-in. baking pan. Sprinkle with cake mix; drizzle butter over the top. Sprinkle with pecans.

2 Bake at 350° for 50-60 minutes or until a toothpick inserted near the center comes out clean.

Cool for 1 hour on a wire rack. Refrigerate for 3 hours or overnight.

3 Remove from the refrigerator 15 minutes before serving. Cut into squares; garnish with whipped topping if desired. **Yield:** 12-16 servings.

Mom's Strawberry Shortcake

(Pictured on page 233)

This spongy shortcake is plain and simple, and my kids love it—but it's also special enough for company. It melts in your mouth.

—*Diane Werner*

2 eggs
1-1/2 cups sugar, *divided*
1 cup all-purpose flour
1 teaspoon baking powder
1/4 teaspoon salt
1/2 cup milk

1 tablespoon butter
1 teaspoon vanilla extract
1 to 1-1/2 quarts fresh strawberries, sliced
Whipped cream
Fresh mint, optional

1 In a large mixing bowl, beat eggs on medium speed for 3 minutes. Gradually add 1 cup sugar, beating until thick and lemon-colored. Combine the flour, baking powder and salt; beat into the egg mixture. Heat milk and butter just until butter begins to melt. Beat into batter with vanilla (batter will be thin).

2 Pour into a greased 8-in. square baking dish. Bake at 350° for 25 minutes or until a toothpick inserted near the center comes out clean. Cool for 10 minutes before removing from pan to a wire rack to cool completely.

3 Just before serving, cut cake into serving-size pieces; cut each slice in half horizontally. Combine strawberries and remaining sugar. Spoon strawberries between cake layers and over the top of each serving. Top with whipped cream; garnish with mint if desired. **Yield:** 9 servings.

TEST KITCHEN TIP

For a change of pace, Diane sometimes replaces the strawberries with raspberries she picks from the large raspberry patch in her garden.

Blackberry Cobbler

This dessert works great with frozen berries. I often make it during the winter.

—*Mark Morgan*

1/2 cup sugar
4-1/2 teaspoons quick-cooking tapioca
1/4 teaspoon ground allspice
5 cups fresh *or* frozen blackberries, thawed
2 tablespoons orange juice
DOUGH:
1 cup all-purpose flour
1/3 cup plus 1 tablespoon sugar, *divided*
1/4 teaspoon baking soda
1/4 teaspoon salt
1/3 cup reduced-fat vanilla yogurt
1/3 cup fat-free milk
3 tablespoons butter, melted

1 In a large bowl, combine the sugar, tapioca and allspice. Add blackberries and orange juice; toss to coat. Let stand for 15 minutes. Spoon into a 2-qt. baking dish coated with nonstick cooking spray.

2 In a small mixing bowl, combine the flour, 1/3 cup sugar, baking soda and salt. Combine the yogurt, milk and butter; stir into dry ingredients until smooth. Spread over the berry mixture. Bake at 350° for 20 minutes. Sprinkle with remaining sugar. Bake 25-30 minutes longer or until golden brown. Serve warm. **Yield:** 10 servings.

Frozen Lemon Dessert

Lots of lemony flavor is packed into this refreshingly simple dessert. Try making it with pink lemonade concentrate and red food coloring.
—*Janet Briggs*

3/4 cup graham cracker crumbs
2 tablespoons plus 2 teaspoons butter, melted
2 tablespoons sugar
FILLING:
1/3 cup lemonade concentrate

2 drops yellow food coloring, optional
1 cup vanilla ice cream, softened
1-3/4 cups whipped topping
Grated lemon peel, optional

1 In a small bowl, combine the cracker crumbs, butter and sugar; blend well. Press onto the bottom and 1 in. up the sides of a greased 6-in. springform pan. Place on a baking sheet. Bake at 375° for 6-8 minutes or until lightly browned. Cool on a wire rack.

2 For filling, in a large mixing bowl, beat lemonade concentrate and food coloring if desired for 30 seconds. Gradually blend in ice cream. Fold in whipped topping. Spoon into crust. Freeze until firm, about 2 hours.

3 Remove from the freezer 10-15 minutes before serving. Carefully run a knife around edge of pan to loosen. Remove sides of pan. Garnish with lemon peel if desired. **Yield:** 6 servings.

Creme Brulee

My favorite dessert is Creme Brulee, so I quickly learned how to successfully make this on my own. Recently I was at a party where the guests finished off their own desserts "broiling" the sugar on their portions with a small torch. What a great idea!
—*Joylyn Trickel*

4 cups heavy whipping cream
9 egg yolks
3/4 cup sugar
1 teaspoon vanilla extract
Brown sugar

1 In a heavy saucepan, heat cream to 180° over medium heat, stirring frequently. Meanwhile, in a large bowl, whisk the egg yolks, sugar and vanilla. When cream reaches 180°, slowly stir into the egg yolk mixture.

2 Pour into eight 6-oz. custard cups; place cups in a baking pan. Add 1 in. of boiling water to pan. Bake, uncovered, at 325° for 45-50 minutes or until a knife inserted near the center comes out clean. Remove from water bath. Cool for 10 minutes.

3 Before serving, sprinkle each cup with 1 to 1-1/2 teaspoons brown sugar. Place on a baking sheet. Broil 6 in. from the heat for 3-5 minutes or until sugar is caramelized. Serve immediately. Refrigerate leftovers. **Yield:** 8 servings.

Chocolate Souffles

For a delicious dessert, try these easy-to-make souffles at your next dinner party. Everyone will think you fussed!
— *Sarah Thompson*

  6 teaspoons plus 1 tablespoon sugar, *divided*
  1 cup light corn syrup
  1/2 cup baking cocoa
  4 eggs, *separated*
  1 teaspoon vanilla extract
Confectioners' sugar

1 Coat six 6-oz. souffle dishes with nonstick cooking spray. Sprinkle 1 teaspoon of sugar into each dish, tilting to cover the bottom and sides; set aside.

2 In a bowl, whisk the corn syrup, cocoa, egg yolks and vanilla until blended. In a large mixing bowl, beat egg whites on medium speed until soft peaks form. Add remaining sugar, beating on high until stiff peaks form. Gently fold a fourth of the egg white mixture into chocolate mixture; fold in remaining egg white mixture.

3 Spoon batter into prepared dishes. Bake at 375° for 15-20 minutes or until a toothpick inserted near the center comes out clean. Dust with confectioners' sugar. Serve warm. **Yield:** 6 servings.

Broken Glass Torte

I find this light and fluffy dessert to be popular at family gatherings and potlucks. — *Sue Megonigle*

  1 package (3 ounces) orange gelatin
4-1/2 cups boiling water, *divided*
  1 package (3 ounces) lime gelatin
  1 package (3 ounces) raspberry gelatin
  1 envelope unflavored gelatin
  1/4 cup cold water
  1/4 cup lemon juice
1-1/2 cups graham cracker crumbs
  3 tablespoons sugar
  1/4 cup butter, melted
  2 cups heavy whipping cream

1 In a small bowl, dissolve orange gelatin in 1-1/2 cups boiling water. Pour into an 8-in. square dish coated with nonstick cooking spray. Refrigerate until set. Repeat with lime gelatin and raspberry gelatin, placing each in a separate 8-in. square dish.

2 In a saucepan, combine unflavored gelatin and cold water; let stand for 1 minute. Add lemon juice. Heat over low heat, stirring until gelatin is dissolved. Remove from the heat; cool.

3 In a bowl, combine the graham cracker crumbs and sugar; stir in butter. Reserve 1/2 cup for topping. Press remaining crumb mixture into a 13-in. x 9-in. x 2-in. dish coated with nonstick cooking spray; set aside.

4 Cut the orange, lime and raspberry gelatins into 1-in. cubes. In a large mixing bowl, beat cream until stiff. Fold in unflavored gelatin mixture, then fold in flavored gelatin cubes. Transfer to prepared dish. Sprinkle with reserved crumb mixture. Cover and refrigerate for 2 hours or until set. **Yield:** 12-15 servings.

Rhubarb Meringue Dessert

I'd say this is one of the best rhubarb desserts I've ever tasted. I can't wait for spring to use the fresh rhubarb in the garden. This is always a hit at church suppers. —Patricia Schmeling

2 cups all-purpose flour
2 tablespoons sugar
1 cup cold butter
FILLING:
2 cups sugar
1/3 cup all-purpose flour
1 teaspoon salt
6 egg yolks, beaten
1 cup heavy whipping cream
5 cups sliced fresh *or* frozen rhubarb, thawed
MERINGUE:
6 egg whites
1 teaspoon vanilla extract
1/2 teaspoon cream of tartar
3/4 cup sugar

1 In a small bowl, combine flour and sugar; cut in butter until crumbly. Press into a greased 13-in. x 9-in. x 2-in. baking dish. Bake at 350° for 20 minutes. Cool on a wire rack while preparing filling.

2 In a large bowl, combine sugar, flour and salt. Stir in egg yolks and cream. Add rhubarb. Pour over crust. Bake at 350° for 50-60 minutes or until set.

3 For meringue, in a large mixing bowl, beat egg whites, vanilla and cream of tartar on medium speed until soft peaks form. Gradually beat in sugar, 1 tablespoon at a time, on high until stiff peaks form and sugar is dissolved. Spread over hot filling.

4 Bake for 12-15 minutes or until golden brown. Cool on a wire rack. Refrigerate for 1-2 hours before serving. Refrigerate leftovers. **Yield:** 12-15 servings.

Coffee Ice Cream Torte

Ladyfingers make an easy crust and a lovely presentation. This is a great dessert if you like coffee.
—Amy Welk-Thieding

2 packages (3 ounces *each*) ladyfingers
1 cup chocolate-covered English toffee bits *or* 4 Heath candy bars (1.4 ounces *each*), crushed, *divided*

1/2 gallon coffee ice cream, softened
1 carton (8 ounces) frozen whipped topping, thawed

1 Place ladyfingers around the edge of a 9-in. springform pan. Line bottom of pan with remaining ladyfingers. Stir 1/2 cup toffee bits into the ice cream; spoon into prepared pan. Cover with plastic wrap; freeze overnight or until firm.

2 Remove from the freezer 15 minutes before serving. Remove sides of pan. Garnish with whipped topping and remaining toffee bits. **Yield:** 12-16 servings.

TEST KITCHEN TIP
Amy keeps extra whipped topping in the freezer to spread over desserts or dollop over individual servings.

Chocolate-Covered White Cheesecake

(Pictured on page 232)

The chocolate glaze and white chocolate drizzle make this delectable cheesecake a showstopper, but you can skip the glaze and still have a fabulous cheesecake. —Janet Briggs

1-1/2 cups chocolate wafer crumbs (about 27 wafers)
   3 tablespoons butter, melted
FILLING:
   3 packages (8 ounces *each*) cream cheese, softened
1/2 cup sugar
1/4 cup heavy whipping cream
   1 teaspoon vanilla extract
   3 eggs, lightly beaten

1-1/2 cups vanilla *or* white chips, melted and cooled
GLAZE:
   2 cups (12 ounces) semisweet chocolate chips
   1 cup heavy whipping cream
   2 tablespoons butter
   2 tablespoons sugar
   1 cup vanilla *or* white chips
Striped chocolate kisses, optional
Raspberries *or* cranberries, optional

1 In a small bowl, combine wafer crumbs and butter; press onto the bottom of a greased 9-in. springform pan. Place pan on a baking sheet. Bake at 350° for 10 minutes. Cool on a wire rack.

2 In a large mixing bowl, beat the cream cheese, sugar, cream and vanilla until well blended. Add eggs; beat on low speed just until combined. Stir in melted vanilla chips. Pour into crust. Place pan on a double thickness of heavy-duty foil (about 16 in. x 16 in.). Securely wrap foil around pan.

3 Place in a larger baking pan. Add 1 in. hot water to larger pan. Bake at 350° for 65-70 minutes or until center is just set. Remove pan from water bath. Cool on a wire rack 10 minutes. Run a knife around edge of pan to loosen; cool 1 hour longer. Remove foil. Refrigerate 4 hours or overnight.

4 For glaze, place chocolate chips in a medium bowl; set aside. In a heavy saucepan, bring the cream, butter and sugar to a boil over medium-high heat, stirring constantly. Pour over chocolate chips. Cool for 3 minutes. Stir until smooth and cool.

5 Remove sides of springform pan. Spread glaze over the top and sides of cheesecake. Refrigerate for 2 hours. Melt vanilla chips; pipe or drizzle over cheesecake. Garnish with kisses and raspberries if desired. **Yield:** 12-14 servings.

Coconut Ice Cream

Scrumptious coconut flavor can be found in every bite of this tropical-tasting ice cream! —Stephanie Marchese

1-3/4 cups sugar
1/2 teaspoon salt
   4 cups milk
1-1/2 cups flaked coconut, *divided*
   4 cups heavy whipping cream
   1 tablespoon vanilla extract
Toasted flaked coconut, optional

1 In a large saucepan, combine the sugar, salt and milk; cook and stir over medium heat just until mixture begins to boil. Stir in 1/2 cup coconut. Remove from the heat; let stand for 30 minutes. Strain, discarding coconut.

2 Place milk mixture in a large bowl; add cream, vanilla and remaining coconut. Freeze in an ice cream freezer according to manufacturer's directions.

3 Transfer to a 2-qt. freezer container. Cover and freeze for at least 4 hours before serving. Garnish with toasted coconut if desired. **Yield:** 2 quarts.

Pretzel Dessert

This is one of my mom's favorite desserts. The salty crust tastes so good with the sweet cream cheese filling.
—*Erin Frakes*

    2 cups crushed pretzels
3/4 cup butter, melted
    2 tablespoons sugar
FILLING:
    1 package (8 ounces) cream cheese, softened
    1 cup sugar
    1 carton (8 ounces) frozen whipped topping, thawed
TOPPING:
    1 package (6 ounces) strawberry gelatin
    2 cups boiling water
1/2 cup cold water

1 In a large bowl, combine pretzels, butter and sugar. Press into an ungreased 13-in. x 9-in. x 2-in. baking pan. Bake at 350° for 10 minutes. Cool completely.

2 In a large mixing bowl, beat cream cheese and sugar until smooth. Stir in whipped topping. Spread over crust. Cover and refrigerate until chilled.

3 For topping, in a small bowl, dissolve gelatin in boiling water. Add cold water; chill until partially set. Carefully pour over filling. Cover and refrigerate for 4-6 hours or until firm. Cut into squares. **Yield:** 12-16 servings.

Turtle Cheesecake

This smooth and creamy cheesecake is a real winner. It's a wonderful dessert because it can be made a day early.
—*Patricia Schmeling*

    2 cups vanilla wafer crumbs
1/2 cup butter, melted
    1 package (14 ounces) caramels
    1 can (5 ounces) evaporated milk
    2 cups chopped pecans, toasted, *divided*
    4 packages (8 ounces *each*) cream cheese, softened
    1 cup sugar
    2 teaspoons vanilla extract
    4 eggs, lightly beaten
    1 cup (6 ounces) semisweet chocolate chips, melted and slightly cooled
Whipped cream, optional

1 Combine wafer crumbs and butter; blend well. Press onto the bottom and 2 in. up the sides of a 10-in. springform pan. Place on a baking sheet. Bake at 350° for 8-10 minutes or until set. Cool on a wire rack.

2 In a saucepan, melt caramels with milk over low heat, stirring until smooth. Cool for 5 minutes. Pour into crust; top with 1-1/2 cups pecans. In a large mixing bowl, beat cream cheese until smooth. Add sugar and vanilla; mix well. Add eggs; beat on low speed just until combined. Stir in chocolate. Carefully spread over pecans.

3 Return pan to baking sheet. Bake at 350° for 55-65 minutes or until filling is almost set. Cool on a wire rack for 10 minutes. Carefully run a knife around edge of pan to loosen; cool 1 hour longer. Refrigerate for 4 hours or overnight.

4 Remove sides of pan. Garnish with remaining pecans and whipped cream if desired. **Yield:** 16 servings.

TEST KITCHEN TIP

The secret to a wonderful creamy cheesecake is in the mixing. Mix ingredients just until blended and do not overbeat.

Lemon Icebox Dessert

I always remember my mom making this for her bridge club and hoping that when I got home from school she would have a piece left for me...she always did! —*Sue Draheim*

- 1-1/2 cups all-purpose flour
- 4-1/2 teaspoons sugar
- 3/4 cup cold butter

FILLING:
- 8 eggs, *separated*
- 2 cups sugar, *divided*
- 2/3 cup lemon juice
- 3 tablespoons grated lemon peel
- 1 tablespoon unflavored gelatin
- 1/2 cup plus 2 tablespoons cold water, *divided*
- 1/2 teaspoon cream of tartar

TOPPING:
- 1 cup heavy whipping cream
- 1 tablespoon confectioners' sugar
- 1 cup flaked coconut
- 1 tablespoon grated orange peel

1 In a small bowl, combine flour and sugar. Cut in butter until crumbly. Press into a greased 13-in. x 9-in. x 2-in. baking dish. Bake at 350° for 18-22 minutes or until lightly browned. Cool on a wire rack.

2 For filling, in a large heavy saucepan, combine egg yolks, 1 cup sugar, lemon juice and peel. Sprinkle gelatin over 1/2 cup cold water; let stand for 1 minute. Add to the egg yolk mixture. Cook and stir over medium heat until mixture reaches 160° and coats the back of a metal spoon. Remove from the heat; cool completely.

3 In another large saucepan, combine egg whites, cream of tartar, and remaining sugar and water. Cook over low heat, beating with a hand mixer on low speed until mixture reaches 160°. Pour into a large mixing bowl; beat on high until soft peaks form. Gently fold into yolk mixture. Spread over crust.

4 For topping, in a small mixing bowl, beat cream until it begins to thicken. Add sugar; beat until soft peaks form. Spread over filling. Combine coconut and orange peel; sprinkle over top. Cover and refrigerate for 4 hours or overnight. Refrigerate leftovers. **Yield:** 12-16 servings.

TEST KITCHEN TIP

One medium lemon will yield 3 tablespoons juice and 2-3 teaspoons zest. Room temperature lemons will yield more juice than those coming right out of the refrigerator. Always thoroughly wash lemons before using their peels. Remove the zest before juicing the fruit.

Citrus Ice

It's hard to resist the refreshing flavor of lemon and lime in this frosty treat for two. It uses ingredients that are normally on hand and doesn't require an ice cream maker.
—*Wendy Stenman*

1-1/4 cups water
1/3 cup sugar
1/4 cup orange juice
2 tablespoons lemon juice
2 tablespoons lime juice

1 In a small saucepan, combine all of the ingredients. Bring to a boil. Reduce heat; cook and stir over medium heat until sugar is dissolved, about 2 minutes. Cool.

2 Pour into a 13-in. x 9-in. x 2-in. dish; cover and freeze for 45 minutes or until edges begin to firm. Stir and return to the freezer. Repeat every 20 minutes or until slushy, about 1 hour. **Yield:** 2 servings.

TEST KITCHEN TIP
This recipe can easily be doubled. Be sure to use two 13-in. x 9-in. x 2-in. dishes.

Chocolate Baklava

Baklava is a sweet, delicious Greek treat. This twist on the classic dessert adds mini chocolate chips to the nutty filling.
—*Sarah Thompson*

1 package (16 ounces, 18-inch x 14-inch sheet size) frozen phyllo dough, thawed
1-1/4 cups butter, melted
1 pound finely chopped walnuts
1 package (12 ounces) miniature semisweet chocolate chips
3/4 cup sugar
1-1/2 teaspoons ground cinnamon
1 teaspoon grated lemon peel
SYRUP:
3/4 cup orange juice
1/2 cup sugar
1/2 cup water
1/2 cup honey
2 tablespoons lemon juice

1 Butter a 15-in. x 10-in. x 1-in. baking pan. Layer eight sheets of phyllo dough in pan, brushing each with butter. Keep remaining phyllo covered with plastic wrap and a damp towel to prevent drying. In a bowl, combine the nuts, chocolate chips, sugar, cinnamon and lemon peel. Sprinkle 2 cups over top layer of phyllo.

2 Layer and brush four sheets of dough with butter. Top with 2 more cups of nut mixture. Layer and brush four more sheets of dough with butter; top with remaining nut mixture. Top with the remaining dough, brushing each sheet with butter. Drizzle any remaining butter over the top.

3 Using a sharp knife, cut baklava into 1-1/2-in. diamonds. Bake at 325° for 50-60 minutes or until golden brown.

4 Meanwhile, combine the syrup ingredients in a saucepan; bring to a boil over medium heat, stirring occasionally. Reduce heat; simmer, uncovered, for 20 minutes. Pour over warm baklava. Cool completely in pan on a wire rack. **Yield:** 50 pieces.

Lemon Dream Crepes

Need a light dessert idea for a luncheon? With a delicate lemon filling, these crepes are even better than lemon meringue pie! I have served them at many summer luncheons, and they seem to be a perfect ending for the meal. —Sue A. Jurack

1-1/2 cups all-purpose flour
1 tablespoon sugar
1/2 teaspoon salt
2 cups milk
3 eggs
2 tablespoons butter, melted
2 teaspoons vanilla extract

LEMON FILLING:
1/2 cup butter
1-1/2 cups sugar
1/2 cup lemon juice
1 teaspoon grated lemon peel
1/8 teaspoon salt
3 eggs, beaten
3 egg yolks, beaten
1 cup heavy whipping cream

1 In a large mixing bowl, combine the flour, sugar and salt. Combine the milk, eggs, butter and vanilla; add to flour mixture and mix well. Cover and refrigerate for 1 hour.

2 Heat a lightly greased 8-in. nonstick skillet; pour 2 tablespoons batter into the center of skillet. Lift and tilt pan to evenly coat bottom. Cook until edges are lightly browned; turn and cook 15-20 seconds longer. Remove to a wire rack. Repeat with remaining batter, greasing skillet as needed. When cool, stack crepes with waxed paper or paper towels in between.

3 For filling, melt butter in a small saucepan over low heat. Add sugar, lemon juice, lemon peel and salt. Whisk in eggs and yolks. Cook over low heat until mixture thickens and coats the back of a metal spoon, whisking constantly. Remove from the heat. Transfer to a small bowl; press plastic wrap over top of filling. Refrigerate until chilled.

4 In a small mixing bowl, beat cream until soft peaks form. Fold half of the whipped cream into lemon filling. To serve, spoon 2 tablespoonfuls of filling down the center of each crepe; fold sides of crepe over filling. Top with remaining whipped cream. **Yield:** 24 filled crepes.

Mocha Fondue

Our Valentine's Day tradition is a fondue meal of beef, chicken and vegetables. We always top it off with this chocolate fondue and fresh strawberries. —Coleen Martin

3 cups milk chocolate chips
1/2 cup heavy whipping cream
1 tablespoon instant coffee granules
2 tablespoons hot water
1 teaspoon vanilla extract
1/8 teaspoon ground cinnamon, optional
1 pound cake (16 ounces), cut into 1-inch cubes
Strawberries, kiwi *or* other fresh fruit

In a heavy saucepan, melt chocolate chips with cream over low heat, stirring constantly. Dissolve coffee granules in water; add to chocolate mixture with vanilla and cinnamon if desired. Mix well. Serve warm, using cake cubes and fruit for dipping. **Yield:** 2 cups.

TEST KITCHEN TIP
For a recipe with more kid appeal, Coleen leaves out the coffee granules and hot water.

Butternut Apple Crisp

This crisp is a great way to use up that abundant fall squash. The topping is crunchy and sweet.
—*Peggy Fleming*

1 small butternut squash (about 1 pound)
3 medium baking apples, peeled and sliced
1/4 cup corn syrup
2 tablespoons lemon juice
3/4 cup packed brown sugar
1 tablespoon cornstarch
1 teaspoon ground cinnamon
1/2 teaspoon salt
TOPPING:
1/2 cup all-purpose flour
1/2 cup quick-cooking oats
1/4 cup packed brown sugar
6 tablespoons cold butter
Vanilla ice cream *or* whipped cream

1 Peel squash and cut in half lengthwise; scoop out seeds. Cut squash into thin slices. In a large bowl, combine the squash, apples, corn syrup and lemon juice; toss to coat. In a small bowl, combine the brown sugar, cornstarch, cinnamon and salt. Add to squash mixture; mix well.

2 Transfer to a 13-in. x 9-in. x 2-in. baking dish coated with nonstick cooking spray. Cover and bake at 375° for 20 minutes.

3 For topping, in a bowl, combine the flour, oats and brown sugar; cut in butter until mixture resembles coarse crumbs. Sprinkle over squash mixture. Bake, uncovered, for 25 minutes or until squash and apples are tender and topping is lightly browned. Serve with ice cream or whipped cream. **Yield:** 6-8 servings.

Creamy Caramel Flan

If you're unfamiliar with flan, think of it as a tasty variation of custard. This particular recipe is a cross between cheesecake and flan. It's a rich and special treat.
—*Coleen Martin*

3/4 cup sugar
1 package (8 ounces) cream cheese, softened
5 eggs
1 can (14 ounces) sweetened condensed milk
1 can (12 ounces) evaporated milk
1 teaspoon vanilla extract

1 In a heavy saucepan, cook and stir sugar over medium-low heat until melted and golden, about 15 minutes. Quickly pour into an ungreased 2-qt. round baking dish or souffle dish, tilting to coat the bottom; let stand for 10 minutes.

2 In a large mixing bowl, beat the cream cheese until smooth. Add eggs, one at a time, beating well after each addition. Add remaining ingredients; mix well. Pour over caramelized sugar.

3 Place the dish in a larger baking pan. Add 1 in. of boiling water to larger pan. Bake at 350° for 50-60 minutes or until center is just set (mixture will jiggle). Remove dish to a wire rack; cool for 1 hour. Refrigerate overnight.

4 To unmold, run a knife around edges and invert onto a large rimmed serving platter. Cut into wedges or spoon onto dessert plates; spoon sauce over each serving. **Yield:** 8-10 servings.

TEST KITCHEN TIP

Pay close attention when melting sugar as it changes quickly. Be sure to find a pan for the water bath before starting to prepare the recipe.

Pumpkin Trifle

To date, this is the most-requested recipe featured in Light & Tasty magazine. It tastes as good as it looks and is great to prepare for fall potlucks. —Mark Morgan

     1 package (14-1/2 ounces) gingerbread cake mix
1-1/4 cups water
     1 egg
     4 cups cold fat-free milk
     4 packages (1 ounce *each*) sugar-free instant butterscotch pudding mix
     1 can (15 ounces) solid-pack pumpkin
     1 teaspoon ground cinnamon
   1/4 teaspoon *each* ground ginger, nutmeg and allspice
     1 carton (12 ounces) reduced-fat frozen whipped topping, thawed

1 In a large mixing bowl, combine the cake mix, water and egg. Pour into an ungreased 8-in. square baking dish. Bake at 350° for 35-40 minutes or until a toothpick inserted near the center comes out clean. Cool for 10 minutes before removing from pan to a wire rack to cool completely.

2 In a large bowl, whisk milk and pudding mixes for 2 minutes or until slightly thickened; let stand for 2 minutes or until soft-set. Stir in pumpkin and spices. Crumble the cake; set aside 1/4 cup crumbs.

3 In a trifle bowl or 3-1/2-qt. glass serving bowl, layer a fourth of the cake crumbs, half of the pumpkin mixture, a fourth of the cake crumbs and half of the whipped topping. Repeat layers. Garnish with reserved cake crumbs. Serve immediately or refrigerate. **Yield:** 18 servings.

EDITOR'S NOTE: This recipe was tested with Betty Crocker gingerbread cake mix.

Creamy Peanut Dessert

This dessert tastes just like a Drumstick ice cream cone. People can't believe it doesn't even have ice cream in it. —Karen Scales

1-1/2 cups graham cracker crumbs
   1/2 cup chopped salted peanuts
   1/4 cup butter, melted
     2 tablespoons peanut butter
FILLING:
     1 package (8 ounces) cream cheese, softened
   1/2 cup peanut butter
   1/2 cup sugar
     2 teaspoons vanilla extract
     1 carton (16 ounces) frozen whipped topping, thawed
     3 to 4 tablespoons chocolate syrup

1 In a small bowl, combine cracker crumbs and peanuts. Stir in butter and peanut butter; mix well. Set aside 1/2 cup for topping. Press the remaining crumb mixture into a greased 13-in. x 9-in. x 2-in. dish. Cover and refrigerate for 30 minutes.

2 Meanwhile, in a large mixing bowl, beat cream cheese and peanut butter until smooth. Beat in sugar and vanilla. Fold in whipped topping. Spoon over crust. Drizzle with chocolate syrup; sprinkle with reserved crumb mixture.

3 Cover and freeze for up to 3 months. Remove from the freezer 15 minutes before serving. **Yield:** 15-20 servings.

TEST KITCHEN TIP
Make graham cracker crumbs in your food processor or put crackers in a large resealable plastic bag and crush them with a rolling pin.

Lemon Cream Dessert

This pretty layered dessert is requested often at family gatherings. I have served it at both bridal and baby showers.
—*Patricia Schmeling*

1-1/2 cups sugar
1/3 cup plus 1 tablespoon cornstarch
1-1/2 cups cold water
3 egg yolks, lightly beaten
3 tablespoons butter, cubed
2 teaspoons grated lemon peel
1/2 cup lemon juice
CRUST:
1 cup all-purpose flour
1 cup finely chopped walnuts
1/2 cup cold butter
TOPPING:
1 package (8 ounces) cream cheese, softened
1 cup confectioners' sugar
2 cups cold milk
2 packages (3.4 ounces *each*) instant vanilla pudding mix
1 teaspoon vanilla extract
1 carton (16 ounces) frozen whipped topping, thawed

1 In a saucepan, combine sugar and cornstarch; gradually stir in water until smooth. Bring to a boil; cook and stir 1 minute or until thickened. Remove from heat. Stir a small amount of hot filling into egg yolks; return all to pan, stirring constantly. Bring to a gentle boil; cook and stir 1 minute. Remove from heat; stir in butter and lemon peel. Gently stir in lemon juice. Refrigerate until cool.

2 For crust, in a bowl, combine flour and nuts. Cut in butter until mixture resembles coarse crumbs. Press onto the bottom of a greased 13-in. x 9-in. x 2-in. baking dish. Bake at 350° for 15-20 minutes or until edges are golden. Cool on a wire rack.

3 For topping, in a large mixing bowl, beat cream cheese and confectioners' sugar until smooth; spread over crust. Spread with cooled lemon mixture. In another bowl, whisk milk, pudding mixes and vanilla 2 minutes or until slightly thickened; let stand 2 minutes or until soft-set. Fold in half of whipped topping. Spread over lemon layer. Spread with remaining topping. Refrigerate 4 hours before cutting. **Yield:** 18-24 servings.

PATRICIA SCHMELING

Serving well-balanced meals is a priority for this mother of four and grandma of two, who has been married for 34 years. Pat collects cookbooks and tries to make at least one new recipe each week—her family is always eager to be her guinea pigs! Before coming to Reiman Publications 7-1/2 years ago, she worked as a food technologist, developing salad dressings and sauces. She also taught evening baking classes at a local college.

Chocolate Eclair Torte

I take this impressive dessert to the table whole, then slice it and serve. It can be made ahead of time and refrigerated until you're ready to serve. —*Janaan Cunningham*

1 cup water
1/2 cup butter
1 cup all-purpose flour
4 eggs
FILLING:
2-1/2 cups cold milk
2 packages (3.4 ounces *each*) instant French vanilla pudding mix
1 teaspoon vanilla extract

1 carton (8 ounces) frozen whipped topping, thawed
ICING:
2 squares (1 ounce *each*) semisweet chocolate
2 tablespoons butter
2 tablespoons milk
1 teaspoon vanilla extract
1 cup confectioners' sugar

1 In a large saucepan, bring water and butter to a boil. Add flour all at once and stir until smooth ball forms. Remove from the heat; let stand for 5 minutes. Add eggs, one at a time, beating well after each addition. Continue beating until mixture is smooth and shiny.

2 Line a large baking sheet with waxed paper. Draw a 10-in. circle on the waxed paper. Grease the paper. Drop batter by rounded tablespoonfuls just inside the circle outline. Bake at 400° for 40-45 minutes or until golden brown. Transfer to a wire rack. Immediately prick with a fork and cool completely. Cut off top third of puffs. Pull out and discard soft dough from inside.

3 For filling, in a large bowl, whisk milk, pudding mixes and vanilla for 2 minutes; let stand for 2 minutes or until soft-set. Fold in whipped topping. Place bottom ring of cream puffs on a serving platter. Spoon filling inside. Top with top ring. Refrigerate.

4 For icing, in a microwave, melt chocolate and butter with milk; stir until smooth. Stir in vanilla. Add confectioners' sugar and stir until smooth. Cool for 5 minutes. Drizzle over top of cake. Serve immediately. Refrigerate leftovers. **Yield:** 12 servings.

Ice Cream Sandwich Dessert

Kids love this recipe! I appreciate that it's so easy to put together but looks like you fussed. —*Wendy Stenman*

19 ice cream sandwiches
1 carton (12 ounces) frozen whipped topping, thawed
1 jar (11-3/4 ounces) hot fudge ice cream topping
1 cup salted peanuts

1 Cut one ice cream sandwich in half. Place one whole and one half sandwich along a short side of an ungreased 13-in. x 9-in. x 2-in. pan. Arrange eight sandwiches in opposite direction in the pan. Spread with half of the whipped topping. Spoon fudge topping by teaspoonfuls onto whipped topping. Sprinkle with 1/2 cup peanuts.

2 Repeat layers with remaining ice cream sandwiches, whipped topping and peanuts (pan will be full). Cover and freeze for up to 2 months. Remove from freezer 20 minutes before serving. Cut into squares. **Yield:** 12-15 servings.

CAKES

Apricot Hazelnut Torte

This showstopping torte is as light as a feather and tastes heavenly.
—*Janaan Cunningham*

> 4 eggs, *separated*
> 1 cup ground hazelnuts
> 3/4 cup all-purpose flour
> 2 teaspoons baking powder
> 1/2 teaspoon salt
> 2 tablespoons water
> 1 teaspoon vanilla extract
> 1 cup sugar, *divided*
> 2 cups heavy whipping cream
> 1/4 cup confectioners' sugar
> 2/3 cup pureed canned apricots
> 1/2 cup apricot jam, warmed
> Whipped cream, sliced apricots and whole *or* chopped hazelnuts, optional

1 Place egg yolks in a large mixing bowl; place egg whites in a small mixing bowl. Let stand at room temperature for 30 minutes. Line two greased 9-in. round baking pans with waxed paper; grease the paper and set aside. In a bowl, combine the hazelnuts, flour, baking powder and salt; set aside.

2 Add water and vanilla to egg yolks; beat until lemon-colored. Gradually add 3/4 cup sugar; set aside. Beat egg whites on medium speed until soft peaks form. Gradually beat in remaining sugar, 1 tablespoon at a time, on high until stiff peaks form. Fold a fourth of the dry ingredients into egg yolk mixture. Repeat three times. Fold in egg white mixture.

3 Spread batter evenly into prepared pans. Bake at 350° for 20-25 minutes or until cake springs back when lightly touched. Cool for 10 minutes before removing from pans to wire racks to cool completely.

4 In a large mixing bowl, beat cream until it begins to thicken. Add confectioners' sugar; beat until stiff peaks form. Fold in apricots. Split each cake into two horizontal layers. Spread filling between layers and over sides of torte. Spread jam over top. Garnish with whipped cream, apricots and hazelnuts if desired. Store in the refrigerator. **Yield:** 12-14 servings.

Mini Pineapple Upside-Down Cakes

Pineapple upside-down cake is one of my family's favorite desserts. These mini versions are just the thing for a large crowd.
—*Megan Taylor*

> 2/3 cup packed brown sugar
> 1/3 cup butter, melted
> 2 cans (20 ounces *each*) sliced pineapple
> 1 package (18-1/4 ounces) yellow cake mix
> 3 eggs
> 1/3 cup vegetable oil
> 12 maraschino cherries, halved

1 In a small bowl, combine the brown sugar and butter; mix well. Spoon into 24 greased muffin cups. Drain pineapple, reserving the juice. Trim pineapple to fit muffin cups; place one ring in each cup.

2 In a large mixing bowl, combine the cake mix, eggs, oil and 1-1/4 cups of the reserved pineapple juice; mix well. Spoon over pineapple, filling each cup two-thirds full. Bake at 350° for 20-25 minutes or until a toothpick comes out clean.

3 Immediately invert onto wire racks to cool. Place a cherry in the center of each pineapple ring. **Yield:** 2 dozen.

Lemon Lover's Pound Cake

*(**Pictured on page 252**)*

With its great lemon flavor, this cake always receives raves. It'll even make a lemon lover out of those who say they don't normally care for the fruit! —*Nancy Fridirici*

1 cup butter, softened
3 cups sugar
6 eggs
5 tablespoons lemon juice
1 tablespoon grated lemon peel
1 teaspoon lemon extract
3 cups all-purpose flour
1/2 teaspoon baking soda

1/4 teaspoon salt
1-1/4 cups sour cream
ICING:
1/4 cup sour cream
2 tablespoons butter, softened
2-1/2 cups confectioners' sugar
3 tablespoons lemon juice
2 teaspoons grated lemon peel

1 In a large mixing bowl, cream butter and sugar until light and fluffy, about 5 minutes. Add eggs, one at a time, beating well after each addition. Stir in the lemon juice, peel and extract. Combine the flour, baking soda and salt; add to the creamed mixture alternately with sour cream. Beat just until combined.

2 Pour into a greased and floured 10-in. fluted tube pan. Bake at 350° for 55-60 minutes or until a toothpick inserted near the center comes out clean. Cool for 10 minutes before removing from pan to a wire rack to cool completely.

3 For icing, in a small mixing bowl, beat the sour cream and butter until blended. Gradually add confectioners' sugar. Beat in lemon juice and peel. Drizzle over the cake. Store in the refrigerator. **Yield:** 12 servings.

Chocolate Raspberry Torte

A packaged mix makes this striking cake fast to fix. I've made this cake for one of my children's birthdays and it was loved by all. —*Wendy Stenman*

1 package (18-1/4 ounces) chocolate cake mix
1 package (3 ounces) cream cheese, softened
3/4 cup cold milk
1 package (3.4 ounces) instant vanilla pudding mix
1 carton (8 ounces) frozen whipped topping, thawed
2 cups fresh raspberries
Confectioners' sugar
Fresh mint and additional raspberries, optional

1 Prepare the cake mix according to package directions, using three greased and floured 9-in. round baking pans. Bake at 350° for 25-30 minutes or until a toothpick inserted near the center comes out clean. Cool for 10 minutes before removing from pans to wire racks to cool completely.

2 In a large mixing bowl, beat cream cheese until fluffy. Combine milk and pudding mix; add to cream cheese and mix well. Fold in whipped topping and raspberries.

3 Place one cake layer on a serving plate; spread with half of the filling. Repeat layers. Top with remaining cake; dust with confectioners' sugar. Garnish with mint and raspberries if desired. Store in the refrigerator. **Yield:** 12 servings.

TEST KITCHEN TIP

Wendy likes to use reduced-fat cream cheese and reduced-fat whipped topping in this recipe to cut back on some of the calories.

Chocolate-Covered Gingerbread Cake

This recipes takes homey gingerbread to a new level that will delight your family and friends. I especially like to serve it for the holidays.
—*Julie Ferron*

6 tablespoons butter, melted
3/4 cup packed brown sugar
1/3 cup molasses
2 eggs
1 tablespoon grated fresh gingerroot
1-3/4 cups all-purpose flour
2 teaspoons ground ginger
1 teaspoon baking powder
1 teaspoon ground cinnamon
1/2 teaspoon baking soda
1/4 teaspoon salt
1/4 teaspoon ground cloves
1 cup warm water
GLAZE:
1/2 cup heavy whipping cream
1/4 cup butter
2 tablespoons light corn syrup
8 squares (1 ounce *each*) semisweet chocolate, chopped
1 teaspoon vanilla extract

1 In a mixing bowl, combine butter, brown sugar, molasses, eggs and gingerroot. Combine flour, ground ginger, baking powder, cinnamon, baking soda, salt and cloves; add to molasses mixture alternately with water, beating just until combined.

2 Pour into a greased 13-in. x 9-in. x 2-in. baking pan. Bake at 350° for 25-30 minutes or until a toothpick inserted near the center comes out clean. Cool for 10 minutes before removing from pan to a wire rack to cool completely.

3 In a medium saucepan, combine cream, butter and corn syrup; bring to a simmer over medium heat. Remove from the heat. Stir in chocolate and vanilla until smooth. Let stand until cool but still pourable, about 20 minutes.

4 Place a baking sheet underneath the wire rack. Reserve 1/2 cup glaze. Pour remaining glaze over cake, spreading with spatula to cover top and sides. Chill cake and reserved glaze until glaze is just firm enough to pipe, about 1 hour.

5 Pipe reserved glaze in a pattern over cake. Cover and refrigerate. Remove from refrigerator 30 minutes before serving. **Yield:** 12-15 servings.

Cream Cheese Sheet Cake

This moist sheet cake with a fudgy chocolate glaze is a favorite at my family gatherings. —*Patricia Schmeling*

1 cup plus 2 tablespoons butter, softened
2 packages (3 ounces *each*) cream cheese, softened
2-1/4 cups sugar
6 eggs
3/4 teaspoon vanilla extract
2-1/4 cups cake flour
FROSTING:
1 cup sugar
1/3 cup evaporated milk
1/2 cup butter
1/2 cup semisweet chocolate chips

1 In a large mixing bowl, cream butter, cream cheese and sugar. Add eggs, one at a time, beating well after each addition. Beat in vanilla. Add flour; mix well.

2 Pour into a greased 15-in. x 10-in. x 1-in. baking pan. Bake at 325° for 30-35 minutes or until a toothpick inserted near the center comes out clean. Cool completely.

3 For frosting, combine the sugar and milk in a saucepan; bring to a boil over medium heat. Cover; cook 3 minutes (do not stir). Stir in butter and chocolate chips until melted. Cool slightly. Stir; spread over cake. **Yield:** 24-30 servings.

Berry Tiramisu Cake

There is no going wrong with this almost-foolproof sponge cake. I enjoy making it in a fancy flower or other patterned tube pan and still layering as the recipe directs.

—Joylyn Trickel

- 4 cups assorted fresh berries
- 1 cup sugar
- 1 tablespoon lemon juice
- 2 teaspoons cornstarch

SPONGE CAKE:
- 1-1/2 cups all-purpose flour
- 1 cup plus 2 tablespoons sugar, *divided*
- 2 teaspoons baking powder
- 1/2 teaspoon salt
- 4 eggs, *separated*
- 1/2 cup water
- 1/3 cup vegetable oil

CREAM FILLING:
- 1 package (8 ounces) cream cheese, softened
- 1/2 cup confectioners' sugar
- 2 cups heavy whipping cream, whipped

1 In a large bowl, combine the berries, sugar and lemon juice. Cover and refrigerate for 1 hour. Gently press berries; drain, reserving juice. Set berries aside. In a large saucepan, combine cornstarch and reserved juice until smooth. Bring to a boil; cook and stir for 1-2 minutes or until thickened. Cool completely.

2 In a large mixing bowl, combine the flour, 1 cup sugar, baking powder and salt. Whisk egg yolks, water and oil; add to dry ingredients, beating until smooth. In another mixing bowl, beat egg whites on medium speed until soft peaks form. Gradually beat in remaining sugar, 1 tablespoon at a time, on high until stiff peaks form; fold into batter.

3 Spread into an ungreased 9-in. springform pan. Bake at 325° for 30-38 minutes or until cake springs back when lightly touched. Cool for 10 minutes before removing from pan to a wire rack to cool completely.

4 In a large mixing bowl, beat cream cheese and confectioners' sugar until smooth. Fold in whipped cream. Split cake into three horizontal layers; place one layer on a serving plate. Spread with a third of the filling; top with a third of the berries and drizzle with 1/4 cup berry syrup. Repeat layers twice. Loosely cover; refrigerate for at least 2 hours before serving. **Yield:** 12 servings.

TEST KITCHEN TIP

The undecorated cake freezes well for up to 3 months. Just let the frozen cake thaw completely in the refrigerator, decorate and serve.

Hazelnut Mocha Torte

(Also pictured on front cover)

The authentic buttercream frosting is the crowning glory to this sensational torte. It is worth all the effort that goes into making it.
—*Wendy Stenman*

 6 egg whites
1/4 teaspoon cream of tartar
 1 cup sugar
 2 cups ground hazelnuts
1/4 cup all-purpose flour
MOCHA GANACHE:
 8 squares (1 ounce *each*) semisweet chocolate
 1 cup heavy whipping cream
 3 tablespoons butter
 2 teaspoons instant coffee granules
BUTTERCREAM:
2/3 cup sugar
1/4 cup water
 4 egg yolks, lightly beaten
 1 teaspoon vanilla extract
 1 cup butter
1/4 cup confectioners' sugar
Additional ground hazelnuts
Whole hazelnuts and chocolate leaves

1 Place egg whites in a large mixing bowl; let stand at room temperature for 30 minutes. Add cream of tartar; beat on medium speed until soft peaks form. Gradually beat in sugar, 2 tablespoons at a time, on high until sugar is dissolved and stiff peaks form. Combine hazelnuts and flour; fold into batter, 1/4 cup at a time.

2 Spoon into two greased 9-in. round baking pans lined with waxed paper. Bake at 300° for 25-30 minutes or until cake springs back when lightly touched. Cool for 10 minutes before removing from pans to wire racks.

3 In a heavy saucepan, combine the ganache ingredients; cook and stir over low heat until chocolate and butter are melted. Remove from the heat. Set saucepan in ice; stir for 3-4 minutes or until thickened. Remove from ice and set aside.

4 For buttercream, combine sugar and water in a heavy saucepan. Bring to a boil; cook over medium-high heat until sugar is dissolved. Remove from the heat. Add a small amount of hot mixture to egg yolks; return all to pan. Cook and stir 2 minutes longer. Remove from the heat; stir in vanilla. Cool to room temperature.

5 In a large mixing bowl, cream butter until fluffy. Gradually beat in cooked sugar mixture. Beat in confectioners' sugar. If necessary, refrigerate until buttercream reaches spreading consistency.

6 Place one cake layer on a serving plate. Spread with half of ganache to within 1/4 in. of edges. Top with second cake layer and remaining ganache. Freeze for 5 minutes.

7 Spread buttercream over top and sides of cake. Gently press ground hazelnuts into sides of cake. Garnish with whole hazelnuts and chocolate leaves. Store in the refrigerator. **Yield:** 12-16 servings.

Raspberry Walnut Torte

(Pictured on page 253)

When you want a dessert that makes a statement, serve this eye-catching, fantastic cake. It's delicious as well as pretty.
—*Janet Briggs*

1-1/2 cups heavy whipping cream
3 eggs
1-1/2 cups sugar
3 teaspoons vanilla extract
1-3/4 cups all-purpose flour
1 cup ground walnuts, toasted
2 teaspoons baking powder
1/2 teaspoon salt

FROSTING:
1-1/2 cups heavy whipping cream
1 package (8 ounces) cream cheese, softened
1 cup sugar
1/8 teaspoon salt
1 teaspoon vanilla extract
1 jar (12 ounces) raspberry preserves

1 In a small mixing bowl, beat cream until stiff peaks form; set aside. In a large mixing bowl, beat eggs and sugar until thick and lemon-colored. Beat in vanilla. Combine flour, walnuts, baking powder and salt; fold into egg mixture alternately with whipped cream.

2 Pour into two greased and floured 9-in. round baking pans. Bake at 350° for 25-30 minutes or until a toothpick inserted near the center comes out clean. Cool for 10 minutes before removing from pans to wire racks to cool completely.

3 In a small mixing bowl, beat cream until stiff peaks form; set aside. In a large mixing bowl, beat cream cheese, sugar and salt until fluffy. Add vanilla; mix well. Fold in whipped cream.

4 Split each cake into two horizontal layers. Place one bottom layer on a serving plate; spread with about 1/2 cup frosting. Top with a second cake layer; spread with half of the raspberry preserves. Repeat layers. Frost sides of cake with frosting.

5 Cut a small hole in the corner of a pastry or plastic bag; insert ribbon tip #47. Fill bag with remaining frosting; pipe a lattice design on top of cake. Using star tip #32, pipe stars around top and bottom edges of cake. Store in the refrigerator. **Yield:** 16 servings.

EDITOR'S NOTE: A coupler ring will allow you to easily change tips for different designs.

Caramel Apple Cupcakes

These cupcakes make a fun treat at a Halloween party or any autumn event.
—*Sue Megonigle*

1 package (18-1/4 ounces) spice *or* carrot cake mix
2 cups chopped peeled tart apples
20 caramels
3 tablespoons milk
1 cup finely chopped pecans, toasted
12 Popsicle sticks

1 Prepare cake batter according to package directions for cupcakes; fold in apples. Fill 12 greased or paper-lined jumbo muffin cups three-fourths full. Bake at 350° for 20 minutes or until a toothpick comes out clean. Cool for 10 minutes before removing from pans to wire racks to cool completely.

2 In a saucepan, cook the caramels and milk over low heat until smooth. Spread over cupcakes. Sprinkle with pecans. Insert a Popsicle stick into the center of each cupcake. **Yield:** 1 dozen.

Peach Cake

This springtime layer cake is peachy and creamy. My mom gets requests for this cake from my brother for his April birthday.
—*Tamra Duncan*

  1 can (15-1/4 ounces) sliced peaches
  1 package (18-1/4 ounces) yellow cake mix
1/3 cup vegetable oil
  3 eggs
  1 carton (8 ounces) frozen whipped topping, thawed
  1 carton (6 ounces) peach yogurt

1 Drain peaches, reserving juice. Add enough water to juice to measure 1-1/4 cups. Cut peaches into 1-in. pieces; set aside.

2 In a large mixing bowl, beat the cake mix, peach juice mixture, oil and eggs on low speed for 30 seconds. Beat on medium for 2 minutes.

3 Pour into two greased and floured 9-in. round baking pans. Bake at 350° for 28-33 minutes or until a toothpick inserted near the center comes out clean. Cool for 10 minutes before removing from pans to wire racks to cool completely.

4 In a small bowl, combine the whipped topping and yogurt; fold in reserved peaches. Spread between layers and over top of cake. **Yield:** 10-12 servings.

Caramel Apple Cake

This cake is very tender and drizzled with a caramel icing. It disappears quickly when I take it to potluck suppers.
—*Patricia Schmeling*

1-1/2 cups vegetable oil
1-1/2 cups sugar
  1/2 cup packed brown sugar
    3 eggs
    3 cups all-purpose flour
    2 teaspoons ground cinnamon
    1 teaspoon baking soda
  1/2 teaspoon salt
  1/2 teaspoon ground nutmeg
3-1/2 cups diced peeled apples
    1 cup chopped walnuts
    2 teaspoons vanilla extract
CARAMEL ICING:
  1/2 cup packed brown sugar
  1/3 cup half-and-half cream
  1/4 cup butter
Dash salt
    1 cup confectioners' sugar
Chopped walnuts, optional

1 In a large mixing bowl, combine the oil and sugars. Add eggs, one at a time, beating well after each addition. Combine the dry ingredients; add to the batter and stir well. Fold in the apples, walnuts and vanilla.

2 Pour into a greased and floured 10-in. tube pan. Bake at 325° for 1-1/2 hours or until a toothpick inserted near the center comes out clean. Cool for 10 minutes before removing from pan to a wire rack to cool completely.

3 In a small heavy saucepan, heat the brown sugar, cream, butter and salt over low heat until sugar is dissolved. Cool to room temperature. Beat in confectioners' sugar until smooth; drizzle over cake. Sprinkle with nuts if desired. **Yield:** 12-16 servings.

Hazelnut Chiffon Cake

The hazelnuts give this beautiful cake a surprising crunch. It's covered with a buttery mocha frosting. —Joylyn Trickel

2-1/4 cups cake flour
1-1/2 cups sugar
   1 cup finely chopped hazelnuts, toasted
   1 teaspoon baking powder
  1/2 teaspoon salt
   5 egg yolks
  2/3 cup water
  1/2 cup vegetable oil
   1 tablespoon vanilla extract
   8 egg whites
1-1/2 teaspoons cream of tartar
MOCHA FROSTING:
  3/4 cup butter, softened
1-1/2 cups confectioners' sugar
   2 tablespoons baking cocoa
   1 teaspoon vanilla extract
   2 to 3 tablespoons strong brewed coffee

1 In a large mixing bowl, combine the flour, sugar, hazelnuts, baking powder and salt. Whisk the egg yolks, water, oil and vanilla; add to dry ingredients. Beat until well blended. In another large mixing bowl, beat egg whites and cream of tartar on medium speed until soft peaks form; fold into batter.

2 Gently spoon into an ungreased 10-in. tube pan. Cut through batter with a knife to remove air pockets. Bake on the lowest oven rack at 325° for 60-70 minutes or until top springs back when lightly touched. Immediately invert the cake pan onto a wire rack; cool completely. Carefully run a knife around edges and center tube to loosen; remove cake.

3 In a small mixing bowl, cream butter and confectioners' sugar. Beat in the baking cocoa, vanilla and enough coffee to achieve desired consistency. Frost cake. **Yield:** 12-16 servings.

Cranberry Cake

Served with a warm cream sauce that melts in your mouth, this cranberry cake is unbeatable, especially for the holidays.
—Amy Welk-Thieding

   3 tablespoons butter, softened
   1 cup sugar
   1 egg
   2 cups all-purpose flour
   2 teaspoons baking powder
   1 teaspoon ground nutmeg
   1 cup milk
   2 cups cranberries
   2 tablespoons grated orange *or* lemon peel
CREAM SAUCE:
1-1/3 cups sugar
   1 cup heavy whipping cream
  2/3 cup butter

1 In a large mixing bowl, cream butter and sugar. Beat in egg. Combine the flour, baking powder and nutmeg; add to creamed mixture alternately with milk. Stir in the cranberries and orange peel.

2 Pour into a greased 11-in. x 7-in. x 2-in. baking dish. Bake at 350° for 35-40 minutes or until a toothpick inserted near the center comes out clean.

3 Meanwhile, in a saucepan, combine sauce ingredients. Cook and stir over medium heat until heated through. Cut warm cake into squares; serve with cream sauce. **Yield:** 8-10 servings.

Pumpkin-Pecan Cake Roll

The pumpkin and spices combine with the delicious cream cheese filling to make this a must-have dessert at our annual Thanksgiving feast. —Coleen Martin

    3 eggs
    1 cup sugar
  3/4 cup all-purpose flour
  3/4 cup canned pumpkin
1-1/2 teaspoons ground cinnamon
    1 teaspoon baking powder
    1 teaspoon ground ginger
  1/2 teaspoon salt
  1/2 teaspoon ground nutmeg
    1 teaspoon lemon juice
    1 cup finely chopped pecans
Confectioners' sugar
FILLING:
    2 packages (3 ounces *each*) cream cheese, softened
  1/4 cup butter, softened
    1 cup confectioners' sugar
  1/2 teaspoon vanilla extract

1 Line a greased 15-in. x 10-in. x 1-in. baking pan with parchment paper and grease the paper; set aside. In a large mixing bowl, beat eggs for 5 minutes. Add the next eight ingredients; mix well. Add lemon juice.

2 Spread batter evenly in prepared pan; sprinkle with pecans. Bake at 375° for 15 minutes or until cake springs back when lightly touched. Cool for 5 minutes. Turn onto a kitchen towel dusted with confectioners' sugar. Peel off parchment paper. Roll up cake in towel jelly-roll style, starting with a short side. Cool on a wire rack.

3 In a small mixing bowl, combine the filling ingredients; beat until smooth. Unroll cake; spread filling over cake to within 1/2 in. of edges. Roll up again; place seam side down on a serving platter. Cover and refrigerate for at least 1 hour before serving. Refrigerate leftovers. **Yield:** 12 servings.

Mandarin Orange Cake

I've taken this cake to potlucks and it's always a hit. Everyone enjoys the light and moist cake with its fluffy orange frosting. —Kris Lehman

    1 can (11 ounces) mandarin oranges
    1 package (18-1/4 ounces) yellow cake mix
  1/2 cup vegetable oil
    4 eggs
    1 teaspoon orange extract
TOPPING:
    2 cups cold milk
    1 package (3.4 ounces) instant vanilla pudding mix
    1 can (8 ounces) unsweetened crushed pineapple, drained
    1 carton (8 ounces) frozen whipped topping, thawed

1 Drain oranges, reserving juice. Set oranges aside. In a large mixing bowl, beat the cake mix, oil, eggs, orange extract and reserved juice on low speed for 30 seconds. Beat on medium for 2 minutes.

2 Transfer to a greased 13-in. x 9-in. x 2-in. baking pan. Bake at 350° for 30-35 minutes or until a toothpick comes out clean. Cool on a wire rack.

3 For topping, in a bowl, whisk milk and pudding mix for 2 minutes. Let stand for 2 minutes or until soft-set. Fold in pineapple and reserved oranges; fold in whipped topping. Frost the cake. Refrigerate for at least 1 hour before serving. **Yield:** 12-15 servings.

Rich Mocha Cake

(Pictured on page 252)

I love chocolate and coffee together…so when I tried this recipe, there wasn't much room for disappointment! —Joylyn Trickel

2 cups all-purpose flour
1-3/4 cups sugar
1/2 cup baking cocoa
2 teaspoons baking soda
1 teaspoon salt
1 egg
2/3 cup vegetable oil
1 cup buttermilk
1 cup strong brewed coffee

FROSTING:
5 tablespoons butter
1 cup sugar
1/3 cup milk
1-1/2 cups semisweet chocolate chips, melted and cooled
1/2 cup caramel ice cream topping
1 cup chopped pecans, toasted

1 In a large bowl, combine the first five ingredients. In another bowl, whisk egg, oil and buttermilk. Add to the dry ingredients and stir well. Slowly add the coffee until combined (batter will be thin).

2 Pour into a greased 13-in. x 9-in. x 2-in. baking pan. Bake at 350° for 35-40 minutes or until a toothpick inserted near the center comes out clean. Cool completely on a wire rack.

3 For frosting, melt butter in a small saucepan. Add the sugar and milk; bring to a boil. Reduce heat; cook and stir for 2-3 minutes. Remove from the heat. Add the melted chips and stir until blended. Pour over cake, spreading evenly. Drizzle with caramel topping and sprinkle with pecans. **Yield:** 12-15 servings.

TEST KITCHEN TIP

To make drizzling easier, spoon caramel topping into a small resealable plastic bag and cut a small hole in the corner of the bag. Press topping out for an even and less messy drizzle.

Santa Cupcakes

Kids of all ages won't be able to resist these easy-to-make and cute-to-look-at cupcakes! They've become a Christmas tradition at our house. —Janaan Cunningham

1 package (18-1/4 ounces) white cake mix
1 can (16 ounces) *or* 2 cups vanilla frosting, *divided*
Red gel *or* paste food coloring
Miniature marshmallows, chocolate chips, red-hot candies and flaked coconut

1 Prepare cake batter according to package directions for cupcakes; fill paper-lined muffin cups two-thirds full. Bake according to package directions. Cool for 10 minutes before removing from pans to wire racks to cool completely.

2 Place 2/3 cup frosting in a small bowl; tint with red food coloring. Set aside 3 tablespoons white frosting for decorating. Cover two-thirds of the top of each cupcake with remaining white frosting. Frost the rest of cupcake top with red frosting for

hat. Place reserved white frosting in a small heavy-duty resealable plastic bag; cut a 1/4-in. hole in one corner. On each cupcake, pipe a line of frosting to create fur band of hat.

3 Press a marshmallow on one side of hat for pom-pom. Under hat, place two chocolate chips for eyes and one red-hot candy for nose. Gently press coconut onto face for beard. **Yield:** about 1-1/2 dozen.

Almond Eggnog Pound Cake

For the Christmas rush, this easy-to-make pound cake is a must. It makes a great hostess gift.
—Joylyn Trickel

6 tablespoons butter, softened, *divided*
2/3 cup sliced almonds
1 package (18-1/4 ounces) yellow cake mix
1-1/2 cups eggnog
2 eggs
1 teaspoon rum extract
1/8 teaspoon ground nutmeg

1 Grease a 10-in. fluted tube pan with 2 tablespoons butter. Press almonds onto the bottom and sides of pan; set aside. Melt remaining butter. In a large mixing bowl, beat the cake mix, eggnog, eggs, rum extract, nutmeg and melted butter on low speed for 30 seconds or just until moistened. Beat on medium for 2 minutes or until smooth.

2 Pour into prepared pan. Bake at 350° for 40-50 minutes or until a toothpick inserted near the center comes out clean. Cool for 15 minutes before removing from pan to a wire rack to cool completely. **Yield:** 12-14 servings.

EDITOR'S NOTE: This recipe was tested with commercially prepared eggnog.

Viennese Torte

I guarantee that this dessert tastes as fabulous as it looks! It's perfect for any special occasion. *—Peggy Fleming*

1/2 cup butter, softened
1-1/2 cups sugar, *divided*
4 eggs, *separated*
1/4 cup milk
1 teaspoon vanilla extract
3/4 cup cake flour
1 teaspoon baking powder
1/8 teaspoon salt
1/8 teaspoon cream of tartar
1/2 cup flaked coconut
1/2 cup sliced almonds
FILLING:
1 cup cold milk
1 package (3.4 ounces) instant vanilla pudding mix
1 cup heavy whipping cream, whipped

1 Line two 9-in. round baking pans with waxed paper and grease the paper; set aside. In a large mixing bowl, cream butter and 1/2 cup sugar. Beat in egg yolks, milk and vanilla. Combine the flour, baking powder and salt; gradually add to creamed mixture. Pour into prepared pans.

2 In a small mixing bowl, beat egg whites and cream of tartar on medium speed until soft peaks form. Gradually add remaining sugar, 1 tablespoon at a time, beating on high until stiff glossy peaks form and sugar is dissolved. Spread evenly over batter, sealing edges to sides of pan.

3 Bake at 300° for 30 minutes. Sprinkle with coconut and almonds. Bake 20-30 minutes longer or until meringue and coconut are lightly browned. Cool for 10 minutes before removing from pans to wire racks. Cool with meringue side up.

4 In a bowl, whisk milk and pudding mix for 2 minutes. Let stand for 2 minutes or until soft-set. Fold in whipped cream. Place one cake layer on a serving plate meringue side up; spread with pudding mixture. Top with remaining cake. Chill overnight. Refrigerate leftovers. **Yield:** 12 servings.

Tiramisu Toffee Torte

Tiramisu is Italian for "pick-me-up," and this treat truly lives up to its name. The high torte is a great ending to a meal. I love the flavorful filling and crushed toffee candy on top. When we first made this in the Test Kitchen, everyone took some home! That's always a good sign a recipe has excellent flavor. —Sue A. Jurack

> 1 package (18-1/4 ounces) white cake mix
> 1 cup strong brewed coffee, room temperature
> 4 egg whites
> 4 Heath candy bars (1.4 ounces *each*), chopped
> FROSTING:
> 4 ounces cream cheese, softened
> 2/3 cup sugar
> 2 cups heavy whipping cream
> 1/3 cup chocolate syrup
> 1/4 cup plus 6 tablespoons strong brewed coffee, room temperature, *divided*
> 2 teaspoons vanilla extract
> 1 Heath candy bar (1.4 ounces), chopped

1 Line two greased 9-in. round baking pans with waxed paper and grease the paper; set aside. In a large mixing bowl, beat the cake mix, coffee and egg whites on low speed until moistened. Beat on high for 2 minutes. Fold in chopped candy bars. Pour into prepared pans.

2 Bake at 350° for 25-30 minutes or until a toothpick inserted near the center comes out clean. Cool for 10 minutes before removing from pans to wire racks to cool completely.

3 For frosting, in a mixing bowl, beat the cream cheese and sugar until smooth. Add the cream, chocolate syrup, 1/4 cup coffee and vanilla. Beat on high speed until light and fluffy, about 5 minutes.

4 Split each cake into two horizontal layers. Place one layer on a serving plate; drizzle with 2 tablespoons of the remaining coffee. Spread with 3/4 cup frosting. Repeat layers twice. Top with fourth cake layer. Frost top and sides of cake with remaining frosting. Refrigerate overnight. Garnish with chopped candy bar. Store in the refrigerator. **Yield:** 12-14 servings.

TEST KITCHEN TIP

Make and bake the cake in advance and split the layers before freezing. Assembling the torte will go very quickly once the filling is made.

Chocolate Almond Cake

My sons request this cake for their birthdays. To decorate, I fill the palms of my hands with almonds and press the nuts into the frosting. —*Patricia Schmeling*

1/3 cup butter, softened
1/3 cup shortening
1-3/4 cups sugar
2 eggs
1-1/2 teaspoons vanilla extract
2 cups all-purpose flour
1/2 cup baking cocoa
1 teaspoon baking powder
1/2 teaspoon baking soda
1/2 teaspoon salt
1-1/4 cups buttermilk
FROSTING:
3 cups heavy whipping cream
1 cup confectioners' sugar
3 tablespoons baking cocoa
1-1/2 teaspoons vanilla extract
6 tablespoons seedless raspberry jam, warmed
1-1/2 to 2 cups sliced almonds, toasted
Fresh raspberries and mint

1 Line two greased 9-in. round baking pans with waxed paper; set aside. In a large mixing bowl, cream the butter, shortening and sugar until fluffy. Add eggs, one at a time, beating well after each addition. Add vanilla. Combine the flour, cocoa, baking powder, baking soda and salt; add to creamed mixture alternately with buttermilk and mix well.

2 Pour into prepared pans. Bake at 350° for 25-30 minutes or until a toothpick inserted near the center comes out clean. Cool for 10 minutes before removing from pans to wire racks to cool completely.

3 For frosting, beat cream in a large mixing bowl until soft peaks form. Add confectioners' sugar and cocoa, beating until stiff peaks form. Beat in vanilla.

4 Spread about 2 tablespoons of jam over each cake layer. Spread 1-1/2 cups whipped cream mixture over one layer; drizzle with remaining jam. Top with remaining cake layer; spread the remaining whipped cream mixture over top and sides of cake. Press almonds onto sides and top of cake. Garnish with raspberries and mint. Store in the refrigerator. **Yield:** 12-14 servings.

TAMRA DUNCAN

As a teenager, Tamra worked at a country club where she made 250 omelets to order every Sunday as part of a weekly brunch. That's also when she discovered *Taste of Home* magazine and dreamed of working for the company—she's been an employee for over 3 years now! She "absolutely" loves cooking and sharing her love of food and recipes with others. Tamra and her husband recently bought their first home and are enjoying furnishing and landscaping it.

Coconut-Topped Oatmeal Cake

This is an old-fashioned cake with mass appeal that was passed down from my husband's grand-mother. It's a classic for everyone's recipe box.
—*Tamra Duncan*

1-1/2 cups boiling water
1 cup quick-cooking oats
1/2 cup butter, softened
1 cup sugar
1 cup packed brown sugar
2 eggs
1-1/2 cups all-purpose flour
1 teaspoon baking soda
1 teaspoon ground cinnamon
1/2 teaspoon salt
TOPPING:
1 cup packed brown sugar
1/2 cup butter
1/2 cup milk
1 cup flaked coconut
1/2 cup chopped pecans
1 teaspoon vanilla extract

1 In a bowl, pour boiling water over oats; let stand for 5 minutes. In a large mixing bowl, cream butter and sugars. Add eggs, one at a time, beating well after each addition. Combine the flour, baking soda, cinnamon and salt; add to creamed mixture alternately with oat mixture until combined.

2 Transfer to a greased 13-in. x 9-in. x 2-in. baking pan. Bake at 350° for 30-35 minutes or until a toothpick inserted near the center comes out clean.

3 Meanwhile, in a saucepan, bring the brown sugar, butter and milk to a boil over medium heat. Remove from the heat; stir in the coconut, pecans and vanilla. Pour over warm cake. Cool completely. **Yield:** 12-15 servings.

Pecan Date Fruitcake

Sometimes I make this fruitcake in larger pans or mini pans. If you try a different pan size, make sure you also adjust the baking time. Pretty slices are an attractive addition to the dessert table.
—*Anita Bukowski*

2 pounds pitted dates, quartered
1 pound pecan halves (4 cups)
1 pound candied cherries, halved (2-1/4 cups)
1 cup all-purpose flour
1 cup sugar
1/2 teaspoon baking powder
1/2 teaspoon salt
4 eggs
2 teaspoons vanilla extract

1 Grease and line three 8-in. x 4-in. x 2-in. loaf pans with waxed paper; set aside. In a large bowl, combine the dates, nuts and cherries. Combine the flour, sugar, baking powder and salt; stir into fruit mixture until well coated. In a small mixing bowl, beat eggs and vanilla until foamy. Fold into fruit mixture and mix well.

2 Pour into prepared pans. Bake at 300° for 1 hour or until a toothpick inserted near the center comes out clean. Cool for 10 minutes before removing from pans to wire racks. Remove waxed paper. Cool completely before slicing. Wrap and store in a cool dry place. **Yield:** 3 loaves.

Nutmeg Pear Cake

I have a favorite apple cake that I used to make each fall, but this recipe has replaced it. We love the creamy apple cider sauce that tops the moist spiced pear cake. —Sue A. Jurack

3 cups all-purpose flour
1-1/2 teaspoons ground nutmeg
1 teaspoon baking soda
1 teaspoon ground cinnamon
3/4 teaspoon salt
1/2 teaspoon baking powder
2 cups sugar
1 cup vegetable oil
3 eggs, beaten
1/2 cup apple cider *or* juice
3 teaspoons vanilla extract

1 can (29 ounces) pear halves, drained and mashed
1 cup chopped pecans
APPLE CIDER SAUCE:
3/4 cup butter
2/3 cup sugar
1/3 cup packed brown sugar
2 tablespoons cornstarch
2/3 cup apple cider
1/3 cup heavy whipping cream
1/3 cup lemon juice

1 In a bowl, combine first six ingredients. In another bowl, whisk sugar, oil, eggs, cider and vanilla. Stir into dry ingredients. Stir in pears and pecans.

2 Pour into a greased and floured 10-in. fluted tube pan. Bake at 350° for 65-70 minutes or until a toothpick inserted comes out clean. Cool for 10 minutes before removing from pan to a wire rack.

3 For sauce, combine the butter and sugars in a saucepan. Cook over low heat for 2-3 minutes or until sugar is dissolved. Combine the cornstarch and cider until smooth; add to sugar mixture. Stir in the cream and lemon juice. Bring to a boil; cook and stir for 1-2 minutes or until thickened. Serve warm with cake. **Yield:** 12-15 servings.

Chocolate Creme Cakes

I make this every year for our subdivision picnic. After the first time I brought it, I was jokingly told to bring it again or not to come back! —Coleen Martin

1 package (18-1/4 ounces) chocolate cake mix
1 package (3.9 ounces) instant chocolate pudding mix
3/4 cup vegetable oil
3/4 cup water
4 eggs
FILLING:
3 tablespoons all-purpose flour
1 cup milk
1/2 cup butter, softened
1/2 cup shortening
1 cup sugar
1 teaspoon vanilla extract

1 In a large mixing bowl, combine the cake and pudding mixes, oil, water and eggs. Pour into a greased and floured 13-in. x 9-in. x 2-in. baking pan. Bake at 350° for 30-35 minutes or until a toothpick inserted near the center comes out clean. Cool for 10 minutes before removing to a wire rack to cool completely.

2 In a small saucepan, combine flour and milk until smooth. Bring to a boil; cook and stir for 2 minutes or until thickened. Cool. In a large mixing bowl, cream the butter, shortening, sugar and vanilla; beat in milk mixture until sugar is dissolved, about 5 minutes.

3 Split cake into two horizontal layers. Spread filling over bottom layer; cover with top layer. Cut into serving-size pieces. **Yield:** 12-18 servings.

German Apple Cake

I love this moist, old-fashioned cake with a rich cream cheese frosting. It's a true taste of the fall.
—Julie Ferron

3 eggs
2 cups sugar
1 cup vegetable oil
1 teaspoon vanilla extract
2 cups all-purpose flour
2 teaspoons ground cinnamon
1 teaspoon baking soda
1/2 teaspoon salt
4 cups chopped peeled tart apples
3/4 cup chopped pecans
FROSTING:
1 package (8 ounces) cream cheese, softened
2 teaspoons butter, softened
2 cups confectioners' sugar

1 In a large mixing bowl, beat the eggs, sugar, oil and vanilla. Combine the flour, cinnamon, baking soda and salt; add to egg mixture and mix well. Fold in apples and pecans.

2 Pour into a greased 13-in. x 9-in. x 2-in. baking dish. Bake at 350° for 55-60 minutes or until a toothpick inserted near the center comes out clean. Cool on a wire rack.

3 In a small mixing bowl, beat cream cheese and butter. Add confectioners' sugar, beating until smooth. Spread over cake. Store in the refrigerator. **Yield:** 12-15 servings.

Peanut Chocolate Cake

This recipe deliciously combines chocolate and peanut butter—two of my favorites!
—Peggy Fleming

1/2 cup butter, softened
2-1/4 cups packed brown sugar
3 eggs
3 squares (1 ounce *each*) unsweetened chocolate, melted and cooled
2 teaspoons vanilla extract
2-1/4 cups all-purpose flour
2 teaspoons baking soda
1/2 teaspoon salt
1 cup (8 ounces) sour cream
1 cup water
FROSTING:
1 cup butter, softened
1 cup peanut butter
4 cups confectioners' sugar
1/4 cup milk
2 teaspoons vanilla extract
1 cup finely chopped peanuts

1 In a mixing bowl, combine butter and brown sugar; beat in eggs, chocolate and vanilla. Combine flour, baking soda and salt; add to creamed mixture alternately with sour cream. Beat in water.

2 Pour into two greased and floured 9-in. round baking pans. Bake at 350° for 35-40 minutes or until a toothpick inserted near the center comes out clean. Cool for 10 minutes before removing from pans to wire racks to cool completely.

3 For frosting, in a large mixing bowl, cream the butter, peanut butter, confectioners' sugar, milk and vanilla until smooth; set aside.

4 Split each cake into two horizontal layers. Spread about 1/2 cup frosting over one bottom layer; repeat layers twice. Top with remaining cake. Frost top and sides of cake. Gently press peanuts into sides of cake. **Yield:** 12 servings.

Pear Tart

(*Pictured on page 272*)

This pretty pastry is quick and easy to prepare yet looks like it came from a fancy bakery. Baked in a tart pan, it's quite delicate looking.
— *Peggy Fleming*

3 tablespoons butter, softened
3/4 cup plus 1 tablespoon sugar, *divided*
3/4 cup all-purpose flour
1/3 cup finely chopped walnuts
1 package (8 ounces) reduced-fat cream cheese

1 egg
1 teaspoon vanilla extract
1 can (15 ounces) reduced-sugar pears, drained and thinly sliced
1 teaspoon ground cinnamon

1 Coat a 9-in. fluted tart pan with removable bottom with nonstick cooking spray; set aside. In a small mixing bowl, beat butter and 1/2 cup sugar for 2 minutes or until crumbly. Beat in flour and nuts. Press onto the bottom and up the sides of prepared pan.

2 In another small mixing bowl, beat cream cheese until smooth. Beat in 1/4 cup sugar, egg and vanilla; spread over crust. Arrange pears over cream cheese layer. Combine cinnamon and remaining sugar; sprinkle over pears.

3 Bake at 425° for 10 minutes. Reduce heat to 350°; bake 15-20 minutes longer or until filling is set and a thermometer reads 160°. Cool for 1 hour on a wire rack. Refrigerate for at least 2 hours before serving. Remove sides of pan before slicing. **Yield:** 12 servings.

TEST KITCHEN TIP
Slice the pears thinly. The more you have to layer over the filling, the more impressive it will look.

Chocolate Cheesecake Pie

This pie's smooth, rich chocolate filling melts in your mouth. The pie can be ready to eat in 30 minutes. I like to garnish it with fresh fruit. — *Amy Welk-Thieding*

1 package (8 ounces) cream cheese, softened
1/4 cup butter, softened
1/3 cup sugar
1-1/2 teaspoons vanilla extract
1-1/2 cups milk chocolate chips, melted and cooled
1 carton (8 ounces) frozen whipped topping, thawed
1 graham cracker crust (9 inches)
Chocolate leaf dessert decorations

1 In a large mixing bowl, beat the cream cheese, butter, sugar and vanilla until smooth. Beat in melted chocolate. Fold in the whipped topping.

2 Spoon into the crust. Cover and chill until serving. Garnish with chocolate leaves. **Yield:** 6-8 servings.

Chocolate Cream Pie

This rich, old-fashioned chocolate cream pie is one of my favorites. The homemade goodness of the filling is unbeatable.
— *Erin Frakes*

1-1/2 cups sugar
   1/3 cup all-purpose flour
    3 tablespoons baking cocoa
   1/2 teaspoon salt
1-1/2 cups water
    1 can (12 ounces) evaporated milk
    5 egg yolks, beaten
   1/2 cup butter
    1 teaspoon vanilla extract
    1 pastry shell (9 inches), baked
Whipped topping

1 In a large saucepan, combine the first six ingredients until smooth. Cook and stir over medium-high heat until thickened and bubbly, about 2 minutes. Reduce heat; cook and stir 2 minutes longer. Remove from the heat.

2 Stir 1 cup hot filling into egg yolks; return all to the pan, stirring constantly. Bring to a gentle boil; cook and stir for 2 minutes. Remove from the heat; gently stir in butter and vanilla. Cool slightly.

3 Pour warm filling into pastry shell. Cool for 1 hour. Refrigerate until set. Garnish with whipped topping. **Yield:** 6-8 servings.

Cherry Almond Pie

My dad loves all kinds of fruit pies, especially this one, so I make it for his birthday every year. — *Megan Taylor*

    2 cans (14-1/2 ounces *each*) pitted tart cherries
    1 cup sugar
   1/4 cup cornstarch
   1/8 teaspoon salt
    2 tablespoons butter
   1/2 teaspoon almond extract
   1/2 teaspoon vanilla extract
   1/4 teaspoon red food coloring, optional
Pastry for double-crust pie (9 inches)
    1 egg yolk, beaten
Additional sugar

1 Drain the cherries, reserving 1 cup juice. In a saucepan, combine the sugar, cornstarch and salt; gradually stir in the reserved juice until smooth. Bring to a boil; cook and stir for 2 minutes or until thickened. Remove from the heat. Stir in the butter, extracts and food coloring if desired. Fold in cherries. Cool slightly.

2 Line a 9-in. pie plate with bottom pastry; trim to 1 in. beyond edge. Add filling. Roll out remaining pastry; make a lattice crust. Trim, seal and flute edges. Brush lattice top with egg yolk. Sprinkle with additional sugar.

3 Cover edges loosely with foil. Bake at 425° for 15 minutes. Remove foil. Bake 20-25 minutes longer or until crust is golden brown and filling is bubbly. Cool on a wire rack. **Yield:** 6-8 servings.

Macadamia Caramel Tart

Chock-full of buttery macadamia nuts, this rich tart is a real crowd-pleaser! —*Peggy Fleming*

- 2-3/4 cups all-purpose flour
- 2-1/2 cups sugar, *divided*
- 1 cup cold butter, cubed
- 2 eggs
- 1 cup heavy whipping cream
- 2-1/2 cups macadamia nuts, toasted
- 1 egg white, beaten

1 In a food processor, combine the flour, 1/2 cup sugar and butter; cover and pulse until blended. Add eggs; pulse until blended. Turn onto a lightly floured surface; gently knead 5 times or until dough forms a ball.

2 Between two sheets of waxed paper, roll two-thirds of dough into a 13-in. circle; press onto the bottom and 2 in. up the sides of an ungreased 9-in. springform pan. Cover and chill. Roll remaining dough into a 9-in. circle; chill.

3 In a large heavy skillet, cook and stir the remaining sugar over medium heat until melted and dark brown, about 20 minutes. Slowly stir in cream until blended. Remove from the heat; stir in nuts. Cool for 15 minutes. Pour into prepared pan. Top with 9-in. pastry circle. Fold pastry from sides of pan over the top pastry; seal edges with a fork. Brush top with egg white.

4 Bake at 325° for 50-55 minutes or until golden brown. Cool on a wire rack for 20 minutes. Carefully run a knife around edge of pan to loosen. Remove sides of pan. Cool completely before cutting. **Yield:** 10-12 servings.

TEST KITCHEN TIP

If you don't have a food processor, the pastry can be made in the traditional manner by cutting the cold butter into the flour mixture.

Graham Cracker Crust

Instead of purchasing a graham cracker crust, make your own with just three everyday ingredients. —*Janaan Cunningham*

- 1-1/2 cups crushed graham crackers (24 squares)
- 1/4 cup sugar
- 1/3 cup butter, melted

1 In a small bowl, combine the crumbs and sugar; add butter and blend well. Press onto the bottom and up the sides of an ungreased 9-in. pie plate.

2 Refrigerate for 30 minutes before filling, or bake at 375° for 8-10 minutes or until crust is lightly browned. Cool on a wire rack before filling. **Yield:** 1 pie crust (9 inches).

Candy Bar Pie

Here's a very rich and creamy pie that tastes terrific. If you prefer, use Milky Way candy bars instead of Snickers in this recipe. —Sue Megonigle

  5 Snickers candy bars (2.07 ounces *each*), cut into 1/4-inch pieces
  1 pastry shell (9 inches), baked
 12 ounces cream cheese, softened
1/2 cup sugar
  2 eggs
1/3 cup sour cream
1/3 cup peanut butter
2/3 cup semisweet chocolate chips
  2 tablespoons heavy whipping cream

1 Place candy bar pieces in the pastry shell; set aside. In a large mixing bowl, beat cream cheese and sugar until smooth. Add the eggs, sour cream and peanut butter; beat on low speed just until combined. Pour into pastry shell.

2 Bake at 325° for 35-40 minutes or until set. Cool on a wire rack. In a small heavy saucepan, melt chocolate chips with cream over low heat until smooth. Spread over filling. Refrigerate for 2 hours or overnight. Cut with a warm knife. **Yield:** 8-10 servings.

Autumn Apple Tart

The crumb topping gives this apple tart a delightfully sweet crunch in every bite. I like to make it year-round, but it's especially good in fall when fresh apples are at their best. —Janet Briggs

1-1/4 cups all-purpose flour
    1 teaspoon baking powder
 1/2 teaspoon salt
    1 tablespoon sugar
 1/2 cup cold butter
    1 egg, beaten
    2 tablespoons milk
    6 medium tart apples, peeled and cut into 1/4-inch slices

TOPPING:
 1/3 to 1/2 cup sugar
4-1/2 teaspoons all-purpose flour
 1/2 teaspoon ground cinnamon
 1/2 teaspoon ground nutmeg
    2 tablespoons cold butter

1 In a medium bowl, combine the flour, baking powder, salt and sugar. Cut in butter until mixture resembles fine crumbs. Combine egg and milk; gradually add to flour mixture, tossing with a fork until dough forms a ball.

2 With lightly floured hands, press dough onto the bottom and up the sides of a 12-in. fluted tart pan with removable bottom. Arrange apple slices in a circular pattern over dough, starting at the outer edge and overlapping slices.

3 For topping, combine the sugar, flour and spices in a small bowl. Cut in butter until crumbly. Sprinkle over apples. Bake at 350° for 50-60 minutes or until apples are tender. Serve warm or cold. **Yield:** 6-8 servings.

Cranberry Cherry Pie

(Pictured on page 273)

The addition of cranberries to this pie is a great way to dress up canned cherry pie filling—the two flavors really complement each other.
—*Rita Krajcir*

Pastry for double-crust pie (9 inches)
   2 cups fresh *or* frozen cranberries, thawed
   3/4 cup plus 2 teaspoons sugar, *divided*
   2 tablespoons cornstarch

1 can (21 ounces) cherry pie filling
1 egg white
1 teaspoon water

1 Line a 9-in. pie plate with bottom pastry; trim even with edge of plate. Set aside. In a large bowl, combine the cranberries, 3/4 cup sugar and cornstarch; stir in pie filling. Spoon into crust.

2 Roll out remaining pastry; make a lattice crust. Trim, seal and flute edges. Beat egg white and water; brush over crust. Sprinkle with remaining sugar.

3 Cover edges loosely with foil. Bake at 425° for 25 minutes. Remove foil; bake 15-20 minutes longer or until crust is golden brown and filling is bubbly. Cool on a wire rack. **Yield:** 6-8 servings.

Glazed Blackberry Pie

I especially enjoy making this pie when visiting my family in Michigan. I use blackberries fresh from their garden.
—*Karen Johnson*

   5 cups fresh blackberries, *divided*
   1 pastry shell (9 inches), baked
   1 cup water, *divided*
 3/4 cup sugar
   3 tablespoons cornstarch
Red food coloring, optional
Whipped cream

1 Place 2 cups blackberries in pastry shell; set aside. In a saucepan, crush 1 cup berries. Add 3/4 cup water. Bring to a boil over medium heat, stirring constantly; cook and stir for 2 minutes. Press berries through a sieve. Set juice aside and discard pulp.

2 In a saucepan, combine the sugar and cornstarch. Stir in remaining water and reserved juice until smooth. Bring to a boil; cook and stir for 2 minutes or until thickened. Remove from the heat; stir in food coloring if desired.

3 Pour half of the glaze over berries in pastry shell. Stir remaining berries into remaining glaze; carefully spoon over filling. Refrigerate for 3 hours or until set. Garnish with whipped cream. Refrigerate leftovers. **Yield:** 6-8 servings.

TEST KITCHEN TIP
Wild blackberries (bramble berries) work nicely as a substitution.

Apple Cranberry Tart

A few simple ingredients are all you need to make this elegant-looking fruit tart. Try it with vanilla ice cream served alongside.
—*Sue Myers*

Pastry for double-crust pie (9 inches)
  2 cups fresh *or* frozen cranberries, coarsely chopped
  2 medium tart apples, peeled and coarsely chopped
1-1/4 cups packed brown sugar
  2 tablespoons all-purpose flour
1/2 teaspoon ground cinnamon
  1 to 2 tablespoons butter

1 On a lightly floured surface, roll out half of the pastry into a 13-in. circle. Press onto the bottom and up the sides of an ungreased 11-in. fluted tart pan with removable bottom; trim pastry even with edge.

2 In a bowl, combine the cranberries, apples, brown sugar, flour and cinnamon. Pour into crust. Dot with butter. Roll out remaining pastry to 1/4-in. thickness. Cut out with a floured 1-in. apple cookie cutter. Place over filling.

3 Place tart pan on a warm baking sheet. Bake at 425° for 35-40 minutes or until filling is hot and bubbly and crust is golden. Serve warm. **Yield:** 12-16 servings.

Strawberry Pie

For my mother's 70th birthday and Mother's Day, I made two of these strawberry pies instead of a cake. Since it was mid-May in Texas, the berries were absolutely perfect. It was a memorable occasion for the whole family.
—*Sue A. Jurack*

  1 unbaked pastry shell (9 inches)
3/4 cup sugar
  2 tablespoons cornstarch
  1 cup water
  1 package (3 ounces) strawberry gelatin
  4 cups sliced fresh strawberries
Fresh mint, optional

1 Line unpricked pastry shell with a double thickness of heavy-duty foil. Bake at 450° for 8 minutes. Remove foil; bake 5 minutes longer. Cool on a wire rack.

2 In a saucepan, combine the sugar, cornstarch and water until smooth. Bring to a boil; cook and stir for 2 minutes or until thickened. Remove from the heat; stir in gelatin until dissolved. Refrigerate for 15-20 minutes or until slightly cooled.

3 Meanwhile, arrange strawberries in the crust. Pour gelatin mixture over berries. Refrigerate until set. Garnish with mint if desired. **Yield:** 6-8 servings.

Test Kitchen Tip

Sue often uses whole fresh strawberries and arranges them pointed side up in the pastry shell for a different presentation. It also is a time-saver because she doesn't have to slice the berries.

Old-Fashioned Custard Pie

My family requests this pie more than any other type I make. It has stood the test of time! —*Betty Reuter*

Pastry for single- *or* double-crust pie (9 inches)
      4 eggs
 2-1/2 cups milk
    1/2 cup sugar
       1 teaspoon vanilla extract
       1 teaspoon almond extract
       1 teaspoon salt
       1 teaspoon ground nutmeg

1 Line pie plate with bottom pastry; flute edges or prepare a braided crust (see Editor's Note). Bake at 400° for 10 minutes. Meanwhile, in a large mixing bowl, beat eggs. Add the remaining ingredients; mix well. Pour into crust.

2 Cover edges with foil. Bake for 20-25 minutes or until a knife inserted near the center comes out clean. Cool completely. Store in the refrigerator. **Yield:** 6-8 servings.

EDITOR'S NOTE: Pastry for a double crust is needed only if a braided crust is desired. To prepare braided crust, trim pastry even with edge of pie plate; brush with water. From the top pastry, cut 12 strips, each 1/4 in. thick. Using three strips at a time, braid pastry on edge of crust, attaching ends together. Press down gently. Bake as directed.

Cappuccino Chocolate Pie

This pie uses some prepared convenience products, but you'd never know it from the taste. It is so rich and creamy. —*Karen Scales*

       1 cup (6 ounces) semisweet chocolate chips
    1/3 cup heavy whipping cream
       1 tablespoon light corn syrup
    1/2 teaspoon vanilla extract
Dash salt
       1 graham cracker crust (10 inches)
       1 cup chopped pecans
       4 ounces cream cheese, softened

 1-1/2 cups milk
       2 tablespoons brewed coffee
       2 packages (3.4 ounces *each*) instant vanilla pudding mix
       2 tablespoons instant coffee granules
       1 carton (8 ounces) frozen whipped topping, thawed, *divided*

1 In a saucepan, melt chocolate chips, cream, corn syrup, vanilla and salt over low heat; stir until smooth. Spoon into the crust. Sprinkle with pecans.

2 In a large mixing bowl, beat cream cheese until smooth. Gradually add milk and brewed coffee; mix well. Add pudding mixes and instant coffee; beat until smooth. Fold in 1-1/2 cups whipped topping. Spoon over pecans. Spread with remaining whipped topping. Refrigerate for at least 3 hours before serving. **Yield:** 6-8 servings.

Peanut Butter Pie

My college roommate made a fabulous peanut butter pie very similar to this one. Even though we both studied nutrition, we still understood the need for comfort food.
—*Tamra Duncan*

1-1/4 cups chocolate cookie crumbs (about 20 cookies)
   1/4 cup sugar
   1/4 cup butter, melted
FILLING:
     1 package (8 ounces) cream cheese, softened
     1 cup sugar
     1 cup creamy peanut butter
     1 tablespoon butter, softened
     1 teaspoon vanilla extract
     1 cup heavy whipping cream, whipped
Grated chocolate *or* chocolate cookie crumbs, optional

1 Combine the cookie crumbs, sugar and butter; press into a 9-in. pie plate. Bake at 375° for 10 minutes. Cool.

2 In a large mixing bowl, beat the cream cheese, sugar, peanut butter, butter and vanilla until smooth. Fold in whipped cream. Gently spoon into crust. Garnish with chocolate or cookie crumbs if desired. Refrigerate. **Yield:** 8-10 servings.

Almond Tartlets

These nutty, rich treats are perfect for setting out on a dessert buffet. Folks can never resist them!
—*Kristin Arnett*

1-1/3 cups all-purpose flour
   1/4 cup sugar
     1 teaspoon grated lemon peel
   1/2 cup cold butter
     1 egg, beaten
FILLING:
   1/2 cup almond paste

   1/3 cup sugar
     4 teaspoons butter, softened
     1 teaspoon vanilla extract
     1 teaspoon rum extract
     2 eggs
   1/3 cup sliced almonds
   1/3 cup apricot jam, melted

1 In a small bowl, combine the flour, sugar and lemon peel; cut in butter until crumbly. Add egg and toss with a fork until dough forms a ball. Cover with plastic wrap and refrigerate for 1 hour.

2 Place almond paste in a food processor or blender; cover and process until crumbly. Add the sugar, butter, extracts and eggs; cover and process until smooth.

3 On a lightly floured surface, roll out dough to 1/8-in. thickness. Cut into thirty 2-1/2-in. circles; press dough into miniature muffin cups coated with nonstick cooking spray. Bake at 350° for 10 minutes.

4 Spoon 1 teaspoon filling into each shell; sprinkle with a few almonds. Bake 10 minutes longer or until filling is set and pastry is lightly browned. Brush jam over tarts. Cool for 10 minutes before removing from pans to wire racks to cool completely. **Yield:** 30 tartlets.

Tin Roof Fudge Pie

*(**Pictured on page 272**)*

This rich pie with peanuts, whipping cream and caramel is a wonderful ending to any meal. I can't wait to indulge a piece!
—Patricia Schmeling

2 squares (1 ounce *each*) semisweet baking chocolate
1 tablespoon butter
1 pastry shell (9 inches), baked
PEANUT LAYER:
20 caramels
1/3 cup heavy whipping cream
1-1/2 cups salted peanuts
CHOCOLATE LAYER:
8 squares (1 ounce *each*) semisweet baking chocolate

2 tablespoons butter
1 cup heavy whipping cream
2 teaspoons vanilla extract
Whipped cream and salted peanuts, optional
TOPPING:
3 caramels
5 teaspoons heavy whipping cream
1 tablespoon butter

1 In a microwave or small heavy saucepan, melt chocolate and butter. Spread onto the bottom and up the sides of pastry shell; refrigerate until chocolate is set.

2 In a saucepan over low heat, melt caramels and cream, stirring frequently until smooth. Remove from the heat; stir in peanuts. Spoon into pastry shell; refrigerate.

3 In a small saucepan over low heat, melt chocolate and butter. Remove from the heat; let stand for 15 minutes. Meanwhile, in a small mixing bowl, beat cream and vanilla until soft peaks form. Carefully fold a third of the whipped cream into the chocolate mixture; fold in remaining whipped cream. Spread over peanut layer; refrigerate until set.

4 Garnish with whipped cream and peanuts if desired. In a small saucepan over low heat, melt caramels, cream and butter. Drizzle over pie. Refrigerate until serving. **Yield:** 8-10 servings.

Peach Pie

The lemon juice in this recipe helps keeps the peaches' pretty color. The fresh flavor of the fruit comes through in every forkful!
—Sarah Thompson

Pastry for double-crust pie (9 inches)
5 cups sliced peeled fresh peaches
1 tablespoon lemon juice
1/2 teaspoon almond extract
1 cup sugar
1/4 cup quick-cooking tapioca
1/4 teaspoon salt
2 tablespoons butter

1 Line a 9-in. pie plate with bottom pastry; trim to 1 in. beyond edge of plate. Set aside. In a bowl, combine the peaches, lemon juice and extract. Add the sugar, tapioca and salt; toss gently. Let stand for 15 minutes. Pour into crust; dot with butter. Roll out remaining pastry; make a lattice crust. Seal and flute edges.

2 Cover edges loosely with foil. Bake at 425° for 20 minutes. Remove foil; bake 20-30 minutes longer or until crust is golden brown and filling is bubbly. Cool on a wire rack. **Yield:** 6-8 servings.

Classic Pie Crust

This is the recipe we use in the Test Kitchen when we test readers' pie recipes that don't include a specific recipe for the pastry.

—*Janet Briggs*

Pastry for double-crust (9-inch to 10-inch pie):
- 2 cups all-purpose flour
- 3/4 teaspoon salt
- 2/3 cup shortening
- 6 to 7 tablespoons cold water

Pastry for single-crust (9-inch to 10-inch pie):
- 1-1/4 cups all-purpose flour
- 1/2 teaspoon salt
- 1/3 cup shortening
- 4 to 5 tablespoons cold water

1 In a small bowl, combine the flour and salt; cut in shortening until crumbly. Gradually add the water, tossing with a fork until dough forms a ball. Cover and refrigerate for 30 minutes if desired.

2 For double crust: Divide dough in half so one ball is slightly larger than the other. Roll out larger ball to fit a 9-in. to 10-in. pie plate. Trim pastry even with edge. Fill crust with desired filling. Roll out remaining pastry to fit top of pie; place over filling. Trim, seal and flute edges. Cut slits in top. Bake according to recipe directions. **Yield:** pastry for double-crust pie.

3 For single crust: Roll out pastry to fit a 9-in. to 10-in. pie plate. Transfer pastry to pie plate. Trim pastry to 1/2 in. beyond edge of pie plate; flute edges. Fill or bake shell according to recipe directions. **Yield:** pastry for single-crust pie.

Strawberry-Rhubarb Crumb Pie

My mother-in-law makes this pie when she has lots of rhubarb in her garden. It has become an often-requested family favorite. —*Stephanie Marchese*

- 1 egg
- 1 cup sugar
- 2 tablespoons all-purpose flour
- 1 teaspoon vanilla extract
- 3/4 pound fresh rhubarb, cut into 1/2-inch pieces (about 3 cups)
- 1 pint fresh strawberries, halved
- 1 unbaked pastry shell (9 inches)

TOPPING:
- 3/4 cup all-purpose flour
- 1/2 cup packed brown sugar
- 1/2 cup quick-cooking oats
- 1/2 cup cold butter

1 In a large mixing bowl, beat egg. Add the sugar, flour and vanilla; mix well. Gently fold in rhubarb and strawberries. Pour into pastry shell. For topping, combine flour, brown sugar and oats in a small bowl; cut in butter until crumbly. Sprinkle over fruit.

2 Bake at 400° for 10 minutes. Reduce heat to 350°; bake for 35 minutes or until crust is golden brown and filling is bubbly. Cool on a wire rack. **Yield:** 8 servings.

Traditional Pumpkin Pie ✓

We host Thanksgiving dinner for about 25 relatives. The holiday wouldn't be the same without a piece—or two—of this pumpkin pie! —*Janaan Cunningham*

  2 cups all-purpose flour
  3/4 teaspoon salt
  2/3 cup shortening
  4 to 6 tablespoons cold water
FILLING:
  6 eggs
  1 can (29 ounces) solid-pack pumpkin
  2 cups packed brown sugar
  2 teaspoons ground cinnamon
  1 teaspoon salt
  1/2 teaspoon *each* ground cloves, nutmeg and ginger
  2 cups evaporated milk

1 In a small bowl, combine flour and salt; cut in shortening until crumbly. Sprinkle with water, 1 tablespoon at a time, tossing with a fork until dough forms a ball. Divide dough in half. On a floured surface, roll out each portion to fit a 9-in. pie plate. Place pastry in plates; trim pastry (set scraps aside if leaf cutouts are desired) and flute edges. Set aside.

2 For filling, beat eggs in a large mixing bowl. Add pumpkin, brown sugar, cinnamon, salt, cloves, nutmeg and ginger; beat just until smooth. Gradually stir in milk. Pour into pastry shells. Bake at 450° for 10 minutes. Reduce heat to 350°; bake 40-45 minutes longer or until a knife inserted near the center comes out clean. Cool on wire racks.

3 If desired, cut the pastry scraps with a 1-in. leaf-shaped cookie cutter; place on an ungreased baking sheet. Bake at 350° for 10-15 minutes or until lightly browned. Place on baked pies. **Yield:** 2 pies (6-8 servings each).

Shoofly Pie ✓

My grandmother made the best shoofly pie in the tradition of the Pennsylvania Dutch. Shoofly pie is to the Pennsylvania Dutch what pecan pie is to a Southerner. —*Mark Morgan*

  1 unbaked pastry shell (9 inches)
  1 egg yolk, lightly beaten
  1/2 cup packed brown sugar
  1/2 cup molasses
  1 egg
1-1/2 teaspoons all-purpose flour
  1/2 teaspoon baking soda
  1 cup boiling water
TOPPING:
  1-1/2 cups all-purpose flour
  3/4 cup packed brown sugar
  3/4 teaspoon baking soda
Dash salt
  6 tablespoons cold butter

1 Line unbaked pastry shell with a double thickness of heavy-duty foil. Bake at 350° for 10 minutes. Remove foil; brush crust with egg yolk. Bake 5 minutes longer; cool on a wire rack.

2 In a small bowl, combine brown sugar, molasses, egg, flour and baking soda; gradually add boiling water. Cool to room temperature; pour into crust.

3 For topping, in a bowl, combine the flour, brown sugar, baking soda and salt. Cut in butter until crumbly. Sprinkle over filling. Bake at 350° for 45-50 minutes or until crust is golden brown and filling is set. Cool on a wire rack. Store in the refrigerator. **Yield:** 6-8 servings.

Cookies
and Bars

Nutmeg Meltaways

These are truly melt-in-your-mouth cookies. A dusting of nutmeg seasons them nicely. —Amy Welk-Thieding

   1 cup butter, softened
 1/2 cup sugar
   1 teaspoon vanilla extract
   2 cups all-purpose flour
 3/4 cup ground almonds, toasted
   1 cup confectioners' sugar
   1 tablespoon ground nutmeg

1 In a large mixing bowl, cream the butter, sugar and vanilla. Gradually add flour; mix well. Stir in almonds. Shape into 1-in. balls.

2 Place 2 in. apart on ungreased baking sheets. Bake at 300° for 18-20 minutes or until bottoms are lightly browned. Cool on wire racks.

3 In a shallow bowl, combine confectioners' sugar and nutmeg. Gently roll cooled cookies in sugar mixture. **Yield:** about 5 dozen.

Cheesecake Cranberry Bars

I like to serve these wonderful bars as one of the desserts for Thanksgiving dinner. Everyone always goes back for seconds! —Kris Lehman

1-1/2 cups all-purpose flour
    1 cup quick-cooking oats
    3 tablespoons brown sugar
  3/4 cup cold butter
    1 cup vanilla *or* white chips
    1 package (8 ounces) cream cheese, softened

    1 can (14 ounces) sweetened condensed milk
  1/4 cup lemon juice
    1 teaspoon vanilla extract
    2 tablespoons cornstarch
    1 can (16 ounces) whole-berry cranberry sauce

1 In a large bowl, combine the flour, oats and brown sugar. Cut in butter until crumbly. Reserve 1 cup for the topping. Stir chips into the remaining crumb mixture. With floured fingers, press into a greased 13-in. x 9-in. x 2-in. baking pan. Bake at 350° for 15-18 minutes or until golden brown.

2 In a large mixing bowl, beat cream cheese until light. Add the milk, lemon juice and vanilla; beat until smooth. Pour over crust. Combine the cornstarch and cranberry sauce until blended; spoon over the cream cheese layer. Sprinkle with the reserved crumb mixture.

3 Bake for 30 minutes or until center is set. Cool for 1 hour on a wire rack. Cut into bars. Store in the refrigerator. **Yield:** 2-1/2 dozen.

Berry Shortbread Dreams

(Pictured on page 287)

These cookies look so pretty on a tray. You can make them with the same flavor of jam or with an assortment of jams.
—Megan Taylor

1 cup butter, softened
2/3 cup sugar
1/2 teaspoon almond extract
2 cups all-purpose flour
1/3 to 1/2 cup seedless raspberry jam

GLAZE:
1 cup confectioners' sugar
2 to 3 teaspoons water
1/2 teaspoon almond extract

1 In a large mixing bowl, cream butter and sugar. Beat in extract; gradually add flour until dough forms a ball. Cover and refrigerate for 1 hour or until easy to handle.

2 Roll dough into 1-in. balls. Place 1 in. apart on ungreased baking sheets. Using the end of a wooden spoon handle, make an indentation in the center. Fill with jam.

3 Bake at 350° for 14-18 minutes or until edges are lightly browned. Remove to wire racks to cool. Spoon additional jam into cookies if desired. Combine glaze ingredients; drizzle over cooled cookies. **Yield:** about 3-1/2 dozen.

Caramel-Filled Chocolate Cookies

You can't eat just one of these cookies! My mother-in-law bakes them throughout the year, and they're always a hit.
—Tamra Duncan

1 cup butter, softened
1 cup plus 1 tablespoon sugar, *divided*
1 cup packed brown sugar
2 eggs
1 teaspoon vanilla extract
2-1/2 cups all-purpose flour
3/4 cup baking cocoa
1 teaspoon baking soda
1-1/4 cups chopped pecans, *divided*
1 package (13 ounces) Rolo candies
4 squares (1 ounce *each*) white baking chocolate, melted, optional

1 In a large mixing bowl, cream butter, 1 cup sugar and brown sugar. Add the eggs, one at a time, beating well after each addition. Beat in vanilla. Combine the flour, cocoa and baking soda; gradually add to creamed mixture, beating just until combined. Stir in 1/2 cup pecans.

2 Shape a tablespoonful of dough around each candy, forming a ball. In a small bowl, combine the remaining sugar and pecans; dip each cookie halfway. Place nut side up 2 in. apart on greased baking sheets.

3 Bake at 375° for 7-10 minutes or until tops are slightly cracked. Cool for 3 minutes before removing to wire racks to cool completely. Drizzle with melted white chocolate if desired. **Yield:** about 5 dozen.

Butterscotch Cashew Bars

This is my husband's favorite bar. He'd eat close to half the pan at one sitting if I'd let him. The recipe makes a big batch, which is good, because they go quickly!
—Megan Taylor

       1 cup plus 2 tablespoons butter, softened
     3/4 cup plus 2 tablespoons packed brown sugar
   2-1/2 cups all-purpose flour
   1-3/4 teaspoons salt

TOPPING:
       1 package (10 to 11 ounces) butterscotch chips
     1/2 cup plus 2 tablespoons light corn syrup
       3 tablespoons butter
       2 teaspoons water
   2-1/2 cups salted cashew halves

1 In a large mixing bowl, cream butter and brown sugar. Combine flour and salt; add to creamed mixture just until combined. Press into a greased 15-in. x 10-in. x 1-in. baking pan. Bake at 350° for 10-12 minutes or until lightly browned.

2 Meanwhile, combine the butterscotch chips, corn syrup, butter and water in a small saucepan.

Cook and stir over medium heat until chips and butter are melted. Spread over crust. Sprinkle with cashews; press down lightly.

3 Bake for 11-13 minutes or until topping is bubbly and lightly browned. Cool on a wire rack. Cut into bars. **Yield:** 3-1/2 dozen.

Candy Corn Cookies

Get a jump on Halloween or Thanksgiving with this buttery cookie that's shaped like candy corn. They're fun to make and eat!
—Sue Megonigle

   1-1/2 cups butter, softened
   1-1/2 cups sugar
     1/2 teaspoon vanilla extract
       3 cups all-purpose flour
       1 teaspoon baking soda
     1/2 teaspoon salt
Yellow and orange paste food coloring

1 In a large mixing bowl, cream butter and sugar. Beat in vanilla. Combine the flour, baking soda and salt; gradually add to creamed mixture. Divide dough in half. Tint one portion yellow. Divide remaining dough into two-third and one-third portions. Color the larger portion orange; leave smaller portion white.

2 Shape each portion of dough into two 8-in. logs. Flatten top and push sides in at a slight angle.

Place orange logs on yellow logs; push the sides in at a slight angle. Top with white logs; form a rounded top. Wrap in plastic wrap. Chill for 4 hours or until firm.

3 Unwrap dough and cut into 1/4-in. slices. Place 2 in. apart on ungreased baking sheets. Bake at 350° for 10-12 minutes or until set. Remove to wire racks to cool. **Yield:** about 5 dozen.

Apricot Meringue Bars

These fruit-filled bars are especially nice for a bridal or baby shower. Their sweet apricot filling and delicate meringue topping make them everyone's favorite. —Karen Johnson

    3 cups all-purpose flour
    1 cup sugar, *divided*
    1 cup cold butter
    4 eggs, *separated*
    1 teaspoon vanilla extract
    2 cans (12 ounces *each*) apricot filling
  1/2 cup chopped pecans

1 In a large bowl, combine flour and 1/2 cup sugar; cut in butter until crumbly. Add egg yolks and vanilla; mix well. Press into a greased 15-in. x 10-in. x 1-in. baking pan. Bake at 350° for 12-15 minutes or until lightly browned. Spread apricot filling over crust.

2 In a small mixing bowl, beat the egg whites until soft peaks form. Gradually beat in the remaining sugar, 1 tablespoon at a time, on high until stiff peaks form and sugar is dissolved. Spread over apricot layer; sprinkle with pecans.

3 Bake for 25-30 minutes or until lightly browned. Cool on a wire rack. Cut into bars. Refrigerate leftovers. **Yield:** 32 bars.

Chocolate-Dipped Macaroons

These macaroons have a great homemade feel to them. The chocolate and coconut combination makes them a rich treat that are well loved. —Joylyn Trickel

      5 egg whites
    1/2 teaspoon vanilla extract
  1-1/3 cups sugar
      4 cups flaked coconut, toasted
    3/4 cup ground almonds
     12 squares (1 ounce *each*) bittersweet *or* semisweet chocolate

1 Place egg whites in a large mixing bowl; let stand at room temperature for 30 minutes. Add vanilla; beat on medium speed until soft peaks form. Gradually beat in sugar, about 2 tablespoons at a time, on high until stiff glossy peaks form and sugar is dissolved. Gradually fold in coconut and nuts, about 1/2 cup at a time.

2 Drop by rounded tablespoonfuls 2 in. apart onto parchment paper-lined baking sheets. Bake at 275° for 25 minutes or until firm to the touch. Remove to wire racks to cool completely.

3 In a microwave-safe bowl, melt chocolate; stir until smooth. Dip the bottom of each cookie in chocolate. Place on waxed paper-lined baking sheets. Refrigerate for 1 hour or until chocolate is set. Store in an airtight container. **Yield:** 5 dozen.

TEST KITCHEN TIP
To make the cookies all white, dip them in melted white chocolate. You can also drizzle with milk chocolate to give them a different look.

Chocolate Malted Cookies

Forget regular chocolate chip cookies—these are the king of chocolate chip cookies! With malted milk powder, chocolate syrup plus chocolate chips and chunks, these are the next best thing to a good old-fashioned malted milk.

—Diane Werner

1 cup butter-flavored shortening
1-1/4 cups packed brown sugar
1/2 cup malted milk powder
2 tablespoons chocolate syrup
1 tablespoon vanilla extract
1 egg
2 cups all-purpose flour
1 teaspoon baking soda
1/2 teaspoon salt
1-1/2 cups semisweet chocolate chunks
1 cup milk chocolate chips

1 In a large mixing bowl, beat the shortening, brown sugar, malted milk powder, chocolate syrup and vanilla for 2 minutes. Add egg. Combine the flour, baking soda and salt; gradually add to creamed mixture, mixing well after each addition. Stir in chocolate chunks and chips.

2 Shape into 2-in. balls. Place 3 in. apart on ungreased baking sheets. Bake at 375° for 12-14 minutes or until golden brown. Cool for 2 minutes before removing to a wire rack. **Yield:** about 1-1/2 dozen.

Three-Nut Cherry Slices

The men in my family have always liked these refrigerator cookies. I'm always happy to make a batch for them.

—Sue Megonigle

1-1/2 cups butter, softened
1 cup packed brown sugar
1/4 cup milk
1 teaspoon vanilla extract
3-1/2 cups all-purpose flour
1 teaspoon ground cinnamon

1/2 teaspoon baking soda
1/2 teaspoon salt
1/2 pound red candied cherries, chopped (1 cup)
1/4 cup *each* chopped walnuts, Brazil nuts and hazelnuts

1 In a large mixing bowl, cream butter and brown sugar. Beat in milk and vanilla. Combine the flour, cinnamon, baking soda and salt; gradually add to creamed mixture. Stir in the cherries and nuts. Shape into three 10-in. rolls; wrap each in plastic wrap. Refrigerate for 4 hours or overnight.

2 Unwrap dough and cut into 1/4-in. slices. Place 2 in. apart on ungreased baking sheets. Bake at 350° for 10-12 minutes or until golden brown. Remove to wire racks. **Yield:** 7 dozen.

Brownie Mallow Bars

(Pictured on page 286)

When you need something sweet and you're short on time, this is a great way to transform a brownie mix into a fabulous treat.
—*Rita Krajcir*

- 1 package fudge brownie mix (13-inch x 9-inch pan size)
- 1 package (10-1/2 ounces) miniature marshmallows
- 2 cups (12 ounces) semisweet chocolate chips
- 1 cup peanut butter
- 1 tablespoon butter
- 1-1/2 cups crisp rice cereal

1 Prepare brownie batter according to package directions for fudge-like brownies. Pour into a greased 13-in. x 9-in. x 2-in. baking pan. Bake at 350° for 28-30 minutes. Top with marshmallows; bake 3 minutes longer (marshmallows will not be completely melted). Cool on a wire rack.

2 In a saucepan, combine the chocolate chips, peanut butter and butter. Cook and stir over low heat until smooth. Remove from the heat; stir in cereal. Spread over brownies. Refrigerate for 1-2 hours or until firm before cutting. **Yield:** 2-1/2 dozen.

Dipped Gingersnaps

Old-fashioned gingersnaps are one of my favorites. These chewy cookies are not only festive-looking, but they taste great, too. The spices are perfectly balanced. These Yuletide treats add a special touch to any cookie platter.   —*Sue A. Jurack*

- 2 cups sugar
- 1-1/2 cups vegetable oil
- 2 eggs
- 1/2 cup molasses
- 4 cups all-purpose flour
- 4 teaspoons baking soda
- 1 tablespoon ground ginger
- 2 teaspoons ground cinnamon
- 1 teaspoon salt
- Additional sugar
- 2 packages (10 to 12 ounces *each*) vanilla *or* white chips
- 1/4 cup shortening

1 In a large mixing bowl, combine sugar and oil; mix well. Add eggs, one at a time, beating well after each addition. Stir in molasses. Combine the flour, baking soda, ginger, cinnamon and salt; gradually add to sugar mixture and mix well.

2 Shape into 3/4-in. balls; roll in additional sugar. Place 2 in. apart on ungreased baking sheets. Bake at 350° for 10-12 minutes or until cookie springs back when lightly touched. Remove to wire racks to cool.

3 In a microwave or small heavy saucepan, melt chips with shortening; stir until smooth. Dip the cookies halfway into melted chips; shake off excess. Let stand on waxed paper-lined baking sheets until set. **Yield:** about 14-1/2 dozen.

TEST KITCHEN TIP

Use a small ice cream scoop to drop the cookie dough onto waxed paper, then roll each into a ball.

Oatmeal Chocolate Chip Bars

This is a great recipe to have in your collection. All of the ingredients are common staples, so you don't have to run out to the store to enjoy these chocolate chip-packed bars. —Peggy Fleming

    1 cup shortening
1-1/2 cups packed brown sugar
    2 eggs
    2 tablespoons molasses
    2 teaspoons vanilla extract
    3 cups quick-cooking oats

    1 cup all-purpose flour
    1 teaspoon baking soda
  1/2 teaspoon salt
    2 cups (12 ounces) semisweet chocolate chips
  3/4 cup chopped pecans

1 In a large mixing bowl, cream shortening and brown sugar. Add eggs, one at a time, beating well after each addition. Beat in molasses and vanilla. Combine the oats, flour, baking soda and salt; gradually add to creamed mixture. Stir in chocolate chips and pecans.

2 Spread into a greased 13-in. x 9-in. x 2-in. baking pan. Bake at 350° for 28-32 minutes or until golden brown and edges pull away from sides of pan. Cool on a wire rack. Cut into bars. **Yield:** 2 dozen.

Test Kitchen Tip

Peggy likes to heat these bars in the microwave for 8-10 seconds and eat with a fork. They're great with a glass of milk.

Double Butterscotch Cookies

I've made this old-fashioned recipe for years. It can also be made with miniature chocolate chips or coconut in place of the toffee bits. —Anita Bukowski

  1/2 cup butter, softened
  1/2 cup shortening
    4 cups packed brown sugar
    4 eggs
    1 tablespoon vanilla extract
    6 cups all-purpose flour
    1 tablespoon baking soda
    1 tablespoon cream of tartar
    1 teaspoon salt
    1 package English toffee bits (10 ounces) *or* almond brickle chips (7-1/2 ounces)
    1 cup finely chopped pecans

1 In a large mixing bowl, cream the butter, shortening and brown sugar. Add eggs, one at a time, beating well after each addition. Beat in vanilla. Combine the flour, baking soda, cream of tartar and salt; gradually add to creamed mixture. Stir in toffee bits and pecans.

2 Shape into three 14-in. rolls; wrap each in plastic wrap. Refrigerate for 4 hours or until firm.

3 Unwrap dough and cut into 1/2-in. slices. Place 2 in. apart on greased baking sheets. Bake at 375° for 9-11 minutes or until lightly browned. Cool for 1-2 minutes before removing to wire racks to cool completely. **Yield:** about 7 dozen.

Root Beer Cookies

When we go to a lodge in northern Wisconsin each Labor Day weekend with a group of friends, I bring these cookies—dozens of them. When I first tasted them in our Test Kitchen, I was intrigued by the flavor and decided it was a must-try cookie. —Sue A. Jurack

    1 cup butter, softened
    2 cups packed brown sugar
    2 eggs
    1 cup buttermilk
  3/4 teaspoon root beer concentrate *or* extract
    4 cups all-purpose flour
    1 teaspoon baking soda
    1 teaspoon salt
1-1/2 cups chopped pecans
FROSTING:
3-1/2 cups confectioners' sugar
  3/4 cup butter, softened
    3 tablespoons water
1-1/4 teaspoons root beer concentrate *or* extract

1 In a large mixing bowl, cream butter and brown sugar. Add eggs, one at a time, beating well after each addition. Beat in buttermilk and root beer concentrate. Combine flour, baking soda and salt; gradually add to creamed mixture. Stir in pecans.

2 Drop by tablespoonfuls 3 in. apart onto ungreased baking sheets. Bake at 375° for 10-12 minutes or until lightly browned. Remove to wire racks to cool.

3 In a large mixing bowl, combine frosting ingredients; beat until smooth. Frost cooled cookies. **Yield:** about 6 dozen.

Very Chocolate Brownies

The truth is I would be willing to abandon all other food for these brownies. You'll never find a thicker, richer or more chocolaty brownie! —Joylyn Trickel

  2/3 cup butter
1-1/2 cups sugar
  1/4 cup water
    4 cups (24 ounces) semisweet chocolate
      chips, *divided*
    2 teaspoons vanilla extract
    4 eggs
1-1/2 cups all-purpose flour
  1/2 teaspoon baking soda
  1/2 teaspoon salt

1 In a heavy saucepan, bring the butter, sugar and water to a boil, stirring constantly. Remove from the heat. Stir in 2 cups of chocolate chips until melted; cool slightly. Stir in vanilla.

2 In a large mixing bowl, beat eggs. Gradually add chocolate mixture; mix well. Combine the flour, baking soda and salt; gradually add to chocolate mixture. Stir in remaining chocolate chips.

3 Spread into a greased 13-in. x 9-in. x 2-in. baking pan. Bake at 325° for 35-40 minutes or until a toothpick inserted near the center comes out clean. Cool on a wire rack. Cut into bars. **Yield:** 3 dozen.

Holly Berry Cookies

I always get comments on how pretty these cookies are—but not too pretty to eat, of course! —*Amy Welk-Thieding*

  2 cups all-purpose flour
  1 cup sugar
  1 teaspoon ground cinnamon
  3/4 teaspoon baking powder
  1/4 teaspoon salt
  1/2 cup cold butter
  1 egg
  1/4 cup milk
  2/3 cup seedless raspberry jam
GLAZE:
  2 cups confectioners' sugar
  2 tablespoons milk
  1/2 teaspoon vanilla extract
Red-hot candies
Green food coloring

1 In a large bowl, combine the first five ingredients. Cut in butter until mixture resembles coarse crumbs. In a small bowl, beat egg and milk. Add to crumb mixture just until moistened. Cover and refrigerate for 1 hour or until easy to handle.

2 On a lightly floured surface, roll out dough to 1/8-in. thickness. Cut with a 2-in. round cookie cutter. Place on ungreased baking sheets. Bake at 375° for 8-10 minutes or until edges are lightly browned. Remove to wire racks to cool.

3 Spread jam on half of the cookies; top each with another cookie. In a small mixing bowl, combine confectioners' sugar, milk and vanilla until smooth; spread over cookies. Immediately decorate with red-hot candies; let stand until glaze is set.

4 Using a new paintbrush and food coloring, paint holly leaves on cookies. **Yield:** 2 dozen.

NANCY FRIDIRICI

A high school home economics teacher first sparked Nancy's interest in food and cooking...and high school is where she met her future husband. They've now been married 34 years and have two college-age children! Nancy even taught home ec classes herself before coming on board our Test Kitchen team. She especially enjoys baking and trying out new recipes. Living in Iran for 2 years introduced her to a whole new cuisine!

Caramel Butter Pecan Bars

This recipe is quick, easy and delicious. It makes enough to serve company or bring to a party.
—*Peggy Fleming*

  2 cups all-purpose flour
  1 cup packed brown sugar
  3/4 cup cold butter
1-1/2 cups chopped pecans

  1 jar (12 ounces) caramel ice cream topping, warmed
  1 package (11-1/2 ounces) milk chocolate chips

1 In a large bowl, combine flour and brown sugar; cut in butter until crumbly. Press into an ungreased 13-in. x 9-in. x 2-in. baking dish. Top with pecans. Drizzle caramel topping evenly over pecans.

2 Bake at 350° for 15-20 minutes or until caramel is bubbly. Remove to a wire rack. Sprinkle with chocolate chips. Let stand for 5 minutes. Carefully spread chips over caramel layer. Cool at room temperature for at least 6 hours or until chocolate is set. Cut into bars. **Yield:** 4 dozen.

Oatmeal Chip Cookies

(Pictured on page 286)

I made this recipe just before we showed our house. Not only did the people buy the house, they requested the recipe!
—Nancy Fridirici

1 cup butter, softened
1 cup sugar
1 cup packed brown sugar
2 eggs
1 teaspoon vanilla extract
2 cups all-purpose flour

1 teaspoon baking soda
1/2 teaspoon baking powder
1/2 teaspoon salt
2 cups old-fashioned oats
2 cups (12 ounces) semisweet chocolate chips

1 In a large mixing bowl, cream the butter and sugars. Beat in eggs and vanilla. Combine the flour, baking soda, baking powder and salt; add to creamed mixture. Stir in oats and chocolate chips.

2 Drop by rounded tablespoonfuls 2 in. apart onto ungreased baking sheets. Bake at 350° for 11-12 minutes. Remove to wire racks. **Yield:** 4 dozen.

Candy Cane Cookies

These cookies were a holiday tradition in my family since I was a young child. Now my own family requests them before any others at Christmas. *—Patricia Schmeling*

1/2 cup shortening
1/2 cup butter, softened
1 cup confectioners' sugar
1 egg
1-1/2 teaspoons almond extract
1 teaspoon vanilla extract
2-1/2 cups all-purpose flour
1/2 teaspoon salt
1/2 teaspoon red food coloring
1/2 cup peppermint candies, crushed
1/2 cup sugar

1 In a large mixing bowl, cream the shortening, butter and confectioners' sugar. Add egg and extracts; mix well. Combine flour and salt; gradually add to creamed mixture. Divide dough in half; mix the food coloring into one half. Cover and refrigerate white and red dough for 2 hours or until easy to handle.

2 Shape 1 teaspoon white dough into a 4-in. rope. Shape 1 teaspoon red dough into a 4-in. rope. Place ropes side by side; twist one over the other. If cracks form in dough, gently press to seal. Place on an ungreased baking sheet; curve top of cookie down to form handle of candy cane. Repeat with remaining white and red dough, placing 2 in. apart on baking sheets.

3 Bake at 375° for 8-9 minutes or until set. Combine the crushed candies and sugar; sprinkle a small amount on each cookie. Remove to wire racks. **Yield:** 4 dozen.

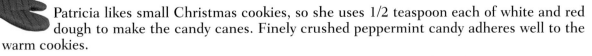

TEST KITCHEN TIP

Patricia likes small Christmas cookies, so she uses 1/2 teaspoon each of white and red dough to make the candy canes. Finely crushed peppermint candy adheres well to the warm cookies.

Michigan Cherry Drops

The staff at our Reiman Publications Visitor Center considers these cookies to be the best! Pretty pink cookies such as these are a wonderful treat.
—*Betty Reuter*

1 cup butter, softened
1 cup sugar
1/2 cup packed brown sugar
4 eggs
1-1/2 teaspoons vanilla extract
4 cups all-purpose flour
1 teaspoon salt
1 teaspoon ground cinnamon
1/2 teaspoon ground nutmeg
3-1/2 cups chopped walnuts
3 cups chopped maraschino cherries
2-2/3 cups raisins

1 In a large mixing bowl, cream the butter and sugars. Add eggs, one at a time, beating well after each addition. Beat in vanilla. Combine the flour, salt, cinnamon and nutmeg; gradually add to creamed mixture. Transfer to a larger bowl if necessary. Stir in walnuts, cherries and raisins.

2 Drop by tablespoonfuls 2 in. apart onto ungreased baking sheets. Bake at 350° for 16-18 minutes or until lightly browned. Remove to wire racks to cool. Store in an airtight container. **Yield:** about 14 dozen.

Chunky Blond Brownies

When I sent these to my husband's office, he received many recipe requests. These rich brownies are easy to make but are so special. Every bite is packed with chunks of white and semisweet chocolate and macadamia nuts.
—*Coleen Martin*

1/2 cup butter, softened
3/4 cup sugar
3/4 cup packed brown sugar
2 eggs
2 teaspoons vanilla extract
1-1/2 cups all-purpose flour
1 teaspoon baking powder
1/2 teaspoon salt
1 cup vanilla *or* white chips
1 cup semisweet chocolate chunks
1 jar (3-1/2 ounces) macadamia nuts *or* 3/4 cup blanched almonds, chopped, *divided*

1 In a large mixing bowl, cream butter and sugars. Add the eggs and vanilla; mix well. Combine the flour, baking powder and salt; add to creamed mixture and mix well. Stir in vanilla chips, chocolate chunks and 1/2 cup nuts.

2 Spoon into a greased 13-in. x 9-in. x 2-in. baking pan; spread to evenly cover bottom of pan. Sprinkle with remaining nuts. Bake at 350° for 25-30 minutes or until golden brown. Cool on a wire rack. **Yield:** 2 dozen.

TEST KITCHEN TIP
The batter is very thick, so be sure to spread it evenly in the pan. Coleen keeps macadamia nuts in the freezer just so she can make this recipe in a pinch.

Lemon Bars

I made these for my friend's bridal shower and received lots of compliments about how delicious they were. The lemon flavor keeps the bars light and flavorful.

—Megan Taylor

1 cup all-purpose flour
1/3 cup butter, softened
1/4 cup confectioners' sugar
TOPPING:
1 cup sugar
2 eggs
2 tablespoons all-purpose flour
2 tablespoons lemon juice
1/2 teaspoon lemon extract
1/2 teaspoon baking powder
1/4 teaspoon salt
Confectioners' sugar

1 Combine the flour, butter and confectioners' sugar; pat into an ungreased 8-in. square baking pan. Bake at 375° for 15 minutes.

2 Meanwhile, in a large mixing bowl, combine the sugar, eggs, flour, lemon juice, extract, baking powder and salt. Beat until frothy; pour over crust.

3 Bake for 18-22 minutes or until light golden brown. Cool on a wire rack. Dust with confectioners' sugar. **Yield:** 9 servings.

Almond-Tipped Shortbread Fingers

These rich and buttery shortbread cookies look like you fussed when really they're quite easy to make.

—Janet Briggs

1 cup butter, softened
3/4 cup packed brown sugar
2 teaspoons vanilla extract
2 cups all-purpose flour

6 squares (1 ounce *each*) white baking chocolate
1-1/4 cups chopped almonds

1 In a large mixing bowl, cream butter and brown sugar. Beat in vanilla. Gradually add flour. Shape 1/2 cupfuls of dough into 1/2-in.-thick logs. Cut logs into 2-in. pieces.

2 Place 2 in. apart on ungreased baking sheets. Bake at 325° for 15-17 minutes or until lightly browned. Remove to wire racks to cool.

3 In a microwave-safe bowl, melt white chocolate; stir until smooth. Dip one end of each cookie into chocolate, then into almonds. Place on waxed paper until set. **Yield:** 4 dozen.

TEST KITCHEN TIP

Sometimes Janet likes to use melted semisweet chocolate instead of the white baking chocolate and chopped pecans in place of the almonds.

Chocolate Caramel Thumbprints

I think these are the best cookies ever! Try them, and I think you'll agree. Covered in chopped nuts and drizzled with chocolate, they are delicious and pretty, too.

—Sue Megonigle

          1/2 cup butter, softened
          2/3 cup sugar
            1 egg, *separated*
            2 tablespoons milk
            1 teaspoon vanilla extract
            1 cup all-purpose flour
          1/3 cup baking cocoa
          1/4 teaspoon salt
            1 cup finely chopped pecans
FILLING:
          12 to 14 caramels
            3 tablespoons heavy whipping cream
          1/2 cup semisweet chocolate chips
            1 teaspoon shortening

1 In a large mixing bowl, cream butter and sugar. Beat in egg yolk, milk and vanilla. Combine the flour, cocoa and salt; add to creamed mixture. Refrigerate for 1 hour or until easy to handle.

2 Roll dough into 1-in. balls. Beat egg white. Dip balls into egg white and coat with nuts. Place 2 in. apart on greased baking sheets. Using the end of a wooden spoon handle, make a 3/8-in. to 1/2-in. indentation in the center of each ball. Bake at 350° for 10-12 minutes or until set. Remove to wire racks to cool.

3 Meanwhile, in a heavy saucepan, melt caramels with cream over low heat; stir until smooth. Spoon about 1/2 teaspoon into each cookie. In a microwave-safe bowl, melt chocolate chips and shortening. Drizzle over cookies. **Yield:** about 2-1/2 dozen.

Peanut Butter Cup Cookies

I can't resist these cookies when they serve them at the Reiman Publications Visitor Center! The classic combination of chocolate and peanut butter is unbeatable. *—Peggy Fleming*

            1 cup butter, softened
          2/3 cup peanut butter
            1 cup sugar
            1 cup packed brown sugar
            2 eggs
            2 teaspoons vanilla extract

          2-1/4 cups all-purpose flour
            1 teaspoon baking soda
          1/2 teaspoon salt
            2 cups (12 ounces) semisweet chocolate chips
            2 cups chopped peanut butter cups (about
                six 1.6-ounce packages)

1 In a large mixing bowl, cream the butter, peanut butter and sugars. Add eggs, one at a time, beating well after each addition. Beat in vanilla. Combine the flour, baking soda and salt; gradually add to creamed mixture. Stir in the chocolate chips and peanut butter cups.

2 Drop by rounded tablespoonfuls 2 in. apart onto ungreased baking sheets. Bake at 350° for 10-12 minutes or until edges are lightly browned. Cool for 2 minutes before removing to wire racks. **Yield:** 7-1/2 dozen.

Toffee Oat Cookies

My six children love these cookies—I can never make enough of them! The crisp yet chewy cookies appeal to young and old alike.
—Kristin Arnett

3/4 cup butter, softened
1 cup packed brown sugar
3/4 cup sugar
2 eggs
3 teaspoons vanilla extract
2-1/4 cups all-purpose flour

2-1/4 cups old-fashioned oats
1 teaspoon baking soda
1 teaspoon baking powder
1/2 teaspoon salt
1 package English toffee bits (10 ounces) *or* almond brickle chips (7-1/2 ounces)

1 In a large mixing bowl, cream butter and sugars. Add eggs, one at a time, beating well after each addition. Beat in vanilla. Combine the flour, oats, baking soda, baking powder and salt; gradually add to creamed mixture. Stir in toffee bits.

2 Drop by rounded tablespoonfuls 2 in. apart onto ungreased baking sheets. Bake at 375° for 10-12 minutes or until golden brown. Cool for 1 minute before removing from pans to wire racks. **Yield:** about 4 dozen.

Marbled Chocolate Cheesecake Bars

My family was surprised to find these luscious bars were lower in fat than most desserts. That may be the case, but they sure are full of flavor!
—Coleen Martin

3/4 cup water
1/3 cup butter
1-1/2 squares (1-1/2 ounces) unsweetened chocolate
2 cups all-purpose flour
1-1/2 cups packed brown sugar
1 teaspoon baking soda
1/2 teaspoon salt
1 egg
1 egg white
1/2 cup reduced-fat sour cream

CREAM CHEESE MIXTURE:
1 package (8 ounces) reduced-fat cream cheese
1/3 cup sugar
1 egg white
1 tablespoon vanilla extract
1 cup miniature semisweet chocolate chips

1 In a small saucepan, combine the water, butter and chocolate. Cook and stir over low heat until melted; stir until smooth. Cool.

2 In a large mixing bowl, combine the flour, brown sugar, baking soda and salt. Add the egg, egg white and sour cream; beat on low speed just until combined. Stir in chocolate mixture until smooth. In another mixing bowl, beat the cream cheese, sugar, egg white and vanilla; set aside.

3 Spread chocolate batter into a 15-in. x 10-in. x 1-in. baking pan coated with nonstick cooking spray. Drop the cream cheese mixture by tablespoonfuls over batter; cut through batter with a knife to swirl. Sprinkle with chocolate chips.

4 Bake at 375° for 20-25 minutes or until a toothpick inserted near the center comes out clean. Cool on a wire rack. **Yield:** about 4 dozen.

CANDY

Dandy Caramel Candies

These candies are a caramel-pecan delight. They take time to make, but it's worth it since the recipe makes a lot. These are awesome!
— *Coleen Martin*

    1-1/2 teaspoons plus 1 cup butter, *divided*
        1 cup sugar
        1 cup packed brown sugar
        1 cup dark corn syrup
        2 cups heavy whipping cream
    3-3/4 cups chopped pecans (about 1 pound)
        1 teaspoon vanilla extract
    Dark *or* milk chocolate candy coating

1 Butter a 13-in. x 9-in. x 2-in. pan with 1-1/2 teaspoons butter; set aside. In a heavy saucepan, combine the sugars, corn syrup, cream and remaining butter.

2 Bring to a boil over medium-high heat, stirring constantly. Cook over medium heat until a candy thermometer reads 248° (firm-ball stage). Remove from the heat; stir in pecans and vanilla. Quickly spread into prepared pan. Cool.

3 Cut into 1-in. squares. Place squares on waxed paper-lined baking sheets; chill thoroughly.

4 In a microwave or heavy saucepan, melt candy coating. Dip candies into candy coating. Return to refrigerator to set. **Yield:** about 9 dozen.

EDITOR'S NOTE: We recommend that you test your candy thermometer before each use by bringing water to a boil; the thermometer should read 212°. Adjust your recipe temperature up or down based on your test.

Angel Food Candy

This angel food makes a tasty present at Christmas or any time of the year. — *Sarah Thompson*

    1-1/2 teaspoons butter
        1 cup sugar
        1 cup dark corn syrup
        1 tablespoon white vinegar

        1 tablespoon baking soda
    1/2 pound white candy coating
    1/2 pound dark chocolate candy coating

1 Butter a 13-in. x 9-in. x 2-in. pan with 1-1/2 teaspoons butter; set aside. In a large heavy saucepan, combine the sugar, corn syrup and vinegar. Cook and stir over medium heat until sugar is dissolved. Cook, without stirring, until a candy thermometer reads 290° (soft-crack stage). Remove from the heat; stir in baking soda. Pour into prepared pan; cool.

2 Break candy into pieces. Melt white candy coating; dip the candies halfway; allow excess to drip off. Place on waxed paper-lined baking sheets to set. Melt dark chocolate candy coating; dip uncoated portion of candies. Return to waxed paper to set. **Yield:** 1-1/2 pounds.

EDITOR'S NOTE: We recommend that you test your candy thermometer before each use by bringing water to a boil; the thermometer should read 212°. Adjust your recipe temperature up or down based on your test.

Truelove Truffles

(Pictured on page 302)

The name of this minty candy says it all—make it for your loved ones on Valentine's Day or any other special day.

—Diane Werner

1-1/2 teaspoons plus 3/4 cup butter, *divided*
1-1/2 cups sugar
   1 can (5 ounces) evaporated milk
   2 packages (4.67 ounces *each*) mint Andes candies (56 pieces total)

   1 jar (7 ounces) marshmallow creme
   1 teaspoon vanilla extract
  22 ounces white baking chocolate, *divided*
1/2 cup semisweet chocolate chips
Green food coloring, optional

1 Butter a 15-in. x 10-in. x 1-in. pan with 1-1/2 teaspoons butter; set aside. In a heavy saucepan, combine the sugar, milk and remaining butter. Bring to a boil over medium heat, stirring constantly. Reduce heat; cook and stir until a candy thermometer reads 236° (soft-ball stage).

2 Remove from the heat. Stir in candies until melted and mixture is well blended. Stir in marshmallow creme and vanilla until smooth. Spread into prepared pan; cover and refrigerate for 1 hour.

3 Cut into 96 pieces; roll each into a ball (mixture will be soft). Place on a waxed paper-lined baking sheet. Chill until set.

4 In a heavy saucepan or microwave-safe bowl, melt 18 oz. of white chocolate with chocolate chips. Dip balls in melted chocolate; place on waxed paper to set.

5 Melt the remaining white chocolate; add food coloring if desired. Drizzle over truffles. Store in an airtight container in a cool place or in the refrigerator. **Yield:** 8 dozen.

EDITOR'S NOTE: We recommend that you test your candy thermometer before each use by bringing water to a boil; the thermometer should read 212°. Adjust your recipe temperature up or down based on your test.

TEST KITCHEN TIP

Depending on the holiday, the drizzle can be colored to suit the mood—such as red and pink for Valentine's Day or green for St. Patrick's Day.

Cranberry Macadamia Bark

This easy three-ingredient candy is great to give as a gift or to bring for a holiday potluck supper. Dried cranberries are a different taste twist.

—Janet Briggs

   1 pound white candy coating, chopped
   1 jar (3-1/2 ounces) macadamia nuts
1/2 cup dried cranberries

1 In a saucepan, melt candy coating over medium-low heat, stirring until smooth. Add nuts and cranberries; mix well.

2 Spread onto a foil-lined baking sheet; cool. Break into pieces. **Yield:** 1-1/4 pounds.

Chocolate Caramel Candy

I make these for Christmas platters. It's nice to have a great looking and tasting candy without spending a lot of time in the kitchen. —Amy Welk-Thieding

1-1/2 teaspoons butter
    1 cup milk chocolate chips
1/4 cup butterscotch chips
1/4 cup creamy peanut butter
FILLING:
    1/4 cup butter
    1 cup sugar
1/4 cup evaporated milk
1-1/2 cups marshmallow creme
1/4 cup creamy peanut butter
    1 teaspoon vanilla extract
1-1/2 cups chopped salted peanuts
CARAMEL LAYER:
    1 package (14 ounces) caramels
1/4 cup heavy whipping cream
ICING:
    1 cup (6 ounces) milk chocolate chips
1/4 cup butterscotch chips
1/4 cup creamy peanut butter

1 Line a 13-in. x 9-in. x 2-in. pan with foil and butter the foil with 1-1/2 teaspoons butter; set aside. In a small saucepan, combine the chips and peanut butter; cook and stir over low heat until melted and smooth. Spread into prepared pan. Refrigerate until set.

2 For filling, melt butter in a heavy saucepan over medium-high heat. Add sugar and milk. Bring to a boil; boil and stir for 5 minutes. Remove from the heat; stir in the marshmallow creme, peanut butter and vanilla. Add peanuts. Spread over first layer. Refrigerate until set.

3 Combine the caramels and cream in a saucepan; stir over low heat until melted and smooth. Spread over filling. Refrigerate until set.

4 In a saucepan, combine the icing ingredients; cook and stir over low heat until melted and smooth. Pour over caramel layer. Chill for at least 1 hour. Cut into 1-in. squares. Store in the refrigerator. **Yield:** about 9 dozen.

Chocolate Peanut Sweeties

This is a great way to dress up a peanut butter ball. The pretzel provides a handle and makes dipping easier. —Karen Scales

    1 cup peanut butter
1/2 cup butter, softened
    3 cups confectioners' sugar

60 miniature pretzel twists (about 3 cups)
1-1/2 cups milk chocolate chips
    1 tablespoon vegetable oil

1 In a large mixing bowl, beat peanut butter and butter until blended. Beat in confectioners' sugar until combined. Shape into 1-in. balls; press one ball onto each pretzel. Place on waxed paper-lined baking sheets. Refrigerate until peanut butter mixture is firm, about 1 hour.

2 In a microwave or heavy saucepan, melt chocolate chips with oil. Dip peanut butter balls into chocolate. Return to baking sheet, pretzel side down. Refrigerate for at least 30 minutes before serving. Store in the refrigerator. **Yield:** 5 dozen.

Brown Sugar Cashew Fudge

(*Pictured on page 303*)

The crunchy cashews and creamy fudge make a sensational flavor combination in this candy recipe. It disappears really fast. —*Coleen Martin*

1-1/2 teaspoons plus 1/4 cup butter, softened, *divided*
   1 cup packed brown sugar
  1/2 cup evaporated milk

2 tablespoons light corn syrup
2-1/2 cups confectioners' sugar
   2 cups coarsely chopped salted cashews

1 Line a 9-in. square pan with foil and butter the foil with 1-1/2 teaspoons butter; set aside. In a heavy saucepan, combine the brown sugar, milk, corn syrup and remaining butter. Cook and stir over medium heat until sugar is dissolved. Bring to a rapid boil, stirring constantly for 5 minutes.

2 Remove from heat. Gradually add confectioners' sugar; mix well. Fold in cashews. Immediately spread into prepared pan. Cool.

3 Using foil, lift fudge out of pan. Discard foil; cut into 1-in. squares. Refrigerate in an airtight container. **Yield:** 3 dozen.

English Toffee Bars

These wonderful toffee candies are a must on my Christmas tray. I need to hide them from my family or I wouldn't have any left for the holiday. —*Patricia Schmeling*

   1 tablespoon plus 1-3/4 cups butter, softened, *divided*
   2 cups sugar
   1 tablespoon light corn syrup
   1 cup chopped pecans
1/4 teaspoon salt
   1 pound milk chocolate candy coating

1 Butter a 15-in. x 10-in. x 1-in. baking pan with 1 tablespoon butter; set aside. In a heavy 3-qt. saucepan, melt the remaining butter. Add sugar and corn syrup; cook and stir over medium heat until a candy thermometer reads 295° (soft-crack stage). Remove from the heat; stir in pecans and salt. Quickly pour into prepared pan. Let stand for 5 minutes.

2 Using a sharp knife, score candy into squares; cut along scored lines. Let stand at room temperature until cool. Separate into squares, using a sharp knife if necessary.

3 In a microwave or heavy saucepan, melt candy coating, stirring often. Dip squares, one at a time, in coating. Place on waxed paper until set. **Yield:** 2-1/4 pounds.

EDITOR'S NOTE: We recommend that you test your candy thermometer before each use by bringing water to a boil; the thermometer should read 212°. Adjust your recipe temperature up or down based on your test. If toffee separates during cooking, add 1/2 cup hot water and stir vigorously. Bring back up to 295° and proceed as recipe directs.

Three-Chip English Toffee

This toffee is so good, it's worth the effort to make it! Three kinds of melted chips are drizzled on top, plus a sprinkling of walnuts.
—*Janaan Cunningham*

1-1/2 teaspoons plus 2 cups butter, *divided*
    2 cups sugar
    1 cup slivered almonds
    1 cup milk chocolate chips
    1 cup chopped walnuts
  1/2 cup semisweet chocolate chips
  1/2 cup vanilla *or* white chips
1-1/2 teaspoons shortening

1 Butter a 15-in. x 10-in. x 1-in. baking pan with 1-1/2 teaspoons butter; set aside. In a heavy saucepan over medium-low heat, bring sugar and remaining butter to a boil, stirring constantly. Cover and cook for 2-3 minutes.

2 Uncover; add almonds. Cook and stir with a clean spoon until a candy thermometer reads 300° (hard-crack stage) and mixture is golden brown. Pour into prepared pan (do not scrape sides of saucepan). Surface will be buttery. Cool for 1-2 minutes.

3 Sprinkle with milk chocolate chips. Let stand for 1-2 minutes; spread chocolate over the top. Sprinkle with walnuts; press down gently with the back of a spoon. Chill for 10 minutes.

4 In a microwave or heavy saucepan, melt semisweet chips; stir until smooth. Drizzle over walnuts. Refrigerate for 10 minutes. Melt vanilla chips and shortening; stir until smooth. Drizzle over walnuts. Cover and refrigerate for 1-2 hours. Break into pieces. **Yield:** about 2-1/2 pounds.

EDITOR'S NOTE: We recommend that you test your candy thermometer before each use by bringing water to a boil; the thermometer should read 212°. Adjust your recipe temperature up or down based on your test. If toffee separates during cooking, add 1/2 cup hot water and stir vigorously. Bring back up to 300° and proceed as recipe directs.

Chocolate Marshmallow Squares

Children of all ages will enjoy these tall squares of marshmallow- and peanut-packed candies.
—*Kris Lehman*

1-1/2 teaspoons butter
    1 package (12 ounces) semisweet chocolate chips
    1 package (10 to 11 ounces) butterscotch chips
1/2 cup peanut butter
    1 package (16 ounces) miniature marshmallows
    1 cup unsalted dry roasted peanuts

1 Line a 13-in. x 9-in. x 2-in. pan with foil and butter the foil with 1-1/2 teaspoons butter; set aside. In a large microwave-safe bowl, microwave the chips and peanut butter at 70% power for 2 minutes; stir. Microwave in 10- to 20-second intervals until melted; stir until smooth. Cool for 1 minute. Stir in marshmallows and peanuts.

2 Spread into prepared pan. Refrigerate until firm. Using foil, lift candy out of pan. Discard foil; cut candy into 1-1/2-in. squares. **Yield:** 4 dozen.

EDITOR'S NOTE: This recipe was tested in a 1,100-watt microwave.

Mixed Nut Brittle

(Pictured on page 302)

This yummy brittle makes a great food gift at Christmas. Nut fanciers have a lot to love about the irresistible candy. The variety of nuts is what makes it so different. —*Janet Briggs*

1-1/2 teaspoons plus 3 tablespoons butter, *divided*
1-1/2 cups sugar
    1 cup water
    1 cup light corn syrup

    1 can (10 ounces) mixed nuts (without peanuts)
    1 teaspoon vanilla extract
1-1/2 teaspoons baking soda

1 Butter a baking sheet with 1-1/2 teaspoons butter; set aside. In a large saucepan, combine the sugar, water and corn syrup. Cook over medium heat until a candy thermometer reads 270° (soft-crack stage), stirring occasionally. Add nuts; cook and stir until mixture reaches 300° (hard-crack stage).

2 Remove from the heat; stir in vanilla and remaining butter. Add baking soda and stir vigorously.

Quickly pour onto prepared pan. Spread with a buttered metal spatula to 1/4-in. thickness. Cool before breaking into pieces. **Yield:** about 1-3/4 pounds.

EDITOR'S NOTE: We recommend that you test your candy thermometer before each use by bringing water to a boil; the thermometer should read 212°. Adjust your recipe temperature up or down based on your test.

Creamy Peppermint Patties

These peppermint patties take some time to make, but it is time well spent! They fill the bill for folks who like a little sweetness after a meal but don't want a full serving of rich dessert. —*Karen Scales*

    1 package (8 ounces) cream cheese, softened
    1 teaspoon peppermint extract
    9 cups confectioners' sugar
3/4 cup milk chocolate chips
3/4 cup semisweet chocolate chips
    3 tablespoons shortening

1 In a large mixing bowl, beat the cream cheese and extract until smooth. Gradually add confectioners' sugar, beating well. Shape into 1-in. balls. Place on waxed paper-lined baking sheets. Flatten into patties. Cover and refrigerate for 1 hour or until chilled.

2 In a microwave or heavy saucepan, melt chocolate chips and shortening; stir until smooth. Cool slightly. Dip patties in melted chocolate; place on waxed paper until set. Store in the refrigerator. **Yield:** about 4 dozen.

General Recipe Index

This handy index lists every recipe by food category, major ingredient and/or cooking method, so you can easily locate recipes to suit your needs.

Alphabetical Recipe Index

This handy index lists every recipe in alphabetical order so you can easily find your favorites.

X